Cultural Readings

of Restoration and

Eighteenth-Century

English Theater

EDITED BY

J. DOUGLAS CANFIELD

AND DEBORAH C. PAYNE

THE UNIVERSITY OF GEORGIA PRESS

ATHENS AND LONDON

© 1995 by The University of Georgia Press
Athens, Georgia 30602
All rights reserved
Designed by Betty Palmer McDaniel
Set in ten on thirteen Sabon
by Tseng Information Systems, Inc.
Printed and bound by Thomson-Shore, Inc.
The paper in this book meets the guidelines for
permanence and durability of the Committee on
Production Guidelines for Book Longevity of the
Council on Library Resources.

Printed in the United States of America
99 98 97 96 95 C 5 4 3 2 1
99 98 97 96 95 P 5 4 3 2 1

Library of Congress Cataloging in Publication Data
Cultural readings of Restoration and eighteenth-century
English theater / edited by J. Douglas Canfield and
Deborah C. Payne.
        p.   cm.
Includes bibliographical references and index.
ISBN 0-8203-1681-4 (alk. paper).
—ISBN 0-8203-1751-9 (pbk.: alk. paper)
1. English drama—Restoration, 1660–1700—History
and criticism. 2. Literature and society—England—
History—18th century. 3. Literature and society—
England—History—17th century. 4. English drama—
18th century—History and criticism. 5. Culture in literature.
I. Canfield, J. Douglas (John Douglas), 1941–   .
II. Payne, Deborah Christine.
PR698.S46C85   1995
822'.409—dc20   94-8524

British Library Cataloging in Publication Data available

Contents

Cultural Readings
of Restoration and
Eighteenth-Century
English Theater

INTRODUCTION

This collection features work by scholars committed to consciously theoretical readings of Restoration and eighteenth-century drama and theater.
That such a collection has not appeared before now perhaps indicates the
field's resistance to those critical methods that have come to dominate literary studies: semiotics, deconstruction, feminism, Marxism (especially
neo-Marxian discussions), new historicism, and cultural studies (which
appropriates the previous methods).[1] Then, too, the drama has always been
something of a foster child within the family of eighteenth-century studies,
especially by comparison with such "legitimate" progeny as satire and the
novel. For one thing, drama has never functioned as the model for regnant
critical theories, such as new criticism, historicism, and poststructuralism.
For another, Shakespeare and his contemporaries have always dwarfed
Restoration drama in the construction of canonical hierarchies. Even today
the annual scholarly output on Renaissance drama, much of it in important collections of criticism, eclipses the attention devoted to our field. This
book attempts to redress this methodological and scholarly neglect.

The authors included herein have all been producing theoretically informed readings, many as recent or forthcoming books. We chose the
rubric *cultural readings* to showcase their work, despite local differences
between essays, because of the methodological inclusiveness of that category. Roughly, cultural studies examines those societal codes that constitute meaning and value. At the same time, cultural studies has responded
to recent critiques, by more materially minded anthropologists and literary
critics, of purely "symbolic" or "discourse"-oriented readings. These critiques warn against a culturalist practice that reifies the text as a product,
thereby detaching it from historically determined processes. As William
Roseberry has argued, one aspect in particular missing from symbolic anthropology is "a concept of culture as material social process. Without a
sense of culture as material process or creation—as writing as well as what
is written—we once again have a conception of culture as product but not
as production" (26). Cultural studies incorporates elements of semiotics
and formalism, but it also seeks to examine what Michel Foucault calls

"discursive formations": those discourses, both verbal and nonverbal, that constitute "normalized," institutionalized power relations within cultures.[2]

We have arranged the essays in chronological order corresponding roughly to the dates or range of dates of plays discussed, partly as a gesture toward the ordering power of chronology but also partly as an acknowledgment of the limits of strict theoretical categories. Nevertheless, as we attempt to summarize below the essays in this collection, we find that *some* conventional categories and labels are heuristically useful, if only for their descriptive power. Therefore, in our summaries we characterize the essays according to approximate theoretical categories, ranging from gender to materialist to historicist readings, an ordering not reflected on the contents page. At the same time, we freely acknowledge the slippage between categories.

The essays that incline toward feminism—the readings by Green, Burke, and Markley—interrogate the construction of gender and the canon. These essays represent the two major intellectual trends in contemporary feminist literary analysis, psychoanalytic and sociological. Yet even here these categories shade into each other. Susan Green's essay on Charlotte Lennox's eighteenth-century edition of Shakespeare, for instance, tends toward the psychoanalytic category yet is consciously "culturalist." Utilizing Julia Kristeva's notion of the "abject," Green seeks to dispel the hackneyed characterization of Lennox as a tasteless and untutored editor of Shakespeare. Rather, Green examines Lennox's simultaneous resistance and response to Shakespeare's intertextual relations with his sources. She sees Lennox as assuming the position of the pre-Oedipal subject, thereby opening "the possibility for analyzing a textual inscription in women's writing that gives to women's abject voice a historical trajectory that can deflect it from a simple enunciation of itself as the repressed." Green argues further that Lennox subverts contemporary theories of invention and representation. By faulting both Shakespeare's originality and his (mis)representation of women, Lennox refused to participate in the mid-eighteenth-century transfiguration of Shakespeare into a cultural hero. Thus, Green's incisive reading of Lennox discloses both the masculinist bases of the emergent Shakespeare industry and the possibility of recuperating a woman's voice within that hostile enterprise.

A feminist reading less "purely" psychoanalytic can be found in the essay " 'Law-suits,' 'Love-suits,' and the Family Property in Wycherley's *The Plain Dealer*." Helen Burke asks that we reconsider the privileging of the male subject—in this instance, Manly—along traditional humanist lines. Rather, Burke sees Manly as a "figure of [the Lacanian] split subject who plays out his drama along a double register, re-creating in the adult sexual domain the experience first encountered in the family domain." She addresses prior complaints of aesthetic weakness in the play by noting how the plot structures work relationally. The central crisis in the play arises from the "disappropriation suffered by the male subject, a crisis that unfolds along a double register: the anxiety about male property at the individual psychosexual level is duplicated by an anxiety about property at the broader social and economic level." The latter anxiety, the central concern of the Blackacre plot, is part of a specific historical anxiety about property secured by patrilinearity. The former, the central concern of the Manly plot, is part of a larger cultural anxiety finally over the signifying function of the male within the Western symbolic order. Burke's critical methodology deftly historicizes the French psychoanalysis of Hélène Cixous and Jacques Lacan within the Anglo-American Marxism of Fredric Jameson and Michael McKeon. The outcome is a rich reading of *The Plain Dealer* that suggests how the play's failure to resolve its anxieties undercuts its attempt to reaffirm the dominant patriarchal order, an insight gleaned from a method that no longer seeks itself to reaffirm that order through the discovery of logical coherence.

Robert Markley's essay, " 'Be impudent, be saucy, forward, bold, touzing, and leud': The Politics of Masculine Sexuality and Feminine Desire in Behn's Tory Comedies," not only departs from these two essays in its methodological approach but also questions the essentializing premises informing both a psychoanalytic feminism and a bourgeois historicism. Part of the difficulty, Markley contends, in developing a theoretical framework by which to read Behn arises from our own participation in the very discourses of domestic morality and repressed sexuality we have inherited from the late seventeenth century. Several of Behn's comedies, specifically, *The Rover, Part II, The Roundheads,* and *The City Heiress,* remain outside a literary and psychoanalytic tradition "centered on the problematics of subjectivity." To read Behn's construction of gender in essentialized rather than ideological terms is to recapitulate a Whig interpretation of literary history, an interpretation, moreover, that limits our notion of what constitutes "great" or canonical literature. The historical neglect Behn has suffered is not, according to Markley, the result of any "weaknesses" in her plays but rather "of the ideological battles in which they participate:

in terms of her Tory politics, aristocratic apologetics, and feminist sexual ideology, Behn is historically on the losing side." In contrast with essentialized or progressive readings of Behn, we are offered here a tough-minded critique of "the historical and theoretical complexities of a radical theatrical practice . . . pressed into the service of a conservative ideology." As Markley sees it, Behn attempts to reconcile an aristocratic ideology of birth as worth with libertinism, and the result—with varying degrees of success—is a superficially monologic nostalgia for a golden age of natural sex and unpoliticized, unproblematized monarchy. In short, Behn celebrates Cavalier sexual/political dominance.

The essays by Deborah C. Payne, Kristina Straub, and Harold Weber ground their readings in the processes of material culture, that is, in the active negotiation of real cultural conflicts involving such things as group identity and rights, actual practices threatening social and political stability (although, as J. S. Peters notes in her contribution, access to material culture remains through the various *texts* that survive). According to Payne, during the Restoration playwrights, theater personnel, and informed spectators (such as Samuel Pepys) were equally fascinated by the public acting and private acts of the first women on the English stage. For the most part, modern criticism has reproduced this split, construing the Restoration actress as either fetishized commodity or emergent professional. In some instances, the two terms are maintained in a kind of symmetry. Clearly, as Payne argues, these are radically different versions of the same story, but which one do we choose: an all too familiar tale of oppression or an equally tired romance of feminine beauty and talent triumphing against all odds? Choosing between the two versions entails, as choice must, the repression of the opposite. By contrast, Payne offers an alternative strategy, something of a cultural deconstruction that not only posits the necessity for both terms but also locates them at the nexus of complex historical forces. In a sense, voyeurism and professionalism, the lenses through which Pepys and his cohorts viewed actresses, demanded each other's existence. As a result, the Restoration actress, doubly inscribed in both cultural economies, was simultaneously diminished and empowered.

Straub's essay, "Actors and Homophobia," deriving from gay-lesbian liberation theory, departs sharply from more traditional (and even laudatory) accounts of actors' lives to denaturalize the changes leading up to that paradoxical moment when the male actor made a living by displaying himself in an age that "increasingly valued men as spectating subjects rather than objects of spectatorship." Moreover, the contiguous relationship between the professionalization and masculinization of actors paralleled an ongoing attempt to define them "in opposition to homosexually 'tainted' others" from the seventeenth throughout the eighteenth century. Straub shows a gradual shift from the antitheatrical discourse of the seventeenth century, which located in passively seductive boy-players an incitement to sodomy, to the more complex misogynist discourse of the eighteenth century, which attempted to disassociate actors' sexuality from a newly accessible gay male identity. A number of residual ambiguities, however, remained unrecuperated by this process. Thus, actors in the eighteenth century are alternately characterized as being oversexed, promiscuous studs or feminine, unmanly peacocks. Both characterizations, Straub argues, inscribe a failed, feminized masculinity in men who earned their living by making a spectacle of themselves on the stage. And she argues persuasively that the sexually ambiguous figure of the fop destabilizes the supposedly "natural" differentiation of gender.

Also concerned with how cultural constructions of sexuality help to organize other aspects of social life is Weber's essay, "Carolinean Sexuality and the Restoration Stage: Reconstructing the Royal Phallus in *Sodom*." Weber boldly interprets a text so notorious for its obscenity as to have been considered virtually uninterpretable in the past. The few extant commentaries on *Sodom* generally render it safe by focusing on "neutral" issues of bibliography and authorship. Perhaps even bolder than the simple act of attempting a reading is Weber's contention that the problem lies not so much with the aesthetics of obscenity as with its misogyny. That misogyny, moreover, cannot be separated from *Sodom*'s political purpose, "its attempt to reconstruct the monarchy and the patriarchal structures that the king represents." Anxious jokes about Charles II's indolent ways, fear that he was "spending" his sexual and political capital in the arms of numerous women, were a mainstay of Restoration satires, anonymous lampoons, and even private letters. *Sodom* reproduces this anxiety but also attempts to resolve it by withdrawing its representation of Charles "from a circulation that threatens to invert the relationship between the male self and the female other." The king's desires are redirected instead through a homoerotic system of exchange. By attempting to eliminate women from the sexual economy, "the play can indulge a frank, even hysterical, renunciation of the female body." Yet, as Weber shrewdly notes, "in spite of its grandiloquent delight in the male homoerotic, the play never presents two men satisfying themselves sexually on stage," thereby suggesting that an exclusively male sexual economy cannot succeed because "masculine identity requires a female other whose construction testifies to male superiority."

Issues of historicism also play a part in this collection. Formerly, to read the plays "in context" meant to relate them either to the history of ideas or to the history of politics. In both instances, the drama was perceived as passively reflecting specific philosophies or topical events, a historical reading that assumes a grounding in a "prior" reality. Recent theory, historiographical as well as aesthetic, challenges this mimetic assumption. Raymond Williams, for instance, would insist that drama is as constitutive of "reality" as any other form of discourse. Moreover, to limit political meaning to specific topical references is to fail to analyze the broader ideological implications embedded in the plays, as several of our readings argue. J. Douglas Canfield's "Shifting Tropes of Ideology in English Serious Drama, Late Stuart to Early Georgian" combines several sociopolitical interpretive strategies to analyze the way in which certain emergent tropes of Restoration drama (1660 to the 1690s) become dominant in plays after the Revolution. In general, he sees drama as helping to constitute a shift from an aristocratic master trope of word-as-bond to a bourgeois master trope of self-reliance. Important supporting tropes are the emergent bourgeois figures of the benevolent patriarch (or "fratriarch" as he coiningly calls him), the neostoic hero or heroine who stands fixed on his or her own firm center and exhibits not so much constancy for a person but constancy of mind, and the uppity woman who is eventually put in her proper place as still subservient to her man. Canfield examines representative plays from four genres—heroic romance, political tragedy, personal tragedy, and tragicomedy. He concludes, "It becomes obvious that, despite their democratic, meritocratic political rhetoric, the plays are exclusionary: they portray the consolidation of power in the hands of a new (male) elite—a power based ostensibly on law but really on the sword and the gun. And their neostoic exemplary morality masks upper middle-class male dominance over gender, class, and even race."

Richard Braverman's essay, "The Rake's Progress Revisited: Politics and Comedy in the Restoration," moves deftly from a traditional developmental reading of the libertine over a thirty-year period, from the 1660s to the 1690s, to considerations of the state/estate analogy embedded within comedies featuring libertines. Although Restoration comedy might not seem overtly political in the manner of the heroic drama, Braverman maintains that "it is political insofar as it conveys the élan of the court through the charismatic presence of a figure so often affiliated with it." The analogy of the political state as a landed estate finds particular expression in the comedies of the sixties; it recedes, though, in the libertine plays of the mid-seventies, which were "less visibly political than earlier Cavalier comedies that had drawn upon the state-estate analogy." Nevertheless, Braverman insists, "the libertine continued to assert Cavalier values, . . . none of which was more important than his eroding autonomy that mirrored the predicament of the Crown." The best examples of this assertion of autonomy, Braverman suggests, are Wycherley's Horner and Manly, whom he proceeds to analyze as egotists dependent upon a status quo while undermining its professed ideals. The last phase in the nineties, according to Braverman, sees the "erotics of power" shift once again as the old libertine rake is replaced by the *honnête homme,* a movement epitomized in the comedies of Congreve and symbolically concluding with *The Way of the World,* where Fainall and Mirabell "represent conflicting political ideals, Fainall the arbitrary power of the Stuarts in the exercise of his libertine will, and Mirabell the new age of parliamentary power that rests on the authority of the legal will." Furthermore, this displacement occurs at both a political *and* a social level, for "in his social intercourse [Mirabell] removes the hard edge of egotism characteristic of the old libertine"; "he will get to [Millamant's] bedroom, but by way of her drawing room."

An essay that follows a more dialectically based historical method is James Thompson's " 'Sure I have seen that face before': Representation and Value in Eighteenth-Century Drama." Thompson attempts to resolve the "contextual" problem for the drama in a classic Marxist manner: "[T]he discourse of political economy and the discourse of dramatic literature are determined by the stage of capital, and, more specifically, the stage of money. . . . Literature then performs cultural work: plays are determined by social and economic change, and in turn, plays represent and effect, solidify, or modify social change—in other words, literature can serve as a space to imagine and to represent social conditions not yet in being." In this particular instance the drama becomes the site for a crisis in value—how are individual subjects named and differentiated? Both economic theory (seen especially in the debates over the Recoinage Act of 1695–96) and the drama for this time pose questions of what or who authorizes an individual subject's social value. Moreover, several works that turn on the recognition or reading of value, specifically, *Marriage à la Mode, Incognita, The Con-*

scious Lovers, The Rivals, and She Stoops to Conquer, replicate linguisti-
cally in their private, domestic realm the political authority represented by
the coin and the economic value that adheres to that representation in the
public realm.

Although the dialectical approach employed by Thompson has become
increasingly accepted as a way to account for the "doubleness" of Restoration drama—its tendency toward split plots, "non"endings, and divided
social worlds[3]—there remains an intellectual historiography that provides
another means of explanation. Richard Kroll's essay, "Instituting Empiricism: Hobbes's Leviathan and Dryden's Marriage à la Mode," argues that
while a dialectical approach to this play (and, by extension, to others) may
well be "one of the most illuminating so far, the success of [the] method
tends to camouflage the extent to which dialectical analysis depends heavily
on historically sedimented vocabularies." Kroll suggests that we might turn
instead to the more locally produced historical model of late-seventeenth-
century empiricism. This philosophical category is not, he cautions, "a
smug instrument of knowledge; rather, it creates a species of knowledge
that, in the Restoration, could scrutinize its own ideological conditioning."
In this sense especially, Kroll's essay is something of a theoretical apologia
for a more traditional "history of ideas" approach to the drama. But unlike
earlier examples of such an approach, Kroll's essay is self-conscious about
the theoretical implications of this philosophical category: "[B]y contrast
with a more genuinely unmediated and unreflective form of knowledge,
figured in numerous Restoration texts as romance, neoclassical empiricism
provided an extraordinarily flexible tool for self-scrutiny and ideological
analysis. Because it sees itself as an inevitably mediated and negotiable
mode, it seeks at once to construct a positive fiction of knowledge and yet
to make us conscious of the devices by which it does so." Thus, Marriage
à la Mode "debates the terms by which desire and performance themselves
obey the epistemological conditions assumed more consistently by the low
plot." The supposedly unmediated signs of the romance plot are shown to
be as problematized, as contextualized as the supposedly mediated signs of
the ironic comic plot. And all the signs point to the need for public institutions that enforce social roles at some cost of the private realm—especially
for women.

Another essay equally skeptical about dialectical methodologies is J. S.
Peters's "The Novelty; or, Print, Money, Fashion, Getting, Spending, and
Glut." Like Kroll, Peters not only questions Marxist and other approaches

that conceive of themselves as purely materialist (without discounting the ways that material production and institutions may shape discourse), but she also makes a case for a more philosophically grounded historicism. She asserts that, whereas we do not know much about causation, we do know something about metaphor, and that metaphors reflect ways of framing particular community anxieties. In this particular instance, Peters locates anxiety in the late seventeenth century's desire for novelty in a culture in which "reiteration ha[d] grown uncomfortable." Moreover, "a number of seemingly unrelated historical conditions and metaphoric habits are part of the story of the general cultural interest in novelty": the increase in printed matter, not to mention the complexity of publishing; the post-Restoration credit and commercial systems, culminating in the establishment of the Bank of England in 1694; and the "new" science and concomitant concern over style and representation. All three of these institutional structures overlap in the spaces of tropic expression they share. And it is this general anxiety about novelty, Peters argues, that puts pressure "on the drama's conception of its own capacity for novelty." In short, she seeks not to "track the mutual conditioning of 'matter' and 'discourse' . . . but rather to identify a series of tropes that interact with material conditions and institutions [and] . . . relate . . . to one another . . . figures that are the expression of a perennial question, and its coda: Why do we wish for novelty, insofar as we do? More important, is there such a thing as novelty?"

A cultural approach to Restoration and eighteenth-century drama inevitably tests the boundaries of the canon, usually in general anthologies limited to Dryden, Etherege, Wycherley, Congreve, Gay, Goldsmith, and Sheridan. Some drama anthologies include, in tragedy, Otway, Rowe, and Lillo and, in comedy, Vanbrugh, Farquhar, Cibber, and Steele. By contrast, our contributors read a wide range of topics and dramatists; in so doing, they suggest implicitly how earlier critical perceptions determined the shape of the canon. Several essays consider such neglected plays as Motteux's *The Novelty* and Pix's *The Innocent Mistress* (Peters); Sedley's *The Mulberry Garden* (Braverman); *Sodom* (Weber); Behn's *The Rover, Part II*, *The Roundheads*, and *The City Heiress* (Markley); and Manley's *Lucius*, Trotter's *Fatal Friendship*, and Shadwell's *Lancashire Witches* (Canfield). While the canon is still represented, it is reread in fresh ways: Thompson discusses *Marriage à la Mode*, *The Conscious Lovers*, *The Rivals*, and *She Stoops to Conquer* in his essay; Kroll also discusses *Marriage à la Mode*;

Burke and Braverman take up *The Plain Dealer;* and Canfield discusses standard plays by Dryden, Rowe, Addison, Lillo, and Steele. Still other essays, notably Green's, Payne's, and Straub's, consider different aspects of the theater world, especially its masculinization. In short, the contributors' choice of plays results not from a predetermined aesthetic of taste but, rather, from the theoretical lens through which they read.

It is this different critical sensibility that seems to us so worthy of representation to scholars and students alike. This volume collects essays from scholars who are doing some of the most innovative work in the field. Most are in early or midcareer, yet their contributions have already made a significant impact on the field. We hope this collection of their work will increase that impact. We hope, in short, that this volume creates a different kind of image, a *re-storying,* if you will, of Restoration and eighteenth-century theater. And we hope that the re-storying will enable an appreciation for the centrality of the drama to the period. The shift from an aristocratic to a bourgeois ideology has been studied especially effectively in the novel, from Ian Watt's pioneering study to recent work by Michael McKeon, Nancy Armstrong, Lennard Davis, John Richetti, Paul Hunter, and John Bender, among others. But the drama was also co-constitutive of that shift. Cultural studies, as a collage of methods particularly adept at examining such shifts, has provided tools for the analysis especially of tropes of gender, race, and class. Although these essays glance only briefly at race (Canfield on *Cato,* for example), they certainly and thoroughly examine tropes of gender and class, applying various strategies from Marxist, feminist, and related historicist and gender-based methodologies.

The results shed light both on contemporary discourses of the period and on the very methods themselves. In their multiple applications and eclecticism, these essays elude the confines of critical taxonomies and of critical orthodoxies as well. Thus the collection evinces the sort of healthy reflexivity about methodology that currently makes cultural studies so interesting a theoretical nexus.

One last word about implications for theory: It seems to us no accident that most of the work our contributors chose to give us focuses on comedy. Even Straub's essay focuses on the figure of the fop—a staple of comedy—and Canfield's essay on serious drama concludes in a discussion of sentimental comedy as the new bourgeois form of tragicomic romance and seems to gather momentum as it does so. The reason has less to do with aesthetics than the malleability of the material. Let us recall John Loftis's distinction between tragedy and comedy in his work. He maintains that one can see the shift from aristocratic to bourgeois ideology more readily— and earlier—in tragedy than in comedy (*Politics* 5). But Loftis's gaze is, by today's standards of cultural studies work, relatively superficial, seeing "ideology" primarily as a matter of topical political events and theoretical debates and looking for changes in society primarily in the presentation of positive images of the newly dominant bourgeoisie (see *Politics* and *Comedy*, respectively). A new generation of critics finds comedy more susceptible to cultural analysis perhaps because it is more "realistic," closer to the material reality of everyday life. Such closeness is, of course, to some extent illusory, for that material reality is itself a mental construct. Yet the ostensibly mimetic world of comedy may give us greater access to observing the power relations that pervade everyday life and its discipline, such power relations as the control of sexuality and gender, information (the news), indecorous behavior, social mobility. Moreover, the most enabling cultural theorists of recent years—Foucault, the rediscovered Bakhtin, the French feminists, the French social anthropologists, and now the theorists of the postcolonial—have brought a new emphasis on the local, the deviant, the popular, the abject, the subversive, the oppressed. Comedy is particularly susceptible to such analysis.

Nevertheless, Restoration and eighteenth-century comedy represents only one discourse in which to study the tropes of shifting ideology. And we have tried to balance our collection with some attention to other aspects of both drama and theater. More always remains to be done. But we hope that this collection will help bring the study of the drama/theater of the period to its rightful place as a shaping discourse—and thus as an important object of study alongside such other discourses as the novel, nondramatic satire, philosophy, periodicals, paintings, masquerades. Especially as the theaters expanded outside London and into the colonies, drama was a central cultural event that did not just passively reflect but actively shaped consciousness as England moved from a late feudal to an emergent, nay, a dominant bourgeois imperial power.

Notes

We would like to acknowledge the invaluable assistance of our graduate assistants: at American University, Pamela Bender and Helen Roach, and at the University of Arizona, Lori Snook and Maja-Lisa von Sneidern.

1. For recent evidence of continuing resistance, see Schwartz; for a response, see Canfield, "Tradition versus Theory."

2. These concepts run throughout Foucault's work.

3. See, for instance, Brown, McKeon, and Canfield, "Ideology."

Works Cited

Brown, Laura. *English Dramatic Form, 1660–1760: An Essay in Generic History.* New Haven: Yale UP, 1981.

Canfield, J. Douglas. "The Ideology of Restoration Tragicomedy." *ELH* 51 (1984): 447–64.

———. "Tradition versus Theory: Defenders of the Faith." Essay review. *Eighteenth Century: Theory and Interpretation* 33 (1992): 90–96.

Loftis, John. *Comedy and Society from Congreve to Fielding.* Stanford Studies in Language and Literature, 19. Stanford: Stanford UP, 1959.

———. *The Politics of Drama in Augustan England.* Oxford: Clarendon, 1963.

McKeon, Michael. "Marxist Criticism and *Marriage A La Mode*." *Eighteenth Century: Theory and Interpretation* 24 (1983): 141–62.

Roseberry, William. *Anthropologies and Histories: Essays in Culture, History, and Political Economy.* New Brunswick, N.J.: Rutgers UP, 1989.

Schwartz, Richard B., ed. *Theory and Tradition in Eighteenth-Century Studies.* Carbondale: Southern Illinois UP, 1990.

Reified Object or Emergent Professional? Retheorizing the Restoration Actress

Deborah C. Payne

Victim or Victor?

On 14 January 1668 Samuel Pepys took a coach to the house of Mrs. Pierce to fetch his wife and her maid. Instead of leaving promptly, as he originally intended, Pepys idled away the afternoon in gossip with the women. Their topic? The previous night's production of Dryden's *The Indian Emperor* at Whitehall, a novel event, since courtiers performed the play while the actors watched. Mrs. Pierce, who sat among the Duke's Company during the performance, provided her auditors with a firsthand account, especially of the actress *even the women wore nude! - jealousy*

> Mis. Davis . . . the most impertinent slut . . . and the more now the King doth show her countenance and is reckoned his mistress, even to the scorn of the whole world, the King gazing on her, and my Lady Castlemayne being melancholy and out of humour all the play, not smiling once. The King, it seems, hath given her a ring of 700£, which she shows to everybody, and owns that the King did give it her. And he hath furnished a house for her in Suffolke-street most richly for her, which is a most infinite shame. (Pepys 9: 24)

Pepys, almost as an afterthought, then links Davis's looks and her terpsichorean skill: "Pierce says she is a most homely jade as ever she saw, though she dances beyond anything in the world" (9: 24).

This modulation, from appraising looks to performance (or the other way around), is evident throughout the *Diary*. Grumpy at the premiere of the earl of Orrery's *Mustapha* ("not good," Pepys notes dourly), the diarist instead derives pleasure from the presence of the king in the royal box and, best of all, "pretty witty Nell . . . and the younger Marshall, [who] sat next us; which pleased me mightily" (6: 73). The play might disappoint, but the proximity of pretty actresses consoles considerably. An otherwise lackluster production of *Hyde Park,* "an old play of Shirly's," to quote Pepys, is rescued by Rebecca Marshall's "excellent" delivery of the epilogue (9: 260). He rejoices upon discovering that "the eldest Davenport [Hester] is it seems gone from this House to be kept by somebody; which I am glad of, she being a very bad actor" (9: 156). And Nell Gwyn earns raptures for her portrayal of Florimell, the madcap heroine of *The Maiden Queen:*

> [S]o great a performance of a comical part was never, I believe, in the world before as Nell doth this, both as a mad girle and then, most and best of all, when she comes in like a young gallant; and hath the motions and carriage of a spark the most that ever I saw any man have. It makes me, I confess, admire her. (8: 91)

Thus, the *Diary* discloses the three topics that inevitably arise whenever Pepys considers actresses: their looks, their liaisons, and their legerdemain. One could argue that Pepys's interest in the appearance and sexual habits of the actresses reifies them as delectable objects to be consumed visually and, in some instances, sexually by appreciative spectators. Yet his admiration for their craft, all the more notable given the brief time women had been acting in England, grants these actresses a professional stature not usually associated with seventeenth-century women. Nor was Pepys alone. Others in Restoration culture—playwrights, critics, and company personnel—shared the diarist's bifocal fascination with the public acting and private acts of the first women on the English stage. It is almost as if either of these terms necessitated the other one or, as Katharine Eisaman Maus notes, as if contemporary discussions of the actress's private life and lovers were "an extension of her histrionic function" (601).

John Dryden's concern that actresses be cast according to their expertise, not their looks, is evident in this letter to his publisher, Jacob Tonson:

> I had spoken with Mr. Betterton by chance at the Coffee house this afternoon . . . and I believe that the persons were all agreed on, to be just the same you mentioned. Only Octavia was to be Mrs. Butler, in case Mrs. Cooke were not on the Stage. And I know not whether Mrs. Percivall who is a Comedian, will do so well for Benzayda. (23–24)

Nonetheless, contemporary comments about Dryden's affair with Anne Reeves, a minor actress in the King's Company, also show how professional regard and sexual objectification coexisted during the Restoration.[1] Dryden may very well have worried about casting the "best" performer for the role, thus implicitly acknowledging thespian ability. But he also used actresses to shore up personal fictions, both of his sexual prowess and class origins. Thomas Shadwell, for one, accused Dryden of openly bragging about his sexual encounters with Reeves:

> He boasts of Vice (which he did ne'r commit)
> Calls himself Whoremaster and Sodomite;
> Commends Reeve's Arse, and says she Buggers well,
> And silly Lyes of vitious pranks does tell.
>
> (4)

Even the roles Dryden created for Reeves, roles requiring exposure of legs or delivery of suggestive songs, not only titillated the audience but also established her value as a precious object, a value, of course, that redounded to Dryden favorably as its possessor. And, finally, by taking a mistress from the playhouse, Dryden imitated Charles II and his inner circle, thus symbolically claiming a noble affiliation denied him by birth.

Critics also intermingled lurid remarks about actresses with professional praise. *A Comparison between the Two Stages*, a dialogue attributed to Charles Gildon, describes Anne Bracegirdle as "a haughty conceited Woman, that has got more Money by dissembling her Lewdness, than others by professing it," but a page later declares Mrs. Verbruggen "a Miracle" for her acting skills and Mrs. Barry "a Wonder" (199–200). A punning exchange between "Sullen" and "Critic," two of the speakers in the *Comparison*, on the "acting" skills of Anne Bracegirdle perhaps best captures the odd elision between professionalism and eroticism:

> *Sull.* But does that *Romantick Virgin* still keep up her great Reputation?
> *Crit.* D'ye mean her Reputation for Acting?
> *Sull.* I mean her Reputation for not acting; you understand me——.
>
> (17)

Even company personnel winked at the sexual exploits of the actresses while extolling their professional merits. In an often cited passage, John Downes, the prompter for the Duke's Company, describes Moll Davis's

apotheosis from humble player in William Davenant's *The Rivals* to royal
mistress in the king's bedroom:

> And all the Womens Parts admirably Acted; chiefly Celia, a Shep-
> erdess being Mad for Love; especially in Singing several Wild and
> Mad Songs. My Lodging it is on the Cold Ground, &c. She perform'd
> that so charmingly, that not long after, it Rais'd her from her Bed on
> the Cold Ground, to a Bed Royal. (23–24)

Downes plays this story on two familiar registers. He slyly mentions the
"Bed Royal," thus exploiting Davis's private life for public consumption.
But he also stresses that Davis's ability to sing "charmingly"—rather than
her looks—won the king's heart, a tacit affirmation of her art.

All of these anecdotes indicate the extent to which actresses were scru-
tinized within Restoration culture, their looks and liaisons enumerated,
their performances and triumphs praised. Modern criticism reproduces
this split, construing the Restoration actress as either a reified object or an
emergent professional. Clearly, these are radically different versions of the
same story, but which one do we choose: an all too familiar tale of oppression or an equally tired romance of feminine skill triumphing against
all odds? Choosing between the two stories entails, as choice must, the
repression of the opposite. By contrast, I want to suggest in the following
pages how these supposedly antithetical terms actually mark the origins of
a cultural logic still current.

Objectification and professionalization, far from opposing each other,
can be seen as an effect of the late seventeenth-century shift toward the primacy of the visual. And, like most cultural "logics," this one is also marked
by contradiction. Thus, while feminist critics are right to show how objectification undoubtedly diminished actresses, they also fail to note how, in a
public sphere with an increasingly pronounced sense of the visual, objectification simultaneously *amplified* actresses, situating them at the new nexus
of power. Professionalization during the late seventeenth century functions
analogically to objectification. It too diminishes the subject, reducing her
human complexity to the adequate performance of a few prescribed tasks.
But the professional also has a peculiar social prominence because of the
distinctive value assigned to her labor, a fictitious commodity that is scruti-
nized and evaluated within the public realm. It is in this sense that objectification and professionalization both participate in the same cultural logic

of simultaneously reifying and foregrounding the human subject: they are, in short, mutually defining terms.

Before continuing, though, it might prove useful to consider the historical sources for previous readings of the Restoration actress as reified object or emergent professional in order to understand the origins of the thesis. Such an inquiry questions the usual categories of evidence; more important, it also suggests how those of us who are self-styled "cultural critics" too often fail to critique the producers of our historical sources. Considering their own embattled position within the literary marketplace results, as I argue below, in a very different reading of the Restoration actress.

Previous Narratives of the Restoration Actress: Their Sources and Problems

As far as we know, the "facts" are these: an experienced actress earned thirty shillings a week; an actor of similar skill earned fifty shillings (Howe 27). Despite this inequity in pay, actresses were expected to furnish their own stockings, gloves, and scarves for performance, all expensive articles of clothing during the Restoration (Adams 99). There were fewer positions for women than for men: "[T]he rosters of the companies at the beginning of each season in the Calendar suggest also that the number of men was ordinarily at least twice as great as the number of women" (Avery and Scouten c). With the rare exception of Elizabeth Barry, actresses were denied the only source of seniority in the theatrical company—becoming a shareholder (Milhous 8). Pregnancy lost them employment. They were sexually harassed in the tiring-room before and after performance, and they did not have the authority to evict troublesome gentlemen (Nicoll 322). They were subject to violence from rejected courtiers: Sir Hugh Middleton hired a ruffian to fling excrement in Rebecca Marshall's face after she rebuffed him (Wilson 27–28). Some women left the stage for the more profitable, if risky, business of being a mistress, or, as the prompter John Downes quaintly put it, they "by force of Love were Erept the Stage" (35). This last was a mixed blessing. A few women, like Nell Gwyn, did well by themselves and their children and seemed happy to boot; others, like Elizabeth Farley, were abandoned or tricked by noble lovers, only to end up on the street, ill and destitute (Wilson 146–48; 142–44).

This basic information, derived from sources such as the lord chamberlain's records, lawsuits, patents, and articles of agreement, seems fairly incontrovertible. More open to debate is how Restoration culture viewed actresses. Not surprisingly, critical conclusions depend upon the overdetermination of either professionalism or objectification, the two terms, as already argued, in binary play during the period. Some critics stress the former. Rosamond Gilder, writing in the 1930s, enthuses over how "this burgeoning of feminine beauty and talent in the English theatre was spectacularly rapid and sweeping" (134). Her narrative, teleological in shape, emphasizes the gradual transition in actresses' status: "[A]t first barely tolerated in the theatre and classed as mere 'hirelings,' they had, by the close of the century, become respected members of the profession" (172).

Other critics emphasize Restoration culture's voyeuristic and sexual use of the actress. John Harold Wilson, as might be expected from the title of his book, *All the King's Ladies,* tells an elbow-nudging tale that plays up pandering far more than professionalism. Chapter headings, such as "Behind the Scenes" and "In Petticoats and Breeches," hint suggestively at the peep show within. While more recent theater histories have told the story of the Restoration actress without gratuitous titillation, nonetheless they still favor one of the two terms. Elin Diamond, noting how Restoration stagecraft "seems to have created a spectator-fetishist," goes on to assert that "nowhere are these meanings of fetishism more relevant than in discourse generated by that other ornament of the stage, the Restoration actress" (522). And Thomas A. King focuses on the "two bodies" of the Restoration actress (i.e., the fictional character she played and her thespian identity) in attempting to show how "the demand to conflate these two bodies underlay the voyeuristic dynamic that has since been characteristic of Western theatre" (80).

Even those critics who grant both sexual objectification *and* professionalization tend to hold these critical categories apart. Elizabeth Howe, for instance, claims that "society assumed that a woman who displayed herself on the public stage was probably a whore" and that "even if an actress's private life seemed exemplary, writers focused on her sexuality rather than on her acting ability" (32, 35). Pages later, though, we are told that "the presence, and the disappearance, of popular and talented actresses changed and shaped the course of the drama to a degree which has gone unrecognised" (66). Nell Gwyn becomes a test case here. She was celebrated (and reviled) as the king's "Protestant whore"; at the same time, her wit, energy, and comic timing proved instrumental to the generic creation of the gay couple: "[T]he dramatist conceived the innovation, but the inspiration of his assertive heroine was Nell Gwyn and thus, albeit indirectly, she brought a new approach to comic love relationships between the sexes" (71).

Readings that emphasize Restoration culture's construction of the actress-as-object (and I take "object" here to encompass both sexual and visual "uses" of the actress) rely for the bulk of their evidence on satires against the stage and prologues and epilogues. Within the first category of evidence, often cited is *The Session of the Ladies,* a scurrilous lampoon set in a playhouse. Three actresses, Boutell, Cox, and Barry, along with several lecherous court ladies, most notably, the countess of Castlemaine, compete for the sexual favors of Cardell Goodman, an actor figured as "Adonis" in the poem. The poem savages everyone; the actresses, though, are treated in a particularly vicious manner:

> There was chestnut-maned Boutell, whom all the Town fucks,
> Lord Lumley's cast player, the famed Mrs. Cox,
> And chaste Mrs. Barry, i'th midst of a flux
> To make him a present of chancre and pox.
>
> (2r)

Often cited too is Robert Gould's *The Play-House,* a vitriolic attack on all aspects of the theater, from critics to spectators, but especially the actresses:

> But most the Women are Audacious seen,
> All Paint their Out-sides and all Pox within.
> Here 'tis our Quality are fond of such,
> Which ev'n their Wiser Footmen scorn to Touch:
> Divested of the Robes in which they're Cas'd,
> A Goat's as sweet, and Monkey's are as Chast.
>
> (311)

Elizabeth Barry, the great tragedian, earns particular scorn; she is, in Gould's words, "insatiate as a Charnell," "a Dowd / So very basely born so very Proud," and "Covetous" that "she'll prostitute with any, / Rather than wave the Getting of a Penny" (311–12).

These two lampoons allegedly confirm that "society assumed that a woman who displayed herself on the public stage was probably a whore" (Howe 32). Or, as Laura J. Rosenthal, using Gould for support, maintains: "[T]he actress as whore representation appears so frequently during the Restoration that it takes on a life of its own, independent of the reference to the women themselves" (4). Linking the terms *lampoon* and *whore,* though, eliminates the crucial mediation provided by the field of production, thus committing what the sociologist Pierre Bourdieu has in an interview called the "short-circuit fallacy" (Bourdieu and Wacquant 69). In other words, before assuming that these lampoons represent dominant cultural attitudes or even, for that matter, function as "a sign within a network of theatrical signification" (Rosenthal 4), we need to examine critically the *producers* of lampoons, especially their embattled position in the literary marketplace. Lampoons, circulated privately in manuscript and anonymously printed, were usually written by alienated writers avenging their own disappointments (a fall from grace, the inability to be noticed) or claiming a place within the literary marketplace. It should not surprise that this group, the dominated fraction of an already dominated class within the culture,[2] would fixate on actresses, another social group on equally precarious social footing.

Robert Gould is a case in point. Servant to the earl of Dorset, Gould lacked the cultural and educational capital necessary to produce "higher" forms of verse; thus he entered the literary marketplace with lampoons and satires, the only generic options available to a self-taught domestic. Gould was uncomfortably aware of his class origins, a discomfort that sometimes took the form of self-loathing. For instance, the preface to his early collection of poems imagines Denham, Waller, and Mulgrave, all of them gentlemen, to be "ideal" poets, largely because they possess the following attributes: an educational "Foundation laid in the University"; "Travel and Correspondence"; "Modern as well as Learned Languages"; "a good Study of Books"; and "Art" and "Nature," both gifts from "Nature" (*Poems* A1v–A3r). Thus Gould constructs a social category that, by its very nature, excludes working-class poets like himself. Indeed, Gould cannot even imagine himself as a cultural possibility.

At other moments, Gould's class anxiety took the form of literary reprisal. Although he claims to have written *The Play-House* as "a Reproof to the Immorality and Prophaneness of the Stage" (*Works* 2: 225), actors—and actresses especially—most likely earned the poet's wrath because of their structural similarity to his own vexed social standing. Technically, players, like Gould, were servants and enjoyed the customary benefits of that station, such as the wearing of livery. They also experienced the accompanying limitations as well. But the Restoration actors were more than servants—they were also professionals—and, once again, like Gould, they formed uneasy friendships and liaisons with the gentry and nobility. Those relationships, of course, were not truly symmetrical in the manner necessary for "pure" friendship (Eisenstadt and Roniger 2), and it should not surprise that the lord chamberlain's records are filled with complaints and actions taken against company personnel who, quite literally, "did not know their place." Gould thus projects onto actresses his own anxiety, an anxiety figured, appropriately enough, in metaphors of exchange and commodification.

Gould, though, miscalculated not only his own social worth but also that of the actresses. After circulating *The Play-House,* he submitted a play to the United Company for consideration; the insulted players, led by Elizabeth Barry and Thomas Betterton, rejected it. Gould turned for assistance to the lord chamberlain and "several People of Quality" who "ingag'd on [his] side." Although he had a warrant commanding performance of the play (*Innocence Distress'd; or, The Royal Penitents*), "all the Notice they took of it was only to Consult how with safety to disobey it; in which they at last, with a great deal of Inhumanity, Succeeded" (*Works* 2: 225). Gould was so desirous of mending relations with the company—especially the actresses—that he not only pleaded the impetuosity of youth ("I put 'em in Mind I was very Young when this Satyr was Written") but also agreed to revisions ("[I] offered to leave out of this Edition any Verses they pleas'd or that any other Person believ'd cou'd be so much as wrested to their Disadvantage" [*Works* 2: 226]). Elizabeth Barry refused the truce: "All that this cou'd obtain from the Mighty Actress was plainly to tell me, She was not so good a Christian as to forgive." To this Gould added spitefully, "[I]ndeed, I really and readily believ'd Her" (*Works* 2: 226).

Ultimately, Barry and the other women, backed by Thomas Betterton, helped ruin the poet. *Innocence Distress'd* was kept from production *and* print; Gould's daughter, Hannah, finally managed its publication by subscription in 1737, many years after the death of Elizabeth Barry, the "Mighty" actress. As for *The Play-House,* that too mysteriously disappeared, not to appear in print until 1709 in the collected works.[3] The one play Gould did manage to see staged, *The Rival Sisters; or, The Violence of Love* (London, 1696), largely through the intervention of Gould's second employer, the earl of Abingdon, received "much interruption and discouragement from some prejudic'd Gentlemen," perhaps catcalling spectators strategically placed in the audience (A2r). Gould, though, had already stopped writing by that time, largely in response to ill treatment from critics as well as the actresses:

> And certainly there is no worse Fate on Earth than being laught at.
> ———But if the Reader will forgive what is amiss, I will never give him any fresh Occasion for that Favour; for here I renew my Promise (made to two great Men) of yielding up all my Engagements to that Study, together, if the Criticks please, with the very Name of a Poet, which I confess I do not deserve; Resolving seriously never more to write a line. (*Poems* A4r–v)

This episode is troubling on several levels. Gould's invective against actresses supposedly represents dominant social views: for positivists, a historical transparency; for poststructuralists, a sign within a culturally determined system of signification. This "short-circuit fallacy" (i.e., linking cultural objects and the society for which they are produced) can occur only by ignoring Gould's vexed position within the social space of the literary marketplace. Once that position is acknowledged, his ravings lose much of their cultural force. Moreover, Gould's views were not even representative of a certain segment of society; the hostile reception of his work and the rapid demise of his career—such as it was—suggest unpopularity at best. This episode also discloses more thespian authority than theater historians admit. Elizabeth Barry and the other women wield enough power to ruin a writer's career and run afoul of the lord chamberlain's commands. As members of a theatrical company, they participate directly in technologies of distribution; Gould, a servant backed by a couple of noble patrons, does not. This is hardly a symmetrical relationship.

In addition, the women recognize and attempt to control—as does Gould himself—the discursive elements at stake. By squelching the poet's career, the actresses suppress his representation of them as whores, mere commodities. Although *The Play-House* finally saw print in 1709 as part of Gould's collected satires, arguably, the actresses—or, by this late date, their wraiths—won that final round too. Gould wrote an advertisement for that edition to justify this "little Sketch," but his defensive tone and feeble excuses in that essay virtually nullify the lampoon that follows (*Works* 2: 226). Gould badmouths the actresses and then, like a toddler discovering that actions produce consequences, wails in print when they slap his hand. It is, perhaps, one of the ironies of history that recent criticism has done more to advance Gould's construction of the actress-as-commodity than

he ever managed during his own time. One also wonders about the extent
to which the sheer availability of Gould's lampoon, *The Play-House*, has
elevated its stature as a "spokesman for the age." Montague Summers reprinted the lampoon as part of "Appendix I" in *The Restoration Theatre*,
originally published in 1934. Prior to Summers's exhumation of Gould, he
rested through the centuries, undisturbed and unnoticed.

Prologues and epilogues to plays provide another kind of evidence for
the presumed commodification of actresses: "[I]n speaking these epilogues,
Butler, Barry and Gwyn lightheartedly reinforced the idea of themselves as
whores, corroborating, as it were, what the satirists and gossips said about
them" (Howe 98). Rosenthal asserts that "prologues and epilogues frequently proclaim the sexual availability of the woman who delivers them"
(4–5). What, though, constitutes "frequently"? Out of twelve hundred
prologues and epilogues written between 1660 and 1700 and compiled by
Pierre Danchin, only ten—fewer than 1 percent—mention either the sexual
availability of the speaker or actresses in general. One of the most offensive
of these, a manuscript epilogue, was most likely never spoken on the stage
(Danchin 6: 429). Another especially lewd piece in this group, an epilogue
written for William Chamberlayne's *Wits Led By the Nose; or, A Poet's
Revenge* (1678), resulted in the arrest of the actor Joseph Haines for "re-
citeing at the Theatre Royall a scurrilous & obscene Epilogue" (Danchin
3: 52). Interestingly, the next play produced by the King's Company, John
Banks's *The Rival Kings*, promises—mainly as an apology to the "ladies"
who were offended by the Chamberlayne epilogue—"a modest Prologue
and a modest Play," in addition to the absence of Haines, who "has left
us all of your displeasure sick" (Danchin 3: 58). It would seem that prologues and epilogues especially offensive on the subject of actresses were
prohibited or resulted in arrest.

The remaining eight are fairly benign by comparison. Three appear in
the 1676–77 season, an especially difficult time for the beleaguered King's
Company; three in 1682, the year the United Company was formed; one
in 1690; and another in 1693, which witnessed the ignominious departure
of one company manager and the installation of two equally unscrupulous
ones. That seven of these prologues and epilogues occurred amid company
tumult and lackluster box office suggests that playwrights and managers
were on rare occasion willing to brave the displeasure of ladies in the audience and the lord chamberlain in order to make provocative statements
about actresses. All of these eight prologues and epilogues comment on

the actresses' availability, sometimes suggesting an exchange relationship (actress/whore for money), other times acknowledging their active love life.

Irony, though, complicates the sexual innuendo in these pieces, as the prologue to William Wycherley's *The Country Wife* reveals. Taken out of context, it would seem that the last four lines blatantly advertise the availability of the actresses:

> We set no Guards upon our Tyring-Room;
> But when with flying Colours, there you come,
> We patiently you see, give up to you,
> Our Poets, Virgins, nay our Matrons too.
>   (Danchin 2: 638)

The prologue, though, draws throughout a distinction between "bully" poets, who "provoke" audiences, and meek actors, who "submit, / Now, and at any time, to a full Pit." So desperate to please are the actors, they will "murder Poets for you, on our Stage," in addition to giving up "Poets, Virgins, nay our Matrons too." The actresses—as well as the poets—are figured as kind of loot to be handed over to invading hordes of spectators. But the humor here is directed against those spineless actors who would kill stage poets and surrender women in order to appease the audience.

Another epilogue in this group was written for Aphra Behn's *The City Heiress*. The actress Charlotte Butler, who played the title role, warns women in the audience not to pillage the available men: "Pray, Ladies, Leave that Province to our care, / A Fool is the Fee simple of a Player, / In which we Women claim a double share" (Danchin 3: 404). Finally, a compromise is reached. The ladies get the wits, the actresses the fools:

> If by Stage-Fops they a poor Living get,
> We can grow rich, thanks to our Mother Wit,
> By the more natural Block-heads in the Pit.
> Take then the Wits, and all their useless Prattles.
> But as for Fools, they are our Goods and Chattels[.]

While these lines stress the economic advantage of liaisons for actresses, nonetheless it is *men* who function as "Goods and Chattels," not women. Thus, the epilogue inverts the usual ratio between subject/male/wit and object/female/body. The actresses, assisted by "Mother Wit," claim their fools, their "fee simples," twice over, once as paying spectators and again as sugar daddies.

Few prologues and epilogues, then, have as their content the commodification of actresses; indeed, as a percentage the number is negligible at best. And those few pieces that *do* discuss their availability often subvert the implied exchange relationship. That actresses, especially by the 1670s, were preferred over actors to deliver these addresses to the audience is well documented: "[I]t has been calculated that of the eighty or so women who became actresses before 1689, at least twenty-six were entrusted with one or more prologues and epilogues; this was far in excess of the number of named male players so entrusted" (Howe 94). But it is far more common for the actress to plead on behalf of the play, almost as a kind of intercessor between the poet and the audience, than it is for her to pander herself. Undoubtedly, the dramatist and company manager expected that an actress, especially one clothed in tight breeches, would curry favor with the audience, as several critics have noted (e.g., Styan 92–93). Less remarked, though, is how the actress-as-intercessor plays off gendered notions of audience behavior during the Restoration, behavior, moreover, that does not necessarily reinforce the commodification of actresses.

Men, commonly figured in these addresses as "hectors," "bullies," "fools," "fanaticks," and "rogues," challenge the theatrical enterprise; women, possessed of "kindness," "beauty," "wit," "gentleness," and "good sense," encourage it. The prologue to Dryden's *All for Love* likens the men in the audience to "Vultures . . . All gaping for the Carcass of a Play!"— an image so horrifying to the poet that "if he might his own Grand Jury call, / By the Fair Sex he begs to stand or fall" (Danchin 3: 83–85). The prologue to Thomas D'Urfey's *Trick for Trick* laments the "Dearth of Witt" among the men in the audience; the epilogue deplores their "Ill Natures" (Danchin 3: 111–12). The dramatist therefore places his poetic fortunes in the hands of women, the favorites of the "Mighty God of Witt" and possessed of "Sacred Influence" (Danchin 3: 112). A manuscript prologue (which features the instructions "To be spoke by a woman") imagines the speaker as a midwife assisting at the painful birth of a male dramatist's play: "He's in hard labour I'le assure you all / In feare and doubt where he shall stand or fall" (Danchin 3: 163). Here it is the laboring poet and his changeling play that function as the object of a collective male gaze, not the actress: "Cause at the labour here's so many men / So many prying, Censureing, busy creatures / that will be finding fault with all its features" (Danchin 3: 163). The actress/speaker/midwife chides the men in the audience, calling them "froward Gulls," "meer bellowing town bulls," "filthy, and . . . filthy still" for attempting to participate actively in the delivery of a play (Danchin 3: 165). The prologue implies that drawing aesthetic distinctions—like assisting at a birth—is the business of women, "the milder halfe." Men, by contrast, are "roaring boys," frenetic bundles of hopping passions and ill judgments.

This cultural dynamic, whereby women are shown to be more receptive to new plays than men, also affects the conception of the actress speaking the prologue and/or epilogue. Although, as David Roberts points out, "the usual appeals to female critical power do not permit the right of vocal approval or disapproval" (35), nonetheless through their assent women could rescue a play's fortunes. If women, then, are "innately" sympathetic to the artistic enterprise, it follows that actresses are especially well positioned to deliver these writerly appeals. Actresses, by the mere fact of their gender, supposedly embody gentleness and sound judgment, virtues that will hopefully inspire and becalm warring (male) factions in the pit. Then, too, there is the traditional image of women as supplicants: between children and fathers, families and clans, nations and gods.

Female sexuality in these "supplicant" prologues and epilogues proves to be powerfully restorative: the actress on the stage asks the women in the audience for a show of indulgence toward the frightened, feminized, or phallically insufficient male author. Dryden imports this dynamic into the prologue to *An Evening's Love*, drawing an anxious comparison between the poet's literary and sexual performance: "When first our Poet set himself to write, / Like a young Bridegroom on his Wedding-night" (Danchin 1: 286–87). Similar to a bored husband performing "ungrateful drudgery," the dramatist must "strain himself" to please the audience, "Wives ill pleas'd." Spectators consider each "writing Monsieur" a "fresh Gallant" and thus prove distressingly fickle: "These are Gallants but for a Holiday. / Others you had who oftner have appear'd, / Whom, for meer impotence you have cashier'd."

It is this fear of literary impotence, this anxiety over authorial puissance, that necessitates the presence of a soothing female as intermediary between the dramatist and his audience. "I am come again," declares Anne Bracegirdle in the prologue to *The Successfull Straingers*, "to plead in the behalf of a weak Pen" (Danchin 4: 788). Not only is the dramatist here, William Mountfort, said to possess a "weak Pen"—one need not invoke Freud—but he sits "quaking . . . to hear the dreadful sentence of the Pit." Bracegirdle summons additional, almost maternal compassion for the author:

"Cou'd but the Females see, how very sad / He looks, they'd pitty such a likely Lad" (Danchin 4: 789). In a similar hope of eliciting female sympathy, the prologue to *Agrippa, King of Alba* likens the dramatist, most likely John Dancer, to a shy virgin, "cloystred in modesty and cloath'd with fear" (Danchin 1: 312–13). He is "unwilling to become expos'd, / Strugled with doubts, was fearful to be stung / With the lewd touch of every Critick tongue." Even Sir Charles Sedley, according to contemporary accounts no blushing flower he, worries in the prologue to *The Mulberry Garden* about "the dangerous Rocks upon the Coast of Praise, / The cruel Critick and malicious Wit" (Danchin 1: 284–85). Ultimately, it is women who will rescue him: "He hopes the Ladies at small faults will wink, / And a new Poet, a new Servant think."

These prologues and epilogues represent actresses in a far different light from what recent criticism suggests. Women players defend male dramatists anxious about the performance of their "pen"; they appease male spectators about to enter the critical fray. Feminist scholars, especially those working on Victorian literature, have taught us to suspect the power differential that permits benign cultural constructions of women—the proverbial "angel in the house." And, undoubtedly, the woman as pleading daughter, petitioning wife, or understanding lover is a limited and, to modern eyes, reactionary cultural role. The woman as supplicant, though, does exert in traditional societies a kind of archetypal force, and it is this force that more commonly informs prologues and epilogues than formulations of the "actress as whore" or "actress as object."

Perspectivism and Power

The critic John Dennis, writing in the early eighteenth century, noted the two main innovations of the Restoration stage, "Scenes and Women; which added probability to the Dramatick Actions and made everything look more naturally" (II: 277–78). One can make the case, as have several critics, that the use of shutters to frame or suddenly reveal an actress posed before perspective backdrops provided a new technology of objectification: "[T]he movement of painted flats, the discoveries of previously unseen interiors, introduced a new scopic epistemology" (Diamond 521).[4] The reverse, though, is also true: that technology amplified the actress by framing her against the most powerful site within the spectacle. Moreover, while the idea of perspective can, in the words of Claudio Guillen, "be readily associated with a growing epistemological dualism—with a rigorous split between subject and object, as in the Cartesian distinction between mind and *res extensa*," by the same logic, that split also signifies the limitations inherent in discovering the "right" perspective (34). In his study *The Curious Perspective: Literary and Pictorial Wit in the Seventeenth Century* Ernest B. Gilman explains: "The very fullness and definition of perspective spaces implies the radical incompleteness of our vision, and the point of view becomes a drastic limitation, a set of blinders, as well as an epistemological privilege" (31). Thus, as Barbara Freedman notes, perspectivism, by implying that the spectator is never outside what she perceives, also points toward an epistemology based on the *subversion* of spectator consciousness (30).

Gilman traces the origins of a spectator consciousness in the seventeenth century, an epistemological model based on an observer who stands apart from the spectacle. This shift is described by Samuel Y. Edgerton, Jr., as "the crucial turning point in Western cultural history when philosophers first understood themselves as detached from nature, as outside observers limited by the inadequacy of their mental *formae* to perceiving and describing phenomena only metaphorically" (40). In part this separation of the sign from the signified depended upon the rediscovery of classical ratios during the Renaissance, a rediscovery that made possible new techniques in architecture, design, navigation, and cartography: "By positing a human centric point and employing an arbitrary unit as a standard, Renaissance thinkers introduced theories of perspective which effectively reshaped their conceptualization of knowledge" (Freedman 11). Leon Battista Alberti, for one, helped to circulate perspectivism and thus to stabilize a position of mastery.

Perspectivism had the same kind of impact on theater architecture and scenic design as it did on other areas of knowledge: "[P]erhaps the most important single feature of the Renaissance theatre was the enormous symbolic influence of perspective in it" (Carlson 136). As a result, a major shift in spatial organization occurred in academic theaters, such as the Theatro Olimpico in Vicenza, the Gonzaga theater at Sabbioneta, the Medici theater in Florence, and the Farnese theater in Parma. It was theaters such as these that influenced the great English scenic designer Inigo Jones during his travels abroad. Jones, according to his successor John Webb, spent "many years" in Italy studying art and architecture (Orrell 6). To the masques staged at court for James I and Charles I, Jones brought sliding wings, movable back shutters, opening clouds, and deep scenes of relief, all elements imported from academic theaters. The painted flats for these theaters focused the audience's gaze on a single vanishing point. From the royal box, the king, as Stephen Orgel demonstrates in *The Illusion of Power*, enjoyed the "best" view, that vantage point alone encompassing the entire perspective (10–11).

This technology, originally reserved for court consumption in the earlier seventeenth century, became a staple of both court and public theater during the Restoration. Charles II and his courtiers desired the scenic innovations at home they had witnessed in exile abroad. So keen was the king to import the latest technology that he commissioned Thomas Betterton, the rising star of the Duke's Company, to report firsthand on latest developments for the Paris stage (Orrell 4). But it was John Webb who forged the strongest link between the earlier academic theaters and the Restoration playhouses: "[M]uch of what the Restoration playgoer found on the stages of the Duke's and the King's Theatres had first been brought to London in the Court theatres of Whitehall and Somerset House" (Orrell 189).

Perspectivism, by framing and objectifying the woman's body, is thought to intensify the "power differential between the watcher and the watched" already present in spectacle (Straub 5). Because women, not men, are traditionally "looked at," so the argument goes, they become especially apt objects of the audience's gaze. This theory of the "gaze" proceeds from Jacques Lacan's theory of *méconnaissance* and has had particular currency in film studies. Critics such as Laura Mulvey and Kaja Silverman maintain that cinema's formal properties reflect the psychic obsessions of society at large. Additionally, they examine how "cinema poses questions about the ways the unconscious (formed by the dominant order) structures ways of seeing and pleasure in looking" (Mulvey 433). In traditional cinema, as Silverman notes, we are sutured into identification with the camera and the story (201–6). Because the camera continually shifts our focus through successive cuts, it encourages us to desire narrative closure rather than to critique the story itself. Other technological aspects of film—editing, its sense of verisimilitude, even the viewing conditions (the darkened room, the flickering image)—reinforce a sense of voyeurism as the viewer gazes at the celluloid picture before him.

Grafting this filmic model onto theater, though, denies the latter its own unique properties. Theater, by virtue of its semiotic texture, cannot claim cinema's privileged relationship to the imaginary order, nor does it excel as the vehicle par excellence for the voyeuristic gaze, for ocularcentric pleasure. As Barbara Freedman has recently argued, theater, unlike film, "displays a fractured gaze, or shows that it knows that it is showing" (69). Cinema may very well encourage direct identification with the seeing eye of the camera, but theater, as Freedman notes, divides and disperses the possibilities of identification, shifting and problematizing the gaze through multiple points of view. The actress is instrumental to this process: when she plays a "role," she displaces presence by showing that the "I" is actually someone else (Freedman 77). While the actress calls the spectator's desire into play through exhibiting herself, the very contingency of the self subverts the spectator's powerful gaze.

In addition, the actress in theater, unlike the film actress, actively returns the look of the audience. Voyeurism depends upon an unseen spectator; in the theater, though, the actress constantly exposes the fundamental imbalance of this dynamic through her evident response to the audience. In effect, the very nature of theatricality is inimical to the voyeurism typical of cinema. And if "the gaze" also depends in part on spatial, as well as psychological, relationship between the spectator and the object, then staging conventions during the Restoration certainly hindered this dynamic. Comedies were performed on the forestage, allowing performers to align themselves with the audience (Holland 29). Asides, ad libs, prologues, and epilogues all provided the actress the opportunity to interrupt the spectator-object dynamic—to "break" character—and challenge the audience's view of things.

There is little doubt that actresses were exploited economically and sexually. The materiality of late-seventeenth-century theater, though, renders questionable the notion of the Restoration spectator as a sort of prurient "peeping Tom" seated in darkness and gazing at a lambent female body. As Marvin Carlson notes, "the auditoriums of Renaissance and baroque theatres were as a rule better illuminated than the stages," paradoxically making it easier for the actress to see the audience than they could her (140). Moreover, the size of the Restoration playhouse allowed the actress to know—and banter with—many of the spectators, a sort of friendly intimacy that would frustrate her transformation into the objectified "other." In the 1660s the theaters could accommodate around four hundred spectators; when the theaters were rebuilt in the early 1670s, the capacity doubled (Styan 20–21). Allan Richard Botica estimates, however, that no more than four hundred to five hundred spectators attended even these larger theaters (cited in Maguire 104). A much smaller percentage of that total number would have been regular theatergoers and, out of that group, still fewer the sort of public or important figures to garner recognition. Even though the Restoration audience was far from homogeneous—as earlier theater histories argued—nonetheless actresses would have known the regulars in the boxes and the pit (Maguire 104–5).

The "tennis court" architectural model that underpins the Restoration playhouse not only produced a hierarchy of viewpoints (the king's being the most perfect) but also in its use of perspectivism limited the multiplicity common to earlier public theaters like the Globe. It can be argued that this architectural model contributed to the development of ocularcentrism on the English stage, a development that "privileged the power of spectatorship at the expense of the power of performance" (King 79). This movement toward spectatorship supposedly made possible the objectification of the actress. But in its very limiting of multiplicity, its perspectivist framing of the actors and actresses who trod the boards, the Restoration playhouse paradoxically embued them with the authority that can only result from being "on stage" in a Western culture moving toward the primacy of the visual.

Professionalization and the Actress

Professionalization, the other term under consideration, also diminishes and amplifies the actress. It functions as another form of objectification and, like its perspectivist cousin, frames the actress's attributes by drawing attention to them (in this instance to skills rather than appearance). Professionalization claims cultural authority for the actress by staging her unique (and painstakingly acquired) talents in the very public realm of the theater. At the same time, the professionalized subject, unlike the apprentice or master craftsman of previous centuries, is subject to public scrutiny of her trade: her skills—in this instance, thespian skills—are evaluated according to commonly held notions of taste. It is in this sense that professionalization, by forcing the subject into the public realm to be judged according to external criteria, functions as another version of Cartesian dualism. Once again the actress is looked at, objectified; only this time she is framed against the perspectivist backdrop of taste.

The actress earned her professional stature simply by being a working member of a theatrical company during the Restoration. The unprecedented interest in the public theater by the court, the adoption of complex aesthetic rules for actors and playwrights, the self-conscious importation of "the best" in playhouse and set design from the Continent all elevated the social status of the Restoration stage. Thomas Killigrew, manager of the King's Company, drew for Samuel Pepys sharp distinctions between the pre–Civil War stage and the Restoration:

> Now, wax-candles and many of them; then, not above 3£ of tallow. Now, all things civil, no rudeness anywhere; then, as in a bear-garden. Then, two or three fiddlers; now, nine or ten of the best. Then, nothing but rushes upon the ground and everything else mean; and now, all otherwise. Then, the Queen seldom and the King never would come; now, not the King only for state but all civil people do think they may come as well as any. (Pepys 8: 55–56)

Sir William Davenant, manager of the Duke's Company, and his wife, Mary, were careful to give the first actresses training in speaking, movement, elocution, and dancing. We know from Thomas Betterton's *History of the English Stage* that when the earl of Rochester, on a bet from friends, took Elizabeth Barry out to a country house to "teach" her to be an actress, he spent most of his time working through classical texts and the canon of "old" plays. Textual exegesis eventually led to the interpretation of roles: "[The earl] made her enter into the nature of each sentiment; perfectly changing herself, as it were, into the person, not merely by the proper stress or sounding of the voice, but feeling really, and being in the humor, the person she represented, was supposed to be in" (17). Playwrights worked closely with the companies during rehearsal, teaching parts, answering questions, and, in response to suggestions from the players, changing lines. This suggests that, far from functioning as passive objects in a spectacle, actresses shaped plays in rehearsal and performance.

Although many aspects of the Restoration stage were elevated, the professional status of the players was intrinsically problematic due to a number of social transformations. Legally they needed the protection of a patron; the court, for instance, supplied livery annually for the King's Company (Avery and Scouten xcii). But they were also paid professionals who labored in a market, not a clientelistic, economy. Additionally, the acting profession during the Restoration and early eighteenth century suffered the same problems that befell other emergent professions as the old guild system receded: practically anybody could become a professional. Philip Elliott notes that "the system of vocational training seems to have finally

disappeared in the period of Cromwell's government" (29). For many professions, "entry procedures had become . . . a matter of routine formalities"
(Elliott 30).

This mid-seventeenth-century transformation from apprenticeship to
professionalism also affected the organization of the acting company.
Earlier in the century, boys were apprenticed to the adult companies and,
according to Andrew Gurr, "bound for a period of several years' training
in their profession before graduating to be hired men and eventually perhaps sharers in their company" (93). Boys could also learn to act within
the children's companies but, unlike their counterparts in the adult companies, they performed with their own age group and "were trained and
directed not by their fellow-actors but by the managers for whose profit
they worked" (Gurr 93). Because most guild-style organizations strictly
limit membership to a few males who are permitted to learn (through a
lengthy and expensive apprenticeship) how to practice the "mystery" of
a trade, the opportunities for women are few. It should not surprise that
women, who do not easily fit the apprenticeship model characteristic of the
English stage, would be prohibited from acting prior to the Restoration.

This model, though, had all but disappeared by the Restoration when
performers came from all walks of life and acting increasingly was regarded
as a profession. A nursery for actors existed during the Restoration (we
know little about its workings), and Michael Mohun and Charles Hart, two
of the early actors, had been apprentices during the pre-Commonwealth
stage (Avery and Scouten xcix). But the system of apprenticeship, whereby
boys are bound for several years' training to an adult company, seems
to have vanished, only to be replaced by an emergent (and intrinsically
problematic) notion of professionalism. Because professionalism is still
unregulated and uncredentialled during the late seventeenth century, it
absorbs new members in a way that the guild/apprenticeship model, by
its very exclusive nature, could not. While the emergent category of the
"professional" provided actresses with new opportunities, it also produced
attendant contradictions.

Professionals sacrifice the secrecy of their art by operating within a public
sphere: the rules governing their trade are public (unlike the secret practices of a guild) and therefore subject to evaluation and criticism, a kind
of objectifying diminishment. Additionally, professional work, as the sociologist Magali Sarfatti Larson notes, is a fictitious commodity: it cannot
be detached from life, it cannot be stored or eaten, nor is it produced as an
object for sale (although a professional might sell "expertise"). If the pro-

fessional product is to be given a distinctive form, one that separates it from prosaic work, then, in the words of Larson, "the producers themselves have to be produced" (14). In other words, professionals must be adequately trained and socialized so as to justify the exchange of their services within a market economy. The closer a profession mimics "common" trades and the people who perform them, the more urgent is the need to circumscribe the emergent profession through the articulation of elaborate rules.

Acting, by its very nature, though, confounds claims to professionalization. Perhaps "antitheatrical prejudice" proceeds not so much from Puritan anxiety over "conscious deception . . . for wicked purposes" (although that too is present) but from the suspicion that thespians are not truly performing "distinctive work" (Barish 158). An actor's artistry paradoxically depends upon its very ordinariness: the closer a performance is to "real life" (or how "realistically" a person might behave under hypothetical circumstances), the higher its valuation. Although Restoration acting appears "artificial" to modern eyes, this proceeds, according to Peter Holland, from "a misunderstanding of the problem of balance between natural acting and the forms of social artifice" (57). Only fools and fops were caricatures; by contrast, the "acting style for the principals was natural" (Holland 59). Thus, Restoration players strained against the same burden that besets modern performers: giving ordinary behavior a distinctive form so as to justify its exchange in a market economy.

Thus, the Restoration theater staged in a cultural narrative apart from the play proper the contradiction of the professional classes during this time: making the ordinary into the suspiciously extraordinary. This begins to explain, I think, the fascination and anxiety that actors and actresses held for spectators and the origins of a star system that is very much part of our culture today. If a professional is created fictitiously within the public sphere, then, of course, the reverse is also true: that professional can just as easily be "unmade," become downwardly mobile. In an odd way, the very practice of performance embodies the contingency of professionalization. And actresses, even more so than actors, because of the subservient position women held within hierarchical models of the family, become a particular focal point for this anxiety: why should ordinary women occupy such a prominent place in the public sphere? (Maus 611). This might explain, as King argues, why "the threat of mobility was at least partly contained by perpetuating the link between the actress and the prostitute" (87).

But evidence suggests, as I have argued above, that the actress-as-whore/

object/commodity formulation was not a major discourse during the Restoration. Admiration for the actresses' technical skill and gossip about their private lives (this is not the same as commodification) were far more prevalent. Rather, perspectivism and professionalism spawn a complex dynamic whereby perfectly ordinary women become simultaneously the object of collective attention and the practitioners of an "art," a doubly powerful yet circumscribed position. The fascination with the lives and skills of actresses can be situated at the intersection of civic prominence, virtuoso display, and professional anxiety. Stories about "stars" are always contradictory, both celebrating upward mobility (the little girl who made it big) and debunking that same mobility (if someone like that could make it . . .). They describe the craft in detail, justifying acting in a market economy, all the while hinting at the dubious nature of it all.

To end at the beginning: Think once more of Pepys, the consummate civil servant trudging dutifully along his own professional path, irritated over that "jade," Moll Davis, strutting about and showing off her £700 ring. Why the irritation? In one sense, the story confirms what alienated lampooners have charged all along—that actresses are no better than whores. But it is also a story about several anxious gossips analyzing the upward mobility of a dubious young woman. Moll rises from the cold ground to the king's bed not because of her looks, nor even her sexual skill, but because of her delivery of a song. She is, as Mrs. Pierce says, a "most homely jade." To put it another way, Charles II, he of prodigious sexual appetites and numerous bastards, had access to many women, ladies and whores alike. He selects actresses like Moll Davis and Nell Gwyn partly because of their talent (Gwyn reportedly amused him), partly because of their prominence. They are, in the end, the new stars, the nouveau aristocrats of an emergent visual culture that rewards a captivating performance more than the reorganization of the British navy. Poor Pepys, lucky actresses.

Notes

1. For the most complete account of Dryden's relationship with Reeves, see appendix D in Winn (532–39).

2. Satires against the stage occur mainly from the 1670s on, the period that also witnessed an influx of commercial playwrights into the literary marketplace. Many of these playwrights, unlike their aristocratic predecessors of the 1660s, were disenfranchised members of the gentry or professional classes: younger sons and the

offspring of Royalists unremunerated by the Crown after the Restoration figure largely in this group. Given that the theatrical marketplace, structured by a strict monopoly, not to mention fairly small playhouses (and, at times, lackluster attendance), could absorb a limited number of plays, competition among writers was intense and feelings ran high. Moreover, many of the patron-client ties characteristic of the 1660s had dissolved by the 1670s: the court, heavily in arrears, owed money to writers; munificent benefactors, such as the duke of Newcastle, were dead. Dramatists paradoxically looked to box office and print for sustenance at the very moment of marketplace saturation. Thus, lampoons such as Gould's *The Play-House* can be seen as an effect of structural dislocations within the literary marketplace rather than as a response to specific grievances or individuals.

3. There is no known first edition of *The Play-House* outside of its appearance, years after the initial composition, in Gould's collected satires. Either it never saw print—a distinct possibility given the actresses' wrath—or early copies were destroyed.

4. Susan Green has a brilliant discussion of Aphra Behn's use of shutters to reveal a "place" on the stage: "On Behn's stage, because there is already place because of the moveable scenery, we can understand that sexual differentiation is evident as a pretext for the drama. The female body is given as present with everyone in the theatre knowing at the start that women are playing women's roles" (27).

Works Cited

Adams, John Quincy. *The Dramatic Records of Sir Henry Herbert.* 1917. New York: Benjamin Blom, 1968.

Avery, E. L., and A. H. Scouten. Introduction. *The London Stage.* Part 1: *1660–1700.* Ed. William Van Lennep, E. L. Avery, and A. H. Scouten. Carbondale: Southern Illinois UP, 1965.

Barish, Jonas. *The Antitheatrical Prejudice.* Berkeley and Los Angeles: U of California P, 1981.

Betterton, Thomas [William Oldys?]. *The History of the English Stage[, from the Restauration to the Present Time].* 1741. Boston, 1814.

Bourdieu, Pierre, and Loïc J. D. Wacquant. *An Invitation to Reflexive Sociology.* Chicago: U of Chicago P, 1992.

Carlson, Marvin. *Places of Performance: The Semiotics of Theatre Architecture.* Ithaca, N.Y.: Cornell UP, 1989.

Danchin, Pierre, ed. *The Prologues and Epilogues of the Restoration, 1660–1700.* 6 vols. Nancy, Fr.: Presses Universitaires de Nancy, 1981–85.

Dennis, John. "The Causes of the Decay and Defects of Dramatic Poetry." *The Critical Works.* 2 vols. Baltimore: Johns Hopkins UP, 1939–43. 1: 275–99.

Diamond, Elin. "*Gestus* and Signature in Aphra Behn's *The Rover*." *ELH* 56 (1989): 519–41.

Downes, John. *Roscius Anglicanus*. 1708. Ed. Montague Summers. 1929. New York: Benjamin Blom, 1968.

Dryden, John. *The Letters*. Ed. C. E. Ward. Durham: Duke UP, 1942.

Edgerton, Samuel Y., Jr. *The Heritage of Giotto's Geometry: Art and Science on the Eve of the Scientific Revolution*. Ithaca, N.Y.: Cornell UP, 1991.

Eisenstadt, S. N., and L. Roniger. *Patrons, Clients, and Friends: Interpersonal Relations and the Structure of Trust in Society*. Cambridge: Cambridge UP, 1984.

Elliott, Philip. *The Sociology of the Professions*. New York: Herder and Herder, 1972.

Freedman, Barbara. *Staging the Gaze: Postmodernism, Psychoanalysis, and Shakespearean Comedy*. Ithaca, N.Y.: Cornell UP, 1991.

Gilder, Rosamond. *Enter the Actress: The First Women in the Theatre*. 1931. New York: Theatre Arts, 1960.

[Gildon, Charles]. *A Comparison between the Two Stages*. 1702. Gen. ed. Arthur Freeman. The English Stage: Attack and Defense, 1577–1730. New York: Garland, 1973.

Gilman, Ernest B. *The Curious Perspective: Literary and Pictorial Wit in the Seventeenth Century*. New Haven: Yale UP, 1978.

Gould, Robert. *The Play-House: A Satyr*. 1709. The Restoration Theatre. By Montague Summers. London: Kegan Paul, Trench, Trubner, 1934. 297–321.

———. *Poems Chiefly consisting of Satyrs and Satyrical Epistles*. London, 1689.

———. *The Rival Sisters; or, The Violence of Love*. London, 1696.

———. *The Works . . . Consisting of those Satyrs which were formerly Printed, and Corrected since by the Author*. 2 vols. London, 1709.

Green, Susan. "Semiotic Modalities of the Female Body in Aphra Behn's *The Dutch Lover*." Unpublished essay.

Guillen, Claudio. "On the Concept and Metaphor of Perspective." *Comparatists at Work: Studies in Comparative Literature*. Ed. Stephen G. Nichols, Jr., and Richard B. Vowles. Waltham, Mass.: Blaisdell, 1968. 28–90.

Gurr, Andrew. *The Shakespearean Stage 1574–1642*. 2d ed. Cambridge: Cambridge UP, 1980.

Holland, Peter. *The Ornament of Action: Text and Performance in Restoration Comedy*. Cambridge: Cambridge UP, 1979.

Howe, Elizabeth. *The First English Actresses: Women and Drama, 1660–1700*. Cambridge: Cambridge UP, 1992.

King, Thomas A. " 'As if (she) were made on purpose to put the whole world into good Humour': Reconstructing the First English Actresses." *Drama Review* 36 (1992): 78–102.

Larson, Magali Sarfatti. *The Rise of Professionalism: A Sociological Analysis*. Berkeley and Los Angeles: U of California P, 1977.

Maguire, Nancy Klein. *Regicide and Restoration: English Tragicomedy, 1660–1671*. Cambridge: Cambridge UP, 1992.

Maus, Katharine Eisaman. " 'Playhouse Flesh and Blood': Sexual Ideology and the Restoration Actress." *ELH* 46 (1979): 595–617.

Milhous, Judith. *Thomas Betterton and the Management of Lincoln's Inn Fields, 1695–1708*. Carbondale: Southern Illinois UP, 1979.

Mulvey, Laura. "Visual Pleasure and Narrative Cinema." 1975. *Feminisms: An Anthology of Literary Theory and Criticism*. Ed. Robyn R. Warhol and Diane Price Herndl. New Brunswick, N.J.: Rutgers UP, 1991. 432–42.

Nicoll, Allardyce. *A History of Restoration Drama, 1660–1700*. 2nd ed. Cambridge: Cambridge UP, 1928.

Orgel, Stephen. *The Illusion of Power*. Berkeley and Los Angeles: U of California P, 1975.

Orrell, John. *The Theatres of Inigo Jones and John Webb*. Cambridge: Cambridge UP, 1985.

Pepys, Samuel. *The Diary of Samuel Pepys*. Ed. Robert Latham and William Matthews. 11 vols. Berkeley and Los Angeles: U of California P, 1970–83.

Roberts, David. *The Ladies: Female Patronage of Restoration Drama, 1660–1700*. Oxford: Clarendon, 1989.

Rosenthal, Laura J. " 'Counterfeit Scrubbado': Women Actors in the Restoration." *Eighteenth Century: Theory and Interpretation* 34 (1993): 3–22.

The Session of the Ladies. London, 1688.

[Shadwell, Thomas]. *The Medal of John Bayes*. London, 1682.

Silverman, Kaja. *The Subject of Semiotics*. New York: Oxford UP, 1983.

Straub, Kristina. *Sexual Suspects: Eighteenth-Century Players and Sexual Ideology*. Princeton: Princeton UP, 1992.

Styan, J. L. *Restoration Comedy in Performance*. Cambridge: Cambridge UP, 1986.

Wilson, John Harold. *All the King's Ladies: Actresses of the Restoration*. Chicago: U of Chicago P, 1958.

Winn, James Anderson. *John Dryden and His World*. New Haven: Yale UP, 1987.

Instituting Empiricism: Hobbes's *Leviathan* and Dryden's *Marriage à la Mode*

RICHARD KROLL

The Problem

Dryden's *Marriage à la Mode* has always teased its critics with its double plot. Accordingly, the formal and ideological relations between the low (comic) narrative of the play and its high (heroic) narrative have attracted a number of increasingly sophisticated readings by, among others, Laura Brown, J. Douglas Canfield, David Rodes, and Eric Rothstein and Frances Kavenick.[1] In the most ambitious interpretation yet, Michael McKeon argues that the terms of the two plots do not resolve easily into a preference for one mode over the other but remain mutually destabilized, thereby revealing a dialectical tension between a set of dying aristocratic values and a more protobourgeois ethos emerging during the late seventeenth century.

Marriage à la Mode evidently tests our ability to conceptualize and interpret doubleness as an aesthetic feature that has a kind of peculiar life in the Restoration. It also challenges us to think about how different rhetorics might coexist in a given text. This doubleness seems to me to explain in large measure the difficulties we have had in interpreting all the works I discuss below; and I link them in this essay not only because they share similar rhetorical features but also because they invite us to consider the theoretical relations between literary form and politics in similar ways. (Without renegotiating the matter, I will take it for granted that Hobbes exerted a pervasive influence on the way the Restoration approached all such issues, if only by reaction.)[2] Moreover, the effort to explain this rhetoric of doubleness reveals some of the weaknesses of Restoration historiography itself, which it is one of my chief aims here to discuss. In this context, it is tempting to appeal to notions of dialectic, for no other conceptual method may seem on the face of it better suited to analyzing the feature in question. Nevertheless, for all that I think McKeon's dialectical approach to *Marriage à la Mode* to be one of the most illuminating so far, the success of his method tends to camouflage the extent to which dialectical analysis depends heavily on historically sedimented vocabularies. That is, the way it imagines oppositions between terms owes a specific debt to post-Romantic and postindustrial cultural analyses. So accordingly, I want here to explore the hypothesis that, however powerful dialectical analysis has proven, pre-Romantic culture may be capable of providing us with equally sophisticated devices for interpreting Dryden's play, as well as related Restoration texts.

To describe a given method as having an undeniably post-Romantic genealogy is not in itself adequate grounds for objection, for without those genealogies, what we now call "theory" as an academic practice would be unrecognizable. But the appeal to a specifically Marxist dialectical model is in danger of eliding the extent to which Restoration texts were capable of providing complex strategies of ironic self-scrutiny, of which the double plot of *Marriage à la Mode* is only the most obvious. So when we treat its two plots as modes of knowledge, we could (heuristically) speak of these oppositions as if they offer a contrast between romance and empiricism (whose values I am about to define); when we treat them as dramatic genres, a contrast between heroic and comic drama; and when we treat them as social models, a contrast between a residual aristocratic and an emerging bourgeois world. I focus below on what we might loosely call "empiricism" for a number of reasons: inasmuch as we think of it as a distinctive epistemological mode, it did indeed become pervasive in England roughly in the middle of the seventeenth century (a trope of canonical histories of ideas, as I have elaborated elsewhere in *The Material Word*); the value of this mode, both as a historical and rhetorical phenomenon, has been much misunderstood (often by those very methodologies most hospitable to post-Romantic theory); and lastly, as I have indicated, it can in fact provide a sort of dialectical, or at least ironic, possibility of its own, which both Hobbes and Dryden exploit. Put simply, it is important to understand how it might describe an approach to knowledge whose values for Dryden's play are historically apt. So understood, empiricism invents its own logic for the move from epistemology to politics, but not necessarily by engaging in the neat ratios between forms of knowledge, genre, and class

I have sketched above. In many historiographies, empiricism connotes a self-evident and ideologically self-congratulatory mode whose emergence in the late seventeenth century and early eighteenth century assisted the rise of "bourgeois individualism," which stands for a host of suspect and mystifying ideologies. Empiricism is made to translate into positivism, the epistemological instrument of capitalism, such that epistemological postulates serve as a direct correlative to the interests of a given social class. But I am here defending empiricism as a historical category not least by attending to the rhetorical devices by which it made its claims; and since these devices are exceedingly complex, they disturb, if not frustrate, interpretations that would treat empiricism as a single entity and assign it a stable historical and ideological value. Thus, by contrast with a more genuinely unmediated and unreflective form of knowledge, figured in numerous Restoration texts as romance, neoclassical empiricism provided an extraordinarily flexible tool for self-scrutiny and ideological analysis. Because it sees itself as an inevitably mediated and negotiable mode, it seeks at once to construct a positive fiction of knowledge and yet to make us conscious of the devices by which it does so. That is, when I speak of empiricism's capacity for irony, I do not oppose irony as a moral mode to certain forms of social and political commitment.

I agree here with Rothstein and Kavenick's view that the Restoration provided an unusually fluid cultural milieu. Specifically, I would emphasize, in the wake of the Interregnum, new institutions were in the process of emerging, while the culture was also elaborating a second-order vocabulary for discussing how and why they emerged. To some degree this essay is a response to an implied challenge by Rothstein and Kavenick: if, as they argue, a compromise formation distinguishes the comedies of the 1670s, how does any analogous motive or rhetoric find wider expression in Restoration literature? Rothstein and Kavenick write that the comedies are "subversive" and the audiences "subvertible" (258). I want to examine the extent to which empiricism as a way of thinking, *as a way of behaving,* and as a defense of social and linguistic behavior could likewise prove subversive. This empiricism is not a smug instrument of knowledge; rather, it creates a species of knowledge that, in the Restoration, could scrutinize its own ideological conditioning. Moreover, so defined, empiricism is also remarkably honest, for this knowledge refuses to pretend that humans can exist outside cultural institutions, as if a consciousness of ideology could free us from the entanglements of power. Rather, it sees such institutions as an inescapable human fact that also involves a cost to those who must inhabit them.

Constructing a Canon

Readers will remember that Dryden's "Preface" to the *Fables* (1700) constructs a literary canon whose aesthetic values we have largely endorsed: after all, it is here that Dryden pronounces Chaucer the father of English poetry, and here that Chaucer, Spenser, and Milton are given a mutual lineage. There is, however, considerable irony in our modern approval of Dryden's choices, for these selections signify for Dryden no self-evident criteria of value but courageous expressions of personal taste, which, in the preference he gives to Chaucer over Ovid, chooses a Modern over an Ancient and, in the preference he gives to Homer over Virgil, confesses a character more "violent, impetuous, and full of fire" than the Roman poet (Watson 2: 274). There is a further irony embedded in Dryden's strategy, because although he aligns his own character with Homeric violence, implying that such a posture befits a writer denied true access to public life, the terms in which he does so recall not so much Homer as the "quiet, sedate" Virgil he describes (Watson 2: 274). The double-edged rhetoric by which Dryden pledges allegiance to one author while pleading in the habit of a rival is a striking feature of his late years, for he does much the same thing, though more pointedly, in his earlier "Discourse on the Original and Progress of Satire" (1693). The "Discourse" appeared as a preface to Dryden's (and others') translations of a number of Latin writers including Juvenal, in which he admits his identification with Juvenal in a prose marked paradoxically by the Horatian values of discretion and privacy. It is those very values that so infuse his last great essay with an autumnal and elegiac beauty.

Dryden's construction and use of a literary canon, then, in no way reinforce some simple ratio between power and the aesthetic values it might prefer. For he creates a double rhetoric, by selecting Juvenal, then Homer to represent his anger, while nevertheless conducting his argument in an urbane and leisurely manner. Thus he establishes an ironic perspective on the very motives—political and personal—that legitimate his peculiar identifications. That those identifications are apt is proven by the degree to which, in the actual exercise of translating Juvenal, the former poet laureate could fully inhabit Juvenal's alienated vision and rugged idiom. Who better than Juvenal could express the condition of life in the midst of a new regime governed by cultural and political imports and operating in the baleful shadow of tyranny (in Juvenal's case Domitian's and Nero's)? By contrast, the late prose is marked by rounded periods, maintaining a series of extended analogies and qualifications, that provide an ethos of delay and retrospection rather than Juvenalian attack (an ethos one might legitimately call Horatian). Similarly, in "Alexander's Feast," we see Dryden exercising his poetic revenge on Alexander by transforming him at the hands of Timotheus into a grotesque and finally lethal automaton: the consequences of firing another Troy are only softened by the arrival, in the last stanza, of divine Cecilia, representing a less lyrical and pagan violence than Timotheus's but in no way displacing it. Timotheus's violence is given full expression within the body of the poem, but Cecilia represents a guardedly ironic turn upon it. Consequently, we witness the old poet showing his anger as a member of a religious minority but able perhaps more than ever to observe himself dispassionately in that guise. This alone might explain the attraction to Juvenal's Satire III, where satiric authority is deflected from the poet to Umbricius's complaints about modern life, made as he stands at the city gate ready to depart. Dryden's construction of the canon—an act that may in hindsight seem to us a moment of literary authoritarianism—has therefore the character of an act of dissent. What is at issue is less the construction of a canon as such than the forms of discrimination brought to an exercise that (we are now relearning) is an inescapable cultural fact. Canons will come and go, but what marks the politics of each movement are the conditions by which they do so and the motives that we remark within them.

By establishing a canon and yet exposing the terms by which it does so, the preface to the *Fables* calculatedly reveals the ideological work that Dryden wants the canon to do. It also suggests that, for Dryden, empiricism itself may also play a role in that ironic economy. For there are two other figures with whom Dryden identifies in his late critical essays, namely Milton and Hobbes. Dryden identifies with Milton in the last stage of his career because, like his present self, the Milton he knew after the Restoration was a remnant from a different political age. Dryden's use of Hobbes, on the other hand, supposes that a given philosophical position—involving certain attitudes toward knowledge and language—bears no necessary or single relation to the values with which we endow different political views. In the preface to the *Fables,* Hobbes stands in part for the translator of Homer that Dryden himself would like to have been, although he criticizes Hobbes as too old to have embarked on translating the *Iliad* (Watson 2: 275). But more significantly, Dryden believes that his relaxed habit of moving among a series of related topics confirms "Mr. Hobbes['s]" view that "thoughts . . . have always some connection" (Watson 2: 271). Dryden is alluding to the early chapters of *Leviathan,* in which Hobbes analyzes the human powers of perception and speech. In contrast with a prevailing modern assumption that the Hobbesian system is both politically and epistemologically authoritarian, Dryden takes chapter 3 of *Leviathan* to denote a kind of mediated and negotiable knowledge whose corollary in Dryden's text is his own highly rhetorical and often digressive method. In fact, Dryden calls on Hobbes's cognitive theory to excuse the very digression on which he just embarked. Because digression does not command but rather invites attention to its own artifice, it reveals the extent to which Dryden's admission of the violent nature attracting him to Homer is, precisely, delivered by an act of confession and mediated so that it can become a local object of critical observation. If Dryden thinks of Hobbes as the apostle of the authoritarian state whose powers are secured by a stable epistemology—what I have called lyric knowledge—it is clear that he is reading Hobbes against himself, because Hobbes also justifies the waywardness of language itself.

Constructing a State

Dryden's view and use of Hobbes do not, it seems, accord with most modern readings of *Leviathan.*[3] Put simply, Hobbes studies have traditionally been dominated by political science or philosophy, such that most major books on Hobbes in the last half century have concentrated on the possibilities and difficulties offered by chapters 13 to 18, those chapters that famously begin with the state of nature and conclude by enumerating the powers of the sovereign. Huge energies have been directed to particular problems that those chapters have raised: the supposedly false philosophical slide from "is" to "ought"; or alternatively, the conundrum by which the law of nature might be binding on the individual before the advent of the sovereign, in the context of an argument in which law appears only to bind when expressly issued by a sovereign. A more recent book has tried to construct a comprehensive Hobbesian analysis of politics almost entirely out of the concerns introduced by books 1 and 2 (see Kavka). There are readings that do not have that analytical urge, like Quentin Skinner's essay arguing that *Leviathan* should be seen as only the most articulate of a series of tracts issued in response to the engagement controversy ("Conquest and Consent") and, uniquely, J. G. A. Pocock's essay urging us to read the whole of *Leviathan* rather than concentrating on books 1 and 2. But even very different kinds of approaches, such as that taken in Steven Shapin and Simon Schaffer's *Leviathan and the Air Pump,* stress the demonstrative and implicitly authoritarian force of the Hobbesian world. Indeed, Shapin and Schaffer confirm rather than challenge a long-held assumption about Hobbes when they argue that Boyle's defense of vacuum against Hobbesian plenism is a proper metaphor for a newly emerging Restoration ideology of contingent social and intellectual relations—propounded by Boyle and the Royal Society—that successfully displaced a rhetoric of authority symbolized by Hobbes. Boyle's commitment to the hypothesis of vacuum as inhabiting the structure of matter provides a metaphor of the voluntarist ethic he sought to foster. So Shapin and Schaffer's argument must suppose a secure analytical ratio between the Hobbesian cosmology (plenist and materialist), an authoritarian reading of the civil politics in *Leviathan,* and Hobbes's own rhetoric, which they treat as if it were functionally geometrical, even in the case of the dialogue that Schaffer translates as an appendix to the book. Because this argument places Boyleian and Hobbesian empiricism in conflict, Shapin and Schaffer's view of Hobbes finally amplifies the widely held conviction that Hobbes is only or primarily systematic and that that system is given to largely prescriptive ends. Appropriately, Shapin and Schaffer rely on J. W. N. Watkins's *Hobbes's System of Ideas* for their interpretation of Hobbes.

We might ask what has happened at this point to the digressive Hobbes that Dryden exploits. The opposition between Boyleian and Hobbesian empiricism should suggest that there are various empiricisms at play; and I will argue that the Restoration (including Hobbes himself) held that a skeptical (contingent) empiricism necessarily qualified the epistemic claims made by an apparently more dogmatic (positivistic) form of empiricism. In so doing, it provides an analysis of the terms by which we might assent to certain dogmatisms, including the dogmatisms that allow institutions of all kinds to exist.

The kinds of reductions I describe thus seem to simplify the political implications of Hobbes's ideas and, more important, his method. The most famous political allegorizing of *Leviathan* occurs in C. B. Macpherson's *The Political Theory of Possessive Individualism*. Here Macpherson treats Hobbes's state of nature as representing the world that Hobbes finally approves: men are naturally competitive, which produces a highly energized social economy, one that only requires the sovereign to supervise. Hobbes thus becomes willy-nilly an apologist for a capitalist world of free-market relations, in which the sole function of government is to secure peace in order to maximize trade, so that "natural man is civilized man with only the restraint of law removed" (29). Later readers have pointed out the obvious weakness of this Marxian interpretation, the chief being the notion that we can describe any aspect of Hobbes's environment as meaningfully *bourgeois*. It is argued that if proper attention is paid to *Leviathan* itself, and to Hobbes's close relations with the gentry, his allegiances seem to varying degrees to favor certain aristocratic ideals. *Leviathan* does not symbolize in any simple sense the "bourgeois mind," which, Macpherson goes on to assert elsewhere, finds its objectification in "mathematical thinking" and "materialist metaphysics" ("Hobbes's Bourgeois Man" 179). Keith Thomas points out that *Leviathan* never discusses capital, assumes many features of feudal societies, and betrays signs of Hobbes's closeness to an aristocratic circle that employed him (189, 193). Hobbes also shares certain assumptions with the rather rarified and quite unbourgeois atmosphere of the Tew Circle, a fact that in part accounts for the theological nature of books 3 and 4 and its proximity to Anglican polemics in the Restoration, even when the materialism of *Leviathan* angered many Anglican apologists (Thomas 207).

To justify the political allegories they wish to derive from *Leviathan*, Shapin and Schaffer and Macpherson equally must create stable thematic correspondences between Hobbes's epistemology, his method, his cosmology, and finally, the logic connecting the state of nature to the sovereign. I have mentioned how this criticism applies to Shapin and Schaffer's argument that purports to attend to Hobbes's rhetorical gestures. For them, Hobbes is as much an epistemological as a political authoritarian, a single, totalizing entity. Flying in the face of general Restoration protocols of reading, they therefore deny that Hobbes's use of dialogue might express a contingent, negotiable epistemology rather like Boyle's experimentalism. And it is this thematic stabilization of relations we also find in Michael Ryan's deconstructive reading of *Leviathan* (esp. intro.). Although Ryan alludes to Derrida as the source of a deconstructive critique of philosophy, his method follows the version of deconstruction found in Paul de Man's essay "The Rhetoric of Temporality." Both in its logic and in its rhetoric, de Man's essay invents equivalences between a stable epistemology (figured in the power of Coleridge's "symbol") and a conservative politics. For de Man, Coleridge's belief that metaphor can partake of the reality to which it refers constitutes an erasure of language itself, since it denies the degree to which language is a highly dense nonreferential medium. Such resistance to the mediations of language—to figuration as such—has political implications, because it attempts to obscure the rhetorical dimension of utterances, desiring to make them appear the transparent, indisputable vehicles of natural as well as political knowledge. For Ryan, Hobbes's absolutism is directly reflected in his linguistic attitudes, since Hobbes proclaims himself hostile to metaphor in speech. Ryan not only misreads what Hobbes means by attacking metaphor, but he also relies on a common implication that Hobbes (standing in for empiricism at large) deludes himself in the search for stable forms of linguistic reference because he is propounding a doctrine suited to the needs of bourgeois mystification. Ryan is correct to assume that Hobbes sees an equivalence between his definitional method in books 1 and 2 and the creation of a sovereign whose powers, once constituted, are incontestable. But Ryan goes much further than this, to argue that "the absolute political state is necessarily logocentric because it depends on law, which in turn depends on the univocal meaning of words, which can be guaranteed only by the metaphysical concept of the logos, a point at which knowledge and language attain an identity that can serve as an absolute source of authority" (3). That authority Ryan has earlier aligned with the value of "conservative liberalism, that amalgam of possessive individualism, philosophic and scientific rationalism, authoritarian statism, and natural law market economics which has served so well as the philosophy of the capitalist class" (2–3).

A reader accustomed to the language of political science would probably find Ryan's reading of *Leviathan* somewhat precious. But Ryan's resort to deconstruction properly accounts for one feature of *Leviathan* that political scientists have by and large ignored—that it is almost obsessively about language. Moreover, it is deeply interested in a question that deconstruction has helped revive, namely the degree to which theories of language must establish the conditions of political analysis. What relates them is their common institutional base, and this is in large part one of Hobbes's descriptive aims. Just as Dryden sees that literary canons are unavoidable cultural facts, so Hobbes sees that humans inevitably create and inhabit institutions: he assumes, first, that language is the primary feature of being human; second, that language underwrites other social institutions (figured in the contract); and, finally, that human life is conducted within a network of power relations. That Hobbes argues positively for the absolute powers of the sovereign can be taken—as indeed it was in the early 1650s—as a requirement that Englishmen should engage with the Cromwellian government. But Hobbes's hortatory rhetoric (say in chapter 18) only follows on an entirely hypothetical picture of the state of nature. This dooms the attempt to treat the state of nature as anything more than a heuristic fiction, which therefore cannot provide a stable analytical point for deriving the conditions by which the sovereign either is or must be created. Michael Oakeshott's response to Hobbes's numerous analytical contradictions is to suggest that he has two different audiences in mind, a technical and general audience, which explains why Hobbes's rhetoric seems to engage two different logics at once—what Oakeshott calls "a core of discrepancy" (117). I would like to suggest something similar: Hobbes is trying both to persuade Englishmen to act at a particular point in history and, most significantly, to show that no member of any society can ever escape the institutional conditions that allow us even to imagine social life. That is, Quentin Skinner is partly right to say that *Leviathan* is a tract in response to the engagement controversy, but he fails to see that his own argument is motivated by a more elemental fascination with *Leviathan* as a masterpiece of sorts whose descriptive power calls for explanation. The geometrical rhetoric reveals what Hobbes believes we must do to contain a state of war; but the argumentative terms that frame that prescription have made *Leviathan* endure as a descriptive analysis of the human condition. Hobbes's epideictic motive is contained within a forensic frame that supposes that human knowledge is not as certain or as absolute as readers of chapters 13 to 18 have usually thought.

We can see the power of Hobbes's descriptive project when we take seriously what Hobbes says about how we should read it. Political scientists have tended to treat the early chapters in *Leviathan* as defining a human as a self-motivated and selfish atom driven by passion and fear (one exception is Johnston). But this is not what Hobbes says, or at least not all he says. Indeed, Hobbes's most paraphrased political argument is in its essentials anticipated by Lucretius's famous description, in *De Rerum Natura,* book 5, 1028–1160, which begins by describing the emergence of human language from animal cries and gestures, the emergence of society after the invention of fire, and the arrival of a state of civil conflict, which is only properly resolved by a contract to establish a commonwealth. Thomas Creech—who translated *De Rerum Natura* in 1682—renders this final moment thus:

> Those former *Kings* now murthered, they or'ethrown,
> The glory of the *Scepter,* and the *Crown*
> Decreas'd; the *Diadem,* that sign of State,
> Now wept in drops of bloud, the *Wearer*'s fate,
> Spurn'd by the *common feet,* who fear'd no more:
> *Tis sweet to spurn the things we fear'd before.*
> Thus *Monarchy* was lost.———
>   That *Sun* once set, a *thousand* little *Stars*
> Gave a *dim* light to *Jealousies* and *Wars,*
> Whilst each among the *many* sought the Throne,
> And thought no head like his deserv'd the Crown.
> This made them seek for *laws,* this led their Choice
> To *Rulers;* Power was given by *publick* voice.
>
> (174–75)

Book 1 of *Leviathan* (itself a kind of Epicurean text) similarly begins by analyzing humans' ability to think and use language before it describes the state of nature that the contract seeks to regulate.[4] Further, the syntax of that argument finds a much more architectonic expression in Hobbes's entire approach to his reader, which marks a vital point at which Hobbes's pervasive skepticism drives his argument. Books 1 and 2 do indeed work by a kind of geometrical rhetoric, but in his introduction, Hobbes has already exposed the purely contingent terms by which any agreement to define words can proceed.[5] Here Hobbes emphasizes the entirely artificial nature of the commonwealth he will describe and outlines the purpose of the four books of *Leviathan.* Hobbes proceeds to gloss the conditions that produce human wisdom, which he defines centrally by using the metaphor of reading. "*Wisedome* is acquired," he says, "not by reading of *Books,* but of *Men*" (82). Hobbes is admittedly trying to warn us against casual reading by producing a distinction between claims to have read men that merely mask "uncharitable censures of one another" (Hobbes 82) and an ability to read that scrutinizes the conditions and circumstances of the activity itself. We have to begin, says Hobbes, by examining the text to hand, namely ourselves. Only then, and only by analogy, can we begin to infer the relations between ourselves and the minds of others. The choice of textuality as the metaphor for self-knowledge already resists a view of Hobbes as committed to a metaphysic of the logos, whatever he might do later in books 1 and 2 to regulate his own text by a geometrical method. Any such move to secure knowledge by agreement depends on a prior stage, that of revealing the purely conditional nature of our relations with the world and the equally conditional nature of the reader's engagement with Hobbes's text. The precept that one should read oneself exists

> to teach us, that for the similitude of the thoughts, and Passions of one man, to the thoughts, and Passions of another, whosoever looketh into himself, and considereth what he doth, when he does *think, opine, reason, hope, feare,* &c, and upon what grounds; he shall thereby read and know, what are the thoughts, and Passions of all other men, upon the like occasions. (82)

The language of identity—where "the similitude of *Passions,* [which] are the same in all men" (82)—occurs within a rhetorical economy that already treats such forms of identity as only *functionally* identical and is immediately questioned in any case by Hobbes's admission that even if passions as such are the same in all individuals, the way they articulate themselves as desire varies widely. Desires "do so vary, and they are so easie to be kept from our knowledge, that the characters of a man's heart, blotted and confounded as they are, with dissembling, lying, counterfeiting, and erroneous doctrines, are legible onely to him that searcheth hearts" (83). Since only God can read our desires, it is "solely by mens actions wee do discover their designe sometimes," but we cannot make anything of the actions we observe "without comparing them with our own, and distinguishing all circumstances, by which the case may come to be altered[. It] is to decypher without a key, and be for the most part deceived, by too much trust, or by too much diffidence; as he that reads, is himself a good or evil man" (83). This comparative form of knowledge underwrites the entire fabric of Hobbes's argument, for though a magistrate must "read in himself . . . Man-kind," that apparent identification between governor and the governed can only be secured by the method enacted in the reader confronting Hobbes's text. The relationship between reader and author depends on a mere analogy between the way minds work, an analogy that Hobbes leaves to his reader to deny or confirm at will: so, he writes, "[W]hen I shall have set down my own reading orderly, and perspicuously, the pains left another, will be onely to consider, if he also find not the same in himself" (83). Only if we admit this analogy as valid will we later find ourselves logically forced to accept the sovereign's authority. In a society bonded by the originary wills of the individuals who compose it and maintained by the expressive will of the sovereign, it is essential that all parties to the contract be registered, visible, and accountable, and so Hobbes's final gesture in the introduction textualizes the author as cultural agent, a phenomenon potentially contracting with other analogous phenomena.

Thus Hobbes, at the threshold of his argument, establishes the conditions by which we must understand its truth claims. These are not absolute, and for good cause: although definition secures a stability and continuity of argumentation within books 1 and 2 that might and often does appear absolute, that kind of science occurs under conditions that treat all knowledge as probable at best. In fact, it is useful to see *Leviathan* as making four simultaneous propositions: that cultures are artificial, that they can only be understood as a network of external signs or symptoms, that they are produced by voluntary acts on the part of individuals, and that paradoxically they are also coercive. These propositions forge a close identification between the politics of *Leviathan* and its linguistic concerns, since the way we approach Hobbes's text symbolizes the conditions under which culture as a whole illustrates Hobbes's analysis. For *Leviathan*, like all texts or all other features of the world we try to interpret, reminds us constantly of the contingencies of human knowledge: the text is filled with moments of hyperbole and sardonic irony that remind the reader of the pleasure of reading, a mediated pleasure to which Dryden alludes in the preface to the *Fables*. Yet Hobbes also offers another pleasure provided by the attempt to build a geometrical knowledge of political life, what Silver has called a "fiction of self-evidence." In this sense, *Leviathan* is an internally conflicted text, since at moments it seems to prefer what Hobbes calls "science" to the more compromised and compromising forms of "prudence." But that doubleness is established in such a way as to enfold the geometrical within the prudential, the contingent. Even in book 1, Hobbes continually insists that our actions should be "voluntary," a fiction of local agency to some extent belied by the force of absolute sovereignty. Hobbes's analytical point is in part that the constructions of ideology are at once voluntary yet coercive: we are asked to confirm the seductions of Hobbes's early analogies, so experiencing a sensation of choice, but find ourselves later coerced by a demonstrative rhetoric whose articulations move us inexorably from axioms or definitions to their logical entailments. (The latter mechanism is also reinforced by typography, where capitals and italics visibly secure the junctures within the larger logical fabric.) But we remain at the same time uneasily conscious that the voluntary and the coercive coexist.[6] So Dryden establishes one kind of institution—a literary canon—while at the same time revealing the conditions and motives that promote it. Similarly, Hobbes establishes the ultimate human institution—the state—which, figured as a geometrical construct, he treats as an inescapable condition of culture. At the same time he shows that it is the product of a complicated network of motives and desires, figured as a very different kind of rhetoric both conditioning and inhabiting the geometrical.

Precisely for this reason, Hobbes urges us to treat books 3 and 4 as integral to his entire argument: they are emphatically not mere theological appendages to Hobbes's primary concern to establish civil sovereignty. The failure to read Hobbes's entire argument, indeed, invites a political danger that Hobbes alludes to in his introduction: the temptation to suspend the rigors of purely analogical reasoning is often the product of too great a trust in or too pressing a fear of authority. To leave a text only partly read is to misconstrue it, to the extent that what is omitted cannot qualify earlier propositions that might by consequence be abstracted as axiomatic and used for arbitrary purposes that Hobbes does not approve. Consequently, Hobbes prefers the displacements implied in uses of analogy (where what is unlike is as important as what is alike) to the kinds of natural and unmediated identification between terms that Ryan assumes Hobbes wants to create. One might say that Ryan's empiricism is not Hobbes's.

Hobbes's warning to us to complete our reading of *Leviathan* as a whole—a kind of formalist imperative—occurs as the final paragraph of book 3. He writes:

> [I]t is not the bare Words, but the scope of the writer that giveth the true light, by which any writing is to bee interpreted; and they that insist upon single Texts, without considering the main Designe, can derive no thing from them cleerly; but rather by casting atomes of Scripture, as dust before mens eyes, make everything more obscure than it is; an ordinary artifice of those that seek not the truth, but their own advantage. (626)

This passage applies to all texts, for which Scripture is the master metaphor, and explains the major purpose behind books 3 and 4. The sovereign in books 1 and 2 comprises the public and visible site of civic interpretation; in the last two books, he becomes the public site of scriptural interpretation, a hermeneutic court of last resort. The nature of the sovereign's decisions in this sphere may be arbitrary inasmuch as they mark the final point beyond which hermeneutical indeterminacy will produce political chaos. But he stands in distinct opposition to the papacy, where the forensic conditions of textual interpretation remain occult and thus genuinely totalitarian. The distinction again is between those modes of knowledge and representation that are analogical in nature and some other way of thinking about knowledge that tries to obscure or subvert the workings of language as we have it. Like the Anglican apologists who also owed a great deal to the Tew Circle, not least William Chillingworth, one focus of Hobbes's assault on Catholic absolutism is the doctrine of transubstantiation, which Hobbes associates with an Aristotelian epistemology and with attempts to legislate the nature of matter despite appearances, or to inspect the conscience of the believer.[7] For Hobbes, "a sign is not a sign to him that giveth it, but to whom it is made; that is to the spectator" (401). Like character, which must perform dramatistically, a sign is only a sign by virtue of its public, externalized constitution; and so, anticipating Locke, Hobbes abolishes mens rea: "[O]f Intentions, which never appear by any outward act, there is no place for humane accusation" (336). Hobbes therefore defines character by recourse to a theatrical metaphor:

> The word Person is latine: instead, whereof the Greeks have [*prosopon*], which signifies *Face*, as *Persona* in latine signifies the *disguise,* or *outward appearance* of a man, counterfeited on the Stage; and sometimes more particularly that part of it, which disguiseth the face, as a Mask or Visard: and from the Stage, hath been translated to any Representer of speech and action, as well in Tribunalls, as Theaters. So that *Person,* is the same as an *Actor* is, both on stage and in common Conversation; and to *Personate,* is to *Act,* or *Represent* himself, or an other. (217)

To read Scripture, we must engage in what was commonly called the "comparing of places," just as to understand the significance of character, we must see it both externally and contextually: in both cases the method is analogical. Neither texts nor character can be known essentially. Thus in chapter 36, Hobbes writes that "the *Word of God*" is not "*Vocabulum,*" an utterance with a stable kind of reference. If it creates meaning, it does so by placing its utterances into a context that continually qualifies them:

Scripture illustrates that language does not mean by referring but by becoming a form of symbolic action. It is "*Sermo,* (in Greek [*logos*]) that is,
some *Speech, Discourse,* or *Saying*" that "a perfect Speech or Discourse,
whereby the speaker *affirmeth, denieth, commandeth, promiseth, threat-
eneth, wisheth,* or *interrogateth*" (451). Jesus is not some direct signifier
for God the Father: he is "called the *Word,* because his Incarnation was the
Performance of the Promise" (455). Similarly, prophecy is not some special form of knowledge but a mode of public cultural performance whose
significance is determined by local context (457), just as the (culturally
determined) utterance that states that God spoke immediately to his instruments actually alludes to the complex of circumstances by which men
come to know God's will (459).

Books 3 and 4 thus constitute an analysis of the conditions that endow
all cultural expressions with meaning. Even prophecy usually occurs "by
mediation of second causes" (466). Hobbes's commitment to mediation in
this sense also has a distinctly satiric purpose, because book 4 develops
into a series of palpable analogies comparing the Catholic Church to the
Kingdom of Fairies, which by the end almost overwhelm the reader. By
this time Hobbes's agency as a rhetorician palpably dominates: he celebrates the wicked power of his own verbal artifice and in so doing has
denaturalized the illusion that his geometrical method is anything but itself
an artifice. To finish reading *Leviathan* entire is to experience in narrative
form the doubleness that inhabits Dryden's construction of the canon: the
institution (the canon, the state, the text) itself appears inevitable, but we
become conscious of our role in making it possible.

Constructing a Play

Leviathan, then, perplexes the kinds of analysis it has often suffered:
it is unsystematic in the analytical sense, such that philosophers have
often concluded that it does—according to philosophical decorum—what
it ought not to do; it does not represent class interests in any simple
way, and certainly not in terms that allow distinctions between "bourgeois" and "aristocratic" values, since the category of "bourgeois" does
not really apply; and its skeptical commitments compromise the urge to
treat its geometrical rhetoric as Hobbesian nostalgia for an unmediated
form of knowledge. It is a fundamentally ironic or critical document,
in that it also plays a descriptive off a prescriptive urge, with the net

result that Hobbes reveals that what he recommends as necessary (an institution invested with power) is also the inevitable condition of any society. Nor should we treat the various dualities that critics have postulated (analytical-contradictory; aristocratic-bourgeois; demonstrative-analogical; unmediated-mediated; prescriptive-descriptive) as dialectical in any simple sense, nor any given pair as a stable allegory of the next.

Put another way, *Leviathan* treats the fact of reading as an inevitability that itself denotes three things: first, a recognition that the activity entails a contingent epistemology—reading is the exercise of inference and analogy whose equivalence is a probable, empirical approach to the world, or other minds; second, a definite kind of pleasure, whether the pleasure we take in Hobbes's geometrical or analogical rhetoric; and third, a kind of pleasure that involves certain political costs—within the geometrical world of books 1 and 2, the sacrifice of political opposition, and within books 3 and 4, the sacrifice of Catholicism. Reading in *Leviathan* exemplifies for the reader the institutions that Hobbes recommends. Hobbesian self-irony makes us observe life within the institutions that make it possible and meaningful, without invoking the liberationist implications often attached to self-consciousness as a textual or political posture. To that degree, it is scrupulously honest.

Marriage à la Mode similarly prefers its empirical to its romantic plot, and, as with *Leviathan*, it recognizes that one pole of the play's rhetoric (the skeptical-empirical) describes the epistemologically constrained conditions of literary—here dramatic—performance better than the other (the romantic or lyric). Hobbesian simile and irony denote the skeptical terms by which any reader might ever assent to the geometrical dimension of his argument. The low plot of Dryden's play likewise signifies the conditions under which any audience assents to knowledge on the stage. Insofar as the high plot as a theatrical performance tries to resist the purely conditional modes of knowledge involved in judging stage character, it tends to perplex itself or invite contradiction. That is, the romance forms of knowing adumbrated by heroic topoi are finally unavailable to ordinary human cognition, which is what dramatic knowledge must seek to satisfy. Unlike Rothstein and Kavenick, I therefore consider it significant that the low plot involves four Restoration stars (Mohun, Hart, Marshall, Boutell) and the high plot only one (Kynaston). Rather than the two plots engaging parallel lines of desire and performance, the play actually debates the terms by which desire and performance themselves obey the epistemological condi-

tions assumed more consistently by the low plot. It also serves to reveal
that dramatic pleasure entails a political as much as a cognitive economy
that, in being committed to end in a way dictated by genre and by the stage
itself, involves certain sacrifices. In this play, as in *The Country Wife*, it
is primarily the female characters who pay to maintain these social and
dramatic decorums.

Dryden's own ambivalence toward simple oppositions is immediately
registered in his dedication. Dryden evidently sees himself as a professional writer, but one who still courts Rochester's patronage. His uncertainty about the nature and value of patronage emerges as he addresses
an aristocrat who represents a certain access to power. But when Dryden
depicts that court as morally dubious, supplying "much of Interest, and
more of Detraction" (221), we could speculate that Dryden is alluding in
part to Rochester's vexed relationship to it. Dryden thus makes himself
Rochester's moral peer on the basis of their shared ability to discriminate,
while at the same time he calls upon Rochester's "favour" for "Protection
and Patronage" (222). That this protection involves its own threat to a
writer's autonomy, however, is also suggested by Dryden's playful promise
to sacrifice his play to the gods as "the Firstlings of the Flock" (221), where
Dryden might find himself playing Abel to Rochester's Cain; or alternatively in his final sentences, Dryden can imagine Rochester sliding from
patronizing wit to "become its Tyrant: [to] Oppress our little Reputations
with more ease than you now protect them" (224).

This little moral drama—created after the play had been performed—
comments rather neatly on the play's own skepticism about noble values,
where noble values might treat themselves as self-evidently to be read, unqualified by the universal constraints on knowledge. Even though we may
finally endorse the fact of social hierarchy—Dryden still dedicates his play
to Rochester—we must do so while recognizing the system's potential for
victimage. To admit Rochester's power too readily might be fatal; to submit at all is still a threat. The point comes across too in the prologue, where
the historical space in which the play is being performed occurs after the
"civil war" (although Dryden is only indirectly alluding to the English
Revolution) and during a "dead vacation" created by the absence of those
fighting the third Dutch war, as if to emphasize that the play is performed
in a culture bounded, like Hobbes's, by different forms of violence. Like
Hobbes's sovereign, Dryden's play represents a space that holds off and so
civilizes wider forms of conflict.

The entire plot of the play is activated by a simple forensic condition,

namely the discovery of jewels and a letter that suggest that Polydamas
might find his long-lost child in this corner of Sicily. The high plot recalls
Oedipus, where Oedipus's curiosity about the past finally undoes him. But
although Oedipus pursues the signs that lead to his destruction, the action
of unfolding also suggests a mechanism beyond the king's control. Dryden
places more pressure on the forensic moments that lead toward the denouement. For example, Amalthea recounts the condition of the evidence
that has set Polydamas on his search:

> . . . some few days since, a famous Robber
> Was taken with some Jewels of vast price,
> Which, when they were delivered to the King,
> He knew had been his Wife's; with these, a Letter,
> Much torn, and sulli'd, but which yet he knew
> To be her writing.
> *Arte.* ————Sure from hence he learn'd
> He had a Son.
> *Amal.* ————It was not left so plain:
> The Paper only said, she dy'd in childbed:
> But when it should have mention'd Son, or Daughter,
> Just there it was torn off.
>
> (I.i.287–96)

Polydamas speaks of the epistemological problem of interpreting scattered
clues about the past as "the dark riddle" (IV.iv.144). This signifies the general condition of the play. The only unequivocal point at which a different,
romance form of knowledge seems to provide a secure relation between
signs observed and what they signify is the conviction held by all that
Palmyra and Leonidas are much too beautifully formed to be children of
peasants (even then, Polydamas says that their beauty makes "it seem suspicious / They are not what they seem" [I.i.306–7], as if to amplify the
seemingness of it all). But that transparent knowledge fails to describe the
workings of the play, since so much arises from Polydamas's ignorance of
whether Palmyra or Leonidas is his true child. Hermogenes acts as a kind
of playwright, determining the direction of the plot, by informing Polydamas first that Leonidas is his child, then changing his mind and telling
the truth. And when he exclaims, "I had 'em from the Gods" (I.i.344),
that utterance has no explanatory force whatsoever: we know that he is
engaging in mystification for his own motives, much as the language of the
divine used to refer to love in the low plot strikes us as self-deluding. The

point is also made slightly differently, in the failure of torture as a forensic instrument. Under torture the robber has revealed no more than is already circumstantially evident. Hermogenes too is led away to torture that "Will teach him other language" (I.i.357), but Polydamas promptly learns more than the rack would produce, for when Hermogenes' wig falls off, he recognizes him for who he is. The low plot raises its own skeptical issues, but the high plot must also make forensic deliberations on the evidences that prompt Polydamas's search for his child.

The most obvious sense in which this principle operates is that Dryden emphasizes the staginess of the play in a way that recalls, for example, Wycherley's use of offstage action in *The Country Wife* and *The Plain Dealer*. Wycherley highlights the audience's inferential condition by asking us to guess what happens offstage when, for example, Horner goes off with Margery behind the hedge, with Margery returning laden with fruit. Dryden, by contrast, emphasizes the fact that no audience can know who a new character is until informed by someone else: the high plot emerges as a condition of the low plot, whose terms have already been established for us in act 1, when Argaleon appears. We depend on Rhodophil and Palamede to tell us who Argaleon is, just as Polydamas is subsequently introduced by Amalthea's account of the jewels and letter. Amalthea is in the high plot, but the role she plays as a spectator means that she has already been translated into a stage character who watches and supplies information like Rhodophil and Palamede. Similarly, important forms of knowledge are supplied to Polydamas because Argaleon acts as a spy. When Palmyra and Leonidas engage in a kind of operatic pastoral duet (II.i.406 ff.), the possibilities of seeing their dialogue as a lyric and unmediated transaction are already compromised by the fact that the entire scene is observed by Argaleon. For the audience, this renders specious the distinctions governing Leonidas's opening complaint that "So many of [my] hours in publick move, / That few are left for privacy, and Love" (II.i.413–14). The opening scene of act 3 reenacts the argument in different terms, for Rhodophil and Doralice play at marital affection for the benefit of Artemis, who looks on. As soon as Artemis leaves, they revert to the language of ennui. The difference between high and low appears in the degree to which the characters in the low plot understand themselves *as* stage characters, even in Melantha's case, where she practices her postures and engages in an imaginary dialogue with Rhodophil (III.i.219 ff.).

Derek Hughes has very neatly parsed *Marriage à la Mode* as involving a series of such contrasts between private and public knowledge: the *pri-*

vate is, precisely, a fiction made possible under terms established by the public. This pseudodichotomy admittedly creates some ironies and disappointments in the low plot, for the would-be lovers are driven by the rather conventional quasi-libertine axiom that when passion has decayed, it is time to seek partners outside conventional marriage. Their attempts to seek a point at which passion might be consummated only produce comic mistakes: all four make separate assignations to meet in the same private place in act 3, scene 2. The scene in and around the grotto translates a potentially private space into a place for a series of intensely stagy effects.

The resistance to the public condition of knowledge in the high plot creates more internal tension, because characters aspire to be self-defining in ways that resist the normal mode in which stage character can in practice be known and stage plots must move. The lyric knowledge apparently shared by Leonidas and Palmyra involves certain internal contradictions: where the intensity of emotion combines with the unthinking quality of the play's pastoral formulations, it supplies a fiction of an unmediated bond between the lovers; yet they cannot help thinking of each other in slightly different terms, also drawn from pastoral convention, that remind us that character is realized always as a kind of representation. Thus, Leonidas recalls the purity of the pastoral world he and Palmyra earlier shared by speaking of sucking "in Love, as insensibly as Ayre" (II.i.430), and concludes the scene by insisting that even in public,

> Our souls sit close, and silently within;
> And their own Web from their own Intrals spin.
> And when eyes meet far off, our sense is such,
> That, Spider-like, we feel the tender'st touch.
>
> (II.i.499–502)

We should remember that neoclassical spiders are given to spinning self-pleasing webs, the ultimate figure for a self-regarding knowledge. By contrast, Palmyra recalls herself rather as the May Queen, which reconverts that world into another stage (II.i.431 ff.). This, it transpires, is the stage of politics itself, because the public manipulation of images of the kind played out in the May festival predicts the device by which Polydamas will publish Palmyra's presumed treachery:

> First, in her hand
> There shall be plac'd a Player's painted Sceptre,
> And, on her head, a gilded Pageant Crown;

> Thus shall she go,
> With all the Boys attending on her Triumph:
> That done, be put alone into a Boat,
> With bread and water onely for three days.
>
> (III.i.300–306)

It is almost as if Polydamas confirms Hobbes's and Davenant's view that politics has to be conducted by example or public spectacle (a "Triumph"). Leonidas continually attempts to frustrate those conditions by declaring that he is an epistemic law unto himself: not unlike Milton's Satan, he declares in one soliloquy, "I have Scene enough within / To exercise my vertue" (III.i.477–78). Later, he asserts that "I have a Kingly Soul yet" (IV.i.22) and argues that "Duty's a Name; and Love's a Real thing" (IV.iv.46). His attempt to identify himself is twice dramatically cut off by Argaleon, so that he never defines himself directly: his quasi-Cartesian assertion "I am—" (V.i.422) significantly ends in a gap. His self-discovery, when it occurs, takes place in Amalthea's report of his escaping arrest (V.i.438–47).

Dryden is attempting a critique of knowledge in the assertion that knowledge of character, including oneself, is dramatistic. That is partly why the masquerade, which regulates the purely inferential nature of social knowledge, serves to distinguish the high from the low. Of course, there are important parallels. Palamede asserts—to Doralice—that he would know his mistress "in any shape" (IV.iii.54). And Doralice can quietly mock him by asking whether he would make a lodestone of his mistress. But the assertion of some stable and self-evident knowledge is more urgent in the high plot and, rather than a local comic irony, produces the possibility of violence. Because lyric or demonstrative knowledge treats its claims as self-evident, the dangers of romance are very real: unlike dramatistic knowledge, which builds up propositions by exposing multiple points of view, it tends to sweep aside or disregard competing kinds of claims. Thus Leonidas glibly assures Amalthea that he will know Palmyra

> by a thousand other signs,
> She cannot hide so much Divinity.
> Disguis'd, and silent, yet some graceful motion
> Breaks from her, and shines round her like a Glory.
>
> (IV.ii.11–14)

That possibility of certain knowledge is belied by Argaleon's ability to impersonate Leonidas and so glean potentially fatal knowledge from Palmyra.

The equivalent in many ways to Leonidas in the low plot is Melantha. Like Leonidas, Melantha attempts to create a private language by fabricating an identity from French that she learns by rote. Dryden is making several points at once: that there can be no such thing as a private language; that language is more than a mere vocabulary—it comes attached to an entire grammar of behavior; and that Melantha's urgency to Frenchify herself is an expression of any woman's fragile political circumstances. Like other women in Restoration comedy—Millamant above all—Melantha is trying to create a kind of leisure that suppresses the fact that women in this culture cannot afford to engage in the same fictions of self-definition as men. As opposed to the vernacular, French stands for the world of romance or lyric figured in the high plot, and in the world outside Sicily: Palamede has just returned from a sojourn in "*Spain* or *Italy,* or some of the hot Countreys" (I.i.49). But Palamede is returning to Sicily—a type of England— in response to another condition that also stands in the wings: his father threatens his inheritance unless he marries. The same applies to Melantha, for she too is threatened by her father; and Palamede reengages with the world of the vernacular at the beginning of the play, just as Melantha must drop her defenses at the end. That is, if, like Doralice, women can play for a while, they must return to those institutions that regulate their social being: marriage for both Doralice and Melantha, and the vernacular for Melantha.

Leonidas perhaps experiences a momentary lapse of identity on stage because Argaleon strong-arms him, but he recovers both his identity and the kingdom. If he remains deluded about the kind of knowledge available to him, the consequences to him are minimal. Melantha experiences a more genuinely tragic collapse when Palamede sings her French into silence: Palamede overcomes her and she weeps, but the figure of this conquest is, significantly, taken from theology. Melantha and Amalthea play out similar roles in the low and high plots respectively: the high plot is constructed as a chiasmus of power (Polydamas-Leonidas; Argaleon-Palmyra), the low plot as a chiasmus of desire (Rhodophil-Melantha; Palamede-Doralice). Amalthea figures the pure exercise of desire within the high plot, and so she is reduced to silence in soliciting for Leonidas and finally retiring to a nunnery. Melantha similarly wants unmediated access to the world of the court—what Doralice speaks of as "the Presence" (III.i.110). Amalthea's desire results in an obvious cost: she must sacrifice herself to Leonidas; but Melantha's desire is figured not only as her comic French but a series of equally surprising rushes from the stage into the wings in pursuit of the court offstage. When she too collapses into silence, it propels her into, not out of, social relations. This move, Philotis explains to her, occurs because Palamede "does but accommodate his phrase to your refin'd language" (V.i.147–48).

Melantha must submit, that is, to the vernacular, the terms of the comic ending, to marriage, which are institutions that foil the attempt to treat knowledge and language as unmediated expressions of desire. Like other institutions, language involves a series of accommodations. Shortly before she finds her French fails to protect her from Palamede, Melantha remarks that in one exchange she has not used all the words in her armory: "*Naiveté* should have been there, but the disobedient word would not come in" (V.i.89–90). And Melantha's final utterance expresses frustration that "our damn'd Language expresses nothing" (V.i.495): language has failed to protect her from her own impotence. This recalcitrance at the heart of language —its refusal to bend immediately to our will—is what also reveals the self-delusions in Leonidas, and indeed the instabilities of the entire high plot. The very body of Melantha as agent in the plot—itself a tactile and negotiable fact—serves as a dramaturgical figure of that recalcitrance. "*Naiveté*" will not submit to Melantha at the one point where she tries to engage Palmyra directly on stage. Palmyra asks, "What is she?"—which curiously objectifies Melantha, as if she were a physical obstruction—to which Artemis replies, "An impertinent Lady, Madam" (V.i.91–92). Melantha's impertinence is of course a lapse of social decorum, but it is also an impertinence of the kind that bothers the Widow Blackacre in *The Plain Dealer*, namely the tendency of the actual, the empirical world to break into the romantic fictions by which we might like to define ourselves. It is unlikely that the two plots in *Marriage à la Mode* can operate independently for five acts, without intruding upon and qualifying each other: the conventions of the stage themselves figure the resistance of the actual, empirical world to the romantic and ideal world. But nevertheless, the high plot still resents the intrusions of the low.

Leviathan asserts the necessity and inevitability of power, the product of the seemingly inescapable logic of Hobbes's geometrical rhetoric. But the larger frame of *Leviathan* presents a different, more voluntaristic rhetoric that accords with Hobbes's linguistics, as if to expose the pure artifice of power that we both construct and inhabit. Similarly, for all that the high plot of *Marriage à la Mode* finally recommends the restoration of a rightful prince, the terms of that institution are examined by its relation to the low plot. The low plot inscribes the inevitability and desirability of marriage, the high plot the inevitability and desirability of the lawfully constituted state. But where the exchange of value in the low plot occurs finally as an empirical recognition of certain realities, whose consequences for women are potentially tragic, the value of monarchy in the high plot is still to some extent the outcome of its romance premises, which lead Leonidas to think of his claims as self-evident. But because Leonidas is a man, he can afford to ignore the epistemological grounds of his power. Dryden invites us to observe the discrepancy between the empirical and self-evident, the dramatistic and the lyrical, as if to scrutinize the gap between the institutions that govern and the terms by which we agree to obey them. One of those institutions is the play itself, whose generic conventions demand an ending after five acts, but again—as in *The Country Wife*—our pleasure is purchased at a visible cost to some of the characters. Dryden always recognizes the necessity of institutions of all kinds but always makes us conscious of the mediations that make them possible: even in *Astrea Redux* he warns us against seeing Charles's restoration as a natural and unmediated event, for if we do, we might fail to remind the king that his rule must follow the precepts of "method," the most valuable product of his experience in exile, which might serve to check the potential excesses of power. If Hobbes and Dryden defend the status quo, they also denaturalize its ideology: their double rhetoric shows that it may be inevitable, but it is not to be treated as transparent.

Notes

1. I owe special thanks to Brean Hammond, Eric Rothstein, and Victoria Silver for commenting on earlier versions of this essay. For Canfield, see both "Ideology" and *Word as Bond* 66–80; for Rodes, see his commentary on Dryden, *Marriage A-la-Mode;* for Rothstein and Kavenick, see 138–64.

2. I would appeal to Carol Kay for a defense for linking with later authors the way Hobbes formulates the mutual relations between epistemology, language, and politics. Kay uses Defoe as her post-Hobbesian example; and I here cite Dryden's criticism as providing evidence that he was as subtly read in Hobbes as in Milton,

both of which figures occupy him. For more on the "influence" of Hobbes on the Restoration, see especially Quentin Skinner's articles.

3. My use of Hobbes in this essay is determined by two factors: Hobbes's general importance to the Restoration and Dryden's sophisticated appreciation of Hobbes as evidenced in the preface to the *Fables* and in the analogies among the rhetorics of Dryden's greatest critical essays, Hobbes's *Leviathan,* and Dryden's *Marriage à la Mode.* I do not assume that neoclassical philosophy, drama, and criticism inhabit different discursive worlds; rather, I see the necessity of seeing them as aspects of a fairly coherent *literate* culture. For further discussion of the methodological issues at stake, see my *Material Word.* Much of my view of Hobbes is influenced by discussions with Alan Ryan.

4. Interestingly, Leo Strauss aligns the Epicurean values of *Leviathan* with the modernism he so clearly dislikes in Hobbes (what he calls "political hedonism"). Not unlike Alasdair MacIntyre, whose argument in *After Virtue* he partly anticipates, he prefers the stabilities of a more Aristotelian polity (and epistemology). Strauss's allegorizing and demonizing of Hobbes accords with mine to the degree that Hobbes's Epicureanism accompanies a more general skepticism, as well as a certain materialism. See Strauss 169.

5. On definition as itself proof of a human propensity to invent cultural symbols of which the first is language, see Burke 3.

6. Something of this doubleness is the focus of Emile Durkheim's analysis of the symbolically constitutive nature of human societies. The force of the symbolic world we inhabit is such that the cultural actor has the sensation that he or she is responding to imperatives from without and yet that those actions occur as individual decisions. Cultural symbolism is both transindividual and individual at the same time. The transindividual power of that symbolism occurs in the form of lyric violence on the individual, of the kind I have described here both as lyric and as romance. Durkheim writes: "[A] very intense social life always does a sort of violence to the organism, as well as to the individual consciousness, which interferes with its normal functioning. Therefore it can last only a limited length of time. . . . [I]f we give the name delirious to every state in which the mind adds to the immediate data given by the senses and projects its own sentiments and feelings into things, then nearly every collective representation is in a sense delirious; religious beliefs are only one particular case of a very general law" (259).

7. This argument more or less determines Lucius Cary, Viscount Falkland's own *Discourse of Infallibility.*

Works Cited

Brown, Laura S. "The Divided Plot: Tragicomic Form in the Restoration." *ELH* 47 (1980): 67–79.

Burke, Kenneth. *Language as Symbolic Action: Essays on Life, Literature, and Method*. Berkeley and Los Angeles: U of California P, 1966.

Canfield, J. Douglas. "The Ideology of Restoration Tragicomedy." *ELH* 51 (1984): 447–64.

———. *Word as Bond in English Literature from the Middle Ages to the Restoration*. Philadelphia: U of Pennsylvania P, 1989.

Cary, Lucius, Viscount Falkland. *Discourse of Infallibility*. London, 1651.

de Man, Paul. "The Rhetoric of Temporality." *Blindness and Insight: Essays in the Rhetoric of Contemporary Criticism*. 2nd ed. Minneapolis: U of Minnesota P, 1983. 187–228.

Dryden, John. *Marriage A-la-Mode. The Works of John Dryden*. Vol. 11. Ed. John Loftis, David Stuart Rodes, and Vinton A. Dearing. Berkeley and Los Angeles: U of California P, 1978. 17 vols. to date. 1956– . 217–316.

———. *Of Dramatic Poesy and Other Critical Essays*. Ed. George Watson. 2 vols. London: Dent; New York: Dutton, 1962.

Durkheim, Emile. *The Elementary Forms of Religious Life*. New York: Free P, 1985.

Hobbes, Thomas. *Leviathan*. Ed. C. B. Macpherson. Harmondsworth, Eng.: Penguin, 1968.

Hughes, Derek. "The Unity of Dryden's *Marriage à la Mode*." *Philological Quarterly* 61 (1982): 125–42.

Johnston, David J. *The Rhetoric of "Leviathan": Thomas Hobbes and the Politics of Cultural Transformation*. Princeton: Princeton UP, 1986.

Kavka, Gregory S. *Hobbesian Moral and Political Theory*. Princeton: Princeton UP, 1986.

Kay, Carol. *Political Constructions: Defoe, Richardson, and Sterne in Relation to Hobbes, Hume, and Burke*. Ithaca, N.Y.: Cornell UP, 1989.

Kroll, Richard W. F. *The Material Word: Literate Culture in the Restoration and Early Eighteenth Century*. Baltimore: Johns Hopkins UP, 1991.

Lucretius. *T. Lucretius Carus The Epicurean Philosopher, His Six Books De Natura Rerum [sic]*. Trans. Thomas Creech. Oxford, 1682.

MacIntyre, Alasdair. *After Virtue: A Study in Moral Theory*. London: Duckworth, 1981.

Macpherson, C. B. "Hobbes's Bourgeois Man." *Hobbes Studies*. Ed. Keith C. Brown. Oxford: Blackwell, 1965. 169–83.

———. *The Political Theory of Possessive Individualism*. Oxford: Oxford UP, 1962.

McKeon, Michael. "Marxist Criticism and *Marriage A La Mode*." *Eighteenth Century: Theory and Interpretation* 24 (1983): 141–62.

Oakeshott, Michael. *Hobbes on Civil Association*. Oxford: Blackwell, 1975.

Pocock, J. G. A. "Time, History, and Eschatology in the Thought of Thomas Hobbes." *Politics, Language, and Time: Essays in Political Thought and History*. New York: Atheneum, 1973. 148–201.

Rothstein, Eric, and Frances Kavenick. *The "Designs" of Carolean Comedy.* Carbondale: Southern Illinois UP, 1988.

Ryan, Michael. *Marxism and Deconstruction: A Critical Articulation.* Baltimore: Johns Hopkins UP, 1982.

Shapin, Steven, and Simon Schaffer. *Leviathan and the Air Pump.* Princeton: Princeton UP, 1985.

Silver, Victoria. "The Fiction of Self-Evidence in Hobbes's *Leviathan.*" *ELH* 55 (1988): 351–79.

Skinner, Quentin. "Conquest and Consent: Thomas Hobbes and the Engagement Controversy." *The Interregnum: The Quest for Settlement.* Ed. G. E. Aylmer. London: Macmillan, 1972. 78–98.

———. "Hobbes's *Leviathan.*" *Historical Journal* 7 (1964): 321–33.

———. "Thomas Hobbes and His Disciples in France and England." *Comparative Studies in Society and History* 8 (1966): 153–67.

———. "Thomas Hobbes and the Nature of the Early Royal Society." *Historical Journal* 12 (1969): 217–39.

Strauss, Leo. *Natural Right and History.* Chicago: U of Chicago P, 1953.

Thomas, Keith. "The Social Origins of Hobbes's Political Thought." *Hobbes Studies.* Ed. Keith C. Brown. Oxford: Blackwell, 1965. 185–236.

Watkins, J. W. N. *Hobbes's System of Ideas: A Study in the Political Significance of Philosophical Theories.* London: Hutchinson, 1965.

Carolinean Sexuality and the Restoration Stage: Reconstructing the Royal Phallus in *Sodom*

Harold Weber

More than three centuries after it was first written, *Sodom* remains a play without an audience. Notorious though it may be, it possesses no theatrical history, and even its existence as a literary text can too easily be ignored: I search my standard reference guide to the period, the literary history of George Sherburn and Donald F. Bond, and find not a single reference to the play. In my decade and a half in the profession I cannot recall hearing, or even seeing a notice for, a convention paper on *Sodom*—surely, amid the diversity of MLA sessions and regional conferences, a singular absence.

The reasons for this omission cannot be entirely aesthetic: the theoretical revolution of the last decades has convincingly demonstrated that artistic judgments cannot be separated from other discourses of value. Not until I actually tried working with *Sodom,* however, did I realize that the professional silence entombing the play stems from the relationship *Sodom* generates between critic and object. Though I have admired the recent critical methodology in which examination of the text is intimately involved with an interrogation of the self, the position of the writing subject being a necessary part of textual analysis, I have not before this moment felt drawn to assume such a pose. If I do so now, it is because the text itself has finally, in ways I attempt to explain below, made my presence necessary.

I first came to *Sodom* in all "innocence," my work on the rake-hero in seventeenth-century drama leading inevitably to this most infamous, if least read, of Restoration plays. And I first considered writing about the play in all innocence, its satiric depiction of Charles II's sexuality being an integral part of a project on literary representations of Charles that now occupies my attention. I might even have retained my innocence had my examination of *Sodom* simply remained part of the book I am in the process of writing. But in the spring of 1988 I was asked to join a panel treating comic character on the Restoration stage, and I decided to deliver a paper on *Sodom* entitled "Comic Character and Restoration History: Reconstructing the Royal Phallus in *Sodom*."

When solitary contemplation of the play gave way to public dialogue, however, it became clear that *Sodom* could not be treated as simply another text. My age of innocence ended a few days before the Midwestern American Society for Eighteenth-Century Studies convention at the University of Notre Dame in October 1988, when I realized that I would soon have to read aloud passages from the play. Reading literature to an audience, both in class and at conventions, probably constitutes for most academics an important part of the pleasure of our profession. Normally I relish the opportunity to read dramatic works to others, and, having dealt with sexual matters while working on the rake, I had reason to believe that I was not abnormally prissy about such things. In contemplating my paper on *Sodom*, however, I felt terribly anxious, implicated in the vulgarity and misogyny of the text.

In the event, nothing of significance happened when I read the paper. The session, scheduled at an awkward, late hour, drew a minuscule audience, only one of whom left in the middle of my paper (bored, perhaps, rather than offended). But a good friend of mine explained at length that he could not possibly have delivered my paper—could hardly believe that I had delivered it; and recently, when showing a rough draft of this essay—which did not include this confessional introduction—to a group of colleagues, another friend admitted that the material so sickened her that she could not understand why I worked with it. She came close to suggesting that my interest in the play was, like the play itself, perverse.

Such charges—and fears I might add—were not deflected by claiming participation in an ongoing scholarly debate about the play, for *Sodom*, as I have already suggested, remains a text with an extraordinarily small critical literature. Few scholars publish on the play, and those who do almost invariably approach it as a problem in bibliography and authorship.[1] In this essay I do not intend to address either of these problems, except to lament the lack of a widely available scholarly text—certainly one reason for the play's absence from the canon—and to suggest that all ascriptions of authorship remain unprovable until further evidence presents itself. I want instead to ask what has made the play to some extent "unreadable," a text treated by the profession as a bibliographical curiosity rather than a literary artifact. Why does this play seem so dangerous?

The answers to such questions must, I believe, involve not the aesthetics of obscenity but its misogyny. Though the obscene, I suspect, usually depends on a misogynistic subtext, *Sodom* fashions its obscenity quite directly as a violent attack on women, an integral part of its attempt not simply to marginalize but to exile, erase, and annihilate the female body. Moreover, the play's sexual disgust with women cannot be separated from its political purposes, its attempt to reconstruct the monarchy and the patriarchal structures that the king represents. In *Sodom* political and sexual anxiety join to create a powerful vision of the male desire for self-sufficiency and transcendence.

We may approach the problems of gender that the play raises by attending to John Evelyn's diary entry for 6 February 1685, where Evelyn, in describing and lamenting the death of Charles II, includes a lengthy catalog of both the dead king's virtues and vices:

> An excellent prince doubtlesse had he ben lesse addicted to Women, which made him uneasy & allways in Want to supply their unmeasurable profusion. . . . certainely never had King more glorious opportunities to have made himselfe, his people, & all Europ happy, & prevented innumerable mischiefs, had not his too Easy nature resign'd him to be menag'd by crafty men, & some abandoned & prophane wretches, who corrupted his otherwise sufficient parts. . . . those wiccked creatures tooke him [off] from all application becoming so greate a King. (4: 410–11)

Complaints about Charles's sexual behavior did not, of course, have to await the king's death. Rochester's famous lines—"His scepter and his prick are of a length; / And she may sway the one who plays with th'other" —which supposedly numbered the king himself among their readers, owe their notoriety to harmonious numbers and epigrammatic compression, not originality. The connection between Charles's scepter and his prick was a commonplace during the 1670s and early 1680s, this example from the anonymous "Flatfoot the Gudgeon Taker" (1680) demonstrating, like Rochester's lines, a satiric political discourse in which the king's prick both represents and undermines his royal identity:

> Methinks I see our mighty monarch stand,
> His pliant angle trembling in his hand;
> Pleas'd with the sport, good man, nor does he know
> His easy scepter bends and trembles so.
>
> (Lord 2: 189–91)

In such a discourse, Charles's sexual self subverts his royal self, his "easy" sexual behavior lying at odds with assertions of his political "might" and authority.

Evelyn's reflections, however, reveal as well that the king's weakness cannot be separated from the insufficiency of the object of his passion. "Women" are the problem precisely because "their unmeasurable profusion" causes a "Want" in Charles. "His otherwise sufficient parts"—the sexual pun is particularly felicitous here—which might have made him "so greate a King," have been compromised by the female sex, whose excess creates a lack in men. These reflections generate grief out of the disparity between what Charles might have been—"an excellent prince," "so greate a King," a monarch who could have made "his people & all Europ happy"—and what his passion for women, "wiccked creatures," made him. The object of these caustic reflections remains Charles, though their moral force depends on a prior construction of the dangerous and corrupt female. Political critique depends on misogynous rhetoric, royal inadequacy constituted primarily through female insufficiency. In such a discourse Charles emerges as an object of satire primarily because of the worthlessness of women.

Neither Evelyn's scapegoating of women nor his nostalgic evocation of a "lost" ideal is unusual; both participate in a conventional conservative rhetoric. *Sodom*'s uniqueness lies in its attempt to realize that ideal by imagining a world in which women play no part, the threat they represent neutralized not by the patriarchal structures that normally limit women but by their banishment altogether from the sexual world. Within the Western patriarchal system, women play a subservient, though necessary, role. They function, Gayle Rubin explains, as "the most precious of gifts," the currency upon which all gender relations depend:

> If it is women who are being transacted, then it is the men who give
> and take them who are linked, the woman being a conduit of a rela-
> tionship rather than a partner to it. . . . The relations of such a system
> are such that women are in no position to realize the benefits of their

own circulation. As long as the relations specify that men exchange women, it is men who are the beneficiaries of the product of such exchanges—social organization. (173–74)

Within such a system, then, heterosexuality possesses significance only as part of a larger homosocial dynamic, relations between men being the primary goal of heterosexual relationships. In her exploration of how such a gender system operates in literature, Eve Kosofsky Sedgwick demonstrates that "the subject as well as the ultimate object of female heterosexuality within what is called patriarchal culture are seen as male" (12). Female heterosexuality, therefore, though marginalized, is nonetheless "necessary for the maintenance of any patriarchy" (4), a point recently reiterated by Jane Gallop when she notes that "men exchange women for heterosexual purposes, but the real intercourse is that exchange between men. The heterosexual object is irretrievably lost in the circuits, and the man is consoled by the homology" (37).

Sodom fractures this system in its attempt to remove women from the exchange between men. The rupturing of this current liberates a hatred and fear of women that, while an inherent part of the conventional system of exchange, must nevertheless be significantly repressed if that system is to function. In attempting to do away with women, to remove them entirely from its sexual economy, the play can indulge a frank, even hysterical, renunciation of the female body, a strategy and tone exacerbated by the profound anxiety generated by perceptions of Charles's sexual weakness. Public discourse, in spite of the king's quite notorious heterosexual prowess, depicted him as a man unable to use women in the proper fashion, his "easiness" transformed in a 1667 conversation between Samuel Pepys and Thomas Povey, treasurer for Tangier, into a "horrid effeminacy," for Charles "hath taken ten times more care and pains making friends between my Lady Castlemayne and Mrs. Steward when they have fallen out, than ever he did to save his kingdom" (Pepys 8: 288). Women, not politics or power, dominate Charles's life, thus inverting the proper structures of authority in which men rule women.[2]

During the Restoration the profound effects of the king's sexuality on his monarchical identity can best be followed in the ephemeral and usually anonymous poems on affairs of state. The king's sexual antics, though known earlier, did not become a fit topic of public discourse until the late sixties. From the early seventies, then, until the early eighties, when Charles

succeeded in great measure in establishing his authority over the London
print trade, verse satires like "Flatfoot the Gudgeon Taker" constituted one
of the public arenas, and certainly the chief literary one, in which constructions of the king's sexuality played an important part in undermining his
royal identity.

Because the theaters were so much more easily controlled and censored
than a fugitive opposition press, dramatists could do relatively little to exploit the king's sexual vulnerability on the public stage. Many insufficient
kings, of course, graced the Restoration stage, but analogies to Charles
were necessarily complex, indirect, uncertain. Elizabeth's angry remarks
concerning the use of Shakespeare's *Richard II* during Essex's ill-fated
rebellion—"I am Richard II. Know ye not that?"—remain the clearest indication of how well England's monarchs understood the subversive power
of the most public of literary forms. Shakespeare's play, in fact, in its
adaptation by Nahum Tate, ran afoul of the lord chamberlain during the
Exclusion Crisis of 1680; like Nathaniel Lee's *Lucius Junius Brutus,* produced during that same year, the play was silenced because of its dangerous
implications at a moment of intense political crisis.[3]

It should therefore not be surprising that the most frank theatrical depiction of Charles's sexualized monarchy should never have been performed
on the Restoration stage, though *Sodom* acknowledges the dangerousness
of its subject by cleverly ignoring its political involvement, imagining, in
the first of its two extant prologues, an audience attending not to matters
of state but of sex:

> By Heaven a noble audience here to day
> Well Sirs, you've come to see this bawdy Play
> And faith it is Debauchery compleat,
> The very name of 't made you mad to see't;
> I hope 't will please you well, by Yove, I think
> You all love bawdy things as whores love chink. . . .
> It is the most debauch'd heroick piece
> That e're was wrote, what dare compare with this,
> Here's that will fit your fancy with delight
> 't Will tickle every vein, and please your sight,
> Nay make your prick to have an appetite.
>
>   (3–4)[4]

The play's unusual frankness about its lascivious intent, its apparently single-minded desire to "make all pricks to stand and cunts to gape" (5), serves to obfuscate its far more dangerous political implications. Yet even as it affirms its goal of arousing desire, the play uses a literary vocabulary—insisting that it will be a "debauch'd *heroick* piece"—employing as the play opens with a speech by the king, Bolloxinion, a satiric discourse that places it firmly among the satires directed against Charles's sexual weakness:

> Thus in the Zenith of my Lust I reign:
> I eat to swive, and swive to eat again;
> Let other Monarchs, who their scepters bear
> To keep their subjects less in aw than fear,
> Be slaves to crowns, my Nation shall be free—
> My Pintle only shall my scepter be;
> My Laws shall act more pleasure than command
> And with my Prick, I'll govern all the land.
>
> (9)

Bolloxinion's rant, with its emphatic mock-heroic accents, should immediately remind us of Buckingham's *Rehearsal* (1671), written probably within a few years of *Sodom* and directed at the same theatrical form, the heroic drama. *The Rehearsal*, however, directs itself chiefly against the literary sins of the form, its major targets Dryden, satirized in the absurd figure of Bays, and the dramatic conventions of the form itself. *Sodom*, on the other hand, focuses on the protagonist of the heroic drama, creating in Bolloxinion a grotesque sexual version of the Dryden hero, an Almanzor of the bedroom whose considerable energies seek only a sexual outlet. As this opening speech reveals, such a figure clearly parodies Charles, the conventional identity between prick and scepter the most obvious indication of the play's political import. In his elevation of pleasure above power and his easy desire to subordinate fear to freedom, Bolloxinion suggests Charles as well, though Bolloxinion represents Charles raised to the *n*th power, his desire to entirely replace scepter with prick—"My Pintle only shall my scepter be"—providing an outlandish comic exaggeration that moves the play into a realm of unrestricted sexual fantasy.

As I have explained, this fantasy depends on the unusual rupture of the heterosexual channels of homosocial expression. From the very beginning the play reveals the extraordinary violence against women liberated by this process, both versions of the prologue expressing a sensual obsession with women that cannot be separated from a pronounced disgust with the female body. The first begins by insisting that "cunts [are] Loves proper center," but it follows this assertion with a long catalog of repulsive images:

> Their ulcer'd cunts by being so abused . . .
> May well be styl'd, Love's nasty common sink;
> When e're your fancy is to fuck inclin'd,
> If they are sound or not, perhaps you'll find
> Some of their cunts so stufft with gravy thick
> That like an Irish Bogg, they'll drown your prick
> Some swive so much their hair's worn off the spot
> They're dead to sin and do beginn to rot.
>
> (3–4)

The second version of the prologue recapitulates this movement from defining cunt as "Loves proper center" to "Love's nasty common sink" by celebrating "Al——ty Cunts" even as it bewails "her tedious toyl" (5). By its end, the second prologue has concluded that "none but fops alone to cunts will bow," for "she that hath a cunt will be a whore" (6).

This radical disjunction in perceptions of the female sex and body produces the central tension of the play, the obvious though unexamined contradiction that animates the play when it becomes attached to the figure of Bolloxinion. As we have seen, Bolloxinion begins *Sodom* as a king who insists that political power can be understood and expressed only as a manifestation of his royal phallus, the male organ that generates and sustains the patriarchal structures of society. Pockenello, described in the dramatis personae as "Prince, Collonel and Favorite of the King," endorses this vision of the political world, insisting that "Your Grace alone hath from the Powers above / A princely wisdom, and a princely Love" (10). In Pockenello's version of the royal state, the sexualized monarch possesses his warrant from heaven.

The uniqueness of *Sodom* lies in its conversion of this political sexuality from a heterosexual to a homosexual bias. What Evelyn regarded as an "addiction" to women is profoundly altered, the object of the king's desires transformed by the play's radically unstable depictions of the female sex. Though Bolloxinion's opening speech in no way restricts the objects of his lust, both the prologues and first-act set—"an Antichamber hung round with Aretine's Postures"—suggest a conventional heterosexual orientation. Immediately following Bolloxinion's speech, however, Borastus, the "Buggermaster-general," when asked to provide for the king's lust, admits, "I no longer Cunts admire; / The drudgery has worn out my desire— / Your Grace may soon to human arse retire" (11). This rejection of hetero- for homosexual delights becomes the structural principle of the play, which portrays the nation's transformation into a homosexual state.

As political satire, this unusual inversion of "normal" sexual practice undermines Charles's royal identity, subverting and feminizing the king's ostensible male authority. The "Merry Monarch," notorious for his heterosexual promiscuity, becomes a worshiper of homoerotic delights, his masculinity transformed into an unmanliness that threatens the kingdom. At the same time, however, in this sexual fantasy generated by a terrible ambivalence toward female sexuality, the play constructs, and validates, a world in which men can abandon and erase the female body altogether. The play generates an unusual literary world of homosexual machismo in which male virility grounds and proves itself on the male body, the female body being a sign only of a sexual difference that haunts and frightens men. Though these two strategies appear contradictory—the first degrading Charles for his homosexuality, the second valorizing homosexuality— both depend on a construction of gender difference that privileges the male even as it questions male superiority. As in Evelyn, female insufficiency easily becomes male want.

Bolloxinion is at first hesitant to adopt the new homoerotic order, even though act 1 reveals that the king and his court are no strangers to the pleasures of buggery; Bolloxinion and Twely, a "Pimp of Honour," reminisce about a past experience in which "Arse did that deed, which kind Hand could not do" (12). Though no homosexual novice, however, the king at first responds to Borastus's advice by insisting, "My pleasures for new Cunts I will uphold / And have reserves of Kindness for the old" (11). He then admits, however, that

> As for the Queen her Cunt no more invites
> Clad with the filth of all her nasty whites
> Come, we miss-spend our time, we know not how
> The choice of Buggery is wanting now.
>
> (11–12)

At the act's end he expresses his ambivalence in a speech that, as Richard
Elias has persuasively argued (432–34), deliberately parodies Charles's
1672 proclamation concerning religious toleration:

> Henceforth Borastus, set the Nation free,
> Let conscience have its force of Liberty.
> I do proclaim, that Buggery may be us'd
> Thro all the Land, so Cunt be not abus'd
> That, the proviso, this shall be your Trust
> (to Borastus)
>
> All things shall to your order be adjust.
> To Buggeranthos, let this charge be given
> And let him bugger all things under h———ven.
> (13)

Bolloxinion's insistence that in sexual matters "conscience have its force
of Liberty" corresponds to Charles's desire to grant a liberty of conscience
to Roman Catholic and Nonconformist subjects. Here the mingling of
religious and sexual discourse reveals the complex sexual anxieties that
animate Bolloxinion's behavior. The speech begins, after all, by insisting
on the "force of Liberty" and that "Cunt be not abus'd." Yet the rhetorical
bombast of the final lines, with their insistence that Buggeranthos "bugger all things under h———ven," expresses not merely a taste for sodomic
pleasures but a forceful attempt on the king's part to re-create the sexual
universe. He determines not simply that buggery shall be permitted but
that it shall form the chief pleasure in all the land.

In imagining a world in which the king insists on the legitimacy of
buggery, the play suggests just how unsettling was Charles's sexual irre-
sponsibility. The play subverts his power not because it necessarily takes
seriously the charge that he enjoyed men but because the act of imagining
such a *world turned upside down* reveals the tremendous gulf between the
dreams and ideals of Stuart absolutism and the doubts and fears generated by the king himself. *Sodom* represents a monstrous inversion of the
royal masque, for in it the king becomes the symbol not of order's triumph
but of its defeat in a climactic sexual apocalypse. The king becomes the
antimasque, his erotic obsessions responsible for the nation's destruction.

From the ambivalences of the prologues and Bolloxinion's initial adoption of buggery, these obsessions move forcefully not simply to marginalize

the female body but to exile it altogether from a male homosexual economy. Yet this procedure contains a grudging admission of female strength, a recognition that the female body possesses a power that cannot be denied. Indeed, the very extravagance of the play's antipathy toward women stems from this recognition of their necessary power; male power can assert itself fully only by eliminating the seductive and dangerous female body that can control and compel male desires.

Act 3 revolves around a scene that perfectly reveals the play's forced and ambivalent recognition of this biological female strength. In it, the adolescent prince and princess, Pricket and Swivia, show their genitals to each other. Pricket, not yet fifteen, is still a virgin, though Swivia already possesses a sophisticated sexual knowledge. Pricket's reaction, as Swivia shows her "thing," emphasizes his astonishment that "the strangest Creature . . . I ever saw" could be "the Beards that keep men in such aw" (23). Swivia continues by insisting that

> This is the ware house of the world's chief Trade,
> On this soft anvil all mankind was made.
> Come 't is a harmless thing, draw near and try
> You will desire no other Death to dye.
>
> (24)

Swivia succeeds in seducing Pricket, providing the "plaisant pain" of his first sexual encounter. When he has recovered his senses, they discuss the organ that has so overmastered him:

> *Swivia.* It was this Cunt, that made your Pintle weep
>   And lull'd you so unto a gentle sleep.
>   You gave those pleasures, which you waking thought
>   On all my senses had amusement brought.
> *Pricket.* 't Is strange to think that such a homely seat
>   With such delight, should all our senses treat,
>   That such a gaping, slimy, hairy beast,
>   Should from its maw give hungry Prick a feast,
>   But its strange influence, I more admire
>   My heart is glutted, yet I still desire
>   And turn my freezing atoms into fire.
>
> (27)

Pricket's desire is again raised when Cunticula, one of the Maids of Honour, enters and frigs him until he spends. The act ends with the two women "*mournfully*" conveying the exhausted and now impotent prince to bed: "Tho he be living, he's as bad as dead" (32).

Act 3 of *Sodom* enacts, then, in a most unusual and even grotesque fashion, a primal scene wherein the young male comes to recognize the fundamental fact of sexual difference. In seeing the female "thing," and its absolute difference from his own organ, Pricket recognizes the power of his penis. To some extent the scene dramatizes masculine superiority, as the attention lavished on the prince's prick by the two women provides what Irigaray has called the "woman's fetishization of the male organ [that] must indeed be an indispensable support of its price on the sexual market" (53).

Yet the scene insists as well on the immense and frightening power of the female genitalia. Though Swivia assures the prince that hers is a "harmless thing," a "soft anvil," again and again Swivia talks of her power to make the prince die, to bring death and then "Resurrection," to "tickle you to live again." The sight of her cunt creates in Pricket "an agony," a "fire" that Swivia insists "I can allay." Pricket does assert that her "Cunt [is] a most obliging friend," but far more often he sees it as "strange," "homely," "a gaping, slimy, hairy beast." Indeed, it is not the cunt that the scene figures, in Irigaray's language, as "nothing you can see . . . No Thing" (48) but the shrunken penis after intercourse, that "poor little thing . . . as cold as steel," which only "cunt and Thigh" can raise again.

The rest of the play moves forcefully to counter this alien and frightening female power. By act 4, Bolloxinion, who began the play uncertain about his taste for buggery, has determined, "Since I have bugger'd human arse, I find / Pintle to Cunt is not so much inclin'd" (36). He images the female genitalia as horrible and unnatural, characterized by a curiously absent presence:

> By oft fomenting, Cunt so big doth swell
> That Prick works there, like Clapper in a Bell.
> All Vacuum, no grasping flesh does hide
> Or hug, the brawny muscles of its side.
>
> (36)

At once unpleasantly large, yet also hardly present—a contradiction revelatory of men's fear of, and desire to erase, the female genitalia—those genitalia can no longer define "Loves proper center." This devaluation of cunt leads to a celebration of buggery, which comes to represent, for Borastus, a noble freedom peculiar to humankind: "Nature to them [animals] but one poor Rule does give / But man delights in various ways to swive" (36). Pockenello even applauds the act in terms that suggest the Promethean gift of fire: "May as the G——ds his name immortal be / That first receiv'd the gift of Buggery" (37). By elevating buggery at the expense of conventional heterosexual sex, the play can remove women from the sexual economy of the kingdom. As Bolloxinion explicitly says, "Faces may change, but Cunt is but cunt still, / And he that fucks is slave to woman's will" (37). The fears generated by the female body can be repressed and denied by making no place for women in the kingdom's new sexual order.

Act 4 further introduces the movement of this court taste out into the nation itself. Buggeranthos, the General of the Army, enters to announce that his men have welcomed the king's proclamation:

> They practise it in honour of your name;
> If lust present they want no woman's aid
> Each buggers with content his own comrade.
>
> (39)

Men have become so enamored of this new taste for pleasure, in fact, that women have had to seek new forms of sexual release: "Dildoes and dogs, with women do prevail" (39). Banished from the kingdom's new sexual economy, women must seek their pleasure elsewhere, no longer part of the civilized order but devalued and forced into a bestial commerce. Buggeranthos tells the "moving" story of a woman he found "frigging with a bob'd Cur's tail"; since men have abandoned women, she has developed a passion for animals, particularly horses. Even here, however, women are scorned, for a horse whose "stateliest Tarse" she admires "Drew back his Engine": "At length I found his constancy was such, / That he would none but his dear Mrs. touch" (40).

What this anonymous woman calls "this vile cunt starving land" suggests the relentlessness of the play's desire to punish women for their sexual power. Even when Bolloxinion takes pity on this woman, declaring that "She shall a Pintle have, both stiff and stout, / . . . She shall be mistress to an Elephant" (40), we recognize the male desire to humiliate the female body that Pricket first discovered in act 3. Ranged with dogs, horses, and elephants, women are effectively removed from a human world that now defines itself solely in masculine terms. Masculine constructions of the sexual world remain true even for the sex that has been banished, for nothing in the play suggests that women may themselves participate in a homosexual universe. In act 2, scene 3, the frustrated queen and her ladies attempt to satisfy themselves with dildos, but these simulacra of the male organ provide no genuine satisfaction. Though one of the queen's ladies, Fuckadilla, blames this lack on "Short Dildoes [that] leave the Pleasure half undone" (21), her mistress's desires fix themselves firmly on a man. The play, for all its ostensible libertine freedoms, never imagines the possibility of women satisfying each other, for it wants to insist that only phallic power possesses genuine erotic potency.

The ruination that the king brings to his kingdom becomes intimately involved with contemporary politics when Bolloxinion receives an emissary from his brother monarch, Tarsehole of Gomorrah, who sends the king forty striplings as a present. There seems little doubt that "Brother Tarsehole" represents Louis XIV, particularly when the conversation immediately turns to war, the concern that Louis's relationship to Charles invariably raised in the minds of Englishmen humiliated by French might:

> Borastus. Pleasure should strive, so much in time of Peace
>   As Power in time of Battle to increase.
> Bolloxinion. The end of war is to make Peace at last—
>   When pleasure pays for all, the sorrow is past.
>
> (42)

Bolloxinion, of course, has no use for war, all his interest being wrapped up in the soft peace that allows him to pursue his pleasures. He forcefully proves this when choosing among the forty boys sent by Tarsehole, elevating his pleasure above all else, his relations with a brother monarch reinforced not through the gift of women but of men:

> Here my valued Gems, these are to me.
>   [pointing to the boys].
> More than the riches of my treasury—
> What does my crown and jewels do me good.
> Jewels and Gold are clay to flesh and blood.
>
> (43)

The introduction of Tarsehole speaks not only to contempt for Charles's passivity but to suspicion of his relationship with Louis. Throughout his reign, Charles's intimacy with, and dependence on, Louis generated a

lack of trust between monarch and subject. This special relationship between Bolloxinion and Tarsehole perhaps gives a dangerous meaning to
the former's boast during this scene that he has "fuckt and bugger'd all
the land" (42)—suspected of being in league with Louis, Charles could be
seen not as a protector but as a despoiler of his own kingdom.

Despoiler is precisely the role that Bolloxinion plays in the final scene
of *Sodom*. Bolloxinion has paraded his heroic pride from the beginning of
the play, his boast that "with my Prick, I'll govern all the land" revealing
his extraordinary sexual narcissism. In this final scene we discover the full
destructive fury of these outsized desires, which lead him to insist on his
sexual domination of even the gods:

> I'll than invade and bugger all the G——ds
> And drain the spring of their immortal c——ds,
> Then make them rub their arse till they cry:
> You've frigg'd us out of immortality.
>
> (51)

Bolloxinion's rage stems from his failure to transform the sexual nature of
his kingdom. He has attempted to deny male insufficiency by banishing the
sexual other, forgetting, as David Lee Miller reminds us, that in modern
constructions of gender "the difference between male and female, then, is
not that 'she' harbors a lamentable gap in being from which 'he' is exempt,
but that 'he' projects onto 'her' a want of sufficiency that lurks within all
subjects" (779). The desire in the play to erase the female body represents
the desire to achieve immortality, to bugger male gods in order to "drain
the spring of their immortal c[o]ds." Such a desire cannot succeed because
masculine identity requires a female other whose construction testifies to
male superiority. Evelyn pretends that female "profusion" generates male
"Want," but the truth is that female want is the condition of male profusion. Without women Bolloxinion cannot re-create the land in his own
sexual image, can only watch as a plague of biblical proportions ravages
the land:

> The heavy symptoms have infected all,
> I now may call it epidemical.
> Men's pricks are eaten of the secret parts
> Of women, wither'd and despairing heart
> The children harbor mournful discontents,

> Complaining sorely of their fundaments.
> The old do curse and envy those that swive;
> Some fuck and bugger, tho they stink alive.
>
> (51–52)

The only redress for these evils, according to the king's physician, lies in restoring the kingdom's sexual balance: "Fuck women and let buggery be no more: / It doth the procreative End destroy" (53). Here the physician invokes the traditional rationale for condemnations of homosexuality, strictures articulated most systematically for medieval Europe in the *Summa Theologica,* in which Aquinas describes sodomy—"copulation with an undue sex, male with male, or female with female"—as one of four manifestations of "the unnatural vice." This vice contradicts "the natural order of the venereal act as becoming to the human race" precisely because it is not "in keeping with the end of human procreation" (2: 1825, 1811). Theologically as well as sexually and politically bankrupt, the king, like Dryden's Morat or Lyndaraxa, refuses to yield to conventional wisdom or natural law, determined to insist until the end on his own measure of heroic sexuality:

> Why did the G——ds, that gave leave to be
> A king, not give me immortality?
> To be a substitute to h——en at will
> I scorn the gift, I'll reign and bugger still.
>
> (53)

Bolloxinion's refusal to yield his sexual delights generates the nation's final destruction, as fiery demons announce the sexual apocalypse that will engulf the nation:

> Kiss, Rise up and Dally
> Prig, Swive and rally;
> Curse, blaspheme and swear
> Those that will witness bear.
> For the Bollox singes
> Sodome off the hinges,
> Bugger, bugger, bugger
> All in hugger-mugger,

> Fire doth descend:
> 't Is too late to amend.
> (53–54)

The childlike rhythms of this verse, which suggest a perverse nursery rhyme, point to both the approaching dissolution of the civilized order and the infantile narcissistic desires that have led the nation to its destruction. Still refusing to sacrifice his mad heroic pride, however, Bolloxinion welcomes the approaching chaos, concerned only for his own safety and pleasures: "Let heaven descend, and set the world on fire— / We to some darker cavern will retire" (55). Here the play's ambivalence toward women prevents the masculine world from enjoying complete success. The attempt to annihilate female sexuality fails; the female body cannot, finally, be denied, and Bolloxinion's homoerotic order remains unable to re-create itself or the royal power it comes to represent.

The play's conclusion, particularly its appeal to customary censures of sodomy, suggests that its ambivalences encompass not only the female body but also the male homosexuality that it attempts to construct as an alternative to heterosexual sex. Only after teaching *Sodom* in a class—a far more intimidating task even than delivering a paper on it—did I recognize an unusual structural feature of the play that should immediately have impressed me. In spite of its grandiloquent delight in the male homoerotic, the play never presents two men satisfying themselves sexually on stage (as noted above, the play's phallic tyranny makes female homosexuality impossible). It shows us women masturbating with dildos, women bringing men to orgasm with their hands, a dance that dissolves into oral and genital intercourse, a sister seducing her brother; though it constantly insists on the joys and virtues of buggery, that act must always take place offstage, never presentable as a dramatic subject.

Though the play probably was not composed with an eye to its production, this curious absence in its sexual ragout suggests not simply the moral condemnation of the age—Restoration England being apparently no less homophobic than our own society[5]—but the impossibility of imagining a patriarchy that bases itself on homosexual rather than heterosexual sex. For all of its rhetorical celebration of buggery, the play cannot eroticize the sexual relationship of men, reveling instead in a conventional heterosexuality that possesses all the predictability of a pornographic movie. The construction of male identity depends on the female other, for, as Miller argues, "in repudiating femininity the masculine subject tends to lose himself as object. . . . The masculine ego recovers itself as object in the person of a feminine 'other' " (782). This recovery, however, continues to privilege the male, for the feminine returns not as an autonomous self but as an object in the service of the male ego.

The reign of no other English monarch could have produced a *Sodom*. To some extent the libertine freedoms of Charles's easy court encouraged a self-congratulatory and unashamed vulgarity that few other royal courts appear to have imitated. Yet the conditions that permitted the composition of *Sodom* involved not only a self-indulgent freedom but a profound anxiety. *Sodom* presents a vision of an erotic apocalypse; a sexual *Dunciad,* the play does not depend on a saturnian Dulness that helps to bring the "Smithfield Muses to the ear of Kings" but a sexual perversity and destruction that the king himself visits on the land. Though Charles's easy, self-indulgent sexuality may seem to have little in common with Bolloxinion's insistent taste for "men's beastly arses," the play's satiric transformation of the one into the other suggests the extent of the fears generated by Charles's antic behavior.

Sexually, for many of his contemporaries, Charles played his own fool, turning himself into a character in *The Country Wife,* where, as Sedgwick explains, "to misunderstand the kind of property women are or the kind of transaction in which alone their value is realizable means, for a man, to endanger his own position as a subject in the relationship of exchange: to be permanently feminized or objectified in relation to other men" (50–51). In this fashion Charles made his kingship a symbol not of an ordered and potent strength but of a chaotic, frightening, and corrupting sexual weakness. Renaissance England created itself around the image of a virgin queen whose undiminished and uncorruptible sexuality bespoke the power of both the monarch and the nation. Elizabeth constructed herself as unique, uncirculated, "mint," aloof from the normal channels of sexual exchange. Charles, on the other hand, "spent" his erotic and political capital, his sexual extravagance degrading his masculine authority and making him, according to the anonymous "A Dialogue between the Two Horses" (1676), less than a woman: "A Tudor! a Tudor! We've had Stuarts enough. / None ever reign'd like old Bess in her ruff" (Lord 1: 274–83).

By redirecting Charles's desires through a homoerotic system of exchange, the play withdraws Charles from a circulation that threatens to invert the relationship between the male self and the female other. The play reveals, in its futile attempt to imagine an impossible ideal of masculine self-sufficiency, the tremendous resentment generated by this unwilling dependence on women, the intensity of male hatred of, and contempt for, the female body that normally lies submerged by the structures of our gender roles. The play practices a type of gender genocide, the intensity of its desire to annihilate the female commensurate with the futility of its attempt to imagine an alternative sexual economy.

In a 1985 essay dealing with research into homosexuality in the eighteenth century, G. S. Rousseau notes that in the scholarly dialogue concerning "such concepts as homosocial behavior, homophobia, and misogyny . . . there remains a sense that the identity of the scholar-critic is as crucial as the surface discussion because the subject is so emotionally charged." He continues:

> More recently—in the last decade—the whole discussion of homoeroticism has been usurped, if not hijacked, by the feminists. The feminists have triumphed in this usurpation as a consequence of genuine intellectual curiosity, as well as their good fortune in meeting with no significant resistance from their male counterparts who in most cases have been relieved that the women have taken on this burden— the black albatross most men would rather not confront. (132–33)

What Rousseau reveals, explicitly in his first remark and unwittingly in the second, are the tremendous changes that have overtaken academic discourse in the last fifteen or twenty years, as an almost exclusively male profession has been transformed by a significant influx of female, and feminist, scholars. Though Rousseau fails to connect the emergence of a new type of discourse with the rising presence of feminists within the profession, I have little doubt that the two phenomena are related, interrogation of the writing subject being fundamental to the feminist project, both as a response to their marginalization within the field and as an expression of their desire to create a new critical methodology. Rousseau's language of "usurpation" and terrorism suggests the bitter conflicts that have accompanied the feminizing of the profession, for it points to the conviction of masculine entitlement and ownership that previously organized the scholarly world, which, like Bolloxinion's court, attempted to establish itself on the banishment of women.

The increasing prominence of feminism within literary studies, then, has helped legitimize a critical practice very much at odds with the ideals of scholarly detachment previously valorized by the profession, and one that *Sodom* makes so difficult to achieve unless it can be treated as an exercise in bibliography. Given the nakedness of *Sodom*'s sexual ambivalences, the intense misogyny that it sets into play, its "emotional charge," to use Rousseau's term, makes the critical distance valued by more traditional modes of scholarship exceptionally difficult to achieve. *Sodom* has remained invisible at least in part because it threatens the privileged invisibility of the critic; to take the play seriously as a text that can be the subject of a paper, a class, or this essay is to feel implicated in its perversity. If the play is to finally achieve a place in scholarly discourse, it will do so because as a profession we now value the personal involvement that a play like *Sodom* seems to demand.

Notes

In this essay I am particularly indebted to Francesca Kazan, Elizabeth Meese, and Sharon O'Dair. A grant from the Research Grants Committee of the University of Alabama supported the research and writing of this essay.

1. For an important, if brief, review of the problems of authorship, see Milhous and Hume. A more recent discussion of authorship, which takes issue with the conclusions reached by Milhous and Hume, is provided by Johnson. Elias, an exception to the general refusal to consider the play as a literary text, has the best analysis of the play's date of composition and political import. For a discussion of the most important surviving texts of the play, see Carver.

2. The term *effeminate* participated in the transformations that overtook the homosexual identity after the seventeenth century. During the seventeenth century the word possessed multiple uses, describing cross-dressed boys, as well as men, like Charles in this example, excessively fond of women. As a descriptive term, *effeminacy* became almost exclusively attached to male homosexuals only after the seventeenth century. For discussions of this change in meaning, see Bray and both essays by Trumbach.

3. Winton discusses theatrical censorship during Charles's reign. In her contribution to a forthcoming volume on satire, Payne considers the complex relationship

between theatrical semiotics and government censorship. In doing so she makes clear that politics, and not obscenity, was the key to state intervention in the theater during the Restoration.

4. All quotations are from *Rochester's Sodom*, edited by von Romer. Despite its inconsistent punctuation I have decided against correcting the text.

5. The last decade has seen a tremendous increase in scholarship devoted to recovering the history of homosexuality, particularly to questions concerning transformations of the homosexual identity that occurred during the seventeenth and eighteenth centuries. Both Trumbach ("Sodomitical Subcultures") and Rousseau provide useful bibliographies of this research up to 1985. For more current bibliographies, see particularly Greenberg, and the collection edited by Duberman et al. In her contribution to this volume Kristina Straub examines just how such changes affected the perception and presentation of actors during the seventeenth and eighteenth centuries.

Works Cited

Aquinas, Saint Thomas. *Summa Theologica*. Trans. Fathers of the English Dominican Province. 3 vols. New York: Benziger Brothers, 1947.

Bray, Alan. *Homosexuality in Renaissance England*. London: Gay Men's P, 1982.

Carver, Larry D. "The Texts and the Text of *Sodom*." *Papers of the Bibliographical Society of America* 73 (1979): 19–40.

Duberman, Martin Bauml, Martha Vicinus, and George Chauncey, Jr., eds. *Hidden from History: Reclaiming the Gay and Lesbian Past*. New York: NAL, 1989.

Elias, Richard. "Political Satire in *Sodom*." *Studies in English Literature* 18 (1978): 423–38.

Evelyn, John. *The Diary of John Evelyn*. Ed. E. S. De Beer. 6 vols. Oxford: Clarendon, 1955.

Gallop, Jane. *Thinking through the Body*. New York: Columbia UP, 1988.

Greenberg, David F. *The Construction of Homosexuality*. Chicago: U of Chicago P, 1988.

Irigaray, Luce. *Speculum of the Other Woman*. Trans. Gillian C. Gill. Ithaca, N.Y.: Cornell UP, 1985.

Johnson, J. W. "Did Lord Rochester Write *Sodom*?" *Papers of the Bibliographical Society of America* 81 (1987): 119–53.

Lord, George deF[orest], et al., eds. *Poems on Affairs of State: Augustan Satirical Verse, 1660–1714*. 7 vols. New Haven: Yale UP, 1963–75.

Milhous, Judith, and Robert D. Hume. "Attribution Problems in English Drama, 1660–1700." *Harvard Library Bulletin* 31 (1983): 5–39.

Miller, David Lee. "The Death of the Modern: Gender and Desire in Marlowe's 'Hero and Leander.'" *South Atlantic Quarterly* 88 (1989): 757–87.

Payne, Deborah C. "Comedy or Satire?: The Generic Indeterminacy of Restoration Dramatic Satire." *Postmodern Studies in Eighteenth-Century Satire*. Ed. James Gill. Special issue of *Tennessee Studies in Literature*, forthcoming.

Pepys, Samuel. *The Diary of Samuel Pepys*. Ed. Robert Latham and William Matthews. 11 vols. Berkeley and Los Angeles: U of California P, 1970–83.

Rochester's Sodom. Herausgegeben nach dem Hamburger Manuscript. Ed. L. S. A. M. von Romer. Paris: H. Welter, 1904.

Rousseau, G. S. "The Pursuit of Homosexuality in the Eighteenth Century: 'Utterly Confused Category' and/or Rich Repository?" *Eighteenth-Century Life* 9 (1985): 132–68.

Rubin, Gayle. "The Traffic in Women: Notes on the 'Political Economy' of Sex." *Toward an Anthropology of Women*. Ed. Rayna R. Reiter. New York: Monthly Review P, 1975. 157–210.

Sedgwick, Eve Kosofsky. *Between Men: English Literature and Male Homosocial Desire*. New York: Columbia UP, 1985.

Sherburn, George, and Donald F. Bond. *The Restoration and Eighteenth Century (1660–1789)*. Vol. 3 of *A Literary History of England*. Ed. Albert C. Baugh. 2nd ed. 4 vols. New York: Appleton, 1967.

Trumbach, Randolph. "Sodomitical Assaults, Gender Role, and Sexual Development in Eighteenth-Century London." *Journal of Homosexuality* 16 (1988): 407–29.

———. "Sodomitical Subcultures, Sodomitical Roles, and the Gender Revolution of the Eighteenth Century: The Recent Historiography." *Eighteenth-Century Life* 9 (1985): 109–21.

Winton, Calhoun. "Dramatic Censorship." *The London Theatre World, 1660–1800*. Ed. Robert D. Hume. Carbondale: Southern Illinois UP, 1980. 286–308.

"LAW-SUITS," "LOVE-SUITS," AND THE FAMILY PROPERTY IN WYCHERLEY'S *THE PLAIN DEALER*

HELEN BURKE

> The realm of the proper . . . the general cultural
> heterosexual establishment in which a man's reign
> is held to be proper.
> —HÉLÈNE CIXOUS

What is emphasized or downplayed in the history of commentary on a literary text, or what is perceived to be a "problem" or a "failure" in a text, is often as much an effect of the critical tradition in which this text has been received as it is an effect of the literary work itself. At least this is so, I suggest, in the case of William Wycherley's *The Plain Dealer* (1676). Two marked tendencies in the tradition of commentary on this play—the tendency to treat the text almost exclusively in terms of character analysis and the habit of overlooking one of the play's two plots—grow out of the humanist tradition of critical thinking that has until recently governed textual interpretation. The reification of the experience of the (male) subject that is characteristic of this tradition has led to a preoccupation with the character of Manly, the "Plain Dealer" of the play's title, a preoccupation that translates into the desire to establish Manly's psychological and ethical motives.[1] But this desire, as Derek Hughes points out in a recent appraisal of the play, is constantly frustrated by the elusive character of the hero. "Variously interpreted as a dupe, a hypocrite, and a moral paragon," Hughes writes, Manly "refuses to be cramped into any single category" (315). The perceived difficulty in categorization is then equated by at least one critic with an aesthetic weakness; the failure of the work of art to answer the critical demands made of it—in this case, its failure to maintain a stable male subject and a coherent moral viewpoint—is defined by K. M. Rogers as a "fatal inconsistency" (148–62).[2]

The failure to address the Blackacre plot[3] is also symptomatic of a humanist ideology that sees the individual as self-determined and autonomous and that consequently fails to locate the private drama (as I suggest Wycherley does) within the broader social drama. The lack of attention to the plot that provides the larger ideological context to the Manly plot is consistent with the critical perspective of those critics who insist that Restoration comedies are not culturally or intellectually significant. John Harwood, for example, warns us against treating the comedies "as sociological treatises and the dramatists as forerunners of Margaret Mead and Vance Packard" (xii), while Robert Hume, deploring the claims of what he calls the "profundity-zealots," argues that Restoration plays "almost without exception . . . aim more at entertainment than at deep meaning" (*Development* 30–31).[4] In keeping with this belief, Hume examines only the surface content of Wycherley's plays and is led to conclude that this writer's works are "not really 'drama of ideas,' " since they do not question values or challenge the audience's worldview ("William Wycherley" 413).

When attention is paid to the internal and external contexts that structure meaning in a play such as *The Plain Dealer*, a very different reading of Wycherley's work emerges, as I propose to demonstrate here. The components of the play, I will suggest, work relationally to construct an image that undermines the liberal notion of the naturalness or autonomy of the subject. The Blackacre plot, a drama of family property and law, provides the semiotic framework within which the Manly-Olivia love plot, a story of betrayal and deception, finds its significance. The central crisis of the play is the crisis of disappropriation suffered by the male subject, a crisis that unfolds along a double register: the anxiety about male property at the individual psychosexual level is duplicated by an anxiety about property at the broader social and economic level. But again it is only in the context of still larger signifying systems—signifying systems that exist outside the text—that this double plot structure means. The play as a whole also functions relationally, as the articulation of broader economic and sociosexual discourses that were under stress in the immediate historical moment in which Wycherley was writing. The full subversiveness of *The Plain Dealer* is apparent only when the play is culturally contextualized.

To argue for the cultural relevance of this text is not, however, to suggest that the play simply mirrors some exterior phenomenon. "Cultural reality" is understood rather in the Althusserian sense of a structure that is "an absent cause": as that which the text can neither evade nor simply reproduce but that is nevertheless a constitutive force. The critical methodology resulting from such a theoretical position is thus neither purely formal nor "historical" in the traditional use of the term but follows the deductive operation formulated by Althusser and Macherey that Jameson describes in his discussion of political interpretation: the analysis "involves the hypothetical *reconstruction* of the materials—content, narrative paradigms, stylistic and linguistic practices—which had to have been given in advance in order for that particular text to be produced in its unique historical specificity" (*Political Unconscious* 57–58). In the case of *The Plain Dealer*, such an analysis requires the reconstruction of the play's economic, social, and sexual ideologies, ideologies that are the product of both an immediate and general cultural context.

The late seventeenth century in England was a period of profound destabilization for a particular economic class, the class that included both the gentry and the aristocracy.[5] This class traditionally achieved and maintained its power, its hierarchical status, through what Michael McKeon describes as an "aristocratic ideology," an ideology that asserts "that the social order is not circumstantial and arbitrary, but corresponds to and expresses an analogous, intrinsic moral order" (131). There is a natural congruence, this ideology suggests, between the gentleman's property and what is proper to him—his right to power, respect, and privilege. External goods, the result of birth, thus become the mark of internal worth. However, several circumstances in the seventeenth century, some of them economic, some demographic, served to expose the fictionality of this seemingly natural equation between birth and worth, resulting in what McKeon calls a "crisis of status inconsistency" (150–75). Throughout the century, for example, members of the newly wealthy merchant class could and did increasingly buy their way into the aristocratic or gentry class, resulting in what Lawrence Stone calls "the inflation of honours," the widespread selling of aristocratic honors, titles, and genealogies to newly wealthy subjects (*Crisis* 65–128). The demographic crisis of the late seventeenth century also made it necessary to absorb into the aristocratic and gentry class subjects who by birth did not belong there. To maintain the illusion of patrilineal descent during a time of a falling birthrate, there was greater recourse to surrogate heirship and to name changing, the deceit of which was acknowledged in at least one legal term of the period: the use of the term *fictive tail male* to describe the husband of a daughter or niece who had adopted the family name to preserve the illusion of male descent (McKeon 153–54). These legal fictions and strategies of patrilineal repair, implemented to maintain the existing power structure, had also the effect of demonstrating the artificiality of the very socioeconomic system they were designed to protect.

The Plain Dealer reproduces this double effect, asserting aristocratic ideology only to demonstrate its fictionality, proclaiming traditional values only to undermine them in the very act of assertion.[6] In this play, however, the focus is on gender and not class, bringing to our attention another source of the contemporary threat to aristocratic property. The destabilization of social classes at this period was only one expression of a broader cultural shift that also made itself felt in the area of sexual privilege, a shift that had equally problematic social and economic implications for the ruling elite. Throughout the seventeenth century, traditional notions of marriage came under attack. The Civil Marriage Act of 1653 and the Interregnum transfer of jurisdiction over marriage from the ecclesiastical courts to the state created significant changes in how marriage was viewed. These legal changes represented a move away from a sacramental concept of marriage to the concept of marriage based on civil contract, thus unsettling received ideas about man's natural authority in the family and introducing a new perception of the woman as a subject in her own right (Staves, *Players' Scepters* 111–18).

Though these Interregnum laws were overturned by Charles II, there is evidence to suggest that the attack on patriarchal power continued, as least as far as can be determined from legal documents pertaining to property. In the Restoration period, Stone argues, the curbing of male privilege was felt in the new kinds of marriage property settlements that were being arranged, an area in which the sexual and economic domains clearly overlapped. The property arrangement known as "strict settlement," for example, acted, on the one hand, to preserve the family patrimony, but it also had the legal effect of guaranteeing each family member his or her share of the property and of protecting family members from the arbitrary control of the father. (The powers of the current owner of an estate were reduced to that of life trustee, since the owner had willed away his rights to his future children in a settlement drawn up before his marriage.) Marriage settlements during this period also seem to have been more concerned about preserving the rights of the wife, who increasingly managed to keep more of her own property under her own name. Of particular interest in the context of Wycherley's play is the fact that widows, at this time, were managing to secure more of their property for their own use by vesting their property in separate trustees before undertaking a second marriage (*Family* 166–68).

As in the area of class, the ruling elite went to work to recuperate its losses, attempting, to the greatest degree possible, to effect a return to the status quo. Susan Staves's recent study *Married Women's Separate Property in England, 1660–1833* documents this recuperative process. A substantial gap, Staves demonstrates, existed between legal theory and practice, between the new rules asserting women's rights to property and the enforcement of these rules.[7] Through litigation, and with the aid of a judicial system that remained deeply attached to a paradigm of patriarchal sexual and economic power, male family members continually managed to negate the property rights of their mothers, wives, and sisters. *The Plain Dealer,* in the Blackacre plot, dramatizes the struggle Staves describes, representing the conflict between a woman and her son over the family property. Insofar as it reinscribes the defeat of this woman, the play would seem to align itself with the historical victors, taking up the ideological position of the contemporary judicial system that sought to restore the rights of the governing elite. However, because this play also clearly re-veals the *process* by which these rights are established, because it displays the constructedness of privileges hitherto considered to be "natural," it also destabilizes the very ideology it reproduces, much as the contempo-rary multiplication of elaborate laws to counter women's rights signaled the very tenuousness of the property they were designed to defend.

The unsettling effect of this strange play, which so many of its critics have noted, can thus be attributed to a radical destabilization in the economic and sociosexual realm. The immediate historical context is not, however, the only determining factor. In giving form to a particular historical ten-sion, the play also represents an unresolved antagonism in the broader psychosexual discourse that underwrites the sociosexual discourse of that age. *The Plain Dealer,* I suggest, recognizes, as Hélène Cixous does, that "the realm of the proper, culture, functions by the appropriation articu-lated, set into play, by man's classic fear of seeing himself expropriated, seeing himself deprived . . . by his refusal to be deprived, in a state of separation, by his fear of losing the prerogative, fear whose response is all of History" (486). The connection between the public and private domain is most overtly established in the Blackacre plot, where the male subject's fear of social and economic deprivation is shown to be inseparably linked to his fear for his manhood. But the structure of the play itself contains the most interesting formulation of this insight. The double plot structure constructs a Lacanian image of the male subject who is driven by the fear of expropriation, one whose experience is constituted in the mediation between an individual and collective experience.[8] Manly and Jerry Blackacre create a complex figure of this split subject who plays out his drama along a double register, re-creating in the adult sexual domain the experience first encountered in the family domain. The play, of course, never makes an explicit connection between Manly's drama and Jerry's, nor does it assert the primacy of Jerry's experience. At the deep structural level of the play, however, there is an implicit recognition of their relationship. Manly, I will argue, is functionally identical to Jerry, the one marked by the familial drama that establishes identity as "lack in being" (Rose, introduction to *FS* 40–44). The repressed or concealed connection between the two dramas then itself takes on the force of a statement about the condition of the subject at the level of the symbolic: the subject who, like Manly, never recognizes at the level of conscious or articulated knowledge its own origin in lack (the fact that it is constituted in the anxiety of castration). In the analysis that follows, I attempt to disengage Wycherley's complex picture of this subject haunted by the fear of disappropriation, a subject who articulates both a historically specific and larger psychosexual anxiety.

The first conversation between Manly, the hero of the love plot, and the Widow Blackacre, the central figure in what I am calling the law plot, establishes the interconnectedness between the two strands of action. In the exchange between the returned sea captain and the widow in the first act, the term "Love-suits" becomes confused with the term "Law-suits" (I, 402),[9] as each character confounds the other character's interests with his or her own. Manly is inquiring about his "suit" with Olivia, his fiancée, but the widow assumes he is speaking of the legal suit in which she wants to engage Manly as a witness. The notion that the love interest cannot be divorced from the legal interest is reinforced again shortly afterward by the conversation between Freeman, Manly's friend and confidant, and the widow. Freeman, who is a "Gentleman" of "broken Fortune" (I, 387)— thus already a type of the disappropriated male—decides to court the widow for her money. In the exchange between them, the wordplay centered on the term "business" makes the same complex point about the nature of sexuality and its relation to broader social structures: one cannot talk of love, it is implied, without also talking about law. Freeman's "sweet business" (his courtship of the widow) and the widow's "*Westminster-Hall* business" (her legal affairs) are inextricably interrelated (I, 404). What the play makes evident here in these conversations is elsewhere implied through the simultaneous "play" of the Blackacre plot and the Manly-Olivia plot. The text makes its statement by the interceptions and overlappings of these two strands of action. For purposes of discussion, however, I will separate out the two lines of action, but with the acknowledgment that in so doing I am inevitably simplifying and homogenizing the text's workings.

From the outset, it is clear that the situation in the Blackacre household represents a threat to the patriarchal order in general, and to the patrilineal system in particular, which encodes these rights. Rather than allowing herself to be the "gift," the precious object that is traditionally exchanged by men to ensure the social order,[10] the Widow Blackacre has appropriated the male property, the patrimony. Her control of the legal deeds to her husband's estate, the "Writings" that she carries around with her in her bag (III, 453), dramatizes her unusual position in relation to the traditional order. She is constituted as a social and legal subject in her own right, as the one who controls the goods: her own sexuality, the Blackacre estate, and the male heir. The widow, as the play recognizes, is thus a problem and an anomaly in the world in which she is constituted. As Freeman states, she is a woman "at Law and difference with all the World" (I, 401), a woman who is, by her own definition, "no common Woman; but a Woman conversant in the Laws of the Land" (III, 445). Her sexual independence is her guarantee of her power in law, as she herself clearly recognizes when she refuses Freeman's marriage proposal: "I that am a Relict and Executrix of known plentiful Assits and Parts, who understand my self and the Law: And wou'd you have me under Covert Baron again? No, Sir, no Covert Baron for me" (II, 437).

In thus portraying the widow as an antagonistic force, Wycherley, it can be argued, is giving expression to the negative perception of such women in his society. Widows in the seventeenth century, Barbara J. Todd points out, inspired contradictory and anxious feelings among men. An ungoverned woman was felt to be a challenge to the social order, and her very presence served as an unpleasant reminder to men of their own mortality (55). Todd's study also shows that remarriage of widows became increasingly less common in the seventeenth century (54–83), a phenomenon that must have added to the already perceived psychological threat of these women. But the Widow Blackacre also represents the more specifically economic threat posed by married women at this time because of changing property doctrines. She is the embodiment of the contemporary patriarchal nightmare, an image of the newly empowered female subject who, it was feared, by resorting to law, wrested property titles away from helpless male heirs. This female subject, like the Widow Blackacre, was often portrayed as controlling property for her own selfish ends. The interests of women, Staves notes, were frequently considered by the contemporary legal system to be the interests of individuals in direct competition with the interests of "family," a term that effectively designated the interests of the male heir (*Married* 203). In the play the widow's son, Jerry Blackacre, expresses the fears of "family" in relation to this sexual upstart. As the play makes increasingly clear, he feels the widow is endangering both his manhood and the Blackacre estate.

When we first meet Jerry, he is suffering from a crisis of identity that is clearly a result of the unprecedented status of his mother. The refusal of the mother to play her assigned role in the patriarchal game leads to a reduction of the male role to that of reflexive signifier, the traditional devalued role played by "woman" in the homosocial contract (Rubin 171–85). Dressed in a barrister's robes and with a green bag in hand, Jerry forms a mirror image of the widow; in his behavior, he imitates her, parroting her legal jargon, accommodating himself to her desire. When she urges that they leave to take care of "our business," he agrees—"I, forsooth, e'en so let's" (I, 404)—apparently identifying her "business" with his own. However, this compliance toward the mother scarcely disguises Jerry's increasing anxiety about his ability to secure either her or his estate, both of which he clearly sees as his property. Noting Freeman's interest in his mother, Jerry seems, at first, to assert his confidence in his own powers of securing her: "Ay, ay, Mother, he wou'd be taking Livery and Seizen of your Jointure, by digging the Turf; but I'll watch your waters" (I, 404–5). The phrase "watch your waters," Gerald Weales notes, is particularly appropriate here as a way of saying "I'll watch out for your interests"; it alludes to the biological body (to watch the urine for complications) and to the body of land (to guard the water rights of one's property), thus recognizing the dual nature of the Widow Blackacre as a sexual and legal property (523–24). But the phrase could also be read as an expression of a doubt on Jerry's part about his ability to control his property. As Weales suggests, citing Blackstone, water is a difficult "body" to claim: "[I]f a body of water runs out of my pond into another man's, I have no right to reclaim it" (523–24). The widow, Jerry may be tacitly admitting, is just such a difficult "body," just such a fluid and unstable resource.

As the play unfolds, this problem of how to control his rights both in his mother and in his estate becomes more and more central for Jerry. The young man imagines with horror the loss of his property if his mother remarries, envisioning the sold "old gilt Plate," the "mortgag'd Apostle-Spoons, Bowls, and Beakers," and the felled "Trees," what he calls the "havock of our Estate personal" (II, 437). He also imagines his loss of property rights in his mother as an equal and related catastrophe. Explaining his problem to Freeman, he says: "Then wou'd she marry, too, and cut down my Trees: Now I shou'd hate, Man, to have my Father's Wife kiss'd, and slap'd and t'other thing too, (you know what I mean) by another Man; and our Trees are the purest, tall, even, shady twigs, by my fa—" (III, 450). The desire evident here to retain all rights in the mother is complicated by Jerry's awareness that the widow also represents an obstacle to the gratification of his desires. "My Curmudgeonly Mother wo'nt allow me wherewithall to be a Man of my self with," he complains to Freeman (III, 450), by which he means, as he later explains, his mother's refusal to give him money or to allow him to go near the garret where the maidservants are sleeping (IV, 473). As a site of ambivalence, the widow is a classic representation of that nightmare figure, the phallic mother, the imaginary mother who is presumed to have power over identity and meaning and is thus desired and feared (Gallop 113–31). At the same time, the widow is also an effective figure of a real sociosexual tension. Jerry's relation to his mother can also be read as a troping of the conflicted relation between male heirs and the women of their own class whom they both needed and resented. On the one hand, of course, the whole patriarchal system could not have continued without the reproductive contribution of women, a debt that was tacitly acknowledged in the provision of the jointure that the Widow Blackacre enjoys. But on the other hand, this kind of economic settlement and the increasing property rights assigned to women by law were felt to encroach upon male privilege, a sentiment that Jerry, in his hostility to his mother, clearly expresses.

In this play, however, the disappropriated subject, like the sexual subject in the Lacanian drama and like the aristocratic subject in the seventeenth century, does not easily tolerate his state of tension and works to resolve it through various fictions, one of which is the fiction of the "Law." To regain control of his threatened property, Jerry invokes this solution of the "Law." Only by going to "Law" with their mothers, he notes, did other men make "Men of themselves": "[T]hey went to Law with their Mothers; for they say, there's no good to be done upon a Widow Mother, till one goes to Law with her" (III, 450). "Law" in this play thus represents the aristocratic social ideology that assigns the property (the estate, the maid-servants, and money) to the male inheritor of the estate, the ideology that maintains the gentleman in his place of privilege. There is, moreover, no pretense that this "Law" is fair. Freeman's advice to a fellow rival for the widow is as follows:

> If you Litigious Widow e'r wou'd gain,
> Sign not to her; but by the Law complain:
> To her, as to a Baud, Defendant Sue
> With Statutes, and make Justice Pimp for you.
>
> (II, 438)

The historical relevance of his advice is borne out by Staves when she concludes that much of her study of seventeenth- and eighteenth-century married women's property "might be regarded as a study of effective avoid-ance practices and of judicial sanction of avoidance practices" (*Married* 208). Freeman's real contemporaries were very skillful at making justice "pimp" for them.

In playing this role, "Law" is also a dramatization of the Lacanian notion of the process that disrupts the mother-son relationship and that gives the boy his male identity, a process Lacan also equates with "Law" and with the concept of the father. "The father is a function and refers to a law," Rose explains, "the place outside the imaginary dyad and against which it breaks" (39). In this play, Freeman represents this function of father. As the mother's suitor and potential second husband, he is Jerry's rival and a threat to his "estate," both sexual and economic, but he also offers to compensate the boy for his loss in return for his cooperation in Freeman's affair with the mother. The bargain struck here between the two men thus effectively represents the bargain that determines the whole sociosexual contract. Rubin describes the compensatory logic of this contract as fol-lows: "[T]he boy renounces his mother for fear that otherwise his father would castrate him (refuse to give him the phallus and make him a girl). But by this act of renunciation, the boy affirms the relationships which have given mother to father and will give him, if he becomes a man, a woman of his own. . . . [T]he boy exchanges his mother for the phallus, the symbolic token which can later be exchanged for a woman" (193).

An identical logic determines the exchange that takes place in act 3 of *The Plain Dealer*. In return for his allegiance, Freeman gives Jerry gold to buy the books that the young man craves (*St. George for Christendom* and *The Seven Champions of England*), books of heroic deeds that, earlier in the play, were denied to him by his mother (III, 448). This acquisition represents Jerry's entry into the homosocial order, the order in which the male (and not the female) is the hero, the instigator of the action. The young man's appearance in "Red Breeches" shortly after this (IV, 472) and his statement in relation to Freeman that he will "do any thing he'll have me, and go all the World over with him; to Ordinaries, and Baudyhouses, or any where else" (IV, 472) are further assertions of his "manhood." The newly acquired access to women that Freeman guarantees him is the price of the exchange of the mother. In recognizing Freeman as "Guardian and Tutor" (IV, 472), thus recognizing the "Name of the Father," Jerry sub-scribes to the economy of the return, the economy of what Lacan calls the "inviolable Debt" that is the basis of the "Law": "the guarantee that the voyage on which wives and goods are embarked will bring back to their point of departure in a never-failing cycle other women and other goods, all carrying an identical entity" (*Language* 42).

What this exchange represents also, of course, is the reassertion of the old aristocratic order with its valorization, as suggested by the books and by Jerry's swaggering gait, of romance and chivalry.[11] In this order, the woman no longer functions as the active subject, a recognition that the play encodes by now reducing the widow to a state of helplessness. With Jerry's passive cooperation, Freeman steals the deeds of the estate from the widow, a change that symbolizes the displacement of one sexual economy by another. Since it is Jerry now who is in possession of the "Writings," it is he who can "Sign, Seal, and Deliver," a change in power that the widow recognizes, as she weeps for the loss of her property (IV, 473). However, the widow's change in function—that she is now established as "lack" (or the one with the lack) in this economy—is most clearly dramatized by the figurative rape performed on her by Oldfox (another pretender to the "Name of the Father" in that he, too, is a suitor). Throughout the play, Oldfox has been trying to impress the Widow Blackacre with his writings, which he calls "the fruits of my leisure, the overflowings of my fancy and

Pen" or "my parts" (IV, 470). To each of his proffered writings, however, the widow counters with her own (legal) writings, so that, much to Old-fox's frustration, there is no discourse between them: "O Lady, Lady, all interruption, and no sence between us, as if we were Lawyers at the Bar!" (IV, 471). In the final act of the play, however, Oldfox prepares to force his "parts" upon her:

> *Widow.* Acquainted with your parts! A Rape, a Rape—What will you
>   ravish me?
>   [*The Waiters tye her to the Chair, and gag her; and Exeunt*]
> *Oldfox.* Yes, Lady, I will ravish you; but it shall be through the ear,
>   Lady, the ear onely, with my well-pen'd Acrostics. (V, 507)

Oldfox never gets to carry out his "ravishment" because of the arrival of Freeman, Jerry, and the bailiffs, but the defeat of the mother is neverthe-less ensured. The widow's arrest "in the King's Name," at the suit of her son and his adopted father, Freeman (V, 507), is the imaginative assign-ment of the woman to her place in the family plot, a punishment for her boldness in assuming the male prerogative of manipulating the law. The widow's crime in forging signatures to property deeds and in using pro-fessional false witnesses is a necessary defense against the subterfuges, the legal "pimp[ing]" (II, 438), that men like her potential husband Freeman use to acquire women's separate property, as she herself argues:

> *Widow.* Well, these, and many other shifts, poor Widows are put to
>   sometimes; for every body wou'd be riding a Widow, as they say,
>   and breaking into her Jointure: they think marrying a Widow an
>   easie business, like leaping the Hedge, where another has gone be-
>   fore; a Widow is a meer gap, a gap with them. (V, 506)

But, as the action of the play demonstrates, this legal move by the woman is not allowed. The "Settlement" (Freeman's "Writings," which she is com-pelled to sign [V, 509]) strips her of a substantial part of her property and renders her virtually powerless, an imaginative expression of the implicit violence done both to woman in the contemporary social and economic power structure and to women in the psychosexual order. In both struc-tures, woman is required to function as the lack that guarantees the fullness of the male property, the "Other" who is "excluded by the nature of things which is the nature of words" (Lacan, *FS* 144).

On the one hand, then, the Blackacre plot seems to reassert the old power

plot, seeming to guarantee once more the traditional "realm of the proper."
However, the phallic and aristocratic victory is not unproblematic, as the
ending of the play reveals. The social and economic instability the play
reveals is not successfully erased by its closure, as we see, for example, in
the problematic nature of the illegitimacy issue that the widow raises as
one of her last resorts in her battle against Freeman and Jerry. When it is
clear that she no longer has any control over her son and thus stands to
lose control of the estate, the widow stuns her listeners by announcing that
Jerry is a bastard and has, therefore, no claim over the Blackacre estate.
Freeman tries to make her back down from this assertion by pointing out
the social implication for her own honor, but the widow tells him, in no
uncertain terms, to "Hang Reputation"; she is, she says, more concerned
to "save her Jointure" than her "Honour" (IV, 475). As we have seen, this
refusal by the widow to subscribe to a belief in the value of feminine chastity proves to be only a temporary setback for Jerry and Freeman, as the
two men later blackmail her into complying with their wishes. Nevertheless, the implied threat of the widow's disavowal of "reputation" cannot
be dismissed so lightly. The social and economic ramifications of the threat
of the gentlewoman who says "Hang Reputation" are obvious. The whole
system of patrilineage is predicated on the notion that a man knows who
his son is, thus the importance of the woman buying into a belief in sexual
fidelity as a value. J. Douglas Canfield has convincingly demonstrated the
ideological importance of this belief during this period in the tragicomic
romances that thrived in Restoration theaters in the 1660s and 1670s. These
tragicomedies, which emphasized the values of loyalty and constancy, had
the ideological purpose, Canfield argues, of reaffirming feudal aristocratic
values grounded in patrilineage, values that were coming under stress from
precisely the kind of social and economic pressures I outlined at the beginning of my essay. Wycherley's representation of a gentlewoman who
publicly flaunts her dishonor to further her own economic ends is thus an
implicit commentary on the fictionality of these romances, an acknowledgment of the fragility of the whole system on which social privilege
is based.

The revelation that the mother can deceive also threatens to undermine
the broader psychosexual fiction of paternal privilege. "Any suspicion
of the mother's infidelity," Gallop writes, "betrays the Name-of-the-Father
as the arbitrary imposition it is. The merest hint of the mother's infidelity
threatens to expose what Lacan calls the symbolic (the register of the

Name-of-the-Father), which is usually covered over, sutured, by the representations of what Lacan calls the imaginary, the imaginary of chivalry,
the woman's presumed honour" (48). The widow's refusal to play her assigned role thus constitutes an exposure of the phallic conceit, an exposure
most apparent in the final "Settlement" that resolves the Blackacre conflict.
Unlike the traditional comic plot that reaches its resolution through a marriage, the Blackacre plot ends with a kind of divorce. The contract between
Freeman and the widow is based on "Separation," on an agreement that
they will find sexual pleasure "elsewhere" (V, 509). As the widow notes,
she is designated by this agreement as "a kind of a *sine cure*," an office in
name only (V, 509). For Wycherley, as for Lacan, recovery of male privilege
is, then, underwritten by loss, by the recognition that the *jouissance* of the
woman is somewhere "beyond the phallus" (*FS* 145). The men regain their
privilege on the basis of an empty contract.

The drama of Manly takes up this drama of the subject at another stage
and replays the whole crisis on another, more explicitly sexual register.
Manly is the subject caught up in what Lacan calls the "closed field of
desire" that the sexual relation occupies, a field constituted by the endless-
ness of the return of the demand. Despite the fact that the subject's entry
into the symbolic order is predicated upon loss, the subject persists in his
belief that somewhere there is satisfaction, a certainty that a member of the
opposite sex, in later life, seems to guarantee. Manly's drama, in Lacanian
terms, is thus the return into the adult sexual field of the demand made
in the primordial mother-child relation or the family plot, a demand that
is doomed to repeat the originary drama of presence and loss, to signify
desire, or the impossibility of fulfillment, twice over (*FS* 81). Like Jerry,
Manly both loses and regains his property, but his final triumph too is a
patent fraud.

When we first meet him, Manly, like Jerry at the beginning of the Blackacre plot, is absorbed in the fantasy of the woman whose interests he seems
to believe are identical with his own. His relationship with Olivia, as he
describes it to his friend, Freeman, is a reflexive one; he loves her, he says,
because she mirrors his own image back to him, thus verifying his truth,
which becomes "all truth": "She is all truth, and hates the lying, mask-
ing, daubing World, as I do; for which I love her, and for which I think
she dislikes not me" (I, 406–7). Much later in the play, Novel and Lord
Plausible, two of Olivia's other suitors, recognize and describe the fantasy
that the woman in this dynamic guarantees, the fantasy of satisfying the

self: "[F]or, as *Freeman* said of another, she stands in the Drawing-room, like the Glass, ready for all Comers to set their Gallantry by her: and, like the Glass too, lets no man go from her, unsatisfi'd with himself" (V, 479). But insofar as Olivia still satisfies Manly's "truth" at the beginning of the play, her illusionary nature is not yet admitted. She is, rather, "this miracle of a Woman" (I, 408) who constitutes his full value, a function that is dramatized by Manly's act of entrusting her with his fortune.

Manly, at the beginning of the play, is thus re-creating what Lacan would term the "mirror stage" of subjectivity, the dyadic economy of the Imaginary, in which the one is preoccupied with the other as a guarantor of the unity of the self.[12] As the one with the property (his jewels and money), Olivia, like the widow in relation to Jerry, is the fantasized object that guarantees the self's security. In asking us and Freeman, as he does at the end of the first act, to "come along with me, and believe" in Olivia (I, 408), Manly is therefore asking us not only to believe in "The Woman" but also in himself, "The Man," or what is Manly. But with Manly as with Jerry, the seeming confidence that both sexual and real properties are safe is undercut by what are, at first, scarcely articulated expressions of doubt. In his initial discussion with Freeman, when he is asserting his faith in his own integrity as a "Plain Dealer," he admits that signs do not always correspond to worth: " '[T]is not the King's stamp can make the Metal better, or heavier: your Lord is a Leaden shilling, which you may bend every way; and debases the stamp he bears, instead of being rais'd by't" (I, 394). The privileged signifier ("the King's stamp")—like the phallus— is a fraud, Manly acknowledges, because it is not equated with what he calls "intrinsick worth" (I, 394; cf. James Thompson's contribution to this volume). That he has doubts about the "miracle of a Woman" is also clear from his actions in giving Olivia his money and jewels to keep her faithful. To play her role as "all truth," to keep her where he wants her, he knows that she is in need of a supplement:

> *Manly.* Yes: for she is not (I tell you) like other Women, but can keep her promise, tho' she has sworn to keep it; but that she might the better keep it, I left her the value of five or six thousand pound: for Womens wants are generally their most importunate Solicitors to Love or Marriage. (I, 407)

The woman, for Manly, is thus simultaneously conceived of as "all" and "not all" (or wanting), a representation of what Lacan believes to be the

paradoxical situation of woman in the phallic order (*FS* 167). To guarantee
his own identity, the man has to believe in the woman, but he also recognizes at an unconscious level that as a guarantor of his identity she is not
to be trusted. "If the unconscious has taught us anything," Lacan says, "it
is firstly this, that somewhere, in the Other, it knows" (*FS* 158).

The crisis for Manly begins when he is made to confront what he, in one
way, already knows about the "Other," when he is made to recognize the
illusionary nature of the "truth" that is meant to secure his property. What
Manly encounters when he goes to visit Olivia is the ironic reversal of the
Odyssean paradigm of the return, the return that guaranteed, in the traditional epic, the recognition of the lost hero and the reinstatement of his
sexual and social power. When Manly, the great sea captain and war hero,
secretly arrives at his lady's dwelling, he observes a faithless Penelope, an
Olivia flirting with her suitors (Novel and Lord Plausible) and abusing his
name. Her laughter at his "heroic Title," her mocking "Panegyrick" of the
"Martial Man" (II, 426–27), constitute a further debunking of the manly,
epic hero and of the concept of manliness that Manly so clearly embodies.
Olivia's revelation that she has married and has given away his "Jewels"
(II, 429) actualizes this verbal violation. She no longer is the keeper of his
property and is thus the site of both her own and his lack.

The full ironic implication of this discovery is only apparent, however,
in the context of the play's double plot structure. What Olivia's unfaith-
fulness clearly demonstrates is the illusionary nature of the compensation
guaranteed by the "Father," by the "Law," in the family plot. The heroic
narratives and the "Wenches" (Jerry's compensation for the loss of the
mother) are always already empty signifiers. This consciousness of a lack
of signification pervades the center of the play, a lack that is represented at
the broadest level by the image of a debased and meaningless "Law." That
this collapse in meaning is instigated by the infidelity of the woman is signaled by the dominance of the widow in Westminster Hall, the ascendancy
of the woman who will later assert her infidelity to the "Father." Under her
sign, under the aegis of the rebellious "Woman," the "Law" is reduced to
nonsense, its function as a conceit revealed. Working for the widow, the
lawyer Quaint demonstrates how he will cause chaos in the court:

> I will, as I see cause, extenuate, or examplifie Matter of Fact; baffle
> Truth, with Impudence: answer Exceptions, with Questions, tho,
> never so impertinent; for Reasons, give 'em Words; for Law and
> Equity, Tropes and Figures. (III, 444)

This exposure of the "Law" as a "Trope," the exposure of social and sexual privilege as a "figure," lies at the center of *The Plain Dealer*. If, as Lacan notes, "it is in the *name of the father* that we must recognize the support of the Symbolic function which, from the dawn of history, has identified his person with the figure of the law" (*Language* 41), then the emptying out of this "name," the detraction from the father's authority, results in the collapse of the whole edifice of signification. We see such a collapse in the third act, a reduction of signs to a flow of meaningless signifiers. Earlier on in the play Manly had described society as "*Bays's* grand Dance," where people "tread round in a preposterous huddle of Ceremony to each other, whil'st they can hardly hold their solemn false countenances" (I, 398). In act 3, this nightmare vision is translated into action in the parade of corrupt lawyers and public officials who follow each other across the stage in an economy in which empty figures circulate in a meaningless flow.

Against this backdrop of an empty "Law," the love drama collapses, becoming instead the drama of a man and woman who "want." Manly's sudden recognition that he is "an Hypocrite" (III, 439) can be translated as the recognition of a failure of signification, as a consciousness that he, too, is not what he seems, that he lacks. This recognition is given figurative representation in his relation to economic property, which he now knows to be lost. As "a Man without Money" (III, 439), he has no worth—"I am not worth a shilling in the World" (IV, 462)—a loss that he equates with the refusal by the woman to return what he is owed. When, in the last act, Freeman suggests that Manly, whose financial state is now desperate, should borrow money from one of his female acquaintances, Manly replies:

> Dam thee! how cou'dst thou think of such a thing? I wou'd as soon rob my Footman of his Wages: Besides, 'twere in vain too; for a Wench is like a Box in an Ordinary, receives all peoples Money easily; but there's no getting, nay shaking any out again: and he that fills it, is never to keep the Key. (V, 496)

The frustration expressed by Manly at his failure to "keep the Key" is an expression of the instability of his own sexual identity, an instability he clearly relates to the nature of "the Box," the woman who does not guarantee an adequate return.[13]

This image of the woman who does not guarantee the return of the male investment because she "wants" something else or something more dominates the play from the fourth act onward. The hero is finally made aware, first in listening to the account by Fidelia of Olivia's pursuit of her (IV, 464–68) and then in watching Olivia actually chase Fidelia (IV, 481), that the love he sought is a fantasy, an illusion, and that the woman is occupied elsewhere. In pursuing her own elusive object (Fidelia), Olivia represents the pursuit by the woman of her own pleasure, the *jouissance* that is not "proper" to the phallus (Lacan, *FS* 145), a revelation that leaves the man also wanting, "not satisfi'd" (IV, 483).

But if Manly is forced to acknowledge finally that women do not pay "just Debts" (IV, 470), the play does not end in the overt consciousness of male expropriation. Wycherley, like Man in History as described by Cixous, seems in the final scenes to reinstate the economy of the return:

> Everything must return to the masculine. "Return": the economy is founded on a system of returns. If a man spends and is spent, it's on condition that his power returns. If a man should go out, if he should go out to the other, it's always done according to the Hegelian model, the model of the master-slave dialectic. (486)

Manly's proposed rape of Olivia (by pretending to be Fidelia) would effect the reimposition of this dialectic and thus the return of the woman to her role as complement to the male: "Yes, so much she hates me," Manly explains to Fidelia, "that it wou'd be a Revenge sufficient, to make her accessary to my pleasure, and then let her know it" (IV, 484). As "accessary" to Manly's "pleasure," Olivia would find herself in her assigned place within the symbolic order, which is to be the support of the male subject: the rape would guarantee that the resistance offered by the woman would no longer figure.

And according to one reading of what happens in act 4, this plan is indeed carried out. As Percy G. Adams notes, one interpretation of what both Manly and Olivia say after Manly emerges from Olivia's bedroom would suggest that Olivia has, in effect, been duped by Manly and has had sex with him, thinking that he is her lover, Fidelia (179–83). Manly's sexual victory would then seem to be completed by his economic victory, when he recovers his jewels and money (Olivia, thinking Manly is Fidelia, gives him the "Cabinet" that contains the goods [V, 511]). Manly's final discovery of Fidelia, the faithful woman who loves him, would seem to constitute a further restoration of this "realm of the proper." Fidelia's emergence is the restoration of woman into the rational structure of a courtly love framework, a framework in which, Peggy Kamuf argues, the disturbing elements of sexuality are negated and neutralized (xv). Fidelia, as her name suggests, is a figure of the faithful lady who is prepared to abnegate her own subjectivity in the name of love. "Believe me, I cou'd dye for you, Sir," she tells Manly early on in the play (I, 399), and this necessary death of woman in her own right now restores order. Fidelia's "virtue," Manly states, saves him from his near madness, "reconcile[s]" him, makes him "Friends with the World" (V, 515).

However, the problem with this final restoration of the status quo is that it is not entirely convincing in its ability either to master disorder (as represented by Olivia) or to assert order (as represented by Fidelia). It is characteristic of this play that we never really know, for example, whether the rape of Olivia takes place. We are never sure whether the rebellious woman has been subjected to the Manly will. Adams, for example, notes that everything that is said after Manly emerges from Olivia's bedroom could also support the reading that Manly did *not* rape her (176–79).[14] The play affords no closure on the question of the sexual relation, a deferral of satisfaction that anticipates the interrupted "ravishment" of the widow in the next act. What we do know is that even if Manly did "it," Olivia was no "accessary" to his pleasure; Manly asserts his phallic power under cover of darkness in the full recognition that he is not who he is supposed to be and that Olivia's desire is located elsewhere. The situation thus once again inscribes what Lacan argues is the absence at the basis of phallic privilege and the subsequent necessity of the phallic signifier playing its role "veiled" (*FS* 82).

The Fidelia solution is equally ambivalent, equally unsatisfactory as a means of shoring up disorder, clearly signaling, as many critics have recognized, its own artificiality as a closure device. Fidelia herself seems to have stepped out of an older romantic world, an Arcadian world glaringly at odds with the bleak and sordid world of *The Plain Dealer*. The conventional happy marriage ending that she is instrumental in creating is likewise unconvincing. To cite Anne Righter, the lovers' agreement is "extra-social, romantic, artificial and almost impossible to believe in"; it is a "victory of excess," which undercuts its own credibility (85–86). The disclosure that Fidelia is not only a faithful lover but also an heiress serves as the clearest example of this undermining excess. While the revelation of her wealth would seem initially to add to Manly's triumph (Fidelia brings to the marriage the two thousand pounds a year she has inherited from her father), it serves finally only to underscore the inadequacy of the initial

Manly property, signaling the lack at the basis of this property by pointing
to the necessity of still further supplementation. The Derridean formulation of the double nature of the supplement thus applies to this ending:
"[I]f it fills, it is as if one fills a void. If it represents and makes an image, it
is by the anterior default of a presence." And most important, as Derrida
says of the supplement, "it provides no relief" (145).

To conclude, then, it could be said of *The Plain Dealer* that it operates through a kind of negativity, producing ideologies only to disclose
their limits, asserting values only simultaneously to cancel and deny them.
Ronald Berman is correct in saying that the play is situated at the point
where "satire gives up," where it becomes "incoherent and incommunicative" (477). Wycherley, Berman suggests, is "more interested in breaking
mirrors than in exposing vices" (466).[15] But breaking mirrors is only a
problem if the viewer wants a unified image reflected back. The play's incoherence, its inconsistency, is dismaying only if there is a desire to re-create
the theater of the identical, to reinscribe "Law." As it stands, the play provides a useful corrective to a kind of legal and social history that has been
intent on providing this kind of therapeutic reinscription, a history that
has been guilty of ignoring the material reality behind its optimistic progressive myth. Historians of the law, Staves points out, continually identify
with the perspective of the male heir (*Married* 204) and, in their pleasure
at an evolutionary functionalist model of legal history, consistently ignore
the discrepancies between the legal gains made by women and their un-
changed economic condition.[16] In constructing the story of the rise of the
"egalitarian family," social historians similarly ignore the complex social
factors that ensured that little actually changed in women's lives. Indeed,
rather than serving to liberate women, Susan Okin argues, the sentimental-
ism, described by historians as a positive feature of this new family, acted
"as a *reinforcement* for the patriarchal relations between men and women
that had been temporarily threatened by seventeenth-century individualism" (74).[17]

In its disclosure of the reactionary function of romantic myth, *The Plain
Dealer* anticipates Okin's insight. As the play acknowledges, behind the
consoling image of a Fidelia, Manly's "little Volunteer" (V, 512), who will-
ingly sacrifices her property to male interests, there is the harsh reality
of a Widow Blackacre and an Olivia, the reality of the contemporary
female subject who, by physical or mental coercion, is frequently "kissed or
kicked" out of her legally acquired property (Staves, *Married* 34). Adorno's

formulation of the unique relation of art to society is particularly relevant here: art, Adorno writes, "negates the conceptualization foisted on the real world and yet it harbors in its own substance elements of the empirically existent" (7). *The Plain Dealer* shows us not only the constructedness of the dominant social and sexual ideology but also the material costs of maintaining the dominant group in power, the economic reality that sustains what is presented as natural privilege. I will add, however, this insight is accessible only to an epistemological structure that is itself open to history: one that is no longer governed by what could be called the "Manly agenda," by the desire to impose on reality its own curative, identitarian logic. To disengage the complexity of *The Plain Dealer*, an "Other" kind of criticism is required, a criticism that is not "proper."

Notes

1. For an overview of the many different critical positions on Manly and on the play's moral standpoint, see Chadwick 133–34 and Hughes 315. For a discussion of the general muddle surrounding Wycherley criticism, see Hume, "William Wycherley."

2. A number of recent studies of *The Plain Dealer*, however, see this "inconsistency" as a mark of the play's complexity rather than of its failure. See Markley, Holland 170–203, and Hume, "William Wycherley." Hume, for example, suggests that "to do worthwhile interpretive work on Wycherley we must first accept a kind of uncertainty principle" (415); he does not, however, see any connection between this "uncertainty principle" and Wycherley's ideology, which he takes to be conservative.

3. See Bode 2 for a review of the dismissive treatment of the Blackacre plot in the criticism of this play. In his discussion of this plot, Bode argues, as I do, that an understanding of the Blackacre plot is essential to an understanding of the play, but his argument, which emphasizes the ethical and normative function of this plot (the widow's crookedness acting as a foil to Manly's "plain dealing"), is very different from mine.

4. Hume acknowledges that the plays are "full of social and political commentary," but he dismisses any argument for their complexity on the grounds that the ideas the plays present are no more than "commonplaces" (30). For a discussion of what she terms this "antiintellectualism" in the criticism of Restoration drama, see Staves, *Players' Scepters* xv–xvi.

5. To avoid getting into the taxonomic controversy that has so engaged historians of this period when they try to label different social and economic groups, I am

here adopting J. H. Hexter's position that the aristocracy and the gentry form one economic class in that both groups drew the larger part of their income from land (cited in McKeon 161).

6. The tenuousness of social privilege must have been particularly acutely felt by the playwright himself because of the legal challenge to the Wycherleys' social privilege around the time the play was being written. Between the years 1676 and 1679, a search was made on the claim of Daniel Wycherley (the playwright's father) to the rank of gentleman. Daniel was accused of assuming arms "by a false and erroneous Pedegree with arms and quartering." The search successfully established the Wycherley claim to bear arms (McCarthy 3).

7. By changing the common-law rules that gave husbands almost total power over their wives' property, equity practices of the eighteenth century, Staves agrees, did prepare the way for the greater degree of property control married women have today. However, such equity doctrines were not, as legal historians claim, an unambiguous gain, since these doctrines also effectively dismantled women's dower rights, the common-law rights a woman had to one-third of all the lands ever owned by her husband during the marriage (*Married* ch. 2). It is also possible, Staves argues, that these new settlements, which robbed women of the security of land, had the effect of making it easier rather than harder to manipulate women out of their property. Women rarely had the legal expertise to protect themselves against the increasingly complex conveyancing techniques that were developed during the eighteenth century, a legal structure that, it could be argued, was specifically designed to undermine any real changes in property ownership (*Married* ch. 3).

8. See Lacan, "The Meaning of the Phallus" and also "The Phallic Phase and the Subjective Import of the Castration Complex" in *Feminine Sexuality,* a collection of Lacan's essays (cited hereafter as *FS*). For an excellent analysis of these difficult texts, see Rose's introduction to *FS*. For a discussion of Lacan's mediation between the individual and the collective, see Jameson, "Imaginary and Symbolic."

9. All quotations are from Weales's edition. The numbers in parentheses refer to act and page numbers respectively.

10. For the notion that marriage is the most basic form of gift exchange, see Lévi-Strauss's influential study *The Elementary Structures of Kinship,* particularly 115–16 and 481.

11. For a discussion of the relation between romance and aristocratic ideology, see McKeon 150–59.

12. See Wilden's commentary for a helpful discussion of the "mirror phase" (Lacan, *Language* 159–77).

13. The phallic nature of the image Manly uses does not have to be labored; we only have to think of Freud's interpretation of Dora's dream: " 'Where is the *key*?' seems to me to be the masculine counterpart to the question 'Where is the *box*?' They are therefore questions referring to—the genitals" (117).

14. The initial ambiguity arises from Manly's statement when he emerges from

the bedroom: "I have thought better on't, I must not discover my self now, I am without Witnesses" (IV, 485). The problem is with the "it," which could refer to the sexual act or to the disclosure of the act. As Adams's reading shows, subsequent statements by Olivia and Manly can be read to support either interpretation.

15. Berman argues, as I do, that Wycherley is concerned with the status of heroic society and that the incoherence of this play derives from the experience of a social and epistemological crisis. However, Berman identifies Manly's heroic ideology with a moral norm that Wycherley endorses, an identification that leads him to conclude that Wycherley's "harshness and misanthropy" are "understandable"; that if his satire is "either incoherent or incommunicative," it is "natural" (477). I would suggest that only if one believes that male aristocratic privilege is natural do Manly's fears become understandable.

16. For a discussion of the masculinist bias of legal historians, see Staves, *Married* 202–5. For a discussion of the celebratory nature of legal history, see 9–10 and 32–33. Staves attributes the "adaption theory" of legal history to Robert Gordon, who states that behind legal history is the assumption that "the natural and proper evolution of a society . . . is towards the type of liberal capitalism seen in the advanced Western nations . . . , and that the natural and proper function of a legal system is to facilitate such an evolution" (cited in *Married* 9–10).

17. The rise of the "egalitarian family" in the eighteenth century is a thesis supported by Trumbach. Stone develops a similar idea when he argues that the development of the "companionate marriage" during this century resulted in an amelioration of the condition of women (*Family*, ch. 8). This kind of analysis has come under attack from a number of sources recently as being implicated in the very capitalist ideology that this thesis was designed to promote. See, for example, Staves, *Married* 222–28, and Pollak's discussion of the myth of passive womanhood throughout her *Poetics of Sexual Myth*.

Works Cited

Adams, Percy G. "What Happened in Olivia's Bedroom? or Ambiguity in *The Plain Dealer*." *Essays in Honor of Esmond Linworth Marilla*. Ed. Thomas Austin Kirby and William John Olive. Baton Rouge: Louisiana State UP, 1970. 174–87.

Adorno, Theodor. *Aesthetic Theory*. Trans. C. Lenhardt. Ed. Gretel Adorno and Rolf Tiedemann. London: Routledge, 1984.

Berman, Ronald. "Wycherley's Unheroic Society." *ELH* 51 (1984): 465–78.

Bode, Robert F. " 'Try Me, at Least': The Dispensing of Justice in *The Plain Dealer*." *Restoration and Eighteenth-Century Theatre Research* 2nd ser. 4 (1989): 1–24.

Canfield, J. Douglas. "The Ideology of Restoration Tragicomedy." *ELH* 51 (1984): 447–64.

Chadwick, W. R. *The Four Plays of William Wycherley*. The Hague: Mouton, 1975.

Cixous, Hélène. "Castration or Decapitation?" *Contemporary Literary Criticism.* Ed. Robert Con Davis and Ronald Schleifer. 2nd ed. New York: Longman, 1989. 479–91.

Derrida, Jacques. *Of Grammatology.* Trans. Gayatri Chakravorty Spivak. Baltimore: Johns Hopkins UP, 1976.

Freud, Sigmund. *Dora: An Analysis of a Case of Hysteria.* Ed. Philip Rieff. New York: Macmillan, 1963.

Gallop, Jane. *The Daughter's Seduction: Feminism and Psychoanalysis.* Ithaca, N.Y.: Cornell UP, 1982.

Harwood, John T. *Critics, Values, and Restoration Comedy.* Carbondonale: Southern Illinois UP, 1982.

Holland, Peter. *The Ornament of Action: Text and Performance in Restoration Comedy.* Cambridge: Cambridge UP, 1979.

Hughes, Derek. "*The Plain Dealer:* A Reappraisal." *Modern Language Quarterly* 43 (1982): 315–36.

Hume, Robert D. *The Development of English Drama in the Late Seventeenth Century.* Oxford: Clarendon, 1976.

———. "William Wycherley: Text, Life, Interpretation." *Modern Philology* 78 (1981): 399–415.

Jameson, Fredric. "Imaginary and Symbolic in Lacan: Marxism, Psychoanalytic Criticism, and the Problem of the Subject." *Literature and Psychoanalysis: The Question of Reading: Otherwise.* Ed. Shoshana Felman. Baltimore: Johns Hopkins UP, 1982. 338–95.

———. *The Political Unconscious.* Ithaca, N.Y.: Cornell UP, 1981.

Kamuf, Peggy. *Fictions of Feminine Desire: Disclosures of Heloise.* Lincoln: U of Nebraska P, 1982.

Lacan, Jacques. *Feminine Sexuality: Jacques Lacan and the école freudienne.* Trans. Jacqueline Rose. Ed. Juliet Mitchell and Jacqueline Rose. New York: Norton, 1982.

———. *The Language of the Self: The Function of Language in Psychoanalysis.* Trans. Anthony Wilden. New York: Delta-Dell, 1968.

Lévi-Strauss, Claude. *The Elementary Structures of Kinship.* Trans. James Harle Bell, John Richard von Sturmer, and Rodney Needham. 1949. Boston: Beacon, 1969.

Markley, Robert. "Drama, Character, and Irony: Kierkegaard and Wycherley's *The Plain Dealer.*" *Kierkegaard and Literature.* Ed. Ronald Schleifer and Robert Markley. Norman: U of Oklahoma P, 1984. 138–63.

McCarthy, B. Eugene. *William Wycherley: A Biography.* Athens: Ohio UP, 1979.

McKeon, Michael. *The Origins of the English Novel, 1600–1740.* Baltimore: Johns Hopkins UP, 1987.

Okin, Susan Moller. "Women and the Making of the Sentimental Family." *Philosophy and Public Affairs* 11 (1982): 65–88.

Pollak, Ellen. *The Poetics of Sexual Myth: Gender and Ideology in the Verse of Swift and Pope.* Chicago: U of Chicago P, 1985.

Righter, Anne. "William Wycherley." *Restoration Theatre.* Ed. John Russell and Bernard Harris. 1965. New York: Capricorn, 1967. 81–86.

Rogers, K. M. "Fatal Inconsistency: Wycherley and *The Plain-Dealer.*" *ELH* 28 (1961): 148–62.

Rubin, Gayle. "The Traffic in Women: Notes on the 'Political Economy' of Sex." *Toward an Anthropology of Women.* Ed. Rayna Reiter. New York: Monthly Review P, 1975. 157–210.

Staves, Susan. *Married Women's Separate Property in England, 1660–1833.* Cambridge: Harvard UP, 1990.

———. *Players' Scepters: Fictions of Authority in the Restoration.* Lincoln: U of Nebraska P, 1979.

Stone, Lawrence. *The Crisis of the Aristocracy, 1558–1641.* Oxford: Clarendon, 1965.

———. *The Family, Sex, and Marriage in England, 1500–1800.* Abridged ed. New York: Harper, 1979.

Todd, Barbara J. "The Remarrying Widow: A Stereotype Reconsidered." *Women in English Society, 1500–1800.* Ed. Mary Prior. London: Methuen, 1985. 54–83.

Trumbach, Randolph. *The Rise of the Egalitarian Family: Aristocratic Kinship and Domestic Relations in Eighteenth-Century England.* New York: Academic P, 1978.

Wycherley, William. *The Complete Plays of William Wycherley.* Ed. Gerald Weales. New York: Anchor-Doubleday, 1966.

"Be impudent, be saucy, forward, bold, touzing, and leud": The Politics of Masculine Sexuality and Feminine Desire in Behn's Tory Comedies

ROBERT MARKLEY

That [Behn] should ever recover her pristine reputation is of course, owing to the
passing of time with its change of manners, fashions, thought and style,
impossible. But there is happily every indication that—long neglected and
traduced—she will speedily vindicate for herself, as she is already beginning to
do, her rightful claim to a high and honourable place in our glorious literature.
—MONTAGUE SUMMERS

In heralding Behn's impending reemergence as a canonical author, Summers and subsequent critics have underestimated the theoretical—and
ideological—problems that her plays present for readers weaned on Whig
interpretations of literary history. Since her own day, Behn has been the
victim both of misogynistic and moralistic critics and of broadly dissemi-
nated critical biases and conceptions of literature that depend upon—and
celebrate—the political and social values of bourgeois economic morality,
sentimental benevolence, and individualist psychology.[1] In this essay I argue that her work resists the critical values and cultural assumptions that
traditionally have informed our notions of what constitutes "great" or
canonical literature, particularly the discourses of domestic morality and
repressed sexuality that seek to depoliticize—and delegitimate—feminine
desire. As a political writer and a feminist, Behn frustrates attempts to
incorporate her work within progressivist ideologies of class and gender;
she is a "radical royalist," to borrow Christopher Hill's phrase (275–316),

whose distrust of partisan politics and incipient capitalism leads her to promote an idealized vision of a monarchical and benevolently paternalistic
order that paradoxically frees women, in particular, from the demands of
the patrilineal ideology on which it ultimately depends. The significance
of Behn's challenges to the critical norms that have marginalized her work
or distorted it to fit conventional notions of seventeenth-century comedy
can be gauged by examining what I shall call her Tory comedies of the
Exclusion Crisis: *The Rover, Part II, The Roundheads,* and *The City Heiress.*[2] These plays, despite their contemporary popularity, have been largely
ignored by recent critics, and Behn herself "long neglected and traduced"
as a writer of comedies. I would argue that this neglect is a result not of
any intrinsic weaknesses in Behn's plays but of the ideological battles in
which they participate: in terms of her Tory politics, aristocratic apologetics, and feminist sexual ideology, Behn is historically on the losing side,
a marginalized figure within the traditionally marginalized field of Restoration drama.[3] Unlike Dryden, Pope, and Swift, Behn has not been read
as the defender of a critical or literary faith against the corruption of her
times; nor has she been the recipient of efforts to demonstrate the timeless "value" of her art, as Etherege, Wycherley, and Congreve have.[4] To
reread her Tory comedies, in this regard, is to confront the historical and
theoretical complexities of a radical dramatic practice—one that defamil-
iarizes seventeenth-century sexual politics—pressed into the service of a
conservative ideology.

Historically, the challenge that has confronted Behn's critics has been
to develop a theoretical framework—a politics of reading—that recognizes the ways in which her comedies resist a literary and psychoanalytic
tradition centered on the problematics of subjectivity.[5] Her plays present
gender roles in ideological rather than essentialist terms. In some respects,
Behn's critique of the mystification of sexuality anticipates the thinking of
the Freudian Left in the twentieth century. Wilhelm Reich, for example,
argues that the Freudian unconscious is an ideological "artifact of a sex-
negating culture; consciously, it is mostly experienced only as a gaping
inner emptiness. Behind it, in the depths, live and work natural sociality
and sexuality, spontaneous enjoyment of work, capacity for love" (204).
If we allow for historical differences, we can hear in Reich's utopian-
ism echoes of a seventeenth-century libertinism that perceives repression
as ideological rather than psychological. Behn's significance, in part, lies
in her politicizing of this utopian vision, her challenges to constructions

of sexuality and desire—in the seventeenth century and the twentieth—
that take as their bases repressive strategies designed to constrain "natural
sociality and sexuality." Behn's comedies savage the Puritan ideology of
self-denial that both historically and conceptually underlies the construction of the gendered self, whose genealogy Nancy Armstrong traces from
the conduct manuals of the late seventeenth century into the literature of
the eighteenth (3–27, 59–95). In this respect, Behn's political attacks on the
Whigs in the 1680s and the Commonwealthsmen of the 1650s are efforts
to demystify what we might call the masculinizing of desire—the creation
of women as other and as object—that is crucial to a sexual ideology that
insists on the indivisibility of feminine chastity and feminine identity.

For Behn, what Foucault calls the "repressive hypothesis" is ideological bad faith; desire is defined in her plays in non-Oedipal terms: not
as lack, not as symbolic castration, but as the striving of the individual
against the constraints of internalized morality and feminized virtue. Because she writes outside—and against—the economy of repression, Behn
is able to present her heroines as desiring subjects who can attain, within
the parameters that her plays describe, what they desire. Her concern is not
so much to detail a transhistorical women's "experience" but to dramatize culturally specific forms of resistance that idealize sexual desire at the
expense of Whiggish conceptions of individual, specifically female, rights.
Rights, for Behn, inhere in the natural order, not in the individual; in *The
City Heiress,* her comic appropriation of the Whigs' discourse of "Rights"
identifies her adversaries with a Hobbesian disorder, a divisiveness that results in endless squabbling and backbiting, with sedition and treason. Her
privileging of natural desire over socially conceived and socially contested
rights recasts notions of masculine and feminine sexuality by allowing us
to perceive the workings of desire from the vantage point of her female
characters; Behn simultaneously deconstructs and idealizes the discourses
of sexual and romantic love, reconstructing them in opposition to the mercenary economies of financial self-interest and the exploitation of women.
This process of defamiliarizing the discourses of desire inscribes in Behn's
plays a counterideology that seems, to those of us who are products of
psychosexual constructions of selfhood, counterintuitive. There is, quite
obviously, a significant element of idealization in Behn's portrayals of feminine desire and in her rewriting—as Cavalier and Tory "good nature"—
of what Lacan terms the "Law of the Father"; but it is an idealization

that Behn embraces (however problematically) and that is essential to her critique of sexual hypocrisy and the ideology of hypocritical self-denial.[6]

In her Tory comedies, Behn idealizes feminine desire and masculine desirability to counter the internalized policing mechanisms that operate, particularly in women, to constrain love: her plays offer both utopian and dystopian visions of "natural sociality." By "poaching," in de Certeau's sense, on the dominant discourses of honor and virtue and subverting them to her own ends, Behn seeks to create female characters who, while passionate, resist misogynist stereotyping as either harpies or fools.[7] Feminine desire—denied and repressed by a patrilineal ideology that must keep women circulating as goods to be exchanged for lands, money, and titles—therefore emerges in Behn's comedies from within and in opposition to the discourses of honor and virtue. The desiring heroines of her plays—particularly La Nuche in the second part of *The Rover* and Lady Galliard in *The City Heiress*—are outsiders, a prostitute and, by the end of the play, a sexually compromised woman. They represent the playwright's idealized separation of feminine desire from masculinist honor, good nature from repression in its extrinsic and self-policing forms; they serve as exemplars of a Royalist ideology that associates, on the one hand, "natural sociality and sexuality" with political loyalty and, on the other, repressive morality and repressed sexuality with hypocrisy and sedition. Within her political satire, then, Behn seeks to demasculinize desire, to find contemporary equivalents—in her Tory heroes and the women who love them—for the nymphs and shepherds of a golden age.

The dramatizing of feminine desire dialectically reinscribes masculine sexuality as both dangerous and desirable. Her Tory heroes—Willmore, Freeman and Loveless, and Wilding—become their plays' dominant sex symbols: both the objects of desire and the infinitely desiring males. Their dual sexuality is presented by Behn as the product of their natural exuberance, a manifestation of their inherent, literally inborn, gentlemanly good nature. The underlying associative logic of Behn's politicosexual economy might be described like this: the innate goodness of her heroes "naturally" leads them to embrace both Royalist loyalties and libertine lifestyles; wenching, drinking, and spending money are "natural" manifestations of their inherent virtue. Conversely, penury and abstinence from women and liquor signal a form of ideological repression, a hypocritical self-policing that internalizes standards of puritanical self-righteousness and can lead only to cowardice and misery. Therefore, for her heroes to violate conventional standards of sexual morality is paradoxically to legitimate aristocratic notions of birth and worth and to challenge the cultural forms of repression identified with the Puritans.

Behn's portrayal of male sexuality, in this regard, is both constitutive and subversive of traditional hierarchical constructions of gender. Because we see male sexuality from the point of view of the female characters, we undergo a process of defamiliarization, of having to reorient ourselves within what at first may seem the familiar terrain of seventeenth-century wit comedy. To construct men as the objects of desire in Behn's plays is to legitimate feminine desire, and therefore to offer the prospect of a reciprocal desire analogous to the sociosexual ideal that she describes in her poem "The Golden Age." Her identification of sexual desirability and Tory politics, in this respect, challenges traditional gender hierarchies—the women as the means to transmit property from one generation to the next—by positing an idealized feminine desire as, in Lacanian terms, the conflation of the penis and the phallus, that is, of physical desire and symbolic empowerment. Yet because Behn seeks to create reciprocal relationships of desire between her male and female characters within Royalist economies of class and privilege, she must idealize this desire as something other than a product of—and as prior to—patrilineal ideology. Her Tory comedies verge on creating a myth of desire as presence, as a form of "natural sociality" that can become a bulwark against the economies of exile and repression symbolized by Roundheads and Whigs.

In this regard, Behn's comedies dramatize what I would call a complex monological discourse that suppresses the dialogical nature of dramatic language, of socioeconomic conflict, in favor of a polemic intended to disseminate Royalist—and quasi-utopian—values.[8] *The Rover, Part II, The Roundheads,* and *The City Heiress*—all produced by the Duke's Company at Dorset Garden between January 1681 and late spring 1682—are designed, as Behn states in dedicating *The City Heiress* to Arundel, to make

> seditious Fools and Knaves that have so long disturb'd the Peace and Tranquility of the World . . . the business and sport of Comedy, and at last the scorn of that Rabble that fondly and blindly worshipt 'em; and whom nothing can so well convince as plain Demonstration, which is ever more powerful and prevailent than Precept, or even Preaching it self. (2: 200)

Although Behn dedicates her Tory comedies to the duke of York, the duke of Grafton, and Arundel, she constructs her audience as the *"Almighty Rabble"* that she invokes in the prologue to the second part of *The Rover* (1: 116); they are the ones who must be prevailed upon by "plain Demonstration." Her emphasis on the polemical nature of comedy distinguishes her work from the plays of her predecessors in the 1670s, notably Etherege and Wycherley. Whereas they demystify conventions of wit and carriage, Behn reinvests Fletcherian ideals of libertine behavior with a political significance that can be conveyed to the "rabble" in "plain Demonstration." Her comedies of the 1680s seek to reclaim the figure of the rake from the ambiguous forms of ironic existence to which he had evolved in the mid 1670s.[9] In Willmore, Loveless, and Wilding, Behn presents dialectical portraits of the rake as both libertine and Royalist, at once antiauthoritarian and passionately committed to king, country, and class. If Wycherley and Etherege render the identity of their heroes as ironic, dialogic, Behn decenters notions of identity—of the moral and, she assumes, puritanical self—to offer culturally based depictions of identity that seek to transcend the constraints of "Custom." The divisiveness of patrilineal ideology dramatized, for example, in *The Country Wife* is subsumed in Behn's foregrounding of mutual desire between the sexes, a vision of unrepressed sexuality that produces and is produced by a political ethos of idyllic Royalism.

    The Rover, Part II was written, Behn tells us in her dedication, at the behest of the duke of York, who, in early 1681 when the play was produced, was in "voluntary Exile" to appease the "ill-gotten Power, and worse-acted Greatness of the Rabble" (1: 113). She compares the plight of her royal patron to the sufferings of his "Glorious Father," Charles I, and to the circumstances of her own hero, the Rover: "[H]e is a wanderer too," she tells the duke, "distrest; belov'd, the unfortunate, and ever constant to Loyalty." He was, Behn continues, "driven from his Native Country with You, forc'd as You were, to fight for his Bread in a Strange Land, and suffer'd with You all the Ills of Poverty, War and Banishment" (1: 113–14). The parallels she draws between her hero's wanderings in the 1650s and the duke's exile in 1681 emphasize her "plain Demonstration" of Royalist good nature that she hopes will work upon the "Rabble." In one sense, the Rover becomes a sexualized embodiment of the duke's virtues, the avatar, like Behn's other Royalist heroes, of "a Prince of . . . Illustrious Birth and God-like Goodness" (1: 113). As he was in part 1 of *The Rover*, Willmore is dispossessed; he suffers the fate that threatens the heir to the throne. Symbolically, however, he retains the erotic power that "naturally," in Behn's eyes, emanates from his gentlemanly birth and loyalty to his monarch, class, and country. His sex appeal, in short, compensates for his political disempowerment and reflects the true measure of his social as well as personal worth: his desirability to the women of Madrid, as the duke of York apparently realized, validates the political and social values that he represents.

A refugee from the puritanical England of the Interregnum, Willmore embodies the idealized Cavalier values that Behn extols in her dedication. In his first exchange in the play with La Nuche he accuses her of being interested in him and in all men only for their money:

> [Y]ou made love to my Breeches, caress'd my Garniture and Feather, an English Fool of Quality you thought me—'Sheart, I have known a Woman doat on Quality, tho he has stunk thro all his Perfumes; one who never went all to Bed to her, but left his Teeth, an Eye, false Back and Breast, sometimes his Palate too upon her Toilet, whilst her fair Arms hug'd the dismembered Carcase, and swore him all Perfection, because of Quality. (I.i; 1: 132)

The image of the dismembered male ironically anticipates Swift's satiric dismemberment of the diseased prostitute in his poem "A Beautiful Young Nymph Going to Bed." What Behn dismembers, however, is the traditional image of masculine sexuality that yokes wit, physical attractiveness, money, and "Quality." A soldier without a war, Willmore spends a good deal of his time on stage disguised as a mountebank, a fitting image of the banished Cavalier who must rely on his wit to survive. At the end of the first part of *The Rover,* he had married Hellena and her fortune; now, having spent her hundred thousand crowns in the months after her death, he is, as his friend Beaumond says, "the same Man still, wild and wanton!" (I.i; 1: 122). Willmore's exile from his country and from his estate paradoxically frees him from the immediate demands of patrilineal ideology—to marry and to father heirs. Even as he embodies the good nature and loyalty that endear him to Royalists, he remains outside the economy of money and "Quality." He is, he says, "for Change . . . of Place, Clothes, Wine, and Women [because] Variety is the Soul of Pleasure, a Good unknown" (I.i; 1: 123). His wildness, his constancy to variety, mark him as a foe to the repressive forces of sanctimonious morality that Behn travesties in her hero's image of the "dismembered Carcase" who symbolizes, for the woman who would close her eyes and have him, the sacrifice of pleasure to mercenary ends.

Neither La Nuche nor Ariadne, however, has to choose a carcass; the two women—the prostitute and the heiress—contend for the favors of Willmore, with the gentlemanly Beaumond, a perfectly good second banana, as their fallback. The fools in the play, Blunt and Fetherfool, court two wealthy "Monsters," a giant and her dwarfish sister, but lose them to Shift and Hunt, Willmore's lieutenants. Blunt and Fetherfool are not, as one might expect, "punished" by being forced to marry "Monsters"; instead, the two women are rewarded with marriages to Shift and Hunt for their help in deluding the two English fools. Even in the comic subplot, then, feminine desire has its way. With the politically suspect Blunt and Fetherfool eliminated as potential comic rivals and the jealous Don Carlo, an aged pursuer of La Nuche, relegated to a few farcical scenes, the audience's interest focuses on how the four lovers—Willmore, La Nuche, Beaumond, and Ariadne—will pair off.

In part 1 of *The Rover* Willmore is pursued by Hellena, a wealthy noblewoman bent on escaping life in a nunnery, who disguises herself as a gypsy. In the course of the play, the penniless hero seduces the fashionable prostitute Angellica Bianca, jilts her to pursue his "little Gipsey," outfaces Angellica when she brandishes a pistol at him, and eventually marries Hellena, whose wit matches his. In the sequel, Behn complicates our responses to the conventional roles of the prostitute and the madcap heiress that she had previously exploited. Willmore's indiscriminate sexuality—his commitment to "Variety"—creates a symbolic space for feminine desire; it enables the women to choose him. As Ariadne tells her kinswoman Lucia after she first sees Willmore, "I'll . . . please my self in the choice of this Stranger, if he be to be had" (II.ii; 1: 149). Her decision to pursue Willmore is based, in part, on her discounting the threat that La Nuche poses as her rival: "[T]hat Stranger's not such a fool," she asserts, "to give his Heart to a common Woman" (II.ii; 1: 149). But as the play goes on, Ariadne's conventional wisdom—heroes go for rich, chaste, and witty women rather than whores—is undone. Beaumond, to whom she is engaged but who is in love with La Nuche, asks,

What difference then between a money-taking Mistress and her that gives her Love? only perhaps this sins the closer by't, and talks of

Honour more: What Fool wou'd be a Slave to empty Name, or value
Woman for dissembling well? I'll to *La Nuche*—the honester o'th'
two—. (IV.i; 1: 179)

La Nuche is not simply the "honester o'th' two" but the woman who in-
spires the Cavaliers to a generous, unfeigned love. When Willmore speaks
to Ariadne of love, he ironically employs and undercuts a conventional
language of seduction:

Come, let's pursue the Business we came for: See the kind Night invites, and all the ruffling Winds are husht and still, only the Zephirs
spread their tender Wings, courting in gentle Murmurs the gay
Boughs; 'twas in a Night like this, *Diana* taught the Mysteries of Love
to the fair Boy *Endymion.* I am plaguy full of History and Simile to
night. (IV.i; 1: 180)

Willmore's use of "Business" to describe his canned rhetoric suggests, as
Beaumond had a few minutes earlier, that the difference between Ariadne,
the virgin, and La Nuche, the prostitute, is socially constructed, not essential. They are, in one sense, the "same" woman: they are sexually desirous
and seeking to cut the best deal possible for themselves. Their sexual identities are not determined by their (lack of) virtue but by the cultural roles
that they play—and resist—within a patrilineal society.

Although Willmore's love scene with La Nuche in act 5 has its share
of history and similes, Behn's stage directions as well as her verse suggest
that their passion is intended to challenge the theatrical conventions—and
ideological imperatives—that turn the hero's earlier encounter with Ariadne into a comic battle of wits. The scene begins with La Nuche "on a
Couch in an Undress, Willmore at her Feet, on his Knees, all unbrac'd."

Willmore. The Blushes on thy Face, thy trembling Arms,
    Thy panting Breast, and short-breath'd Sighs confess
    Thou wo't be mine, in spite of all thy Art.
La Nuche. What need you urge my Tongue then to repeat
    What from my Eyes you can so well interpret?
            [*Bowing down her Head to him and sighing.*]
    —Or if it must—dispose me as you please—
Willmore. Heaven, I thank thee!   [*Rises with Joy.*]
    Who wou'd not plough an Age in Winter Seas,

Or wade full seven long Years in ruder Camps,
To find out this Rest at last?—
                         [*Leans on, and Kisses her Bosom.*]
Upon thy tender Bosom to repose;
To gaze upon thy Eyes, and taste thy Balmy Kisses,
                         [*Kisses her.*]
—Sweeter than everlasting Groves of Spices,
When the soft Winds display the opening Buds:
—Come, haste, my Soul, to Bed—
La Nuche. You can be soft I find, when you wou'd conquer
absolutely.

                         (V.i; 1: 189–90)

Willmore's verse both invokes and seeks to escape from the conventionality of stage-show passion and from traditional gender roles: Willmore as the conqueror, La Nuche as the woman powerless to resist him. His imagery is not that of conquest but of "Rest" and "repose," of "mutual Love." But because she is a prostitute and he an exiled soldier of fortune, the power relationship between them is complicated: his love can neither ennoble nor enrich her. The obstacle that Willmore faces is not the heroine's honor but her economic self-interest. When Beaumond interrupts their love scene, La Nuche's thoughts turn to her cash flow. "And must I be undone because I love ye?" she asks. "This [either the couch or possibly Beaumond] is the Mine from whence I fetcht my Gold." Willmore's response is telling: "Damn the base trash: I'll have thee mine; / 'Tis nobler far, to starve with him thou lov'st / Than gay without, and pining all within" (V.i; 1: 191). Punning on "mine" and divorcing love from money, Willmore ironically enables himself to choose the prostitute over the heiress. La Nuche matches him in wit and offers him the possibility of "a Calm of Love" (V.i; 1: 190) outside the constraints of marriage and the responsibilities—as husband and patriarch—that it entails.

But as their exchange indicates, it is La Nuche as well who does the choosing. Unlike Angellica in part 1 of *The Rover,* she is not excluded from the realm of romantic comedy; she is, arguably, its focus. The psychological interest in the play centers on her struggle between mercenary self-interest and generous love, a standard dilemma for comic heroines but an unusual one for prostitutes. Torn between Beaumond's money and Willmore's passion, La Nuche finally opts for the "wild Inconstant": "He has," she asserts, "he shall, he must compleat my ruin" (V.i; 1: 195). Her ruin, however, is financial rather than moral; Behn, in this instance, uses the familiar rhetoric of seduction to undermine the audience's conventional moral expectations. The Rover and the prostitute become the fitting rewards for each other's passion. What La Nuche learns during the course of the play is to reject the fears of poverty and old age—the ideological economy that equates love and loot and the moral economy that decrees sexual "sins" must be punished—that she, as a businesswoman, has internalized and to embrace the values that lead the Rover "o'er the habitable World . . . [to] live and starve by turns." These Cavalier values suggest a perpetuation of the freedoms of exile, of remaining outside the constraints of patrilineal responsibility. The untrammeled desire that Willmore represents signals his escape into a realm of Cavalier idealism that potentially frees La Nuche to shed her role as sexual object and act upon her desire. The lovers make "a Bargain . . . without the formal Foppery of Marriage" and leave Ariadne and Beaumond to take formal vows (V.iii; 1: 208). Willmore ends the play by telling his friend and former rival,

> You have a hankering after Marriage still, but I am for Love and Gallantry.
>> So tho by several ways we gain our End,
>> Love still, like Death, does to one Center tend.
>>> (V.iii, 1: 211)

"Love and Gallantry" is not the conventional promise of living happily ever after, especially if we stop to think about the fate of La Nuche as a camp follower. But Behn, having sent her hero off with a prostitute and her heroine off with a "wild and wanton" soldier, discourages the audience from responding conventionally. In this regard, the key phrase in the play's closing lines is Willmore's invoking "one Center" for love. The center can suggest passion, with or without bawdy connotations, but its proximity to death suggests that love's center is being invoked as an ideal that transcends the vicissitudes that love and gallantry have gone through in the play. Willmore's couplet, in effect, is an invitation to remain in a golden age of Cavalier loving and carousing, in which heroes get their women but escape or forestall the responsibilities of marriage. The end of the play, then, depicts a nostalgia for the freedom of exile, for "Love and Gallantry" as sufficient proofs of resistance to puritanical sanctimony and moneygrubbing. The Toryism that Behn identifies in her dedication with the Rover's constancy, in this regard, is manifest as loyalty and generosity rather than as a sociopolitical program; the commitment that the play encourages is to ideals rather than to policies.

What is missing, in one sense, from Willmore's adventures in part 2 of *The Rover* is an onstage enemy, a foil for his Cavalier wit and virtues, an avatar of the "seditious Faction" that Behn excoriates in her dedication. In *The Roundheads,* a brilliant adaptation of John Tatham's 1660 satire *The Rump,* she provides her Royalist heroes with enemies aplenty by restaging the fall of the Commonwealth as a morality play for the Exclusion Crisis. In dedicating the play to the king's illegitimate son, the duke of Grafton, as a "small Mirror, of the late wretched Times," Behn makes explicit the connections she perceives between the Roundheads of the 1650s and the Whigs of the 1680s who "wou'd be at the *Old Game* their fore-Fathers play'd with so good success" (1: 338). Puritans and Whigs are one and the same: "*Traytors,*" "Meane . . . Villains," "*Phanatick[s],*" and "Rogues" (1: 338). Although Behn claims the play depicts "honest Truths," she takes a good deal of freedom with history to extend her satiric attack beyond politics. What distinguishes this comedy from other Royalist plays of the period—and what may account, in part, for the violent reaction the play elicited from Shaftesbury's followers—is that her political satire is cast in sexual as well as socioideological terms.[10] Her Roundheads are not only scoundrels, thieves, petty tyrants, and hypocrites, they are also sexually unattractive or incompetent, unable to keep their wives from loving and lusting after the play's Royalist heroes, Loveless and Freeman. The sexual inadequacies of the Puritans mark them as trespassers within the symbolic order of phallocratic law; they have, according to Lady Lambert, "the most slovenly, ungrateful, dull Behavior; no Air, no Wit, no Love, nor any thing to please a Lady with" (II.i; 1: 363). A patrilineal order, after all, needs patriarchs; therefore, the Puritans' sexual incompetence and hypocrisy emphasize their political illegitimacy. The fall of the Commonwealth at the end of the play, in this regard, heralds a restoration of both sexual and political power to the Tories. What is at stake in Loveless's and Freeman's courting the wives of Commonwealth leaders, then, is the ideology of restoration: the utopian union of desire and law, of golden age sexuality and a benevolent, even divine, paternalistic authority.[11]

The Roundheads freely mixes historical fact and invention. The play's comic villains and their wives are all historical figures prominent in the

1650s—Fleetwood, Lambert, Wariston, Duckenfield, Whitlock, Desborough, Lady Cromwell, Lady Lambert, Lady Fleetwood, and Lady Desborough—but they are transformed to suit Behn's satiric and ideological purposes. Political conflicts in the play become functions of contrasting sexual ideologies. The satiric scenes of the Roundheads sitting in committee to perpetrate their villainies are drawn from Tatham's play; in adapting *The Rump,* Behn lavishes most of her attention on Loveless's and Freeman's pursuit of Lady Lambert and Lady Desbro. The two wives of the Puritan leaders become the dramatist's means to demonstrate the failures of repressive morality and to reveal the bankruptcy of the Commonwealth as an ideological ideal as well as a political entity. Lady Desbro is trapped in a loveless and politically repellent marriage; she is in love with Freeman but has married Desbro to further the interest of her lover's party. She is, Freeman tells Loveless at the beginning of the play, "not of [the Puritans'] Persuasion, but an errant Heroick in her Heart, and feigns it only to have the better occasion to serve the Royal Party" (I.i; 1: 349). Her marriage to the man who has sequestered her lover's estate is her attempt to preserve these lands until she can restore them to her Cavalier. Her love, her desire to serve the "Royal Party," subverts the Roundheads' usurpative order from within. Lady Desbro remains chaste, however, despite Freeman's entreaties and is rewarded at the end of the play when her husband conveniently dies (the historical Desborough survived until 1680) so that she can marry her lover. However distasteful her marriage, her fidelity to her husband and to her party ensures that she remains above moral and political reproach.

Lady Lambert is a more complex and problematic character. The former mistress of Oliver Cromwell, she is obsessed with furthering her husband's ambitions to secure her own "greatness." She nonetheless falls in love with Loveless at first sight and is taken aback when Lady Desbro informs her that he is a Royalist:

> *Lady Lambert.* Ah, Heav'ns, that they [Freeman and Loveless] should prove Heroicks!
> *Lady Desbro.* You might have known that by the Conquest; I never heard any one o't' other Party ever gain'd a Heart; and indeed, Madam, 'tis a just Revenge, our Husbands make slaves of them, and they kill all their Wives. (I.i; 1: 350–51)

This exchange reveals the sexual and ideological economy that celebrates Cavalier good nature and vilifies Puritan hypocrisy and injustice: the bases of the Roundheads' tyranny are their sexual insecurities and jealousies. Their acts of sequestration are a form of overcompensation for their failures as lovers: their seizing of land, of property, is symbolically a measure of their inability to control the "property"—women—that they exchange callously among themselves. The subordinate positions of women in patrilineal society—as wives, daughters, and mistresses—allow Behn to insulate Lady Lambert and Lady Desbro from the savage satire leveled at their husbands and the other male members of the committee. Precisely because they are disempowered, the women cannot be held morally responsible for the political corruption of England. Their political ties to the Commonwealth are the consequences of their having been bartered or coerced into marriage. Because Puritanism is equated with false standards of masculinity, Lady Lambert gradually emerges as a figure of resistance within the Roundheads' debased political order, even though her character seemingly cries out for satiric broadsides: she is socially and politically ambitious, power hungry, self-important, both sex starved and adulterous, and the wife of General Lambert, the most dangerous and hypocritical of Behn's villains. Significantly, however, she is not presented as a satiric butt, as the audience recognizes at the beginning of the play when Loveless falls instantaneously in love with her despite his disgust for everyone associated with the Good Old Cause. In the course of the play, Behn develops the mutually reinforcing actions of Lady Lambert's seduction by Loveless and her political reformation as an ideological heuristic: her heroine is reclaimed by sex and to a sexualized ideology of Royalist good nature. Lady Lambert serves, in this regard, as a manifestation of the "Rabble" and the audience—Behn conflates the two in her epilogue to the play—who must be taught by "plain Demonstration" to make the correct political choices. We are invited to participate vicariously in, and to learn from, her reformation.

   The Roundheads' movement toward political restoration is cast in sexual and religious terms; in the relationship of Loveless and Lady Lambert, the two are conflated to reinvest monarchical and upper-class authority with transcendent significance. Loveless's manner of seducing her is to rail at the "mungrel, mangy, Mock-Monarchy" that she represents and to denounce the "new-rais'd Rascals, Canters, Robbers, Rebels / [who] Do lord it o'er the Free-born, Brave and Noble" (II.i; 1: 361). Lady Lambert, though, is exempt from this critique because Loveless constructs her ambition as "Madness": "Sure she's mad," he observes at their first meeting, "yet she walks loose about, / And she has Charms even in her raving Fit" (II.i; 1:

361). His cure, of course, is sex. Loveless's seduction of Lady Lambert is an act of both moral restoration and political defiance, a mark of his refusal to acquiesce in the sexual hypocrisy and political corruption of the Commonwealth. For her, their love becomes a form of ironic liberation from the tyranny of her husband: she embraces Loveless as the exemplar of a Royalist order to escape the pleasure-denying effects of masculinist and Puritan tyranny. The lovers' political differences, in this respect, are overcome by the ideology of desire. "[L]eave we Politicks," Loveless entreats, "and fall to Love, / Who deals more Joys in one kind happy moment / Than Ages of dull Empire can produce" (II.i; 1: 367). His rhetoric is that of the golden age, in Behn's theatrical re-creation of 1660, about to be restored.

Loveless's disparaging of partisan politics is characteristic of Behn's efforts to contrast the pettiness and double-dealing of Puritans and Whigs with what she wants her audience to see as the broad appeal of Tory ideology. Nowhere in her works does she suggest that opponents of the monarchy or of James II's succession have legitimate grievances; nowhere does she offer a rationale to explain how or why the Civil War and Exclusion Crisis occurred except to vilify her enemies as irrevocably corrupt and vindictive. The tyranny of the Puritans in *The Roundheads* is explained only in terms of greed, hypocrisy, and sexual jealousy:

> *Lady Lambert.* . . . As thou say'st, these Heroicks have the strangest
>   Power—
> *Lady Desbro.* I never knew a Woman cou'd resist 'em.
> *Lady Lambert.* No marvel, then, our Husbands use 'em so, betray 'em,
>   banish 'em, sequester, murder 'em, and every way disarm 'em—[.]
>   (II.i; 1: 368)

This exchange displaces political struggle into the sociosexual ideology of Royalist "Power." Identified with Puritan chicanery, politics itself is corrupt and corrupting. As in *The Rover, Part II*, Cavaliers have no political program save their loyalty; they do not talk politics but reassert the tautologies of birth and worth, good breeding and good nature. In this regard, Cavalier sexuality—"the strangest Power" of the "Heroicks"— merges symbolically with the natural rights of a golden age that antedates and transcends the evils of corruption and repression.

The basis of the Royalists' ideology—their claim to transcend politics— is brilliantly dramatized by Behn in the fetishizing of Charles I's crown and scepter that occurs in act 4. This bedroom scene conflates Cavalier

sexuality with images of political—and religious—martyrdom and resurrection. Lady Lambert and Loveless rest on a couch while she gives him a
diamond bracelet that was given to her by Cromwell. "*Oliver, illustrious
Oliver,*" she tells her lover, "[w]as yet far short of thee" (IV.iv; 1: 399).
Behn's sexual pun underscores the political implications of the scene: the
Protector was not the man that the dispossessed Cavalier is; the Commonwealth in 1660 is being supplanted by the restored order sexually and politically. Lady Lambert then offers Loveless, as a sexual come-on, a greater
gift—the crown and scepter—that he refuses:

> *Loveless.* Have I been all this while
>   So near the sacred Relicks of my King;
>   And found no awful Motion in my Blood,
>   Nothing that mov'd sacred Devotion in me? [*Kneels.*]
>   —Hail sacred Emblem of great Majesty,
>   Thou that hast circled more Divinity
>   Than the great Zodiack that surrounds the World. . . .
> *Lady Lambert.* Is't not a lovely thing?
> *Loveless.* There's such Divinity i'th' very Form on't,
>   Had I been conscious I'd been near the Temple,
>   Where this bright Relick of the glorious Martyr
>   Had been enshrin'd, 't had spoiled my soft Devotion. . . .
> *Lady Lambert.* Thou art a Fool, the very sight of this—
>   Raises my Pleasure higher[.]
>   (IV.iv; 1: 399–400)

Lady Lambert, still fixated on her dreams of glory, nonetheless makes a crucial connection between power and pleasure. Loveless's "Devotion[s]"—
"sacred" and "soft"—belong to the same Royalist homology. Charles I
is not a political figure, a rallying point for political resistance, but a
"Divinity." His "Relicks" are sanctified to the extent that they are depoliti-
cized; they represent Cavalier nostalgia for a golden age that transcends—
and represses the knowledge of—the political circumstances that led to
the Civil War.[12] In one sense, the crown is a symbol of the phallic power
that has been taken from the Royalists; in another, it appears in the play
as a foreshadowing of the restoration. Lady Lambert, by trying to place
the crown on Loveless's head, offers him a political symbol of the sexual
power that he has just demonstrated: she seeks the union of penis and phal-

lus that Loveless, a faithful Cavalier rather than a monarch, resists. Her desires, however, are not unlawful, only premature. Before she can have what she desires, she must come to recognize the "Divinity" that the crown represents, the ideology of divine right that transcends the squabbling of partisan politics, and Loveless and the Royalist order he symbolizes must be restored to power. In act 5, Lady Lambert moves from madness to loyalty as the Commonwealth collapses about her. After sneaking Loveless out of her room, she outfaces her husband, who, the audience learns, had prostituted her to Cromwell for his own advancement; later, she quarrels with Cromwell's widow and condemns the committeemen for their cowardice as General Monck and his forces enter London. Once her husband is imprisoned, she renounces her ambitions and becomes penitent, telling Loveless, "I do not merit thy Respect." Only then can she be reclaimed by the hero and converted to the Royalist standard he upholds:

> *Loveless.* By Heaven, you were never great till now;
>   I never thought thee so much worth my Love,
>   My Knee, and Adoration, till this Minute. . . .
>   [*Kneels.*]
> *Lady Lambert.* Is there such God-like Virtue in your Sex?
>   Or, rather, in your Party.
>   Curse on the Lyes and Cheats of Conventicles,
>   That taught me first to think Heroicks Devils,
>   Blood-thirsty, leud, tyrannick, salvage Monsters.
>   —But I believe 'em Angels all, if all like Loveless.
>   What heavenly thing then must the Master be,
>   Whose Servants are divine?
>
>   (V.iii; 1: 418)

Loveless goes from adoring the relics of Charles I to adoring his newly great mistress. Her madness, it turns out, is the result not of natural ambition or weakness but of "the Lyes and Cheats" practiced upon her by the Roundheads. Lady Lambert becomes paradigmatic of Behn's heroines who are empowered by their desire for Cavaliers and Tories. Seduction by the Royalist rake represents woman's entry into a utopia of fulfilled sexual desire and symbolic empowerment as an "equal." This is why Behn's rake-heroes must be unmarried, exiled, sequestered, or otherwise disinherited Royalists: paradoxically, they must stand outside the economy of patrilineal inheritance, and they must have the inherent power to bestow upon women a consensual freedom. They must, in other words, have the power to relinquish the power of "Custom," of repressive sexual and masculinist morality, as Loveless does when he kneels to Lady Lambert. The conclusion of *The Roundheads* suggests strongly that the ideology of restoration—the revivifying of the myths of 1660—is the only means that Behn finds cultur-ally available to legitimate within a patrilineal society an idealized vision of reciprocal desire.

In *The City Heiress* Behn adapts the political satire of *The Roundheads* to the conventions of wit and intrigue comedy. Updating the setting of socioideological conflict between the Royalists and their adversaries to the 1680s, she singles out for ridicule the first earl of Shaftesbury, who is trav-estied in the figure of Sir Timothy Treat-all. While the play identifies the Whigs with hypocrisy, greed, and nearly impotent lust and the Tories with loyalty, high spirits, sexual desirability, and a devil-may-care impecunious-ness, its tone is comic rather than bitingly satiric. The main plot involves Wilding's efforts to outwit his uncle, Sir Timothy, and to juggle the atten-tions of three women: Charlotte, a wealthy city heiress whom he has hidden in private lodgings but has neither married nor seduced; Lady Galliard, a rich widow he is trying to seduce and who is also being courted—ineptly— by his friend Sir Charles Meriwill; and his mistress, Diana, who upbraids him for not having found a rich wife whose fortune he can lavish on her. Unlike both parts of *The Rover* and *The Roundheads*, *The City Heiress* examines Tory values as they are established in and by the ruling order, not as the oppositional ideals of disenfranchised nobility. The threat posed by Sir Timothy and the Whigs he represents is contained within the generic constraints of wit comedy. Ironically, though, if the play offers an example of Toryism triumphant, it also reveals the extent to which Behn's sexual counterideology is parasitic upon the repressive morality that it attacks. In dramatizing the conflicts between desire and honor, *The City Heiress* is, at once, more incisive and more ambiguous than her other Tory comedies.

Wilding's efforts to seduce Lady Galliard run into a form of oppo-sition—her honor—with which Willmore and Loveless do not have to contend. Although some of Behn's heroines remain chaste—Lady Desbro and Ariadne, for example—none are given the extended defenses of their honor that fall to Lady Galliard. Money, for the widow, is not a problem; she is financially free to act upon her desires if she can free herself from the masculinist conceptions of virtue and honor that she has internalized. Her exchanges with Wilding become an ongoing debate between different moral and socioideological commitments: he is for pleasure; she is forced repeatedly to deny herself what she desires. Wilding, employing the golden-age rhetoric of unrepressed desire, upbraids Lady Galliard repeatedly for failing to be true to her passion. "I thought you'd lov'd me," he tells her,

> But when I beg'd to reap the mighty Joy
> That mutual Love affords,
> You turn'd me off from Honour,
> That Nothing, fram'd by some old sullen Maid,
> That wanted Charms to kindle Flames when young.
>
> (I.i; 2: 213–14)

Wilding contrasts "mutual Love" and "Honour," but his speech suggests that the two are dialectically rather than antithetically related. Throughout the play, Behn explores the implications of love as a violation of moralistic prohibitions against pleasure. For Wilding, "the mighty Joy" is enhanced by the resistance that he imagines he will encounter:

> The stealths of Love, the midnight kind Admittance,
> The gloomy Bed, the soft breath'd murmuring Passion;
> Ah, who can guess at Joys thus snatch'd by parcels?
> The difficulty makes us always wishing,
> Whilst on thy part, Fear makes still some resistance;
> And every Blessing seems a kind of Rape.
>
> (I.i; 2: 215)

The overcoming of Lady Galliard's fear and resistance provokes Wilding's desire and the desire—"always wishing"—to violate her fear and resistance again. The "Rape" that the hero envisions is symbolic as well as literal: he seeks to master the ideology that the woman has internalized as well as her body. In this regard, the Tory ethic of masculine love is rendered dialectically: the desire to violate repeatedly the ideologically constructed fears that motivate feminine chastity—the tyranny of honor that Behn decries—demonstrates the rake's intrinsic good nature, his commitment to "mutual Love." This dialectic makes sense, however, only if Lady Galliard and other resisting women are constructed as alienated from their own desires, as suffering from a self-imposed repression that must be challenged by "a kind of Rape" in order to enable the possibility of "mutual Love."

Lady Galliard's struggle against self-policing honor dominates her encounters with the hero. She desires Wilding and is aghast at her desires.

She claims that she "understand[s] not these new Morals" that hold, as Wilding says, "All the Desires of mutual Love are virtuous" (IV.i; 2: 264). What she does understand, however, is that she loves him precisely because he represents what she has been taught to shun. She tells him, "Your very Faults, how gross soe'er to me, / Have something pleasing in 'em" (I.i; 2: 265), but quickly slips into the language of internalized honor and moralistic self-condemnation:

> . . . and have I promis'd then to be
> A Whore? A Whore! Oh, let me think of that!
> A Man's Convenience, his leisure Hours, his Bed of Ease,
> To loll and tumble on at idle times;
> The Slave, the Hackney of his lawless Lust!
> A loath'd Extinguisher of filthy Flames,
> Made use of, and thrown by—Oh, infamous!
>
> (IV.i; 2: 266)

Wilding's response—"You start at Words, and turn away from Shadows" (IV.i; 2: 266)—reduces Lady Galliard's virtue to a reflexive and repressive discourse that constructs the standards it imposes on her. The heroine suffers because she is trapped between her desires and a morality of shame and repression. She differs from, say, La Nuche and Lady Lambert because her virtue—which she recognizes as an imposed and oppressive morality—is nearly an equal match, through much of the play, for her desire.[13] Lady Galliard's struggle ends with her asking, "[W]ho can always her own Wish deny?" and then admitting, "My Reason's weary of the unequal Strife; / And Love and Nature will at last o'ercome" (IV.i; 2: 267). Her seduction by Wilding is thus more ambiguous than those of La Nuche by Willmore and Lady Lambert by Loveless; paradoxically, it represents both her capitulation to her lover's entreaties and her rebellion against the dictates of honor. The masculinist mode of "Love and Nature" is the only means available for Lady Galliard to overcome the "shivering Fit of Honour" (IV.ii; 2: 272) that plagues her until she at last relinquishes Wilding for Sir Charles and an honorable marriage. Her seduction, then, both frees her from self-policing repression and marks her implication in the very systems of morality and reason against which she rebels.

Sir Charles, like the woman he desires, learns to reject the conventions of honorable love for unmediated passion. For much of the play, he is the victim of his own mystifications of desire; his courtship of Lady Galliard—

cast in the language of "whining love"—turns his romantic sentiments into hash. His uncle, Sir Anthony Meriwill, who serves as a satiric chorus during his scenes with the widow, upbraids him constantly for addressing her like "a Fore-man o' th' Shop, to his Master's Daughter" (I.i; 2: 216). When Charles protests, "I've try'd all ways to win upon her Heart, / Presented, writ, watcht, fought, pray'd, kneel'd, and wept," his uncle's advice is to imitate the style of Wilding and other rake-hell heroes, to be "very impudent and saucy, Sir, / Leud, ruffling, mad" (I.i; 2: 218). Repeatedly, Sir Charles's "whining love" is described as less than masculine or, what may be worse in Behn's plays, as "puritanical." His attempts to declare his love for Lady Galliard can neither distract her from her dressing table nor please his bluff, Tory uncle:

> *Sir Charles.* [Your] Beauty needs no Ornament, Heaven has been too bountiful.
> *Sir Anthony.* Heaven! Oh Lord, Heaven! a puritanical Rogue, he courts her like her Chaplain.   [*Aside, vext.*]
> *Lady Galliard.* You are still so full of University Complements—
> *Sir Anthony.* D'ye hear that, Sirrah?—Ay, so he is, indeed, Madam— To her like a Man, ye Knave.   [*Aside to him.*]
> *Sir Charles.* Ah, Madam, I am come—
> *Sir Anthony.* To shew your self a Coxcomb.
> *Lady Galliard.* To tire me with Discourses of your Passion—Fie, how this Curl fits!   [*Looking in the Glass.*]
> *Sir Charles.* No, you shall hear no more of that ungrateful Subject.
> *Sir Anthony.* Son of a Whore, hear no more of Love, damn'd Rogue! Madam, by *George,* he lyes; he does come to speak of Love, and make Love, and to do Love, and all for Love—Not come to speak of Love, with a Pox! Owns, Sir, behave your self like a Man; be impudent, be saucy, forward, bold, touzing, and leud, d'ye hear, or I'll beat thee before her: why, what a Pox!
> [*Aside to him, he minds it not.*] (II.iii; 2: 235)

Informing the comedy of this scene is the standard of masculinity that Sir Anthony and, in her jibe at Charles's "University Complements," Lady Galliard uphold. Sir Anthony upbraids his nephew by insulting his manhood, his politics, and his social status: Sir Charles's "whining" language of romantic sentiment renders him a "puritanical Rogue," a "Knave," a "Coxcomb," and a "Son of a Whore." His language is not so much deconstructed—that is, shown to be divided against itself—as it is demasculinized by the overdetermined satire directed against it. Sir Charles makes no progress in his courtship of Lady Galliard until he gets drunk and forces his way into her chamber. Wilding, who has just slept with her, is forced to sneak out of her lodgings, leaving the widow to her newly "forward, bold, touzing, and leud" lover who extracts a promise of marriage from her and vows to "keep her . . . by constant Consummation" (IV.ii; 2: 277). Lady Galliard does not choose a new lover so much as succumb to an "impudent" form of courtship that she cannot resist, regardless of who employs it. To win her, Sir Charles must become a clone of Wilding, less an individual than a reconstructed version of Tory sexuality—"the same Man still, wild and wanton." He and Lady Galliard can marry only after they have dropped their languages of honorable repression in favor of physical love. Behn, however, takes pains to ensure that the audience sees neither their marriage nor Wilding's and Charlotte's as examples of true love winning out against lust. Lady Galliard, even though she has gratified her sexual desires, seems more a victim of circumstance and of the threat of a lost reputation than a woman who has attained what she wants. Throughout the final scene, Wilding and Lady Galliard trade accusations of infidelity in asides that suggest the hero will make good on his promise to cuckold Sir Charles. She does not embrace her new lover so much as his advice to avoid being left "To infamy, to Scandal, and to Wilding"; she marries him to save her reputation (V.v; 2: 292). Wilding marries Charlotte out of revenge rather than love:

> *Charlotte.* I have thee, and I'll die thus grasping thee;
>   Thou art my own, no Power shall take thee from me.
> *Wilding.* Never; thou truest of thy Sex, and dearest,
>   Thou soft, thou kind, thou constant Sufferer,
>   This moment end thy Fears; for I am thine.
> *Charlotte.* May I believe thou art not married then?
> *Wilding.* How can I, when I'm yours?
>   How cou'd I, when I love thee more than Life?
>   [*To Lady Galliard.*]
>   Now, Madam, I am reveng'd on all your Scorn,
>   —And, Uncle, all your Cruelty.
>
>   (V.v; 2: 296)

The marriages that are promised at the end of the play are subordinated to the Cavalier ideology that finds Wilding, like Willmore, "the same Man still." His language of love is comically undercut by his aside to Lady Galliard, but his rakishness paradoxically depends upon his violating his vow to Charlotte. Wilding voices a language of fidelity that he also travesties, a language that he has used before on Lady Galliard and that must be equally true—and equally feigned—to both women. As his line to Sir Timothy suggests, desire remains implicated in violation, in transgressing the morality that his uncle, however hypocritically, represents. Wilding ends up in the ironic position of being the presumptive cuckold of his uncle, who marries Diana; conceivably, the hero could beget a son who would displace him as Sir Timothy's heir. In this respect, Wilding seems intent on remaining "the same Man still," even to his own detriment. His marriage, like Lady Galliard's, offers less a happy ending than a grudging descent into the responsibility that Willmore and Loveless evade.

The comic instabilities of the love matches at the end of *The City Heiress*, however, are contained within a language of loyalty that seeks to transcend the duplicity of sexual and partisan politics. At the beginning of act 5, Wilding has his henchmen stage a robbery of his uncle's house to secure the writings that will make him the heir to Sir Timothy's estate. What they find in addition to these papers is "A whole Bag of Knavery, damn'd Sedition, Libels, Treason, Successions, Rights and Privileges, with a new-fashion'd Oath of Abjuration, call'd the Association" (V.i; 2: 282). Behn turns the stealing of writings—a familiar device in seventeenth-century comedy—to political ends. Sir Timothy's exposure as a plotter against the king parallels his being duped into marrying Wilding's former mistress. Having married the city heiress and her fortune, Wilding allows Sir Timothy to retain the use of his estate during his life but only on the condition "that he makes not use on't to promote any Mischief to the King and Government" (V.v; 2: 298). Whatever disputes exist among the Tories and their women in the play are subsumed within their united opposition to the Whigs and the "Knavery" they represent. To emphasize her point, Behn closes the play with overtly political lines that celebrate the defeat of the Whigs' "Treason" and an idealized vision of order restored:

> Let all things in their own due Order move,
> Let *Caesar* be the Kingdom's Care and Love;
> Let the hot-headed Mutineers petition,
> And meddle in the Rights of just Succession:
> But may all honest Hearts as one agree
> To bless the King, and Royal *Albany*.
>
> (V.v; 2: 298)

These lines perform a sophisticated ideological sleight of hand. The first couplet issues commands, the second suggests a violation of the "due Order" that Behn has just evoked. "Rights" are appropriated from "hot-headed Mutineers," like Shaftesbury, and given to the patrilineal and Royalist imperative of "just Succession." There is no solution, however, offered to mutiny except to elevate the king and his brother above the political fray, symbolized by the univocal blessing they receive from "all honest Hearts" acting "as one." The tensions that existed before the play, before the travestying of Shaftesbury, remain. In this regard, the closing does not look forward to a millenarian order or to sixth acts of happy marriages and male heirs but backward to a golden age before politics, before repression, when all hearts were honest and all could agree. The "due Order" that Behn invokes is a nostalgic invocation of Cavalier unity, the myth of an idyllic past before the divisiveness of civil war.

The appeal of Behn's Tory comedies depends ultimately on the audience's accepting a socioideological framework that represses and mystifies the causes of political strife in seventeenth-century England. Class relations, religious discontent, the upper class's monopoly on property, and the economic problems of trade, mining, and agriculture are violently effaced from her plays, replaced by her invocations of a golden age that paradoxically can be represented only in the refracted images of her heroes' exile and dispossession. But her friendships with Rochester and Buckingham, and her affair with John Hoyle, who may have had republican leanings, suggest that Behn was anything but a knee-jerk conservative (Duffy 289–90). Her fascination with exile, dispossession, and a lost golden age—themes that she reworks in Oroonoko—suggests that the unity, the "due Order," Behn envisions is ecological and holistic rather than rigidly hierarchical. Her radical Royalism, her idealizations of desire, suggest her inclinations to cut rather than untie the Gordian knot of political and sexual repression, self-policing morality, and bourgeois materialism. Behn has remained half-outside the canon of English literature precisely because her works resist explanation by the discourses of Richardsonian psychology and Popean formalism. And yet, I would argue, we cannot rehistoricize Restoration drama without recognizing the significance of her plays. They bring us face to face with our complicity in the economies of sociosexual repression that she satirizes and seeks to transcend.

Notes

1. Whig interpretations of Restoration literature persist in a variety of forms, some quite compelling. See, for example, Zimbardo 277–88, who draws on the work of Reiss to argue against the significance of Behn's plays in favor of her contributions to the developing genre of the novel. On the relation of dramatic form to the rise of the novel, see Brown.

2. Behn uses the terms *Tory* and *Whig* frequently in her prefaces and dedications in both specifically political and broadly ideological ways. In this essay, I use these terms to suggest that her ideological concerns go beyond narrow questions of party loyalty. I discuss the relationship of politics to ideology in the Restoration in *Two-Edg'd Weapons* 41–48. Behn wrote other plays during the period and, at least since part 1 of *The Rover* (1677), had made explicit connections between loyalty, libertinism, and the problematics of masculine sexuality and feminine desire. In concentrating on these three comedies I hope to provide a means to discuss the ways in which gender, class, and politics relate in other of her works.

3. On the complexities of Behn's sociopolitical stance, see Markley and Rothenberg.

4. Finke argues that Behn explicitly challenges the standards of critical value that were commonplace in the late seventeenth century.

5. For recent interpretations of Behn's plays, see Langdell, Pearson, DeRitter, and Gallagher, "Masked Woman." On Behn's relations with her patrons, see Payne.

6. See Lacan, particularly 123–36, and Rose's introduction 32–38. Kristeva (191–208) deals with the problems of idealization in libertinism. I should emphasize that I am arguing for Behn's rejection of Lacanian models of sexuality, not my own. My purpose is not to use Behn's plays to confirm or deny postulates of Lacanian psychoanalysis but to indicate ways in which Behn's comedies slip out from under definitive theoretical as well as thematic formulations.

7. Gallagher, "Masked Woman," has called attention to the ways in which Behn metaphorically describes her position as a woman writer in terms of prostitution and the significance of her ironic reading of the masculinist construction of women-as-prostitutes in *The Lucky Chance.* In "Embracing the Absolute," however, Gallagher presents a less convincing reading of the politics of feminine identity—one that presupposes an "absolutism" divorced from the politics and ideological warfare of late-seventeenth-century Britain.

8. The significance of Bakhtin's concept of dialogics for Restoration drama is discussed in my *Two-Edg'd Weapons* 17–29. To some extent, working on Behn has led me to reconsider the implications of my critical vocabulary in that earlier study. I would emphasize that my use of dialogy and monology does not imply a value judgment about the relative merits of Etherege, Wycherley, and Behn; the terms *dialogical* and *monological* are descriptive rather than evaluative. I would

argue that Behn is attempting a fundamentally different form of comedy from those developed by Etherege and Wycherley and that to describe her plays by the same standards that we use to describe theirs distorts her intentions and downgrades her achievement.

9. I argue for ironic portrayals of Dorimant and Horner in *Two-Edg'd Weapons* 121–37, 159–77. The intractability of these characters to analysis has been something of a commonplace in criticism of Etherege's and Wycherley's plays since the 1970s.

10. Other Royalist plays produced during this period include John Crowne's *City Politiques* (1683), Thomas Southerne's *The Loyal Brother* (1682), Thomas D'Urfey's *Sir Barnaby Whigg* (1681), *The Royalist* (1682), and John Dryden's and Nathaniel Lee's collaborative *The Duke of Guise* (1682). For Behn's account of the reception accorded *The Roundheads*, see *Works* 1: 337–39.

11. The ideological implications of the Restoration for English literature in the 1660s have been studied by Jose. Behn's desire to draw historical parallels between 1660 and 1681 leads her to reintroduce a good deal of the imagery of martyrdom, resurrection, and millennial expectation into her dedications to *The Rover, Part II,* and *The Roundheads;* see particularly 1: 114; 1: 339–40.

12. See Neill for a discussion of the problem of Restoration attitudes toward the generation of the 1630s.

13. Lady Galliard's struggle may, in some respects, reflect the difficult relationship Behn found herself in with John Hoyle in the late 1670s and early 1680s, which she describes in poems such as "On Desire" and *Love Letters to a Gentleman.* See Duffy 130–39.

Works Cited

Armstrong, Nancy. *Desire and Domestic Fiction: A Political History of the Novel.* New York: Oxford UP, 1987.

Behn, Aphra. *The Works of Aphra Behn.* Ed. Montague Summers. 6 vols. 1915. New York: Phaeton, 1967.

Brown, Laura. *English Dramatic Form, 1660–1760: An Essay in Generic History.* New Haven: Yale UP, 1981.

de Certeau, Michel. *The Practice of Everyday Life.* Trans. Steven F. Rendall. Berkeley and Los Angeles: U of California P, 1984.

DeRitter, Jones. "The Gypsy, the Rover, and the Wanderer: Aphra Behn's Revision of Thomas Killigrew." *Restoration* 10 (1986): 82–92.

Duffy, Maureen. *The Passionate Shepherdess: Aphra Behn, 1640–1689.* New York: Avon, 1977.

Finke, Laurie. "Aphra Behn and the Ideological Construction of Restoration Literary Theory." *Rereading Aphra Behn: History, Theory, and Criticism.* Ed. Heidi Hutner. Charlottesville: UP of Virginia, 1993. 17–43.

Foucault, Michel. *The History of Sexuality.* Vol. 1. Trans. Robert Hurley. New York: Pantheon, 1978.

Gallagher, Catherine. "Embracing the Absolute: The Politics of the Female Subject in Seventeenth-Century England." *Genders* 1 (1988): 24–29.

———. "Who Was That Masked Woman? The Prostitute and the Playwright in the Comedies of Aphra Behn." *Women's Studies* 15 (1988): 23–42.

Hill, Christopher. *The Collected Essays of Christopher Hill.* Vol. 1. Brighton, Eng.: Harvester, 1985.

Jose, Nicholas. *Ideas of the Restoration in English Literature, 1660–1671.* Cambridge: Harvard UP, 1984.

Kristeva, Julia. *Tales of Love.* Trans. Leon S. Roudiez. New York: Columbia UP, 1987.

Lacan, Jacques. *Feminine Sexuality: Jacques Lacan and the école freudienne.* Trans. Jacqueline Rose. Ed. Juliet Mitchell and Jacqueline Rose. New York: Norton, 1982.

Langdell, Cheri Davis. "Aphra Behn and Sexual Politics: A Dramatist's Discourse with Her Audience." *Drama, Sex, and Politics.* Ed. James Redmond. Cambridge: Cambridge UP, 1985. 109–28.

Markley, Robert. *Two-Edg'd Weapons: Style and Ideology in the Comedies of Etherege, Wycherley, and Congreve.* Oxford: Clarendon, 1988.

Markley, Robert, and Molly Rothenberg. "Contestations of Nature: Aphra Behn's 'The Golden Age' and the Sexualizing of Politics." *Rereading Aphra Behn: History, Theory, and Criticism.* Ed. Heidi Hutner. Charlottesville: UP of Virginia, 1993. 301–21.

Neill, Michael. "Heroic Heads and Humble Tails: Sex, Politics, and the Restoration Comic Rake." *Eighteenth Century: Theory and Interpretation* 24 (1983): 115–39.

Payne, Deborah C. " 'Poets shall by Patron-Poets Live': Aphra Behn and Patronage." *Curtain Calls: Women Dramatists, 1660–1800.* Ed. Mary Anne Schofield and Cecilia Macheski. Athens: Ohio UP, 1990. 105–19.

Pearson, Jacqueline. *The Prostituted Muse: Images of Women and Women Dramatists, 1642–1737.* New York: St. Martin's, 1988.

Reich, Wilhelm. *The Function of the Orgasm: Sex-Economic Problems of Biological Energy.* Trans. Vincent R. Carfagno. New York: Farrar, 1961.

Reiss, Timothy. *The Discourse of Modernism.* Ithaca, N.Y.: Cornell UP, 1982.

Zimbardo, Rose. "Aphra Behn in Search of the Novel." *Studies in Eighteenth-Century Culture* 19 (1989): 277–88.

THE RAKE'S PROGRESS REVISITED:
POLITICS AND COMEDY
IN THE RESTORATION

RICHARD BRAVERMAN

On 25 May 1660 Charles II stepped ashore on Dover beach, bringing an end to his long exile. An enthusiastic crowd was on hand to greet the young king, who was officially welcomed by General George Monck and the mayor of Dover. Four days later Charles entered London, where he was cheered by large and jubilant crowds as the royal procession slowly made its way from the City to Whitehall.[1] The spirit of the miraculous touched off by the king's return was contagious, spreading from London to the rural communities in the first days of June; it continued for several weeks after, during which time the Crown had more to fear from its drunken supporters than from the remnants of the army (Hutton 126). Before the high spirits had ebbed, the Crown moved to revive the trappings of monarchy in order to restore the appearance of the old regime. Court ceremony was resurrected after a hiatus of nearly twenty years and with it the rituals that reestablished the sacred status of the king's person. The most conspicuous of these was the practice of touching for the king's evil: recognizing its value in reasserting the mystique of monarchy, Charles touched nearly a thousand of his subjects over the course of two days in mid-June, presenting them with "gold pendants and assurances of miraculous recovery" (Hutton 128).

Later that summer, Charles acknowledged the value of another cultural institution within the Crown's purview when he granted theatrical patents to Thomas Killigrew and William Davenant. Grasping the ideological value of the stage, Charles took an active interest in Restoration theater from the start (Sutherland 251). Not long after issuing Killigrew and Davenant patents, he persuaded Charles Boyle, later earl of Orrery, to write a rhymed play in imitation of French tragedy (Clark 2: 23). The result was *The Gen-*

erall, a thinly veiled allegory commemorating the Restoration and its hero, George Monck. *The Generall* was a hit, but it was soon overshadowed by Orrery's next play, *King Henry the Fifth,* which was performed in costumes that had been worn by royalty in the coronation of Charles II.[2] With *King Henry the Fifth* the heroic play came into its own as a vehicle for the aura of the restored court. But this popular genre was far from its sole theatrical vehicle, because comedy had already been summoned to convey the spirit of restoration as well. Abraham Cowley and Robert Howard were among the first to write what might be termed comedies of restoration, Cowley with *The Cutter of Coleman Street* and Howard with *The Committee;* but the first true Restoration comedy did not appear until 1664, when Etherege's *The Comical Revenge; or, Love in a Tub* was produced.

If *The Comical Revenge* announced the arrival of the Restoration mode, it was also significant for the evocation of one of its characteristic figures, the theatrical libertine.[3] Critics who have charted the development of the figure, and the Cavalier values he represents, conveniently divide his progress into three distinct phases.[4] In the first, which runs through the early seventies, he appears as a broadly comic figure who breathes new life into a society recently freed from the Puritan yoke. Here he resembles the new Cavalier of the Interregnum, and he behaves according to a code of manners that prompted Robert Jordan some years ago to label him "extravagant."[5] In the early seventies extravagance generally turns to cynicism as the Cavalier, particularly in his strongest evocations, is transformed into the predatory rake-hero who exploits wit and sexual presence at the expense of comic potential. This, the period of the great libertine comedies, was relatively short-lived, running roughly from *Marriage à la Mode* (1671) to *Mr. Limberham* (1678). In the traditional scheme, the libertine's development leaps directly to the nineties, but as revisionist critics have recently shown, the figure reappeared in the comedies of Behn, Durfey, Ravenscroft, Lee, Otway, Crowne, and Sedley, among others. Behn in particular put him to striking use, notably in the plays she wrote in the wake of the Exclusion Crisis, plays that gave new life to the Puritan-Cavalier axis prevalent in the sixties (see Robert Markley's contribution to this collection). But the tide, despite its importance, was relatively short-lived as comedy on the whole suffered a marked decline in the 1680s, when few new works appeared in an unfavorable climate for the theater in general. The genre, however, made a steady comeback in the nineties, and along with it came the libertine. Here, however, the character showed signs of a changed man, particularly in the hands of Whiggish revisionists who in due course transformed him into an *honnête homme* as they reconfigured a new, postrevolutionary erotics of power.[6] The transformation, which precipitated the predatory rake's fall from grace, reflected a postrevolutionary spirit, a spirit, writes Maximillian Novak, that was accompanied at the same time by a broad philosophical shift: "By the 1690s, many libertine ideas had become part of the general philosophy of the Enlightenment" with the result that by the end of the century many of them had become part of a "gentleman's creed" (*Congreve* 42).[7]

With the transformation, the *honnête homme* restored some of the comic potential to the manners idiom that had been undermined in the satiric phase of the seventies. He also restored some of its political potential, particularly, I will argue, in the case of Congreve. The political dimension of Restoration comedy has, I think, been undervalued, yet, as Michael Neill and Nicholas Jose have recently shown, the vehicle could serve as a political medium, too.[8] This essay takes up their lead in an attempt to shed further light on the way that a social figure like the libertine has a political side. Naturally, the comedy of manners does not deal with politics in the manner of the heroic play, yet it is political insofar as it conveys the élan of the court through the charismatic presence of a figure so often affiliated with it. The libertine's status may differ over time (and in the nineties he comes in for a rude political awakening with the Stuart exile), but the idiom in which it is inscribed finds political expression through a prevalent analogy that it shares with the heroic play: the analogy of the political estate as a landed estate. While the analogy is manifest in the romance, where the royal heir restores patrilineal descent through dynastic marriage, it serves comedy, too, with its latent political end displaced into social conflicts over women and the property they control (see Helen Burke's contribution to this volume).

This pattern of displacement, I will argue, follows the general contour of the rake's progress from the sixties to the nineties. The analogy is particularly clear in the first part of this essay, which deals in turn with three comedies from the sixties that incorporate the action of restoration itself. In the mid-seventies, however, the analogy recedes as the restoration trope becomes more or less anachronistic following the defeat of the Indulgence and the confirmation of the Test. When Catholicism replaced dissent as the principal threat to church and state, the older configuration of Puritan and Cavalier was overshadowed for a time, although it was not forgotten as the Royalist reaction to the Exclusion Crisis would testify. But in the mid-seventies the growing rift between court and country took precedence, and it was in that gap that the rakish libertine tested a range of social and political values associated with the court. In this regard, writes Jose (140–41), the best comedies of this period were attuned to historical and political preoccupations despite the fact that they were displaced to the social sphere:

> In these plays the focus has shifted from historical and political my-
> thology to a version of *social* reality, yet the idealized language of
> Restoration political and religious thought has largely, ironically, been
> maintained. This allows the playwrights at their best to achieve a dis-
> interested, yet penetrating insight into the complexities of their age,
> impossible for the apologising or chastising "serious" plays.

Jose may be a bit harsh on the "apologetics" of so-called serious plays, but he is in tune with the comedies when he stresses the evocation of broader concerns than mere social ones by means of ironic displacement. It is in that sense that the libertine can, I think, be seen as the avatar of a "sovereign" idiom in which autonomy is not simply a social but a political preoccupation as well. It is this concern that defines the libertine's subse-quent development, because in the nineties the postrevolutionary shift in what I have termed the "erotics of power" turns once again to the figure as a vehicle for "historical and political mythology." The development, in which the rakish hero is displaced by the *honnête homme,* parallels the gradual acceptance of the new dynastic idiom, so that as he comes into his own in the social sphere, the "reformed" libertine takes symbolic posses-sion of the political estate at the same time. This phase proceeds by varying degrees in the works of Cibber, Vanbrugh, Shadwell, and Southerne; but as an incremental progression that reflects the political climate it is, I think, clearest in the case of Congreve, who creates the most fully realized comic hero of the time in Mirabell. Mirabell not only displaces the old libertine in Fainall; he has genuine comic powers that synthesize a new sociopolitical paradigm consistent with the political views of the court Whigs. And as part and parcel of that process, he provides the Whig answer to the Stuart élan at the same time.

"The best 'Restoration Comedy,' " Michael Neill has written, "is properly so called not merely from historical convenience, but because, in its sly, allusive fashion, it is actively concerned with the nature of 'restoration' itself" (120). Neill's assertion is particularly true of some of the first Restoration comedies, Cowley's *The Cutter of Coleman Street* (1661), Robert Howard's *The Committee* (1662), Etherege's *The Comical Revenge* (1664), and Sedley's *The Mulberry Garden* (1668), works that complement the political message of heroic romance—that the natural order of things was restored with the monarchy—at the same time they part from its rhetorical world.[9] The first of these, *The Cutter of Coleman Street* and *The Committee*, are comedies of restoration, yet they are too heavily indebted to earlier traditions to be considered true Restoration comedies. That claim properly goes to *The Comical Revenge; or, Love in a Tub*.[10] Despite its historical importance, the play has generally been overlooked as a comedy of restoration. Yet it has a political edge that cuts against Puritan and old Cavalier alike in the character of the libertine, Sir Frederick Frollick, who embodies the vitality of the new age that displaces the moribund world of the Commonwealth.

The Comical Revenge has an unusual triple plot that incorporates three genres as it weaves together distinct levels of romantic action, farcical intrigue, and comedic maneuvering. The highest plot level is occupied by a Cavalier romance that dramatizes the rivalry of Lord Beaufort, a new Cavalier, and Colonel Bruce, an old Cavalier, for Lord Bevil's daughter, the Lady Graciana. Its romantic idealizations are sharply countered in ethos and action by a Middletonian farce in which two Royalist sharpers, Palmer and Wheadle, plot the ruin of a Cromwellian knight, Sir Nicholas Cully. Both the romance and farce plots are subordinated to the comedy of manners that features the libertine-courtier Sir Frederick Frollick, who pursues, or to put it more accurately, is pursued by, Lord Bevil's sister, the Widow Rich. Although he goes unchallenged in the comic plot, the libertine discovers a mock rival—Sir Nicholas Cully—in the farce plot, where he descends to "regain" the political estate from the Puritan knight who seeks the Widow Rich's estate. Sir Nicholas, however, woos the widow by design rather than desire. Having been swindled out of a thousand pounds at cards by Wheadle and Palmer, he is talked into impersonating Sir Frederick Frollick in order to capture the widow's fortune and pay off his debt. But the plot is discovered by Sir Frederick, who marries Cully, Palmer, and Wheadle to his former mistresses. Having defeated his "rival," the libertine at last takes possession of the widow and her property, the real estate of England. It is a comic triumph that legitimates the Cavalier and, by his association with its values, the restored court.

Although the three plots of *The Comical Revenge* are thematically linked, the levels are distinguished by respective patterns of sexual politics that express their sociopolitical ethos. As a result, the rhetorical style and narrative action of each plot are defined by its feminine object of desire: in the romance, the chaste Graciana symbolizes the status quo ante desired by Bruce but eclipsed by Beaufort; in the farce, mistress Grace represents a corrupt prize that elicits the public humiliation of the Royalist conspirators; and in the comic plot the Widow Rich favors the opportunist, who seizes the real estate of England. Since the comic plot is the central plot in the play's overall design, the Widow Rich is distinguished by an important difference from her feminine counterparts, whose names associate them with the feminine idealizations of Cavalier romance. Only Graciana is an ideal heroine, and even then she is satirically doubled in the farce by her namesake, the prostitute Grace; consequently, the parodic pairing equates the lofty sentiments of romance with the lascivious passions of farce. They are equated because all displays of passion are treated alike as expressions of self-aggrandizement and failure: Bruce loses the duel for Graciana and even in his freedom is a reminder of the Royalist defeat and the Cromwellian yoke; Sir Nicholas Cully learns that he cannot control the Widow Rich's fortune, let alone his own; and Palmer and Wheadle discover that they are subject to the game of chance that they think they control. All of these failures are set against the triumph of Sir Frederick, who angles and wins the Widow Rich—and her estate—with expected aplomb. For this reason, Sir Frederick gets the last word of the play. But it is the Widow Rich who delivers the epilogue, and in the brief speech that she delivers behind her husband-to-be's back she adds a final twist to the play. While she accepts her husband and the restored court, she has nevertheless made provisions to control her estate, and with it, Sir Frederick:

> Sir *Frederick,* now I am reveng'd on you;
> For all your Frollick Wit, y'are cozen'd too:
> I have made over all my Wealth to these
> Honest Gentlemen; they are my Trustees.
> Yet, Gentlemen, if you are pleas'd, you may
> Suply his wants, and not your Trust betray.
>   (italics reversed)

Before she married Sir Frederick, the widow exercised her right to keep her estate from her husband, vesting it in trustees who have the responsibility for its maintenance. In doing so, she is protected under the doctrine of separate use, which permitted women to retain legal ownership by assigning beneficiary control. As J. H. Baker explains: "The Court of Chancery enforced such trusts by giving the married woman beneficiary the same independence of ownership, in respect of the equitable estate, as if she had been single" (397). Exercising her rights as a *femme sole,* the widow has entrusted her estate to the men of the audience, whom she entreats to supply her husband's wants according to the conditions of the trust. But why is it she makes the men of the audience trustees, and what is it they are supposed, or able, to pay out? Their "*Wealth*" is, first of all, applause, the admiration that the widow, and Etherege, believe the trustees should bestow upon the hero and the play. But the retention of the trust is at the same time a politically subversive gesture, suggesting that England will be governed only upon condition of her will. Deeply attracted to Sir Frederick, she is wary of his commitment because she knows the libertine to be a man devoted above all to personal pleasure. But given the prospect of his vitality, and the fact that there are no other options on the horizon, she is willing to chance her heart—though not her head. Her reservations suggest that her trust in Sir Frederick, like the nation's in the restored court, is conditional, meaning that the libertine will retain it only as long as he can sustain his performance.

The nation's trust was severely tested by the series of disasters that struck in succession between 1665 and 1667: first came the plague, which at its height in the summer of 1665 claimed more than fifty thousand lives; then the great fire, which destroyed twelve thousand houses and eighty-nine churches; and finally the invasion by the Dutch fleet under Admiral de Ruyter. The Chatham disaster led to the first political crisis of the restored court, but when Charles gave in to the demand for Clarendon's impeachment, he defused the situation and soon regained the popularity he enjoyed before the crisis. The episode had a measurable effect on literature, in particular the satiric poetry that circulated during the crisis; but official culture continued to reflect the ideals of the restored court. Heroic plays continued to be written, and the libertine appeared as a consensual figure in comedies of the succeeding few years. This was particularly true of two plays that appeared in 1668, Etherege's *She Would If She Could* and Sedley's *The Mulberry Garden.*[11]

She Would If She Could translates the restoration theme into a generational conflict of young Cavaliers and aging Puritans who are played, respectively, as wit and humors characters. The play opens shortly after the principal humors characters, Lady Cockwood and her husband, the Cromwellian knight Sir Oliver Cockwood, arrive in London. The couple hope to take the pleasures of the town: Sir Oliver expects to play the libertine with his country companion, Sir Joslin Jolly; Lady Cockwood, the "she" of the title, hopes to satisfy her sexual longings by seducing the young Cavalier, Courtall. When Courtall is interested in other prey, namely Sir Joslin's niece, Lady Cockwood forges letters to break them up, and when that fails, she complains to Sir Oliver that Courtall has made unseemly advances. But she finds no satisfaction, and her frustration has a political edge because her husband has gone to seed as a vestige of the Commonwealth, which resounds in his name.

While Lady Cockwood pursues her amorous designs, Sir Oliver searches for the delights promised by Sir Joslin: "Brother, I have bespoke Dinner, and engag'd Mr. *Rake-hell*, the little smart Gentleman I have often promis'd thee to make thee acquainted withal, to bring a whole Bevy of Damsels" (III.ii.20–23). But the "Bevy" never arrives, and Sir Oliver is never put to the test. Nor does he seem fit for it, as he himself admits in a drunken song he sings with Sir Joslin:[12]

> Love and Wenching are Toys,
> Fit to please beardless Boys,
> Th'are sports we hate worse than a Leaguer;
> When we visit a Miss,
> We still brag how we kiss,
> But 'tis with a Bottle we fegue her.
> (III.iii.407–12; italics omitted)

A mock libertine at play in the tavern, Sir Oliver is as impotent at home, where he is unable to enforce his husbandly prerogatives even though he has pledged to fight a "perpetual civil War" (III.iii.267). But he cannot contain his wife by conventional means because she makes him "more impotent than an Eunuch" (II.ii.143), nor is he any more successful with the "military" option, registering his frustration in the threat he issues to the servant, Sentry: "I will have thee executed for petty Treason; thy skin flay'd off, stuff'd and hung up in my Hall in the Country" (II.ii.148–50). A braggart soldier, Sir Oliver is unable to wield a husband's arbitrary power, but the fact that he speaks the language of paternal rule distinguishes him from the representative of the younger generation, Courtall. Sir Oliver is too much of a fool to be his serious rival, and for that reason he has no claim on the political estate, which passes from him to the libertine in the double pairing that concludes the comic action. The spirit of appeasement extends to the Cockwoods, too, since both husband and wife will be spared further humiliation. The Act of Oblivion that Sir Joslin alludes to, and that Sir Oliver importunes as the plays closes, confirms the comic ambience that Courtall stewards. And in the face of obvious political irony, it reconfirms a satiric assumption that underlies *The Comical Revenge*—that the Commonwealth collapsed under the weight of its own corruption.

The passage from Commonwealth to Restoration was the focus of another comedy produced in 1668, *The Mulberry Garden*. While it shares the ambience of *She Would If She Could*, *The Mulberry Garden* has more in common with *The Comical Revenge,* because it resolves the social conflict leading to the Restoration by means of a divided plot that contains a comedy of manners and a Cavalier romance.[13] In the romance plot, two Cavaliers, Eugenio and Philander, are pursued by parliamentary forces who suspect them as Royalist conspirators. The Cavaliers are suspected to be in London because they are in love with the daughters of the Puritan knight Sir Samuel Forecast, who hopes to marry them to men in better standing with the Interregnum government than the impoverished Cavaliers. It appears that he will get his way when the Cavaliers are captured and arrested in act 4. But they are soon free when it is announced that General Monck has declared his support for King Charles. Foiled, Forecast can no longer stand between his daughters and the Cavaliers, whose unions reinforce the restoration of the political estate to its rightful lord.

While *The Mulberry Garden* closes in the Cavalier romance, it opens in the comedy of manners. The comic plot sets the Puritan knight, Sir Samuel Forecast, against the Cavalier, Sir John Everyoung, whose name identifies him as the spirit that defines the Cavaliers. The difference of Puritan and Cavalier is summed up in the opening scene, in which Sir Samuel and Sir John discuss paternal responsibility with regard to their marriageable daughters. Forecast believes in keeping a tight rein, while Everyoung answers that such a policy can lead only to disaster, because "those women who have been least us'd to Liberty [are] most apt to abuse it, when they come to't" (I.i.68–69). In the course of the action it is Everyoung's tolerant view of family government that wins out, even though Sir John does not participate directly in the comic action. However, the spirit that he represents is carried on by the young Cavalier, Ned Wildish, who courts his own daughter Olivia.

In the meantime, Sir Samuel opportunistically pursues a wealthy widow, but he is foiled when he is arrested on suspicion of harboring the two Cavaliers, who were arrested at his house.[14] Sir John Everyoung bails Sir Samuel out of the tower just in time for the dispirited knight to witness the betrothal of his daughters to the Cavaliers. Meanwhile, in the comic plot, Wildish wins Olivia, renewing the spirit of the restored court that is passed on to him from the archetypal Cavalier, Everyoung. The "*great shout within*" that closes the play (V.v.193 *s.d.*) reminds the audience that General Monck was the hero of the Restoration. But Sedley, like Etherege, revises history to imply that the irrepressible Cavalier, as much as the timely action of Monck, was responsible for the events of 1660.

In the plays from the sixties just examined, the libertine, despite his antics, has a broadly comic capacity whose consensual status resonates in the discourse of restoration. Constructed upon the political difference of Puritan and Cavalier, that potential continued to be resonant through the early seventies until the political wind shifted with the parliamentary reaction to the Declaration of Indulgence. What followed, in political terms, was a renewal of the earlier division between country and court, though it was fueled this time by the widespread suspicion that the Crown was in favor of pro-Catholic policies at home and abroad. While the political fissure had a manifest effect on satiric writing, it had a latent effect on the literature of libertinage, in which the social division of country and court was conveyed through the erotics of power. The libertine continued to assert Cavalier values, accommodating them, however, by means of the social antithesis that underlay the majority of libertine plays of the seventies, town and country.[15] The antagonism, conveyed through wit, manners, and sexuality, abrogated the comic potential of the libertine by virtue of his ambivalent relationship to the values of the restored court. But in spite of a manifest contempt for heroic idealizations he nonetheless held fast to courtly-aristocratic values, none of which was more important than his eroding autonomy that mirrored the predicament of the Crown. The Crown, needless to say, was far more secure, but the libertine was a barometer of its ideological underpinnings insofar as he projected the climate of growing antagonism through his own problematic independence—which could be measured in the seductive power of his own "sovereign" will. Given this scenario, the libertine plays of the mid-seventies were less visibly political than earlier Cavalier comedies that had drawn upon the state-estate analogy. But the works of this phase were nonetheless political, and in reflecting the élan of the court they presented a contradictory picture.

In his influential essay on the "libertine offensive" of the seventies, Novak argues that the group of plays that appeared in the relatively brief span from 1671 to 1677 were inspired by *Marriage à la Mode* ("Margery" 3). Not only did the play initiate the vogue for the marriage debate that set town and country at odds, it also evoked a libertine far more skeptical of conventional mores than had hitherto been the norm. What might be called a tonal shift has been widely noted, but Novak adds an important twist to the account, one that implies a nexus between politics and culture, when he suggests that the impetus for the play originated within the court itself. It was, in this sense, something of a reminder that its habitués considered themselves denizens of a world apart. That world was predictably condemned as irredeemably corrupt by "country" moralists, as the pamphlets written in response to the "libertine offensive" attest. But as excess always looks different at the center than it does from the margin, whatever the real or imagined excesses of the court, it remained, as Dryden for one put it, the provenance of a far more refined culture than England had previously known:

> Now, if any ask me, whence it is that our conversation is so much refin'd? I must freely, and without flattery, ascribe it to the Court; and, in it, particularly to the King; whose example gives a law to it. His own misfortunes, and the nations, afforded him an opportunity, which is rarely allow'd to Sovreign Princes, I mean of travelling, and being conversant in the most polish'd Courts of *Europe;* and, thereby, of cultivating a Spirit, which was form'd by Nature to receive the impressions of a gallant and generous education. At his Return, he found a Nation lost as much in Barbarism as in Rebellion. And as the excellency of his Nature forgave the one, so the excellency of his manners reform'd the other. The desire of imitating so great a pattern, first waken'd the dull and heavy spirits of the English, from their natural reserv'dness; loosen'd them, from their stiff forms of conversation; and made them easy and plyant to each other in discourse. Thus, insensibly, our way of living became more free.[16]

It is tempting to take Dryden's prose as a brief apologia in itself. In transforming the defeat at Worcester into an opportunity for the king to see the world, he reminds his readers of royal hardship to make cultural capital out of the exilic past. The king had no choice but to make the best of circumstances, but the gesture deftly feints in the direction of France to emphasize "conversation" in the broadest sense. Stiffness and ease, these are politically as well as socially charged, and in the seventies, through the developing antithesis of court and country, they were accommodated to an ideological conflict in which the theatrical libertine played an important role in reinforcing Dryden's assumption that "our way of living had become more free" under Stuart rule. That freedom was conveyed in venues beyond the theater, but on the stage it was expressed, among other places, in works of the early to mid-seventies that appeared in the wake of *Marriage à la Mode* (1671), the most notable of these *Epsom Wells* (1672), *The Morning Ramble* (1674), *The Mall* (1674), *The Country Wife* (1675), and *The Man of Mode* (1676). Such works sustained the courtly ethos that had been renewed in the earlier comedies of restoration, although they do not share the dynastic idiom of others such as *The Comical Revenge* and *The Mulberry Garden*. The pursuit of women and their fortunes naturally remained a principal trope here (as Burke points out in her essay in this collection), but it did not return in its full political form until Exclusion, when the dynastic question revived the earlier matrix of political antagonism. It was, instead, the antagonism of court and country that underlay the comedies of the seventies. Antithetical in their embrace of courtly values, and ambivalent toward the libertine while presenting him as a figure of social emulation, they convey a deep skepticism toward the metaphorics of restoration. Skepticism of this sort infects the dramatic romance, too, as such figures as Almanzor and Aureng-Zebe begin to express themselves in the idiom of libertine self-interest and excess.[17]

If the luster of heroic individualism declines with the romance, there is little question that it degenerates even more dramatically in comedy; yet rakish types hold fast to the principles and privileges of an honor culture, even if they do not share its idealism. They do so because of the vital tie that binds them with their heroic counterparts, a tie that cuts across both social and political spheres: autonomy. The sine qua non of gentility, autonomy is, in its analogous political form, the essence of sovereignty. Sovereigns are by definition independent, their power inherent rather than derived. The libertine aspires to a social variation of this, a variation registered in the erotics of power insofar as his desire for sexual dominion displaces his "sovereignty" to the social sphere (see the essay by Harold Weber in this

volume on the problem of Charles II's sexual proclivities and their concomitant analogies of political potency). If sexual politics takes the place of
dynastic politics here, it is nonetheless clear that the rakish libertine wants
to maintain his autonomy and the status quo that sustains it. John Traugott
puts the matter a little differently on the analogy of rakish egotism: "For
all his insistence upon the absurdity of life, the rake is a creature of the Restoration's powerful nostalgia for the pompous virtues of the heroic play"
(388). The rakish hero is struck with "powerful nostalgia" at the same time
that the autonomy of the Crown was subject to dynastic pressures that
eroded confidence in the Restoration consensus. The rakish libertine re-
asserts the spirit, if not the conviction, of that consensus, and he does so in
egotistical rather than comic fashion. As Neill points out, he "is an instinc-
tive 'tyrant' whose insurrection against the civil order of society aims at
the usurpation of absolute authority; for arbitrary pleasure, as Collier implied and Hobbes knew, requires the exercise of an arbitrary power" (132).
While a number of candidates fit the bill, none internalizes the sovereign
ego in its contradictory aspects more completely than Horner, who seems
to "conquer" with the ease of a Don Juan. His power, however, does not
lie in feigned impotence because his disguise only provides a convenient
vehicle for his seductive prowess. He has what women want and what their
husbands cannot give them, and he provides it to sustain his own reputation. In this respect the play is about honor as a value above and beyond
the marriage bed. The women he seduces may be obsessed with reputation,
but he is driven by a more traditional form of honor. It is honor that drives
him in the pursuit of what seems to be echoed in his name, and for that
reason he must not slacken his expenditure if he is to sustain his standing,
so to speak, which he renews by taking others' honor.

When Horner convenes the principals (minus Alithea and Harcourt) at
his lodgings in the last act, he seems to have accomplished that goal. The
dinner party for dishonored wives and cuckolded husbands confirms him
as the master of a sexual economy that brings him honor at others' expense
as Lady Fidget reminds him: "[P]eople eat most heartily of another man's
meat, that is, what they do not pay for" (Wycherley, *Country Wife* V.iv.83–
84). Throughout, Horner has eaten "of another man's meat" without paying for it, and in the final scene he serves up his "benefactors" one last time.
In spite of his apparent control, however, he nearly loses his grip on the
situation when Margery fails to recognize that she cannot have Horner all
to herself. But the dishonored wives silence her, just as Horner silences the

men whose honor he holds. Horner is honor, and he gets the last word as
the play's sovereign:

> Vain fops but court, and dress, and keep a pother,
> To pass for women's men with one another;
> But he who aims by women to be priz'd,
> First by the men, you see, must be despis'd.
>
> (V.iv.408–11)

That Horner is "despis'd" by the husbands he cuckolds is obvious; his need
to dominate men through women is, on the other hand, an expression of
the rivalry that he projects onto the husbands who despise him. An "absolutist" in Neill's sense, he seeks this double mastery in order to assert what
turns out to be an elusive autonomy.[18] Though Sir Jasper and Pinchwife
are comic butts, they seem to pose a threat to Horner's status quo insofar
as they have gentry status. Both, moreover, are financially secure, Fidget
having profited through trade while Pinchwife traded in the rakish life for a
more secure place. Horner, meanwhile, clings to rakish privileges, exploiting his status to win what others have earned by more legitimate means.
So, while Sir Jasper and Pinchwife bring on their fate by delivering their
wives, providing their antagonist with the symbolic sustenance by which
he survives, the ease of Horner's "conquests" does not entirely mask the
animosity that moves him. It moves him because these men, who fit more
securely into civil society than he is able to, pose a challenge to his autonomy—his sovereignty, as it were. But then, it should be remembered
that his power is seductive rather than coercive. Nonetheless, his predicament resonates in contemporary satiric images of the king himself, images
that undercut the seductive illusion of Stuart power that the Widow Rich
had suspected some years earlier in *The Comical Revenge*.

If conquest for Horner is inscribed in the carpe diem tradition, he never
considers a future beyond the status quo. Yet he still holds to the principles
of an honor culture even if he denies its idealizations. The same, however,
cannot be said of Captain Manly of *The Plain Dealer*, who is enraged at a
society that does not recognize the honor he believes himself to uniquely
possess. *The Plain Dealer* is not generally thought of as a libertine comedy,
but the figure is central to the play: he is divided between two characters, Manly and Freeman, whose names reinforce the libertine sine qua
non, manliness. Seeking to restore the patriarchal status quo to a society
that has in effect been feminized, the two are united in the libertine quali-

ties they possess: Freeman is the sly fortune hunter, Manly the misogyn. Together they pursue designs that complement each other through sexual politics: Freeman vies for the Widow Blackacre's estate, while Manly seeks vengeance upon his former mistress, Olivia, for betraying him. Having left Olivia under the protection of his friend Vernish, Manly sets out to punish the two for having fallen into the trap that he set up. In so doing, he undermines the bonds of civil society: male friendship and heterosexual love. But the primary target of his wrath is Olivia, who has spent his fortune and taken up with his friend. She is the blot on his reputation, and in plotting to disguise himself in order to gain access to her bed, he goes so far as to entertain thoughts of taking her by force.

His anger, while directed at Olivia, is symptomatic of the deeper rage that he has against a society that does not reward honor as he anachronistically defines it. Manly expects to be recognized by the principle of intrinsic worth (see James Thompson's contribution to this volume), a principle he locates in the utopian past. He sets out this view in an early conversation with Freeman, who remarks upon the fact that Manly treats Lord Plausible "with very little ceremony":

> A lord! What, thou art one of those who esteem men only by the marks and value fortune has set upon them, and never consider intrinsic worth. But counterfeit honor will not be current with me. I weigh the man, not his title. 'Tis not the king's stamp can make the metal better or heavier. Your lord is a leaden shilling, which you may bend every way; and debases the stamp he bears, instead of being raised by it. (Wycherley, *Plain Dealer* I.178–85)

Manly may hold to intrinsic value, but he consistently violates the principle because, like Molière's misanthrope, he needs the social world that he dismisses. For that reason he is not measured by intrinsic worth at all but by the social value of his reputation. Freeman recognizes this fact to get what he wants, namely the Blackacre estate, but Manly refuses to resort to such mercenary means. In the end he is apparently rewarded when Fidelia reveals her identity and her love. The romance like ending restores a symbolic rather than substantive status quo; the fact that Fidelia is (as her name itself insinuates) complicit in it suggests that the reward the plain dealer gets is precisely the illusion he needs to perpetuate. In this respect he resembles Horner, who is likewise anxious about his autonomy. But while the rake displaces his rivalry with Sir Jasper and Pinchwife as he pursues their wives, Manly embraces the status quo that Fidelia offers. And in doing so he holds on to lost illusions that Horner cavalierly converts for present consumption.

After 1678, writes Robert Hume, there was a "rapid decline in cuckoldry and free gallantry" (*Rakish* 153). But the rakish stage was not closed to developments because, as Markley shows, the figure was subject to revision. In the hands of Behn, in particular, the erotics of power were refigured to fit a post-Exclusion scenario that revived the old Puritan-Cavalier matrix. Its development was both timely and nostalgic; it was also relatively short-lived, because with the Williamite succession the erotics of power shifted once again. That shift, which began with Shadwell's *Squire of Alsatia* and continued in works by Cibber, Congreve, Pix, and others, involved the rakish hero generally with the excesses of the past age, and in the particular case of Congreve, the exiled Stuarts. As Hume puts it: "There are rakes aplenty in nineties comedy, but they tend to be viewed with a harshness almost unknown twenty years earlier" (*Rakish* 165). He attributes this development for the most part to the social legacy of the Revolution. While there was a concerted effort to reform manners in the postrevolutionary period, just as significant was the ongoing debate that prompted questions of order and obligation within the context of dynastic politics. The debate naturally carried over to the theater, where comedy, like tragedy, registered the effects of revolutionary events, though both did so more to deride the Stuarts than to idealize the new regime.[19] In fact, only by the end of the decade did a major comic hero appear who embodied the revolutionary principles of the Whigs, Mirabell; and in the last part of this essay I trace the development of the *honnête homme* from Congreve's early comedies to *The Way of the World*—in which he presents an answer to the Stuart romance through a charismatic figure who would remain unrivaled in Whig annals until Tom Jones came to life in the wake of The Forty-five nearly half a century later.[20]

Congreve's first comedy, *The Old Bachelour* (1693), contains a sustained critique of the libertine. The play, argues John McComb (361), presents the libertine in various incarnations; but he is always a dissolute figure whose excesses lead to impotence:

> Congreve presents the stock characters of Restoration comedy—the rake, the fop, the railing satirist satirized, and the impotent cuck-

old—as stages in a single life's process. . . . In particular, Congreve shows Bellmour, Vainlove, Heartwell, Fondlewife, and Spintext to be metamorphoses of the same figure, the sexual libertine. Congreve is of course drawing upon the implications of earlier plays, especially the implication that the impotent cuckold has brought his fate upon himself by his youthful excesses. His originality, however, lies in expanding these implications with a satiric anatomy of unbridled lust.

While Congreve casts a shadow over the so-called sexual libertine, he sympathizes with his creation at the same time, conspicuously so in the case of the old bachelor, Heartwell. A "misanthrope and misogynist" (Holland 134), Heartwell falls in love with Bellmour's cast mistress, Silvia, but Bellmour, the master of circumstances, saves him from his fate. If the play presents a sustained critique of libertinage, it nevertheless fails to provide an effectively appealing alternative in the insouciant bonhomie of Bellmour. While he may be measured against the social standard of the *honnête homme*, Bellmour is, after all, an opportunist rather than a master of comic fortune. We sympathize with him as he negotiates the obstacles that confront him, but he offers little in the way of a comic option, so that if the play casts the rakish hero as something of an anachronism, it in no way assures us that circumstances can be anticipated so that excess may be contained and social motion regulated. It is in this sense that I think Harold Love is right when he writes that the play's "concluding tableau is to be seen not as an image of comic renewal, but as a giving of emblematic form to a series of rankings which have been implicit in the play's material since the moment it began" (37).

The problem haunts Congreve's second play, *The Double Dealer* (1694), which takes up some of the issues of *The Old Bachelour* but deals with them in a far more sophisticated manner. Superior to the first in plot, dialogue, and characterization, the play also makes use of a common device in nineties comedy in dividing the libertine figure between two characters: the *honnête homme*, Mellefont, and the cynical rake, Maskwell. Maskwell's double dealing is set in the high aristocratic world in which he is the obvious intruder. The friend and rival of Mellefont, he hopes to rise in it by taking advantage of the fact that the aristocrats who dominate it are, as a class and a dynasty, in serious, if not irreversible, decline. Maskwell's hopes are pinned above all on the ability to exploit Sir Paul Plyant's failure to produce a male heir in order to perpetuate family and dynastic lines.

It is for this reason that Sir Paul turns to Mellefont, whom he hopes will
continue the line by marriage to his daughter Cynthia. The play sets up
the expectation of their union, but in due course it becomes clear that it
is the lowborn upstart who possesses the vitality that not only Mellefont
but the aristocracy in general lack. Maskwell almost carries off his scheme
when he takes possession of Cynthia in the last act, but just as he is about
to succeed with the putative usurpation, Mellefont's uncle, Lord Touchwood, exposes the plot and sends Maskwell off to be punished. Aubrey
Williams interprets the abrupt reversal as evidence of divine providence in
the play's overall design (152). While there is textual support for this reading, it undervalues a critical thematic point stressed by Love: "*The Double
Dealer* . . . is not just a comedy about a pair of lovers, nor just a comedy
about a family, but a comedy about a dynasty and a class" (53). If Love
sees dynasty and class as mutually reinforcing signifiers of the old regime,
as I think he does, then the dynastic theme defines the problem of the play
as the inability of the powers that be to perpetuate the status quo ante.
Love pulls up a bit short of the political implications of his assertion, because in pushing them to their logical end it appears that the play conveys
the corruption of a dying line that is both sexually licentious and symbolically impotent by drawing upon the predominant political subtext of the
later seventeenth century, the succession. It is in this light that *The Double
Dealer* questions the principle of genealogical inheritance as the linchpin
of familial and political order through the analogy of state and estate. But
while it conveys the internal corruption of the old regime—with an eye, I
think, to the Revolution settlement—it does not offer a legitimate (in terms
of both character and descent) alternative to it. Love observes that the play
shows "the ways in which a family decays or somehow proves unsatisfactory in one generation and is renewed more happily in the next" (50), but
the new regime presumably to follow from the dynastic union of Olivia
and Mellefont is no more than a marginal improvement at best. Mellefont
plays the *honnête homme*, but he lacks the necessary élan to either repair
or transform a declining line. Add to this the providential conclusion that
Lord Touchwood brings off, and it appears that *The Double Dealer*, like
The Old Bachelour, cannot elicit the demonstrable alternative to the old
regime that the play seems implicitly to call for.

Congreve's next play, *Love for Love* (1695), features another conflict
between old and new regimes, but like *The Double Dealer* it does not
offer a legitimate comic hero either, even though it presents an appeal-

ing *honnête homme* in Valentine. Like *The Double Dealer, Love for Love* is built on a generational conflict that carries a political subtext. While the rivalry between Sir Samuel Legend and his son, the once-profligate-but-soon-to-be-reformed Valentine, is for the most part over money, the language in which it is expressed makes it redolent of the nation's recent struggle against the political yoke of James Stuart. When Sir Samuel, fed up with Valentine's profligacy, decides to exercise his paternal prerogative and disinherit his heir in favor of his younger son Ben, he flaunts the paternal ideology associated with the past age. Despite his efforts, however, Valentine successfully delays the design, and in that time he rededicates himself to the pursuit of Angelica and her thirty thousand a year. Meanwhile, Sir Samuel becomes his rival but is predictably humiliated when he vainly courts the woman. Paternal humiliation is the prelude to the son's long-delayed marriage, which brings the play to an abrupt close. The finale of *Love for Love* resembles the end of *The Double Dealer* in this respect, using Angelica as a deus ex machina who resolves not only the familial but the broader generational antagonisms that the *honnête homme* cannot. Her role (as well as her name) suggests that romance prevails over comedy here, since Valentine's legitimacy is synonymous with an act of grace.

Judging by his first three plays, Congreve seems to be a critic of the old regime. Yet he can hardly be said to be an uncritical supporter of the new one. That, however, was to change, because in *The Way of the World* he at last created a demonstrably comic hero able to master fortune by his own devices. Why didn't Congreve create such a figure earlier, particularly in light of the fact that he seemed to be committed to the libertine as *honnête homme* from the time of *The Double Dealer*? The answer lies, I think, in his personal circumstances in the later nineties, circumstances connected to the political climate of the time. In 1695, Congreve accepted a minor government post as commissioner of hackney coaches. The post paid a modest stipend, forty pounds, but it was probably awarded in the hope that Congreve would continue to support the Crown as he had done already in the commemorative poems "To the Queen, on her Death" and "To the King, on His Taking NAMURE." In 1697, he produced his first and only tragedy, *The Mourning Bride*, which dramatized revolutionary myth as it was revised by the court Whigs and their supporters. That the play was a hit is not surprising; Congreve, after all, had already written three successful comedies. Yet some of the credit for its reception should be attributed to the political atmosphere. The play was produced the year after the Assassination Plot, which the Crown exploited to purge Tories from the government and secure William's claim (Garrett 145). The next year, as a condition of the Peace of Ryswick (1697), Louis publicly recognized William and withdrew support for a Stuart restoration. It was in this atmosphere that political dramatists began to vigorously demonstrate their support for the Williamite regime, support for which had been relatively measured before this time. It is in this context, as well as in light of Congreve's sinecure, that his last two plays should be read. No one would dispute the assertion that *The Mourning Bride* is a political play that attempts to justify Revolution principles; but so is *The Way of the World*, which, I argue, is an attempt at the same time to appropriate the Stuart élan to the Whig cause through the figure of the reformed libertine, Mirabell.

The Way of the World is a legacy play that takes on political meaning through the state-estate analogy that was especially prevalent in the nineties. The parties who vie for a legacy that includes half of Millamant's marriage portion and Mrs. Fainall's trust, Mirabell and Fainall, compose the two halves of the divided libertine: Fainall is the heir of the rakish tradition, Mirabell the *honnête homme* of the postrevolutionary period. While the two duel in the social world of comedy, there is a political edge to their conflict because it is the political estate—controlled by that survivor from the old regime, Lady Wishfort—for which they ultimately vie; and in their struggle they represent conflicting political ideals, Fainall the arbitrary power of the Stuarts in the exercise of his libertine will, and Mirabell the new age of parliamentary power that rests on the authority of the legal will.

The play opens as Mirabell and Fainall rise from cards. Fainall wins the card game that the two have just finished:

> *Mirabell*. You are a fortunate man, Mr. Fainall.
> *Fainall*. Have we done?
> *Mirabell*. What you please: I'll play on to entertain you. (Congreve, *Way of the World* I.i.1–3)

Fainall is "fortunate" because he has won the card game that the two men have just finished playing. But the opening is a setup: Fainall wins when the stakes are small, but he will be the loser in the pursuit of the legacy as well as Lady Wishfort's estate because it is Mirabell who holds the trump card in that game: the black box. That trump, the trust that Mrs. Fainall has given to him before the action of the play begins, is the basis of his moral and legal power. It is the means by which he controls comic and legal fortune, and it permits him to defeat Fainall's fifth-act trump, the threat of divorce with which he expects to win control of the Wishfort estate.

Some critics have argued that the black box is merely a deus ex machina. Such an interpretation suggests that Mirabell exercises little control over the outcome of the play. This reading, which reduces Mirabell to a figure who merely triumphs over circumstances, overlooks the degree to which he defines the comic ambience and shapes the comic action. Mirabell is not a magus like Prospero, but by his name, which means "miracle" or "wonder," Congreve suggests, I think, that his character and actions have something out of the ordinary about them. Though his desire is fixed on Millamant, his design is aimed at Lady Wishfort. There is an immediate reason for this: he wants to win her consent to his marriage to Millamant in order to secure that part of her portion that Lady Wishfort controls. And so he plans, with the help of his servants, to humiliate Lady Wishfort with the mock marriage to Sir Rowland. But there is another reason for such an elaborate plan: he wants to show that Lady Wishfort is obsessed with romantic illusions that keep the ideal of the old libertine alive. When she is to receive Sir Rowland, for example, she is the model of feminine submission:

> *Foible.* All is ready, *Madam.*
> *Lady Wishfort.* And—well—and how do I look, *Foible?*
> *Foible.* Most killing well, *Madam.*
> *Lady Wishfort.* Well, and how shall I receive him? In what figure shall I give his Heart the first Impression? Shall I sit?——No I won't sit—I'll walk—aye I'll walk from the door upon his entrance; and then turn full upon him——No, that will be too sudden. I'll lie——aye I'll lye down——I'll receive him in my little dressing Room, there's a Couch—Yes, yes, I'll give the first impression on a Couch.
> (IV.i.14–24)

Despite the fact that Lady Wishfort thinks she is the seductress, she is in fact the seduced because she has already given Sir Rowland what he wants by the fact that she plans to take him, so to speak, lying down. Her romantic illusions are at odds with the play's normative sexual politics, which are expressed later in the same act in the proviso scene. Out of the playful jawing that goes on between Mirabell and Millamant comes a genuine concession from Mirabell: he promises to submit to the "Dominion of the

Tea-Table" (IV.i.263). He promises, that is, to compromise. Such "reform" should be understood as a rejection of the rakish libertine ethos, based as it was on conquest in the bedroom rather than compromise in the drawing room. Mirabell rejects the old ethos for the new, that of the *honnête homme;* it is, moreover, the condition of Millamant's acceptance. But Lady Wishfort is still enamored with the old ethos, and she expects to find in Sir Rowland the libertine that she did not find in Mirabell, who refused her advances before the action of the play began. The old lady is, to put it a little differently, still taken by the Stuart mystique, and it is that illusion that Congreve hopes to cure.

The romantic illusions of Lady Wishfort would not be so important were it not for the fact that she controls the estate of the late Sir Jonathan Wishfort, who died without a male heir. It is that prize—the estate as political estate—that is the real stake in the game between Fainall and Mirabell, which is why the conflict of libertine and *honnête homme* is over Lady Wishfort rather than Millamant. Lady Wishfort is the center of the action in the fifth act because it is she who must be convinced that the Stuart mystique is a sham. Like the nation, she should not be swept off her feet by the romantic seducer who persists in the collective imagination. But Lady Wishfort is not so wise, and for that reason she is forced to confront her humiliation when, in the last act, the other representative of the Stuart mystique, Fainall, attempts to usurp the Wishfort estate. The act is something of a symbolic rape, and it reveals the reality beneath the Stuart mystique by figuring it in the image of the old, predatory libertine.[21] When Fainall lets his wishes be known, Lady Wishfort comes face to face with the reality of Stuart power. Only then does she defer to Mirabell, who reveals the contents of the black box to defeat Fainall. Mirabell holds the trust that Mrs. Fainall conveyed to him before the play began, and he uses it to defeat Fainall because Congreve wants to dramatize the triumph of legal over arbitrary will in the Glorious Revolution and its aftermath.

In defeating his rival, Mirabell proves himself to be not only in control of comic fortune but also the worthy successor to the "Stuart mystique" insofar as he appropriates libertine vitality to new sociopolitical circumstances. He is not only the most desired man in the play; he is also the only man we suspect of potency. If Mrs. Fainall reminds Mirabell that he broke off their affair because he feared she was pregnant, it is to remind us that her present marriage, like her previous one to Mr. Languish, has produced no heir. And since the collateral heir to the Wishfort estate, Sir Wilfull Witwoud, is non compos mentis, that leaves Mirabell as the only male capable of producing one and carrying on the Wishfort estate through his marriage to Millamant.

But it is not by potency alone that Mirabell appropriates the Stuart élan to the Whig cause. He does so through another libertine virtue, wit, which functions as the correlative of his potency. Here, too, he is governed by the spirit of compromise. Mirabell uses all his wit to defeat Fainall, but in his social intercourse he removes the hard edge of egotism characteristic of the old libertine. This is clear not only in his good-natured mockery of Sir Wilfull but in the genuine conversations he has with Mrs. Fainall and Millamant, too. Like the old libertine, Mirabell is both potent and witty. Yet he is not interested in seducing either woman. In contrast to Fainall, whose relationship with Mrs. Marwood is built from passions that have grown out of revenge, Mirabell entrusts Mrs. Fainall with the secret of his plans, and he courts Millamant in good faith. He has been with Mrs. Fainall before, but he seeks Millamant on her own terms. He will get to her bedroom, but by way of her drawing room: that is, he will have Millamant only on condition that he will translate his passions into manners. That Mirabell agrees with Millamant's proviso sets him apart from the predatory rake, whose quest forgoes the drawing room for the space of feminine compromise, the bedroom. That is the path that Lady Wishfort has internalized; it is also the path that the nation has internalized with regard to the Stuart mystique—which lives on even after their abdication. The danger it poses is the admonitory message of *The Way of the World*. Yet in that regard the play provides something Congreve's earlier comedies did not—an alternative. That alternative is Mirabell, a comic avatar of Revolution principles who exposes the Stuart myth as he attempts to establish a kindred Whig myth in its place.

Notes

A small portion of this essay was taken from chapter 2 of my book *Plots and Counterplots*, published by Cambridge University Press.

1. John Evelyn, who viewed the scene from the Strand, expressed a widespread belief when he declared the restoration of the monarchy to be the work of providence: "Such a Restauration was never seene in the mention of any history, antient

or modern, since the returne of the Babylonian Captivity, nor so joyful a day, and so bright, ever seene in this nation; this hapning when to expect or effect it, was past all humane policy" (182).

2. "Betterton in his part as Owen Tudor was allowed to wear the coronation suit of King Charles; Harris, who played King Henry V, was given a similar garment belonging to the Duke of York; and Smith in his role of the Duke of Burgundy was able to attire himself with the coronation robe of the Earl of Oxford" (Clark 2: 167).

3. Markley notes that the libertine of the piece, Sir Frederick, "comes as close to being as sheer an original as one finds on the stage in the early 1660s: a Fletcher-ian defier of all order, protected from harsh condemnation by his Royalist good nature, negotiating his way through the idealized implications of aristocratic abso-lutism" (107).

4. For the development of a libertine intellectual milieu, see Underwood 10–40; Traugott (384–402) traces his path from court to comedy; Novak ("Margery" 1–4) suggests that the darker libertine of the 1670s may have appeared at the sug-gestion of the court; and Hume (*Rakish* 138–70) sets out the development of the figure in the three phases, warning at the same time that the darker libertine of the seventies is a minority figure. Hume (*Rakish* 164–68) concurs with Novak on the limitations of Underwood, whose static libertine milieu does not account for the development of the character in the 1690s, and with Novak's assessment of the "philosophical libertine" or *honnête homme* at that time (Novak, *Congreve* 42–51). The model is convenient but not entirely accurate, since it does not sufficiently take into account developments following in the wake of the Exclusion Crisis. Yet in its general shape—with the exception of what might be called the Royalist revi-val of the eighties—I find it adequate to my larger concern in this essay, namely the erotics of power as they translate into comic form through the state-estate trope.

5. On the identities and conflicts of old and new Cavaliers, as they were for-mulated during the Interregnum and persisted beyond the Restoration, see Under-down.

6. The trend, set in motion by Shadwell with *The Squire of Alsatia* (1688) and *Bury-Fair* (1689), is continued by Cibber, Pix, and others. As I later argue in the case of Congreve, the new erotics of power linked the rakish libertine to the excesses of the Stuart court.

7. "It was through making an art of life that the ideal of the 'honest man,' or *honnête homme*, might be attained" (Novak, *Congreve* 43–44). Hume is in broad agreement with Novak, though he prefers the term "philosophical libertine" (Hume, *Rakish* 145).

8. Neill writes that the audience would have recognized fundamental matters of order and obligation as they were addressed through the analogy of family and

polity: "It is probably fair to say that theater audiences in the post-interregnum period were more extensively politicized than at any other time in English history, and the crises of the period directly affected lives of many of the dramatists who catered to them. . . . [T]he dramatists are often able to endow the most seemingly frivolous material with surprising and impudent suggestiveness, turning the dizzy round of sexual competition, erotic combat, and parental oppression into a figure for more serious forms of power struggle" (118, 120).

9. All four are set in the late Interregnum and end in anticipation of the Restoration.

10. *The Comical Revenge* was very popular in its time. The modern critical assessments that are most favorable to the play include Underwood 43–58, Holland 20–27, Birdsall 41–57, and Markley 100–111. Some political aspects of the play have been touched upon by Neill: "Sir Frederick, as his name implies . . . is yet another incarnation of the Lord of Misrule, his subversive energies directed towards the undermining of the Commonwealth establishment through the humiliation of 'Oliver's' Knight, Sir Nicholas Cully, whom he triumphantly marries to his own whore" (125). On the play as the first Restoration comedy of manners, see Hume (*Development* 144) and Lynch (143), who stress its Caroline origins. For a more detailed account of the play, see my *Plots and Counterplots* 64–82.

11. On *She Would If She Could*, see Holland 28–37, Birdsall 57–76, Brown 43–48, and Markley 111–21. On *The Mulberry Garden*, see Staves 123–26.

12. Cordner calls the song "a rather cowardly variation on those lyrics from the cavalier defeat which turned their back on the war and looked to the pleasures of the flesh for consolation" (170). A leaguer is a siege.

13. For a full account of the tragicomic genre, see Canfield, "Ideology."

14. In Sir Samuel's unsuccessful pursuit of the widow, Sedley may be suggesting a goal similar to that of *The Comical Revenge*.

15. "In Restoration comedy during the 1670's there was what seems like a deliberate effort to praise the city and court as the center of civilization and to see the country as stupid, barbaric, and dull" (Novak, "Margery" 1). See also my "Libertines and Parasites."

16. *Defense of the Epilogue*, appended to *The Conquest of Granada* (second part), Ker 1: 176.

17. See Hughes 15–19. For a different view, see Canfield, "Significance."

18. On Horner's symbolic impotence, see Vieth 346, Freedman 424, Weber 115–18. For a feminist reading that stresses Horner's limitations in a different light, see Burke. Like his glory-seeking counterpart from the heroic play, Horner seeks honor, but his desire is an expression of power rather than passion because it is a desire for mastery rather than love. Horner does not seduce for the pleasure of it; he is driven to it time and again to sustain his reputation. And since he must

perpetually perform in order to sustain himself, he is, in a manner of speaking, a prisoner of his own name.

19. Loftis (22) notes the tepid theatrical response to the Revolution on the part of the Whigs. Potter confirms it in more detail (186–97). Cf. Canfield's contribution to this collection.

20. See Paulson 190–208.

21. Though Fainall relies on fraud rather than force, the potential for libertine rapine was exploited by Whig writers. At the same time, however, Jacobites also used the imagery of rape to denounce William's claim as conquest. Given this context, discussion of the right of conquest was quickly quashed when it was brought up in 1693 in *King William and Queen Mary Conquerors,* though it remained a staple of Jacobite discourse for a long time to come (see Erskine-Hill).

Works Cited

Baker, J. H. *An Introduction to English Legal History.* 2nd ed. London: Butterworth, 1979.

Birdsall, Virginia Ogden. *Wild Civility: The English Comic Spirit on the Restoration Stage.* Bloomington: Indiana UP, 1970.

Braverman, Richard. "Libertines and Parasites." *Restoration* 11 (1987): 73–86.

———. *Plots and Counterplots: Sexual Politics and the Body Politic in English Literature, 1660–1730.* Cambridge: Cambridge UP, 1993.

Brown, Laura. *English Dramatic Form, 1660–1760: An Essay in Generic History.* New Haven: Yale UP, 1981.

Burke, Helen. "Wycherley's 'Tendentious Joke': The Discourse of Alterity in *The Country Wife.*" *Eighteenth Century: Theory and Interpretation* 29 (1988): 227–41.

Canfield, J. Douglas. "The Ideology of Restoration Tragicomedy." *ELH* 51 (1984): 447–64.

———. "The Significance of the Restoration Rhymed Heroic Play." *Eighteenth-Century Studies* 13 (1979): 49–62.

Clark, William Smith, ed. *The Dramatic Works of Roger Boyle, Earl of Orrery.* 2 vols. Cambridge: Harvard UP, 1937.

Congreve, William. *The Complete Plays of William Congreve.* Ed. Herbert Davis. Chicago: U of Chicago P, 1967.

Cordner, Michael, ed. *The Plays of Sir George Etherege.* Cambridge: Cambridge UP, 1982.

Dryden, John. *Essays of John Dryden.* Ed. W. P. Ker. 2 vols. Oxford: Clarendon, 1926.

Erskine-Hill, Howard. "Was There a Rhetoric of Jacobitism?" *Ideology and Conspiracy: Aspects of Jacobitism, 1689–1759.* Ed. Eveline Cruickshanks. Edinburgh: J. Donald, 1979. 49–69.

Etherege, Sir George. *The Dramatic Works of Sir George Etherege.* Ed. H. F. B. Brett-Smith. 2 vols. Oxford: Blackwell, 1927.

Evelyn, John. *The Diary of John Evelyn.* Ed. John Bowle. Oxford: Oxford UP, 1983.

Freedman, William. "Impotence and Self-Destruction in *The Country Wife.*" *English Studies* 53 (1972): 421–31.

Garrett, Jane. *The Triumphs of Providence: The Assassination Plot, 1696.* Cambridge: Cambridge UP, 1980.

Holland, Norman N. *The First Modern Comedies: The Significance of Etherege, Wycherley, and Congreve.* Cambridge: Harvard UP, 1959.

Hughes, Derek. *Dryden's Heroic Plays.* Lincoln: U of Nebraska P, 1981.

Hume, Robert D. *The Development of English Drama in the Late Seventeenth Century.* Oxford: Clarendon, 1976.

———. *The Rakish Stage: Studies in English Drama, 1660–1800.* Carbondale: Southern Illinois UP, 1983.

Hutton, Ronald. *The Restoration.* Oxford: Oxford UP, 1985.

Jordan, Robert. "The Extravagant Rake in Restoration Comedy." *Restoration Literature: Critical Approaches.* Ed. Harold Love. London: Methuen, 1972. 69–90.

Jose, Nicholas. *Ideas of the Restoration in English Literature, 1660–1671.* Cambridge: Harvard UP, 1984.

Loftis, John. *The Politics of Drama in Augustan England.* Oxford: Clarendon, 1963.

Love, Harold. *Congreve.* Totowa, N.J.: Rowman and Littlefield, 1974.

Lynch, Kathleen. *The Social Mode of Restoration Drama.* New York: Macmillan, 1926.

Markley, Robert. *Two-Edg'd Weapons: Style and Ideology in the Comedies of Etherege, Wycherley, and Congreve.* Oxford: Clarendon, 1988.

McComb, John. "Congreve's *The Old Bachelour:* A Satiric Anatomy." *Studies in English Literature* 17 (1977): 361–72.

Neill, Michael. "Heroic Heads and Humble Tails: Sex, Politics, and the Restoration Comic Rake." *Eighteenth Century: Theory and Interpretation* 24 (1983): 115–39.

Novak, Maximillian. "Margery Pinchwife's 'London Disease.'" *Studies in the Literary Imagination* 10 (1977): 1–23.

———. *William Congreve.* New York: Twayne, 1971.

Paulson, Ronald. *Popular and Polite Art in the Age of Hogarth and Fielding.* Notre Dame, Ind.: U of Notre Dame P, 1979.

Potter, Lois. "Politics and Popular Culture: The Theatrical Response to the Revolution." *The Revolution of 1688–1689: Changing Perspectives.* Ed. Lois G. Schwoerer. Cambridge: Cambridge UP, 1992. 184–97.

Sedley, Sir Charles. *The Mulberry Garden. The Poetical and Dramatic Works of Sir Charles Sedley.* Ed. V. de Sola Pinto. 2 vols. London: Constable, 1928. 1: 98–186.

Staves, Susan. *Players' Scepters: Fictions of Authority in the Restoration.* Lincoln: U of Nebraska P, 1979.

Sutherland, James R. "The Impact of Charles II on Restoration Literature." *Restoration and Eighteenth-Century Literature.* Ed. Carroll Camden. Chicago: U of Chicago P, 1963. 251–63.

Traugott, John. "The Rake's Progress from Court to Comedy: A Study in Comic Form." *Studies in English Literature* 6 (1966): 381–407.

Underdown, David. *Royalist Conspiracy in England.* New Haven: Yale UP, 1960.

Underwood, Dale. *Etherege and the Seventeenth-Century Comedy of Manners.* New Haven: Yale UP, 1957.

Vieth, David M. "Wycherley's *The Country Wife:* An Anatomy of Masculinity." *Papers on Language and Literature* 2 (1966): 335–50.

Weber, Harold. "Horner and His 'Women of Honor': The Dinner Party in *The Country Wife.*" *Modern Language Quarterly* 43 (1980): 107–20.

Williams, Aubrey. *An Approach to Congreve.* New Haven: Yale UP, 1979.

Wycherley, William. *The Country Wife.* Ed. Thomas H. Fujimura. Lincoln: Bison–U of Nebraska P, 1965.

———. *The Plain Dealer.* Ed. Leo Hughes. Lincoln: Bison–U of Nebraska P, 1967.

The Novelty; or, Print, Money, Fashion, Getting, Spending, and Glut

J. S. PETERS

In his dedication to *The Novelty. Every Act a Play. Being a Short Pastoral, Comedy, Masque, Tragedy, and Farce* (1697), Peter Motteux begs protection: "Novelties, and their Introducers," he writes, "have generally most need of powerful Patrons." But in impatient modernity, "a Muse, like a Mistress, tho pleasing at first, is seldom long so to the man that's wedded to her, or indeed to any others" (A2). In his presentation of a "Dramatic Entertainment that may be said to want a precedent," Motteux encapsulates the late seventeenth century's ambivalent attitude toward novelty: innovation may still need a good defense; but repetition too has become unacceptable, the desire for novelty pressing. *The Novelty* takes up the circular refrain that marks the first scene of Buckingham's *The Rehearsal*. The poet Bayes, emblem of the post-Restoration dramatic world (as well as parody of its values), proclaims repeatedly the urgency of novelty. The audience's hunger for "novelty" and "variety," which Motteux cleverly identifies in his title as central to late-seventeenth-century theater ("Pastoral, Comedy, Masque, Tragedy," or "Farce"), is a fragment of the larger cultural desire for novelty, which is at the same time marked by deep ambivalence. The "Augustan" mistrust of things novel is merely the flip side of the general collective enthusiasm, in the 1690s, for novelty.[1] The hunger for novelty must be served by the innovating poet in the theater, just as it is served by the innovating wit in the coffeehouse. That need for dramatic novelty has its parallel not only in the wish for the novelty of the everyday witticism but also in the desire for sexual novelty, novel fashions, news. Etherege's *Man of Mode* or Cibber's *Love's Last Shift*, for instance, set up the analogy between the appetite for sexual variety and that for the variety of new fashion, in the parallelism of the rakish Dorimant and the foppish

Sir Fopling Flutter, and of the rakish Loveless and the foppish Sir Novelty
Fashion. Mr. Novel in *The Plain Dealer,* like Sir Novelty Fashion, "affects
novelty as much as the fashion, and is as fantastical as changeable and as
well known as the fashion, who likes nothing but what is new, nay would
choose to have his friend or his title a new one" (*PD* II.i, 41).[2]

A number of seemingly unrelated historical conditions and metaphoric
habits are part of the story of the general cultural interest in novelty (and the
accompanying suspicion of it) in the late seventeenth century. The increase
over the course of the century in printed matter ("news" and "novels,"
among other things), culminating in the 1695 lapse of the Licensing Act
and the flood it released, and the increasing complexity of publishing and
authorship as commercial enterprises helped condition the ambivalent relation to novelty that Motteux's *The Novelty* identifies: the enduring obligation to justify innovation, the suspicion of it, and, simultaneously, the
desire for novelty in a culture in which reiteration has grown uncomfortable. The post-Restoration credit and commercial system (culminating in
the monuments of Williamite banking, the 1694 institution of the Bank of
England in particular) and the expansion of commodity circulation and
consumerism in the context of English trade (the "new" science, the battle
of the Moderns with the Ancients, the struggle of the inheritors of Bacon
in the Royal Society to validate innovations in the understanding of nature,
in systems of representation, and in style)—these are both cause and effect
of the self-consciousness about the new.[3]

Metaphors emerging from changes in the material and institutional aspects of print, credit, and science, like the uses of these technologies,
overlap. The Bricklayer in *City Politiques* makes, for instance, the parallel
between paper credit and printed pamphlets explicit:

> We will print a narrative of The Pilgrim under the Gown. As paper
> in Holland passes for money, pamphlets with us pass for religion and
> policy. A bit of paper in Holland, from a man of credit, takes up goods
> here, pays debts there; so a pamphlet will take up fools here, make
> fools there. (*CP* IV.i, 82)

But more interesting are the less explicit shared spaces of expression. The
concern for novelty, the anxiety about its status, is one of those spaces—
the fluid in which the material products and institutions of print, credit,
and science move in the second half of the seventeenth century.

The general cultural anxiety about the new puts pressure on the drama's conception of its own capacity for novelty. Some of the drama's involuntary metaphoric tics (like those outside the drama)—the obsessive jokes about sexual, alimentary, sartorial, and poetic consumption and the fear of glut—are products, in part, of the self-consciousness about the threat of sameness in proliferating production. That anxiety about sameness is a translation of the desire for novelty: new lovers or mistresses, new fashions, new gossip, news, new plays. And so, like the more explicit and larger culturewide demand for novelty, these recurring tropes are also conditioned by money and books, by the decreasing materiality of credit-world finance (complicated credit systems that would turn into the South Sea Bubble a few decades later) and the increasing materiality of print-world expression (books filling the St. Paul's bookstalls). Those changes in the way the society stored money (in banks) and the way it stored knowledge (in print) encouraged an intensification of the ideal for the rapidly consumed and the rapidly obsolete, an ideal modulating the period's modes of expression and cultural products, among them the theater—its institutions and classifications, its stylistic, formal, and metaphoric articulations.[4]

I am not concerned here directly with the philosophical formulation of the idea of progress, which developed in the late seventeenth century, or even its offshoots (whether the Moderns are better than the Ancients, for instance).[5] Rather, I am concerned with the attitude toward the phenomena that made the issue of novelty seem urgent in the culture as a whole, an attitude that the theater's metaphors reflect. "Novelty" here is not, principally, new ideas but newness on a smaller scale. If the late seventeenth century is the era in which the modern idea of progress is born, in which people come to feel that they have at last been liberated from the narrow vision of Aristotelianism (and there is another side), this is a different kind of conviction than the conviction that one must have a new-fashioned peruke, even if the larger philosophical perspective has bearing on the minute detail of lived experience. I would like here not to track the mutual conditioning of "matter" and "discourse" (as if we knew how to distinguish these two) but rather to identify a series of tropes that interact with material conditions and institutions. It is a late-seventeenth-century habit to relate these tropes to one another. They have shared patterns of occurrence and parallel relative positions. They are metaphors that get clustered, figures that are the expression of a perennial question, and its coda: Why do we wish for novelty, insofar as we do? More important, is there such a thing as novelty? These questions have a kind of urgency for the period and its theater; they are the shadows behind the most insistent of the jokes, the habitual metaphors, the homologous tropes of the comedy.

Bayes, like Sir Novelty or Mr. Novel, "aim[s] at" the "new." He strives for originality: "I despise your *Johnson,* and *Beaumont,* that borrow'd all they writ from Nature: I am for fetching it purely out of my own fancy, I" (*RSL* II.i, 14). Bayes's value for originality is bound up with the fact of print, whose productions flood the late-seventeenth-century theater. That theater builds itself on the quartos and folios, on bills and posters, on advertisements for new editions; it confounds itself by the volumes of the scholars, worries about the "private Press" that "prints your *Amsterdam* and *Leyden* Libels" (*LC* IV.i, 47), resists the broadsheets and ballads, the printed pictures of cuckolds "hang'd in Effigy" on the wall of the "necessary Houses."[6] Bayes, the man of novelty, has compiled his play from the books and thinks of it in terms of its printed version: "Now there are some Critics that have advis'd me to put out the Second *Dare,* and print *Must* in the place on't" (*RSL* IV.i, 43). He works "by the Rule of Romance," whose authors "divided their things into three, four, five, six, seven, eight, or as many Tomes as they please" (IV.i, 38). He will "take a way the Book," will "Lampoon 'em all," will say "farewel to this Stage," while the players "set up Bills" (V.i, 59). In *The Rehearsal,* the play cannot get past rehearsal, so burdened is it by print-world accumulations, the dramaticocritical detritus that clouds the mind of Bayes.

Here, in a world in which the bookshops hold matter for the "Transprosi[tion]" and "invention . . . by way of Table Book" of thousands of Bayeses (*RSL* I.i, 4), one is haunted by a sense of the books unread, the paths one may be retreading in untrodden naïveté (ignorant that the great Jonson has gone before, that Dacier said it better in a book for which there was never time, that Scaliger's brilliant exegesis of the Theophrastan notion of character, transmogrified through the Rapinian reading of Aristotle, has perfected the analysis one is clumsily trying to "invent"). Poor Bayes! ever rehearsing for the rehearsal of the rehearsal of the performance that will have already happened (not once but hundreds of times in the libraries of the Estiennes and Bodleys and Pepyses) and so never happens. Before the new play even begins (because the new play is never new but has already taken place in the places without action), the actors desert. Bayes is abandoned by those who were to transform book into motion. And yet, for him, the real world is finally his solitude with the book, heedless of "the company that comes to see it acted": "That's all one," says Bayes. "I must reserve this comfort to my self, my Play and I shall go together, we will not part indeed, Sir" (V.i, 59). Nothing to be done but to cede to the conditions of pastness through the medium of the future, to join with the press against itself and its own perpetual posteriority, to write lampoons, to hug one's book to oneself.

"The rehearsal" is the emblem of a community asking itself whether there is such a thing as novelty. The "rehearsal" is a rehearsal for a play that never takes place, explicated to critics made anonymous by their blandness of identity ("Smith" and "Johnson"), critics detheatricalized (no "Truewit" or "Dorimant" these). The "rehearsal" for what is new means that there cannot be anything new but merely recombinations of the fragmentary and imperfect, the collected and repeated. Here, theater is rehearsal, in its necessary incompletion, and rehearsal is repetition—not the ontological kind that establishes events by reinscribing them or proceeds necessarily from universal finitude, nor the kind that means the coming back to a primal place of beginning.[7] Return to the *original* has become a kind of novelty. Repetition, here, is the opposite: the unceasing reiteration of the moment's sameness, the mechanical gesture of the press, the imitative duplication of the mirror. Rehearsal can be the mark of performance only as antithesis to the imagined ur-text of "primitive purity," which cannot be uncovered from the enfolding leaves of the press.

A print world creates a play about rehearsal, about repetition, because it is conscious of the repetition of its own material forms, because (in a world in which knowledge is easily storable on the page) it cannot be certain that life is bettered by the repetitions that once served preservation. But while print is repetition of the old, mechanical reproduction of identical copies (and imitations of those copies in ever expanding branches), it is also "news": the generation of new "stories" in the form of the newspaper; the circulation of information on political change (the fall of states or of mistresses), which breaks into the sameness of quotidian life.[8] If the possibility of preservation helps to create a need for novelty, so does the possibility of novelty itself. The press, the production of "news," sets up an "itch of curiosity after News,"[9] an expectation for the new that is self-generating. It also sets up a reaction, the kind of irritation with the novelty-hungry that shows up in dramatic satire or in Johnson's *Dictionary* in the eighteenth century.[10] Finally, the ever increasing demand for the new, which urges the circulation of stories as news, makes those in search of the new wonder just how new that "news" really is. Print may urge a value for "novelty" and "originality," but simultaneously, by putting pressure on "novelty," it calls into question the very identity of that novelty.

The sensationalist news press (the "*Gazet*" in which cuckoldry, for instance, can be published [LC IV.i, 53]) makes a consumable product out of the theatrical events of London. The theater usually represents the news press with irony: the press as gossipmonger ("my news does come wet out o' the press" [CP III.i, 76]) shows an unseemly garrulity. But the news press and the philosophical folio, the romance and the learned tome, are not necessarily on two sides of an opposition. Those who, as a way of opening late-seventeenth-century comedy, enter "reading on a book," like Hamlet at the beginning of the century (II.ii), are, it is true, holding forth the enduring world of Epicurus and Lucretius (principally) against the modish whirl of urban flux that the news and the print-world ephemeral theater try to capture:

> [Bruce *in his gown, reading*.]
> *Bruce*. Thou great Lucretius! . . . Thou reconcil'st philosophy with
> verse and dost almost alone demonstrate that poetry and good sense
> may go together. (*V* I.i, 9)

But the pages of Lucretius and Epictetus or of Epicurus, with their images of consumption and atomic flux, do not always counter the pages of the gossip rag. Valentine's stoical folios, "Three or Four musty Books, in commendation of Starving and Poverty," serve as displacement for the real food of which Valentine and Jeremy are starved in Congreve's *Love for Love*: "Humph, and so [Epictetus] has made a very fine Feast, where there is nothing to be eaten," complains Jeremy (LL I.i, 216). Congreve, here, parallels these books with the plays that Valentine will write: Valentine will join those scribbling "drudges of the stage" (as Shadwell refers to them [*V* 7]), making his entrance into the Grub Street world in which the Spirit of Famine reigns and one has nothing to eat but the books themselves. And so the philosophical volumes enter the economy of consumable and disgorgeable pages in the print world in which both great tomes and broadsides participate.

Those rapidly produced pages, whether philosophical treatises or news of the outside world, remind the reader of the limitations of the reader's small boudoir or closet, its boundedness. The importation of the news "commodity," like the importation of other exotic wares (pineapples from the South Seas, elephants from the East Indies), makes one wonder just

how interesting one's own life is. Print's productions remind the individual
of the world and its novelties: the duchess of Cleveland's latest amour,
which enters the life of the reader of the roman à clef; the "*Centiloquium
of Trismegistus*" (*EL* II.i, 242), which enters the life of the reader of the
almanac; the madman transfused with sheep's blood, who "bleated perpetually," "had wool growing on him" and "a Northamptonshire sheep's
tail [emerging] from his anus" (*V* II.ii, 51), which enters the life of the
reader in natural history. Life without news seems ever the same. Print—
along with the expansion of markets and the development of visual and
navigational instruments—erects a vast world structure. The constraints
of an individual's life begin to look circumscribed. The virtuoso wants to
get outside its boundaries in order to find something new, whether in the
distance across the seas, which may show the reader of the travel narrative the "Shoulder of an *Egyptian* King . . . purloyn'd from one of the
Pyramids, powder'd with Hieroglyphicks" (*LL* II.i, 242), or in the nearer
distance of the microscope, which shows "the nature of ants, flies, humble-
bees, earwigs, millepedes, hog's lice, maggots, mites in a cheese, tadpoles,
worms, newts, spiders, and all the noble products of the sun by equivocal
generation" (*V* III.ii, 68).

The credit economy—the scarcity of coins and hence the production of
and reliance on "Paper . . . Specie," "Coin'd Paper," "imaginary Money"—
as well as the consciousness of increased trade in the development of the
"Exchange," and so the need for participation in the circulation of consumer novelties, also helps to set up a desire to get out of the container of
one's life by buying foreign wares, as Sir Fopling does when he wears only
French designer clothes: "The suit? . . . Barroy . . . The garniture? . . . Le
Gras . . . The shoes? . . . Piccar . . . The periwig? . . . Chedreux" (*MM* III.ii,
66–67).[11] The anxiety, during the recoinage crisis of the 1690s, over the
scarcity of coins (and the clipping that was decreasing the silver content
of those that were circulating) and the anxiety over the scarcity of solid
tokens of exchange (as opposed to airy credit) were acute. But the coin
shortage only focused with greater intensity a more general anxiety about
the growth of trade and credit and its impact on consumerism, particularly of fashionable luxuries. Lady Wishfort's threat to "spoil [Mirabell's]
Credit with his Taylor" (*WW* III.i, 428) might be taken as emblematic.
Young Worthy, in *Love's Last Shift*, analogizes the debasement of money
and sexual debasement ("Maidenheads are as scarce as our mill'd half
crowns" [*LLS* III.ii, 43]). And Sir Francis, in Pix's *Innocent Mistress*, ex-

plicitly identifies the scarcity of coins (and thus greater reliance on credit) with the increase in fashion (and sexual) consumption when he says that in town "the Money is indeed very much scarcer, yet what perhaps you'l think a wonder, dressing and debauchery increases" (I.i, 1). The theater is unnerved by this fashion consciousness, since buying fashion goods—"the Cravat-string, the Garter, the Sword-knot, the Centurine, the Bardash, the Steinkirk, the large Button, the long Sleeve, the Plume, and full Peruque" (LLS II.i, 31)—creates a kind of theater of the Mall, a theater of the side-box, which competes with the performance on stage: "Nat that I pretend to be a beau," says Lord Foppington, "but a man must endeavor to look wholesome, lest he make so nauseous a figure in the side box, the ladies should be compelled to turn their eyes upon the play" (R II.i, 39).

"Appetite" (spun out, in its various forms, from Hobbesian appetitive desire) is the larger rubric under which are collected the various equivalencies that the comedies establish amid the desire for consumerist novelty—fashion, food, books, bodies—equivalencies that become the most habitual clichés.[12] The homology that The Man of Mode or Love's Last Shift sets up between modishness of dress and modishness of sexual behavior becomes an unthinking figural equation: "Sir, tailors and periwigmakers are now become the bawds of the nation; 'tis they debauch all the women" (R I.iii, 20). The Man of Mode's "sword-knots," "cravats," and "periwigs" (MM, epilogue) are the other Man of Mode's Mrs. Loveits and Bellindas, consumable like the exotic fruits from orient climates, disposable like last year's "Doily Stuff" (WW III.i, 433). In the world of the fashion commodity, characters become the very thing for which appetite hungers. Sir Novelty Fashion, who is an "Ornament to [his] Cloaths" (LLS II.i, 26), metamorphoses into his appurtenances, the goods that dress him. "Why, thou essence bottle," says Young Fashion, "thou musk cat. . . . Soh! Farewell, snuff box" (R III.i, 60–61). Women (as always, goods) are traded and cease to be in fashion, like fashions themselves, which must be cast off long before decay (one gives one's old "Drap-du-berry . . . to one's Chambermaid after a day or two" [WW III.i, 433]). As Welldon says to Lucy at the beginning of Southerne's Oroonoko, "Women in London are like the rich silks; they are out of fashion a great while before they wear out" (I.i, 12). Fashion is part of a system of trade that depends on novelty, on not being yet "worn":

> You may tumble [women and fashions] over and over at their first coming up and never disparage their price; but they fall upon wear-

ing immediately, lower and lower in their value, till they come to the broker at last. (O I.i, 12) [13]

The Indies (Jamaica, Suriname), in the plays, are the origin for all those strange commodities that bawds with baskets ply (the silks, the scented powders, the spices), and so they are the place where commerce and sensuality meet (where the "Offspring of foolish plodding Cits" find sullied, blooming "Jilts" like Mrs. Flywife in *The Innocent Mistress*, "as fine as a Queen covered with Jewels" [*IM* I, 8; I, 5]), at once a site for the kind of trade on which are founded modern credit systems and an exotic locus of sensual pleasures. "The Indies," or the house of "the Indian woman," allow a kind of compression in offering a location for the more pervasive meeting of sexual and commodity consumption.

In London, where the "*Indian* Groves" are only a dream behind the "Smoak" (*IM* I, 8), the urbane world of books becomes part of the sexual/mercantile homology. In *The Innocent Mistress*, Spendall is the monetary equivalent of Sir Francis Wildlove, who *spends all* his *wild love* on "common Jilts," "kept Mistress[es]," and "noisy Coquette[s]" (I, 1–2). Spendall offers to do the duties of public expenditure (as mouthpiece and parasite) for Sir Charles Beauclair, so that Sir Charles, who is willing to read romances rather than spend his sexual all, may make his expenses in literary terms. As novel readers, Sir Charles and Bellinda use the page as barrier to physical presence, closeted from each other in the chastity of their literary and book-inspired Platonism. Books displace sex for the two Platonic lovers (who reconstitute in themselves the books of their literary forebears, *Les précieuses ridicules* and a reimagined print-world Plato): "Too Studious for her Sex, [Bellinda] fell upon the Seducers of the women, Plays, and Romances" (I, 4), rather than falling onto the seducer himself; and so, transmuting her own displacement onto her unseducing seduced one, she "never allows him greater favours then to read Plays to her" (I, 3). (We cannot help but imagine that, on the day when marriage and thus physical union between them become possible, they will, like Paolo and Francesca, "read no farther" [*Inferno* 5.138].)

Bellinda ingests books as a stay against ingestion, for rapid consumption, the need for new objects of appetite, means superannuation, no longer only through natural decay but now also through the search for novelty. By the early eighteenth century—in Swift and Pope, for instance—physical decay and the rapid obsolescence of consumer culture become inseparably intertwined (Swift's dressing room poems exemplifying the union), but the union is already established here. Women (like Mrs. Flywife) are daughters of Eve not only in that they have appetites but also insofar as their appetites make them responsible for having brought on the Fall, the condition of time, of change, of consumption and expenditure that needs renewal in novelty. Since they are imagined as responsible for time, they must find a solution to the Fall in the predominantly female seventeenth-century version of Platonism of which Bellinda partakes. Platonic lovers, through the refusal of consumption, escape the modern system of compulsory novelty and obsolescence and so enter into the realm of eternity. The rapid archaism that Platonism resists compresses time. As part of the world of novelty, Sir Novelty (now Lord Foppington) does not have the old leisurely sense of days but collapses ordinary cycles into hours: "His patent has not been passed eight-and-forty hours, and he has already sent how-do-ye's to all the town to make 'em acquainted with his title" (R II.i, 36).

In the compression made by speedy superannuation, wares (which one consumes and which, in being consumed, consume one) become dangerous. Mrs. Beauclair, in *The Innocent Mistress,* disguised as a young fop who has, like Spendall, spent all, explains that "he" is "follow'd by the several Actions of my *Taylor, Sempstress, Perruke-maker, Hosier,* and a long *Et cætera;* besides, the swingingst Debt my *Perfumer;* Essence and sweet Pouder has compleated my Ruin" (*IM* IV, 28).[14] Things are ever in danger of being consumed. Searchwell complains of his master's "Whores": "The Pox, the Plague, that belongs to 'em, consume 'em all I say" (III, 20–21). Those who engage in sexual consumption, according to Searchwell, will be consumed by disease. But according to Mrs. Beauclair, the woman who refuses herself pleasures (and marries an old squire) "either dies of a Consumption (Pining after pleasures more refin'd) or else o'recome [*sic*] with Vapors runs melancholly mad" (III, 21). Women, daughters of Eve, are consumed from within if they do not consume without. When Mrs. Flywife cannot consume sexually, she wishes all mankind "were in one consuming blaze, tho' I were in the midst of 'em" (IV, 38).

Novelty cannot satisfy itself, for it ceases to be novelty as soon as it is born. The appetite for novelty looks insatiable, as insatiable as Widow Lackitt's sexual appetite in *Oroonoko* ("Satisfied! No indeed. . . . To be satisfied is to have enough of you. . . . I shall never think I can have enough of you" [O IV.i, 80]). It looks as insatiable as the "roving flights" of Loveless's "unlimited desire" (R V.iv, 129), as Horner's, or as Willmore the Rover's in Behn's *The Rover,* ever sniffing the air for the odor of new woman: "a

girl! . . . Ha! Where?" (II.i, 30), "Ha! Whose picture's this? 'Tis a fine
wench!" (III.i, 60), "I'm a dog if it be not a very wench!" (III.v, 66).[15] "Nor
muse nor miss . . . can please" the "disease[d] . . . appetite" of the wits and
libertines in the playhouse (*RVR* 128). For some rovers (rakes, libertines,
male or female), the desire for sexual novelty is based on a fiction of permanent satiety, in which the rover, ever wandering, seeks an object that
will offer finitude to appetite, like the lover's long-lost other half in Aristophanes' myth.[16] But most of the plays remind us that it is only a fiction.
For these, there is always a *Rover, Part II*, a *Relapse*.

There is always a relapse partly because the world is too full of possibilities, because it provides an excess with which appetite can be crammed.
Appetite (sexual and alimentary, as always, conflated) is inseparable from
the threat of glut. The attempt to disengage from ingestion is (for men
at least) an attempt to resist surfeit, the condition of being "cloyed,"
"crammed," which besieges the characters. In Congreve's *Old Bachelour*,
Vainlove (whose name reveals both the self-reflexive vanity of his love and
the vanity of loving him) has a "puny Stomack" whose "nicety" is "cloy'd
with the preparative" (I.i, 43). Sir John Brute, in Vanbrugh's *Provoked
Wife*, is "a savory dish," but "as savory as 'tis," Lady Brute is "cloyed with
it" (V.ii, 95).

The oral excess of alimentary glut, the crammed mouth, is inverted in
the oral excess of verbal glut, the mouth uncramming itself. Beaumont's
"cloyed" stomach suggests to him the usual identification of alimentary (or
alcoholic), sartorial, and verbal excess, and an encyclopedic female excess
(the kind that once got female "scolds" punished on the cucking stool),
when he tells Sir Francis: "Excess of drinking cloys my Stomach, and Im-
pudence in Women absolutely turns it; then I hate the vanity of Dress and
Fluttering, where eternal Noise and Nonsence reigns" (*IM* I, 1).[17]

The print-world representation of oral/verbal excess—gossip, noise,
nonsense—holds a paradoxical double position. The disdain for oral excess represents, on the one hand, a sophisticated print world's mistrust
for the oral. It reflects the attitude of the gentleman of polite letters (often
parodying the woman of impolite "illiteracy"), who has come to appreciate the decorum that can be maintained in the library and who mistrusts
the noise of the live theater, whether the theater at Drury Lane or that
of the coffeehouse. The disdain for oral excess represents, on the other
hand, a discomfort with verbal excess in general. Oral excess is synecdoche
for a more broadly understood verbal excess, that, for instance, generated

by the press. Print-world literary glut, then, shows up metonymically in
the comedies: it is wit glut, the glut of "Similitudes" ("truce with your
Similitudes," says Millamant, "*Mincing,* stand between me and his Wit"
[*WW* II.i, 419]). It is carping critics ("loud gentlemen of the pit" [*PD* 10]);
it is gossip ("Tattle" and "Scandal" [*LL*]); it is "Noise"; it is "Nonsense."
The "wit" fights the verbal glut of sameness by attempting a "surprize," as
Bayes would have it (*RSL* II.iv, 19). Like Bayes, self-footnoting half-wits are
trapped in the parasitic critical economy, an infertile economy not unlike
their autoeroticism before the mirror (Lord Foppington's, for instance),
their onanism in the closet. (It is not hard to imagine what the false wit
Tattle, for instance, does in his "Closet of Beauties," fetishized portraits
of those who "have done him [imaginary] Favours," portraits "Sacred to
Love and Contemplation" [*LL* I.i, 232]).[18]

Appetite (alimentary, literary, sartorial, sexual) is a paradox. It is at once
insatiable and sated, glutted like thirst given an ocean of salt water to drink.
It is never satisfied, and so always consuming, and so cloyed with plenty,
and so all the less satisfied, for plenty is not what it is hungry for. The
problem is that appetite does not know what it is hungry for. The world
of plenty is, in part, responsible. There will always be more fashions, more
books; there will always be more women (or men) for the libertine. Plentiful supply makes novelty seem possible as much as the need for novelty
insists that supply be plentiful. As Lucy in *Oroonoko* complains:

> The men would have us at their own scandalous rates. Their plenty
> makes 'em wanton; and in a little time, I suppose they won't know
> what they would have of the women themselves. (*O* I.i, 12)

The problem with the system of rapid obsolescence and plentiful supply
(of fashions or bodies or books) is that it confuses the nature of desire:
it is hard to know what one "would have" when one is constantly in the
process of having something new. The multiplication of objects obscures
both the identity of that thing appetite wants and the fact that appetite has
no particular object. Fashions, bodies, texts, which multiply, become infinitely repeatable concealments of the fact that we do not know the object
of our own desire:

> When I languish'd, and wish'd you wou'd something bestow,
>   You bad me to give it a Name;

But, by Heaven, I know it as little as you,
Tho' my Ignorance passes for Shame.
(*IM* III, 21–22)

Insistence on the indeterminacy of the object of appetite reflects, in part, the stance of the aristocrat who wishes to be distinguished from all those who, in the flooded centers of trade, are so busy getting and spending (the condition Wordsworth, a century later, will recognize as the outcome of urban capitalism). When the "Exchange" (textual, alimentary, sartorial, sexual) is flooded, there is a democratization of participation in circulation—of things, money, printed matter—even if only at second hand. When there is enough and more than enough, ladies' maids quickly inherit their mistress's cast-off petticoats, shoemakers like that in *The Man of Mode* inherit the gentleman's cast-off vices (*MM* I.i, 18), and servants like Jeremy inherit their masters' cast-off wit. Loveless, in *The Relapse,* reminds us of the identity of the cast-off object, verbal and amorous excess, and the cloyed appetite, when he tells Amanda that the town, "that theater of noise," is "an old cast mistress / Who has been so lavish of her favors, / She's now grown bankrupt of her charms" (*R* I.i, 12).

Democratization of consumption also means democratization of production, particularly on the literary level: "want of money" brings "the scribbling fit" (*R* 5); anyone, even the servant Jeremy—educated by a master who was a student at Cambridge—can "tag the ends of Acts" (*LL* I.i, 218). Even "the reformers," with their "awkward, jangling rhymes," now "all poets turn" (*CP* 8–9). With a climate in which "drudges of the stage must . . . be bound to scribble twice a year" (*V* 7), wit (in the later plays in particular) becomes an item of trade that parallels clothing and women. Wit is an expendable commodity when works are salable, and so must be new, like bodies or fashions. These changes in letters intensify the impression of literary glut (as Pope suggests all too powerfully a few decades later from his invented aristocratic perch in *The Dunciad*).[19] And although courtly sex was always democratic (the courtesan's transgression of class lines does not begin only when King Charles seduces former orange girls), when women become scribblers, then literary glut (from democratization) is figured as sexual glut. Scribblers, and women scribblers in particular, are figured as "Whores," their sexual equivalents in the economic structure: "For Punk and Poetess agree so Pat, / You cannot be This and not be That."[20] When, in *The Innocent Mistress*, Lyewell tells Spendall, "[A]ll the Whores in Town can scrawl" (*IM* I, 7), he creates an emblem for the relation of the democratization of letters to the figural interaction of literary and sexual excess. There are plenty of "Whores" to do the scrawling or the activity for which they are better known, and there will continue to be plenty. The world of commerce may be a world of consumption, but there seems to be no disposal; things do not disappear.

In the glutted Exchange, the system of ready circulation, the wrong kind of writing becomes not invention of the new or disposal of the old but rather conduit for verbal waste. Bayes the transverser uses his porous body as medium:

> If I am to write familiar things, as sonnets to *Armida*, and the like, I make use of Stew'd Prunes only; but, when I have a grand design in hand, I ever take Phisic, and let blood: for, when you would have pure swiftness of thought, and fiery flights of fancy, you must have a care of the pensive part. In fine, you must purge the Belly. (*RSL* II.i, 15)

Feminized (he bleeds for fertility's sake), Bayes here serves as conduit for literary/alimentary matter (like the whores and wives who serve as conduit for seminal matter), which he swallows and then excretes.[21] Glut leads to purging ("Surfeits" of wine lead to "Puking in the morning" for Bellamy in Shadwell's *Bury-Fair* [III.i, 34]); and, in purging himself, Bayes gluts the market with his productions, a market that can serve only "deprav'd . . . Appetite" (*WW* II.i, 418). In feeding off that market through the rules of "inventive" transversion, he feeds off his own blood and excreta. The reflexive anthropophagy inherent in the consumption of one's own bodily productions is a figure for the impossibility of novelty, the impossibility of escape from repetition. (When Saturn eats his own children, he tries to prevent the overthrow of the old that is necessary to make way for the new.)

This circulation of waste makes novelty impossible. Waste is what novelty tries to exclude; waste is what repetition, reiteration (rehearsal) generate; waste is what happens when the libertines waste the bodies that fall across their paths—the Mrs. Loveits or Bellindas in *The Man of Mode* (the Dorimants eventually themselves, like Hogarth's rake, wasted in the wake of the pox). There is, of course, a gentlemanly pleasure, an ease in the wasting of women, time, food—Dorimant, one imagines, throws the ripe peach back to the Orange Woman ("Give the bawd her fruit again" [*MM* I.i, 9]). But waste was different in the old world in which less surplus meant that waste was a privilege. Here, the Dorimants respond to the waste of glut with a gesture of economy (the economy of gesture in "ease" is analogous to the "economy" of structure in decorous literary production). The rejection of waste is a disposal of excesses, a kind of aesthetic throwing away that attempts to compress experience into a few necessary and original gestures, that favors the few over the many, that excludes repetition in favor of novelty: prodigality becomes a version of economy. To throw away is another attempt to refuse repetition. But the attempt at economy fails; where there will always be more, prodigality merely perpetuates the excess that serves repetition.

In a world grown pregnant with a novelty that is merely repetition, things get old and tiresome. Boredom comes. The characters here are bored. They are bored with everything, with nothing. "What a dull, insipid thing is a billet-doux," says Dorimant in his slippers (*MM* I.i, 7). It is out of fatigue rather than dislike that characters stop what they are doing. Clothes are boring ("I'm quite tir'd with wearing the Breeches" [*IM* IV, 30]). Acquaintances are boring ("If we had the liberty, we shou'd be as weary of one Set of Acquaintance . . . as we are of one Suit," says Marwood [*WW* III.i, 432–33]). Books are boring ("I'm weary of *Cook* upon *Littleton*," says Lyewell [*IM* IV, 36]). Like the books in Lord Foppington's gallery ("gilded . . . and ranged . . . so prettily, before Gad, it is the most entertaining thing in the world to walk and look upon 'em" [*R* II.i, 38]), they are all the same. The desire for originality itself leads to sameness. Lord Foppington's disaffection from "the inside of the book" springs from his affection for his own originality: "I think a man of quality and breeding may be much better diverted with the natural sprauts of his own" (II.i, 39). The desire for novelty, for originality, has effaced the differences between the books, transformed them into looking glasses, mirrors of the solipsistic and introjected mind; the desire for difference has made sameness.

The use of masks is, like that easy prodigality, a resistance to the ennui that arises from a surfeit of sameness. The mask disguises the old mistress (or one's friend's mistress) as a new one: Sir Francis thinks his familiar mistress Mrs. Beauclair "a Woman well Shap'd, well Drest, Mask'd and alone!" (*IM* II, 17); Loveless thinks his wife, the metaphorically masked Amanda, "a tempting Creature!" (*LLS* IV.iii, 56); Wilmore thinks his friend's mistress Florinda "a very wench!" (*RVR* III.v, 66).[22] The mask, however, also effaces difference. It elides the plasticity of the mobile human face, with its infinite particularities, into the reified sameness of the silk's

marrying
within your
class

unruffled surface. Masks seem to broaden the pool of available women; they turn endogamy to seeming exogamy. But the translation is only apparent. Don Pedro runs after his masked female prey: " 'Tis but in vain to fly me; you're fallen to my lot" (*RVR* V.i, 109). But under the mask, the "wench" is his sister Florinda: with the lifting of the mask, near incest is revealed; same confronts same.

Bayes or Lord Foppington, the men of novelty, end up in repetition. Horner, the man of repetition, by throwing away "the ladies," seems to end up with novelty incarnate: the fleshy country wife, "new" in her emotional virginity, "novel" as a citizen's wife who has not yet created a cuckold. But the play promises circularity: the country wife will become one of the "women of honor" (*CW* II.i, 46), and a new country wife will arrive in town for the indefatigable, mechanical Horner. The double-horned cuckold (already redoubled in the cry "cuck-ckoo") will repeat indefinitely. Print-world prophecy (the repetitions of the mechanically reproduced almanac) can depend on such reiterations: "Oh things will go methodically in the City, the Clocks will strike Twelve at Noon, and the Horn'd Herd Buz in the Exchange at Two" (*LL* IV.i, 289).

The attempt to find novelty fails because the appetitive agents do not know what they want and so they keep consuming more of the same thing. It fails for individuals in their private worlds, constructing a life around desire, because the appetites cannot escape repetition. And it fails for individuals in the context of the larger world because print seems to have uncovered all that there is to know. For many, in the unlimited productions of print, print shows the limitations of knowledge, of words, of poetry, which seem now merely to repeat on the library shelves.

The playwrights, then, transpose this sense of the limitations and repetitions of print to the laboratory. Sir Nicholas Gimcrack's swimming experiment in Shadwell's *Virtuoso*, although it may be "curious," is the result of the virtuoso's mistaken belief in novelty. The virtuoso errs in believing that something new can be discovered from attention to sensory (empirical) data—the frog's movement "upon the superficies or surface of this humid element" (*V* II.ii, 44)—just as the libertine errs in believing that something new can be discovered from attention to the sensory experience of sensualism. Of course, there *is* novelty in science, the kind of novelty that real natural historians or "mechanic philosopher[s]" (*V* II.ii, 43) can produce: Hooke's microscope or Newton's optics. But the power of all those scientific instruments that represent modernity must be belittled by travesty: Sir Nicholas's "microscopes, telescopes, thermometers, barometers, pneumatic engines, stentrophonical tubes, and the like" (V II.ii, 55). The playwrights' work and the work of natural history are beginning to go separate ways, as Bruce suggests in *The Virtuoso* when he clings desperately to Lucretius, who "reconcil[es] philosophy with verse" (I.i, 9), in whom science and poetry are married.

Sir Nicholas is mistaken in his parallel of science and oratory: "Were I as precelling in physico-mechanical investigations as [Sir Formal Trifle] in tropical rhetorical flourishes, I would yield to none" (II.i, 46). Or, rather, he properly identifies his pseudoscience's redundancy (its labored reiteration of the self-evident) with Sir Formal's rhetorical redundancy. The surplus involved in expatiating on breathing ("which is a motion of the thorax and the lungs whereby the air is impell'd by the nose, mouth, and windpipe into the lungs" [II.ii, 47]) is like the surplus of Ciceronian copia. There are already too many words in the world, and they say the same things. In language and love (or appetite) there is no novelty; there is no novelty in the medium of the comic playwright. To translate the eagerness for scientific novelty into the world of words or things is to be a Mr. Novel, a Sir Novelty Fashion, a Bayes. It is necessary to accept repetition in the print world, where characters who refuse to be made ludicrous by the desire for novelty must cede to the conditions of repetition, not fight them, and where they must somehow find renewal in that willingness to accept that there may be nothing new, at least in the world of theater and life.

If one cannot find true novelty, if one can find only sameness through the repetition of novelties, that repetition may be recuperated. For women in particular (and some men), repetition may be averted in the willingness to step away from getting and spending, ingestion and superannuation, into the Platonic realm, outside time. When women choose the sameness of Platonic atemporality, they move outside the cycle of repetition. When Loveless chooses sameness in Amanda, when he chooses dailiness, he too moves outside the cycle of repetition into a species of novelty. All he need do is change his perspective, like Mellefont in Congreve's *Double Dealer*, who, as Cynthia tells him, has "look'd through the wrong end of the Perspective all this while" (IV.i, 168). At the same time that, in the print world, from the virtuoso's perspective the personal world is small, from the perspective of the reader of spiritual autobiography or the novel the personal world has grown larger, the vicissitudes of the heart infinitely interesting. A life may, with the "enlightenment" of the libertine's knowledge (religious and sexual), cease to have a cosmic telos. But the journal, diary, news-paper—the novel with its "to the minute" detail—remind one of the ways in which dailiness can formulate a new series of ends that constitute a life.[23] The dynamic theatrical self, for whom a single appetite along the lines of Jonsonian "humour" would be boring ("*Ah, l'étourdie!*" says Millamant of the "humourous" Sir Wilfull [*WW* IV.i, 448]), refuses the possibility of becoming finished in a life that is a single act and insists on new thoughts, moment by moment. Cosmic telos is transformed into what one might call diurnal telos, design by dailiness; and the desire for the novelties of ever new appetites may be transformed into a willingness to accept the many small quotidian ends in the pleasure of repetition.

Strangely enough, the kind of renewal inherent in the rejection of the ephemeral temporal world or the embrace of sameness in the once-abandoned wife may be parallel, not opposed, to the impulses of the Epi-curean libertine. When Bellmour cries, "Pleasure [be] my Occupation; and let Father Time shake his Glass. . . . I rowl in a higher Orb" (*OB* I.i, 37–38), he is proclaiming the typical Cavalier-Epicurean creed. But he is also iden-tifying and marrying two apparent opposites: the movement outside time inherent in Platonism (an unlikely bedfellow, so to speak, for Bellmour), outside getting and spending ("Business"); and the movement in time that is earth-bound (daily, temporal) pleasure. For the late-seventeenth-century libertine, unconcerned with time and celebrating pleasure, or for the Pla-tonic mistress, the sacred and unique space of timelessness, ostensibly re-moved from either repetition or novelty, is retranslated into an earthliness to redeem repetition and allow it to seem the locus of novelty. Whether Loveless discovers renewal in his familiar wife Amanda or in his new mis-tress Berinthia may not make a difference; like many of the comedies, *The Relapse* does not resolve the issue of sexual novelty by taking one side or another but by showing the two side by side. It does not really matter, perhaps, whether you choose Amanda or the masked punk or the Platonic orbs, as long as you give up the struggle for something new. And in giving up the struggle for something new, in ceding to that condition of repetition, you may just find novelty.

"*Quicquid est idem, est idem*" ("that which is the same is the same"), says the Bricklayer in Crowne's *City Politiques* (IV.i, 82), but he is wrong. That which is the same may be different. The desire for originality itself leads to sameness; and, so, by looking for sameness, we may find novelty, as Loveless does when he renounces his appetite for the new, as Bellinda does when she surrounds herself with her Platonic books, as even Bellmour may if he is willing to accept that his daily appetitive condition ("Why what a Cormorant in Love am I!" [*OB* I.i, 40]) is chronically repetitious. Perhaps there is no true novelty; perhaps time cannot be either transformed or regained; perhaps there can be no progress nor a return to an "original," to a "primitive purity"; perhaps we are stuck in the sameness of repetition. But we can grant permission to things to be the same, and, in granting permission, we may find in them a kind of renewal. It is exactly what Mirabell means when he answers Millamant's question at the end of *The Way of the World* ("[W]ou'd you have me give my self to you over again?"): "Ay," says Mirabell, "and over and over again" (*WW* V.i, 477).

Notes

1. There has been surprisingly little discussion of the importance of "novelty" to the late seventeenth and early eighteenth centuries, and the few comments that do exist are limited to identifications of the use of the term in discussions of wit and plot. See, for instance, Fujimura ("Critics were generally in agreement over the importance of novelty and surprise in wit" [32]), and Thorpe, who identifies a few seventeenth-century comments. The most extended and interesting discussion is that of Hunter, who identifies the relation between print, the active news press, and the interest in contemporaneity, rightly pointing out the interpenetration of the oral and written realms of discourse, for instance in the newsprint-filled coffeehouses with their emphasis on up-to-date conversation.

2. All parenthetical play references in the text or notes are to act, scene, and page—not line—number in the edition given in the Works Cited. The following abbreviations identify the plays indicated (all dates are of first performance and are from *The London Stage*):

BF	Shadwell, *Bury-Fair* (1689)	N	Motteux, *The Novelty* (1697)
CP	Crowne, *City Politiques* (1683)	O	Southerne, *Oroonoko* (1695)
CW	Wycherley, *The Country Wife* (1675)	OB	Congreve, *The Old Bachelour* (1693)
DD	Congreve, *The Double Dealer* (1693)	PD	Wycherley, *The Plain Dealer* (1676)
EL	Dryden, *An Evening's Love* (1668)	PW	Vanbrugh, *The Provoked Wife* (1697)
IM	Pix, *The Innocent Mistress* (1697)	R	Vanbrugh, *The Relapse* (1696)
LC	Behn, *The Lucky Chance* (1686)	RSL	Buckingham, *The Rehearsal* (1671)
LL	Congreve, *Love for Love* (1695)	RVR	Behn, *The Rover* (1677)
LLS	Cibber, *Love's Last Shift* (1696)	V	Shadwell, *The Virtuoso* (1676)
MM	Etherege, *The Man of Mode* (1676)	WW	Congreve, *The Way of the World* (1700).

I am grateful to Rael Meyerowitz for discussions that gave focus to this paper.

3. These institutional structures have overlapping histories in the late seventeenth century: "Modern" natural history relies on modern financial interests to

finance its work and on print to disseminate, for instance, the graphs and engravings crucial to it; print as a trade develops and diversifies with the help of credit and improves its technology (in the mezzotint, for instance) with the help of science; banking comes increasingly to rely on printed instruments of credit. See my essay "The Bank, the Press" for detail on the historical conditions that led to the recoinage crisis of the 1690s, and the relationship between credit systems and print. Although particular dates are important to the configuration of cultural responses I am describing, the looser historical span in which I am working ("late seventeenth century," roughly 1660–1700) implies a set of arbitrary boundaries. I prefer to call attention to the randomness of choice in historical identification by not pretending to any more "meaningful" series of markers. (To choose 1688 and 1702, for instance, would suggest a political argument that I am not making.)

The shift between 1660 and 1700 from the "hard" to the "soft" comedy—what Novak calls increasing "douceur" (25)—is a real one. Staves describes the philosophical shift aptly: "Man, it is decided toward the end of the seventeenth century, is not essentially a creature of lust and vengeance, but a tranquil social animal animated by benevolence" (302; see also Fujimura 156–96). For the issues I address it is less revealing to pay attention to the differences between eras (or, for that matter, among dramatists, or between genders) than to pay attention to the identity of the comedies as a whole. There is no series of dichotomies (pre-1688/post-1688, Whig/Tory, or even Ancient/Modern) that can make better sense of the figural relations I am tracking. The "Ancients and Moderns" discussion is part of the story but does not offer an appropriate way of bifurcating attitudes toward the various relevant metaphoric clusters. On the Ancients and Moderns, see R. F. Jones. On science and seventeenth-century poetry, see Nicolson. On the connection of science to ideas of innovation in Cowley, see Guibbory. On the Royal Society's dependence on modern finance, see the preface to Hooke's *Micrographia*. On print's use of credit and credit's use of print, see my essay "The Bank, the Press."

Eisenstein discusses the relationship of print to scientific innovation (520–635) and science's particular use of print (543–66). Almost all who have written on "print culture" have stressed the identification of print and the value for the new. See Eisenstein 119–26, Ong 41–42. I will not go over all the arguments and historical evidence for this position, which is clearly important to my present discussion and is convincing as far as it goes. However, as Eisenstein argues, and as I would like to suggest here, to assert a monolithic print-identified value for the new is to oversimplify the manifold ways print interacts with cultural impulses and expression.

4. What is really at issue here is not the "impact" of the press or the bank as such, nor their agency in a process of mutual conditioning, although there certainly is a process of mutual conditioning at work, but rather a continual and fluid interaction among metaphors, material products, and institutions. To read out the moments in which metaphoric clusters, homologies, and cultural products are critical to par-

ticular theatrical and larger community meaning, and to understand the nature of the axis that turns these places of attention—the attention to novelty, news, novels, fashion, food, sex, the attention to varieties of getting, spending, and glut—can tell us something about the ways one kind of energy, as expressed in one medium, may have multiple manifestations during a particular period.

5. Nisbet writes that "by common assent the first expression of the modern idea of progress" is Fontenelle's 1688 assertion that "men will never degenerate, and there will be no end to the growth and development of human wisdom" (104). Nisbet points out, rightly, that the late seventeenth and eighteenth centuries are as full of doubts about the possibility of human progress as they are of belief in it. Whitney also delineates both sides of the idea of progress in the eighteenth century. Fussell identifies the Augustan humanist as one who, among other things, "either possesses or affects such broad and historical awareness of actual human nature as to justify grave doubts about the probability of any moral or qualitative 'progress,'" even while admitting "the reality of experiential or material progress" (4).

6. The phrase is a common one. If courtesans such as Angellica Bianca in Behn's *The Rover* have their pictures hung before their chambers to advertise their goods, cuckolds have their pictures hung on latrine walls to advertise the loss of their goods, in the same way that one would advertise such things as a "lost melancholy Person" in the newspapers. In both cases, the image serves to call attention to the disruption of the closed and finished distribution of goods in the marriage world, to the continued public circulation of women outside the closed space of the marital household. Cheatall, in *The Innocent Mistress*, fears, "In a short time I shall be made Ballads on, and my Picture set before 'em just like the Summons to *Horn-fair*" (*IM* II, 11). The ballad with the cuckoldry print, the "Summons to *Horn-fair*," like the playbill, is an invitation to the theater/Exchange (fairground) in which circulation is freed from the constraints enforced by the closed space of the boudoir.

7. Return to an originary condition, to a "primitive purity," is the same as novelty for the late seventeenth century and the opposite of the print-parasite's productions. Just as Thomas Sprat, in his *History of the Royal Society* (1667), urges a return to a "primitive purity" in language (113), Dennis praises Rymer's intention "to restore Tragedy to its primitive purity" (1: 30), and Farquhar wishes to "discover Comedy in its primitive Institution" (377).

8. On the news press, see Sutherland. Although both Charles and James kept a tight hand on the press, there was a flurry of newspaper publication in the few years during the temporary lapse of the Licensing Act at the beginning of the 1680s, and in 1688 a weekly paper began to appear alongside some unlicensed ones. Although the final lapse in 1695 by no means meant complete freedom, as Sutherland points out, it permitted a fully established news press, publishing a number of thrice-weekly newspapers and, in 1702, the first daily newspaper (31).

9. Preamble to the first *London Courant* (1688). Qtd. in Sutherland 23.

10. The quotations Johnson chooses to illustrate "novelty" and its variants are hardly neutral: "the Presbyterians['] . . . *novel* injunctions"; "*novel* usurpation"; "freed from prejudice or *novelty*"; "our *novelists* impeach . . . that great soul"; "the fooleries of some affected *novelist*."

11. "Paper . . . Specie," "Coin'd Paper": Defoe 214, qtd. in Southerne 78 n. "Imaginary Money": Samuel Lambe, *Seasonable Observations humbly offered to His Highness the Lord Protector,* qtd. in Richards 99. On the history of English banking, trade, and credit for the late sixteenth and early seventeenth centuries, see Thirsk, and, for the late seventeenth and eighteenth centuries, see Dickson. On the crisis of the 1690s in particular, see D. W. Jones, and, for an analysis of the ideology behind seventeenth-century economics, see Appleby 199–241 and throughout. Agnew suggests much about the metaphoric relationship between theater and market from 1550 to 1750.

The use of "paper credit," culminating in the printing of money in 1694 (Richards 156–60, Beresiner and Narbeth 22), both enhanced the sense of the rapidity of circulation in modern commerce and added to the impression that printed matter could be identified with commercial trade and circulation. Shell, in his rich analysis of the relationship between money and language, gives a subtle reading of the meaning of paper money, ideas of inscription, and Faust (105–11) and offers something like a poetics of the literary-economic relation.

12. There has been so much discussion of Hobbesian appetite and alimentary imagery that it would be redundant to offer more examples. Comments are sprinkled throughout discussions of general intellectual background. See especially Underwood 26–28, Holland 114–30, and Fujimura 39–57. The central passage in Hobbes on the primacy of appetite and aversion is *Leviathan* (31–39).

13. When a woman is no longer tradable as one kind of commodity, she must become a trader, but women can be traders only in others, and it is difficult to trade if one continues to be merchandise. "For your part," Welldon asks Lucy, "what trade could you set up in? You would never arrive at the trust and credit of a guinea-bawd. You would have too much business of your own ever to mind other people's" (O I.i, 13–14). In *The Way of the World,* Millamant and Marwood (as always, inverting the presumptions of the male world by parodying them, each in different ways) struggle against the commodification of women by attempting the same on men, proposing to throw out "one's Acquaintance [fools and lovers] as one does one's Cloaths" (WW III.i, 432).

14. Cross-dressing here acts, among other things, as an impractical response to the anxiety over what happens to desire after consummation, after the consumption of the sexual commodity. Cross-dressing permits a form of courtship that bars the possibility of consumption: virgins cannot be "used up" if he is a she or she is a he.

15. Hobbes, in the *Leviathan* (ch. 11), offers a philosophical version of chroni-

cally roving desire and insatiability when he writes: "Felicity is a continual progress of the desire, from one object to another; the attaining of the former, being still but the way to the latter. The cause whereof is, that the object of man's desire, is not to enjoy once only, and for one instant of time; but to assure for ever, the way of his future desire" (63).

16. Vanbrugh reminds us of the extent to which appetitive finitude is a fiction when he shows Berinthia trying to trick Amanda about the nature of male desire. The fates get in the way for men in search of a "woman they are capable of being fond of," Berinthia says, "and this makes them wander about from mistress to mistress, like a pilgrim from town to town, who every night must have a fresh lodging and's in haste to be gone in the morning" (*R* V.ii, 120). Like Aristophanes' fiction, Berinthia's, suggests Vanbrugh, is a promise of appetitive finitude that is a lie.

17. Spacks (123 ff.) has an interesting discussion of the relationship between sexual and verbal promiscuity, the tongue as "common whore, for she lies with all men" (according to Lord Burghley's *Precepts*), the identification of female generativity with the verbal generativity of gossip.

18. Similarly, an actor's gestures might reveal the relationship between the false wit's literary and erotic onanism when Bayes invites Smith and Johnson to do his new play "the honour to see it in its Virgin attire": "Though, perhaps, it may blush, I shall not be asham'd to discover its nakedness unto you.———I think it is in this pocket [*Puts his hand in his pocket*]" (*RSL* I.i, 3). Performance might also bring out the onanistic sodomite voyeur in Lord Foppington's pleasureful using of the mirror to see himself "behind" (*R* I.iii, 19).

19. See Kernan 8–47 on the destruction of "courtly letters" and the new print-based regime. For Pope, print glut (too many books) is the source not only of Nonsense but also of the madness that emanates from nonsense and that identifies Grub Street with Bedlam. In late-seventeenth-century plays, "madness" is often sexual license: "Sr [sic] *Francis Wildlove* is too mad even for me" (*IM* I, 6). (Hogarth and others will not let us forget that untamed sexual consumption leads to the madhouse.) One wonders if the glut and repetition of a surfeit of books that lead to nonsense and madness in Pope are here also suggested in the love madness that parallels and acts as counterpart to the nonsensical wit madness in so many of the plays (for instance, Lady Touchwood's love madness and Lady Froth's wit madness in Congreve's *Double Dealer*).

20. The satirist Robert Gould, in a piece addressed to Behn (qtd. in Woodcock 103).

21. The identification of bodily emission as literary production in the conditions of Grub Street is more explicit in Swift's analogy between the critic and the man who makes his way through the "Ordure" of the streets—"not that he is curious . . . to be padling in, or tasting it" (*Tale of a Tub*, 56)—or in the flowing urine of Pope's booksellers in *The Dunciad*, "Renew'd by ordure's sympathetic force" (II.103),

and even more explicit in Freud who, two centuries later, will identify excreta with literary "creativity."

22. Lord Foppington suggests the relation between the mask and the fashionable wig when he analogizes the two ("Far a periwig to a man should be like a mask to a woman, nothing should be seen but his eyes" [*R* I.iii, 24]): the theatrical mask, which responds to appetite with concealment, is displaced in the former Sir Novelty Fashion's world with shifting periwigs, sizable buttons, and new Steenkirks, which respond to appetite with apparent novelty.

23. On the creation of the diurnal in the late seventeenth and eighteenth centuries, Sherman is suggestive. Eventually, psychoanalysis fulfills the eagerness for the narrative repetitions of quotidian experience. For Freud (in "Remembering," for instance), the narrative enactment of repetition, which must be translated into memory through the repetitions of the analysis, is essential to change—and so to happiness.

Works Cited

Agnew, Jean-Christophe. *Worlds Apart: The Market and the Theater in Anglo-American Thought, 1550–1750*. Cambridge: Cambridge UP, 1986.

Appleby, Joyce Oldham. *Economic Thought and Ideology in Seventeenth-Century England*. Princeton: Princeton UP, 1978.

Behn, Aphra. *The Lucky Chance; or, An Alderman's Bargain*. London, 1687.

——— . *The Rover*. Ed. Frederick M. Link. Lincoln: Bison–U of Nebraska P, 1967.

Beresiner, Yasha, and Colin Narbeth. *The Story of Paper Money*. Newton Abbot, Devon, Eng.: David and Charles, 1973.

Buckingham, George Villiers, Duke of. *The Rehearsal*. 3rd ed. London, 1675.

Cibber, Colley. *Three Sentimental Comedies*. Ed. Maureen Sullivan. New Haven: Yale UP, 1973.

Congreve, William. *The Complete Plays of William Congreve*. Ed. Herbert Davis. Chicago: U of Chicago P, 1967.

Crowne, John. *City Politiques*. Ed. John Harold Wilson. Lincoln: Bison–U of Nebraska P, 1967.

Defoe, Daniel. *Defoe's Review* 3: 55. Ed. Arthur Wellesley Secord. Facsimile Book 7. New York: Columbia UP, 1938.

Dennis, John. *The Critical Works of John Dennis*. Ed. Edward Niles Hooker. 2 vols. Baltimore: Johns Hopkins UP, 1939–43.

Dickson, P. G. M. *The Financial Revolution in England: A Study in the Development of Public Credit, 1688–1756*. London: Macmillan, 1967.

Dryden, John. *An Evening's Love; or, The Mock Astrologer. The Works of John Dryden*. Vol. 10. Ed. Maximillian E. Novak and George Robert Guffey. Berkeley and Los Angeles: U of California P, 1970. 195–314.

Eisenstein, Elizabeth. *The Printing Press as an Agent of Change: Communications and Cultural Transformations in Early-Modern Europe*. Cambridge: Cambridge UP, 1979.

Etherege, Sir George. *The Man of Mode; or, Sir Fopling Flutter*. Ed. W. B. Carnochan. Lincoln: Bison–U of Nebraska P, 1966.

Farquhar, George. "A Discourse Upon Comedy, In Reference to the English Stage." 1702. *The Works of George Farquhar*. Vol. 2. Ed. Shirley Strum Kenny. Oxford: Clarendon, 1988. 364–86.

Freud, Sigmund. "Remembering, Repeating, and Working-Through." *The Standard Edition of the Complete Psychological Works of Sigmund Freud*. Trans. and ed. James Strachey and Anna Freud. Vol. 12. London: Hogarth P, 1958. 145–56.

Fujimura, Thomas H. *The Restoration Comedy of Wit*. Princeton: Princeton UP, 1952.

Fussell, Paul. *The Rhetorical World of Augustan Humanism*. Oxford: Clarendon, 1965.

Guibbory, Achsah. "Imitation and Originality: Cowley and Bacon's Vision of Progress." *Studies in English Literature* 29 (Winter 1989): 99–120.

Hobbes, Thomas. *Leviathan*. Ed. Michael Oakeshott. Oxford: Blackwell, 1947.

Holland, Norman N. *The First Modern Comedies: The Significance of Etherege, Wycherley, and Congreve*. Cambridge: Harvard UP, 1959.

Hooke, Robert. *Micrographia*. London, 1665.

Hunter, J. Paul. " 'News, and new Things': Contemporaneity and the Early English Novel." *Critical Inquiry* 14: 3 (Spring 1988): 493–515.

Johnson, Samuel. *A Dictionary of the English Language*. New York: Arno, 1979.

Jones, D. W. "London Merchants and the Crisis of the 1690s." *Crisis and Order in English Towns, 1500–1700*. Ed. Peter Clark and Paul Slack. Toronto: U of Toronto P, 1972. 311–55.

Jones, Richard Foster. *Ancients and Moderns: A Study of the Rise of the Scientific Movement in Seventeenth-Century England*. Berkeley and Los Angeles: U of California P, 1965.

Kernan, Alvin. *Printing Technology, Letters, and Samuel Johnson*. Princeton: Princeton UP, 1987.

Motteux, Pierre. *The Novelty. Every Act a Play. Being a Short Pastoral, Comedy, Masque, Tragedy, and Farce*. London, 1697.

Nicolson, Marjorie Hope. *The Breaking of the Circle: Studies in the Effect of the 'New Science' upon Seventeenth-Century Poetry*. Rev. ed. New York: Columbia UP, 1960.

Nisbet, Robert A. *Social Change and History: Aspects of the Western Theory of Development*. New York: Oxford UP, 1969.

Novak, Maximillian. *William Congreve*. New York: Twayne, 1971.

Ong, Walter J. *Orality and Literacy: The Technologizing of the Word*. London: Methuen, 1982.

Peters, J. S. "The Bank, the Press, and the Illusory 'Return of Nature': On Currency, Print, and Dramatic Property in the 1690s." *Conceptions of Property in the Seventeenth and Eighteenth Centuries.* Ed. John Brewer and Susan Staves. London: Routledge, forthcoming.

Pix, Mary. *The Innocent Mistress.* London, 1697.

Richards, R. D. *The Early History of Banking in England.* New York: Augustus M. Kelley, 1965.

Shadwell, Thomas. *Bury-Fair.* London, 1689.

———. *The Virtuoso.* Ed. Marjorie Hope Nicolson and David Stuart Rodes. Lincoln: Bison–U of Nebraska P, 1966.

Shell, Marc. *Money, Language, and Thought: Literary and Philosophical Economies from the Medieval to the Modern Era.* Berkeley and Los Angeles: U of California P, 1982.

Sherman, Stuart. "Telling Time: Clocks and Calendars, Secrecy and Self-Recording in English Diurnal Form, 1660–1795." Diss. Columbia U, 1990.

Southerne, Thomas. *Oroonoko.* Ed. Maximillian E. Novak and David Stuart Rodes. Lincoln: Bison–U of Nebraska P, 1976.

Spacks, Patricia Meyer. *Gossip.* Chicago: U of Chicago P, 1985.

Sprat, Thomas. *History of the Royal Society.* Ed. Jackson I. Cope and Harold Whitmore Jones. St. Louis: Washington UP, 1958.

Staves, Susan. *Players' Scepters: Fictions of Authority in the Restoration.* Lincoln: U of Nebraska P, 1979.

Sutherland, James. *The Restoration Newspaper and Its Development.* Cambridge: Cambridge UP, 1986.

Thirsk, Joan. *Economic Policy and Projects: The Development of a Consumer Society in Early Modern England.* Oxford: Clarendon, 1978.

Thorpe, Clarence DeWitt. "Addison and Some of His Predecessors on 'Novelty.'" *PMLA* 52 (1937): 1114–29.

Underwood, Dale. *Etherege and the Seventeenth-Century Comedy of Manners.* 1957. Hamden, Conn.: Archon, 1969.

Vanbrugh, Sir John. *The Provoked Wife.* Ed. Curt A. Zimansky. Lincoln: Bison–U of Nebraska P, 1969.

———. *The Relapse; or, Virtue in Danger.* Ed. Curt A. Zimansky. Lincoln: Bison–U of Nebraska P, 1970.

Whitney, Lois. *Primitivism and the Idea of Progress in English Popular Literature of the Eighteenth Century.* New York: Octagon, 1965.

Woodcock, George. *The Incomparable Aphra.* 1948. London: Oxford UP, 1986.

Wycherley, William. *The Country Wife.* Ed. Thomas H. Fujimura. Lincoln: Bison–U of Nebraska P, 1965.

———. *The Plain Dealer.* Ed. Leo Hughes. Lincoln: Bison–U of Nebraska P, 1967.

SHIFTING TROPES OF IDEOLOGY IN ENGLISH SERIOUS DRAMA, LATE STUART TO EARLY GEORGIAN

J. DOUGLAS CANFIELD

In "Dramatic Shifts: Writing an Ideological History of Late Stuart Drama," I recently called for a history of the drama of the late Stuart and early Georgian periods that analyzes shifts in dramatic tropes, tropes that do not just reflect but help to constitute the transformation from an aristocratic, late feudal to a newly dominant bourgeois ideology. The work of John Loftis pointed the way down this critical path, and work by Susan Staves and Laura Brown a decade ago began to blaze a trail. But Loftis inferred change more in terms of topical than ideological politics, that is, more in terms of topical allusion than tropic transformation. And Staves and Brown employ an evolutionary model that posits early Restoration forms unproblematically representing Royalist ideology followed by forms emptied of any ideological content before they are filled with bourgeois ideology. Moreover, Staves focuses on transformations of portraits of authority ostensibly leading to more democracy in both political and domestic realms, and Brown (references are to *English Dramatic Form* unless otherwise noted) on transformations of generic form leading to the "moral action" of drama and the novel in the new era—the former failing and the latter succeeding in embodying a supposedly exemplary morality.

While I greatly admire their work, perhaps a better model for historical change is not gradual but rather sudden transformation—what Thomas Kuhn calls a *paradigm* or Michel Foucault an *epistemic* shift. It is as if, right up to the Glorious Revolution, an aristocratic force field holds the elements of official discourse together; afterward, we can detect a new, bourgeois configuration of discursive elements. While histories of literary form have proven particularly fruitful in the analysis of the emerging bourgeois form par excellence, the novel, they have not proven fruitful for the drama, probably because dramatic genres were so well established. Instead, we might fare better by analyzing these configurations of elements—what Fredric Jameson calls *ideologemes* but which I prefer to call by the more common, more euphonious name of *tropes*.

Employing useful concepts from Raymond Williams, we can follow tropes that shift from *emergent* status in the aristocratic to *dominant* status in the bourgeois era. For while dramatic *genres* remain quite consistent, the tropes within them shift rapidly over the fulcrum of the Glorious Revolution. By representative sampling in the four main genres of English "serious" drama—heroic romance, political tragedy, personal tragedy, tragicomic romance (as I have defined and deployed them in *Word as Bond*)—I should like in this essay to trace some key tropes, especially of class and gender, from their emergent status in Restoration drama (1660–88) to their dominant status in Revolutionary (1689–1714) and early Georgian drama. Previous formalistic, teleological analysis, by focusing on wholes more than parts, has obscured what a tropic analysis can reveal. It becomes obvious that, despite their democratic, meritocratic political rhetoric, the plays are exclusionary: they portray the consolidation of power in the hands of a new (male) elite—a power based ostensibly on law but really on the sword and the gun. And their neostoic exemplary morality masks upper middle-class male dominance over gender, class, and even race. Lockeian social contract theory, which underlay the bourgeois revolution in England and later in America, actually meant in practice, as these plays despite their inculcation of the new ideology unwittingly reveal, that only a few (good) men are created equal.

Heroic Romance

If the heroic play par excellence of the Restoration, Dryden's *Conquest of Granada* (1670–71), essentially reaffirms Royalist ideology,[1] most intriguing is how Dryden invests so much of the play's energy into two anarchic characters, Almanzor, the "noble Savage" (Part 1, I.i.209), who owes allegiance to no power, and Lyndaraxa, the seductive ambitious woman, who would be queen no matter who wears the crown. Michael McKeon's analysis of Leonidas in Dryden's *Marriage à la Mode* (155) also applies to Almanzor. Following the typical romance plot, Almanzor discovers his royal lineage and kneels to his cousin-sovereign. Nonetheless, he also articulates a radical individualism ("I alone am King of me" [1.I.i.206]) that claims for the savage a new kind of nobility based on merit. Moreover,

Almanzor's discovery of his lineage is complicated by his origins as a love child. The king's sister secretly married beneath her status. She and her husband, the duke of Arcos, were forced into exile, and she died in childbirth. They were thus rebels against the strict control of the patrilineal system especially in the royal family. The princess's death can be read as a condign retribution for such a crime against status. And Almanzor's relegation to the role of a subject can also be seen as a consequence of that crime. Furthermore, as the most attractive and most powerful agent in the play, for the ideological intentionality of the play to work he must be won from fluctuating allegiances and socialized into the service of legitimate power, lending his powerful phallic sword to the growing imperialism of Spain's "Conqu'ring Crosses" (2.V.iii.346). By the end, then, the dominant class ideology subsumes the emergent trope of the bourgeois self-made man. But can we forget it?[2]

Something similar occurs with Lyndaraxa. Characterized as enormously seductive and ambitious, she transcends the normal stereotype in these plays through her brilliant and attractive wit. Observe the way she verbally toys with her suitors, Abdelmelech and Abdalla. At the end she suffers her own condign punishment: killed at the moment of her apparent triumph by a cast suitor who knows her evil wiles, she is finally troped into the figure of the uppity woman put in her place by the phallic sword of gender dominance. Yet does she not too represent an emergent figure that will not go away forever?[3]

In other words, if we proceed by a more dialectical method than I have heretofore employed, we might see *The Conquest of Granada* as a play that allows the genie of emergent bourgeois ideology, particularly concerning the class status of men and the gender status of women, to strut and fret on the stage until charmed back into the lamp. Is there any significance to the contrast between Almanzor's being socialized and Lyndaraxa's being so harshly punished? Perhaps one could speculate that English society was more prepared to embrace the bourgeois trope of the self-made man than it was that of the self-made woman. Meanwhile, the romance form attempts to contain emergent male individualism by enlisting it in the service of imperialism just as Dryden's *Annus Mirabilis* attempted to co-opt rebellious London into a joint venture for a world emporium.[4]

By the time of Rowe's *Tamerlane* (1701), the most popular heroic romance of the eighteenth century, at least the male genie was out of the bottle for good. Previous critics have read the play as a political allegory, attempting to identify characters as prominent persons, from Tamerlane as William III and Bajazet as Louis XIV on down.[5] Loftis goes further, reading the play as "war-inspired Francophobia" at the beginning of the War of the Spanish Succession and Whig propaganda for Lockeian constitutional theory (*Politics* 32–34). Staves (107–9) reads *Tamerlane* as "democratic romance" but focuses on the single trope of reduced authority for sovereigns. Brown (151) reads it as "the direct embodiment of the bourgeois ideals of the Glorious Revolution" but limits her treatment to the contrast between "Herculean" and "exemplary" hero. The figure of Tamerlane is important but not so much in isolation as in his connection to a network of ideological tropes.

Tamerlane indeed portrays the ideal bourgeois leader, the constitutional monarch, primus inter pares, contrasted with his class antithesis, the absolutist monarch Bajazet, whom the new ideology portrays as a runaway autocrat bound by no laws, human or divine. The emergent bourgeois political model is fraternal rather than paternal. Bajazet mocks Tamerlane's dependence upon the advice and consent of "debating Senates," with whom he shares "a precarious Scepter" (II.ii, 24).[6] In the prologue Rowe underlines this bourgeois appropriation of the Roman model of government. When Tamerlane is roused to war against the tyrant, Rowe anachronistically narrates,

> The peaceful Fathers, who in Senates meet,
> Approve an Enterprize so Just, so Great;
> While with their Prince's Arms, their Voice thus join'd,
> Gains half the Praise of having sav'd Mankind.
>
> (italics omitted)

In other words, like the new bourgeois political theorists, Rowe makes Parliament a supposedly equal partner with the king, though the latter's "Scepter" now depends upon the former's will.

Loftis plus Staves plus Brown will take the interpretation this far. But the figure of Tamerlane is part of a larger pattern. Rowe suggests that meritocracy has supplanted aristocracy. Tamerlane's followers insist that "had not Nature made him Great by Birth, / Yet all the Brave had sought him for their Friend" (I.i, 2). When accused by Bajazet of "vile Obscurity," Axalla, who has come to court his daughter as well as peace, scorns to "borrow Merit from the Dead" by citing his Roman lineage but asserts instead "that inborn Merit, / That Worth" of his own "Virtue" that distinguishes him.

Besides, the most salient feature of those "Heroes, and God-like Patriots" among his ancestors is that they "Scorn'd to be Kings" (III.i, 40).

But meritocracy remains a system essentially *between men* (to borrow a key concept from Eve Sedgwick). What complicates the democracy of this romance is the gender politics of its subplot, the tragic story of Moneses and Arpasia, Greek lovers whose solemn betrothal has been ruptured by Bajazet, who has forced Arpasia into marriage with him. When Moneses appeals to Tamerlane, in effect, to annul the forced marriage and reinstate the prior vows, Tamerlane is as absolute as a legislature or tribunal of men refusing to allow an abortion after rape: "[W]ould'st thou have my partial Friendship break / That holy Knot, which ty'd once, all Mankind / Agree to hold Sacred, and Undissolvable?" "All Mankind" has established a system of genealogical control in which woman is nothing more than an incubator, and bourgeois ideology upholds this patriarchal sentiment. Tamerlane enjoins Moneses to "cure this amorous Sickness of thy Soul" and come engage with him in the "manly" art of conquering war: "Nor will I lose thee poorly for a Woman" (III.ii, 50–51). Meanwhile, Arpasia is allowed divorce only in her sleep with its song-induced dream. As with Lyndaraxa, women are not allowed full participation in the new order. They are confined to chambers while the men engage in a displaced version of Britain's new imperialism under King Billy and his wars. The Providential rhetoric of the play insists that bourgeois right now makes might; Bajazet's own daughter may rebel against her father's tyranny and aid the juster side; but the real agency of power remains the phallic sword installing and expanding middle-class male dominance.

A new ethic shrouds the naked point of this political sword, neostoicism. Rowe focuses on the master trope of the bourgeois era, self-reliance. Tamerlane stands fixed on his own firm center (the figures of Marlborough, Nelson, Wellington, and Washington are merely his avatars). Rowe complicates the focus with the heart-rending emotions of the subplot, but finally, when Arpasia is forced to watch Moneses' strangulation, she too becomes a figure for self-reliance as Rowe appropriates the aristocratic trope of constancy and changes its emphasis from constancy or fidelity to a person to constancy of mind. Yet like the martial arts, this too is manly activity: Arpasia must overcome the "Woman" in her "Soul" (IV.i, 63) and endure this "Tryal" of her resolve (V.i, 73). She does, then dies from the strain, confident that she and Moneses will be united in an afterlife. At the end of the play, Bajazet, confined to his cage as an exemplum, has been defeated by those who stand fixed on the firm center of self-control as opposed to those who yield to lawless passion, now a trope for the decadent aristocracy. But the new ethic remains patriarchal, between men, and is enforced by a still quite patriarchal god.

From Delarivier Manley, author not only of notorious attacks on prominent (male) Whigs that incurred the wrath of the government (not to mention Alexander Pope) but also of several numbers of the *Examiner* that earned her temporary co-editorship with Jonathan Swift, one might have expected a more enlightened treatment of gender in her late heroic play *Lucius, the First Christian King of Britain* (1717). Indeed, Jack Armistead and Debbie Davis, editors of a recent facsimile edition, maintain that the heroine Rosalinda, erstwhile queen of Aquitaine and future queen of Britain and Albany (here, Scotland), is a "crucial feminine agent" (iii). They mean that, as the object of what René Girard would call mimetic desire among warring rivals, as the cause of Lucius's killing the usurper of his own throne, and as the converter of Lucius to Christianity, she is responsible for the transmission of Christian authority in England from pope to monarch—a version of history that helps constitute and reinforce early-eighteenth-century Tory ideology (vi–vii).

I shall return to this putative Tory ideology in a moment. Let me first examine Rosalinda's putative agency. As the *object* of mimetic desire, she can hardly be said to be an *agent*. Only as passive object of Lucius's desire, about to be raped by the executioner (really the usurper Vortimer in disguise), does she *cause* the death of the usurper. She does convert Lucius to Christianity, but that action occurs before the play and results in their death sentence by the pagan Gauls. We can infer only from the play's title the kind of implication for British history Armistead and Davis claim: there is no explicit reference in the text to the future Christian reign of Lucius and Rosalinda.

Within the play, however, Rosalinda exercises agency in a very important action, ignored by Armistead and Davis. Set "free" by Honorius, the Gallic king (II.i, 17), though a recent widow to the rebel king of Aquitaine, she defies conventional mourning, *chooses* Lucius as her new consort, and marries him clandestinely. Moreover, she doubly defies convention in that Lucius is the son of the man who murdered her father, the king of Albany. In addition, she defies that parricide (Vortimer), who murdered her father in revenge for denying his daughter's hand to him, who pursued her husband into Gaul and waged war against him, and who now desires her as the victor's spoils. And she lives to triumph with her new husband over that lawless renegade and over her scheming cousin, Arminius, who is also willing to violate all codes of honor to possess her and thus possess double power as the new king of Albany married to its heir presumptive.

Such successful agency is rare indeed in English serious drama. Witness what happens to the duchess of Malfi or Almeyda in Dryden's *Don Sebastian* or Almanzor's mother or Felicia in Trotter's *Fatal Friendship* (see below) when they attempt clandestine marriages to men of their choosing. Witness the painful resistance to such a marriage by Dryden's maiden queen in the play of that subtitle. Even in comedy, where feisty women often marry behind the backs of male protectors, those protectors are almost invariably brought to bless the marriages at the end. No real (class) rebellion takes place. Rosalinda needs and gets no one's blessing. At the end she is queen of Albany, married to the king of Britain—an ending we may view as more an emblem of England's current union with Scotland than any Tory myth of historical origins. Note, however, the implicit superiority, despite Rosalinda's agency, of Lucius over her, England over a feminized Scotland.

More probable than reading the play as a myth of origins is reading it as Jacobite allegory.[7] But if *Lucius* is Jacobite propaganda written during The Fifteen, there are problems with its Tory ideology. First, the trope of kingship. Vortimer sounds like Bajazet when he characterizes Honorius as an inept king, hamstrung by his people despite his desire to void the sentences of Lucius and Rosalinda:

> The Coward *Gaul*, durst not release the *Christians,*
> Durst not command, ev'n in his Capital,
> Lest his good People shou'd, forsooth, grow angry.
> We laugh'd to see the Royal Dastard's Fears;
> Whilst, by our seeming Zeal, and Gold well-plac'd,
> We gain'd a Sentence hateful to their King.
>
> (V.i, 49)

Vortimer is vile, and we are invited to see the Gallic people, through their institutions of religion and justice, as corrupt or corruptible—like an English Parliament that twice in one century would remove a legitimate king from his throne. But Vortimer is wrong about Honorius, for he sends troops, under Lucius's uncle, prince of Cambria (Wales), to rescue the condemned despite his people's decree. Obviously, though no explicit mention of it is made, the decree is set at nought at the end and Lucius and Rosalinda are free to return to England and be the co-sovereigns of a united Great Britain, England, Scotland (and Wales).

Does Manley here offer the image of a king not fettered by Parliament, one who could act independently and forcefully for the good of his people? If so, how would such a ruler escape the Whig accusation of *arbitrary*, especially when Honorius appears to have suspended the laws and institutions of his country, particularly its religion? Moreover, Honorius's intentions are contaminated by his manipulation throughout the play by his sister Emmelin, who is activated by no higher motive than her desire to have Lucius for herself. If Manley intended to provide a positive Tory alternative image of kingship, she failed.

Second, the trope of restored king. Even though Lucius does not know the rapist executioner is his father; even though he constantly defers to his father in filial piety and refuses to fight him in rivalry for Rosalinda; and even though we discover after he accidentally kills him that Vortimer is not his real father and that Lucius has avenged his real father's death at Vortimer's hands, nevertheless the play portrays Oedipal parricide. The audience is forced to experience—and to secretly applaud—the killing *as* parricide, discovering only afterward the truth. Whatever her intention, it is as if Manley is not allowed refuge in myth but is forced to acknowledge history: whether she and the Tories like it or not, succession in England had often been parricidal, and not even a return to the Stuarts could expunge the blot on the escutcheon.

In addition, the approving experience of parricide in the play works to legitimate de facto succession. It is as if the audience is invited to say, "All our theorizing about legitimate succession notwithstanding, whether aristocratic or bourgeois, this is our history; we are heirs of the success of its usurpations and regicides. Behind any myth of legitimacy lurks naked power." Perhaps Manley's own ambivalence about the renewed, Hanoverian usurpation is mirrored in her rapprochement with Sir Richard Steele, one of those prominent Whigs she had attacked, through her dedication of the play to him.

Political Tragedy

If right up to the Revolution Royalist political tragedy, pace Staves and Brown, reaffirmed its master trope of word-as-bond in the teeth of growing opposition (see my "Royalism's Last Dramatic Stand"), nevertheless we see emerging from it in the hands of its last defenders—Dryden, Crowne, and Southerne—another example of the new bourgeois master trope of self-reliance, the figure of the deserted leader in exile, who, at least in the case of Cleomenes in Dryden and Southerne's play of that name (1692), seems no longer reliant even on a god (see my "*Regulus* and *Cleomenes* and 1688").

Joseph Addison's *Cato* (1713) was the most popular political tragedy of the eighteenth century and remains the best-known example of the paradigm shift from the old to the new master trope. It appropriates the aristocratic language of loyalty, though Cato's loyalty is not to an individual but to Rome, to the *patria*, or as Cato puts it throughout, thus transforming a bogeyword of the Royalists into an honorific term, to the *commonwealth*. The older aristocratic loyalty to a person is portrayed as leading all too often not to bonds but bondage. As in *Tamerlane* the proper form of social organization is fraternal; the proper body to govern, the Senate (read *Parliament*). And though constancy of lovers is still important, the main constancy the play celebrates is that of mind. Cato remains true to himself and dies the One Just Man. He becomes the prototype for a series of republican patriotic heroes who regret that "we can die but once to serve our country!" (IV.iv.82; see Loftis, *Politics* 44).

In the subplot concerning Cato's children and their lovers, the trope of neostoic constancy of mind is doubled. Cato's passionate son Marcus's liabilities would, in Restoration drama, have recommended him. Lucia, beloved of both brothers, describes him to the self-controlled Portius thus:

> Marcus is over-warm: his fond complaints
> Have so much earnestness and passion in them,
> I hear him with a secret kind of dread,
> And tremble at his vehemence of temper.
>
> (I.vi.49–52)

But not only is she won by the new man of reason and control, Lucia must overcome her "own weak sex" (I.vi.22) and imitate Cato's daughter, who in emulation of the great self-reliant hero "tow'rs above her sex" (I.iv.147). She makes a sacred vow not to "mix plighted hands" with Portius until the storm above them—Caesar's impending defeat of Cato, Marcus's rash pursuit of her—clears (III.ii.31–36). Though she feels "the woman breaking in upon" her (48), she successfully resists it, regains stoic composure, and re-calls Portius to his self-control as well. Later, she needs to help Marcia rely on her "wonted strength and constancy of mind" when Marcia believes her lover Juba, from whom she has stoically hidden signs of her affection in these troubled times, to be dead (IV.iii.14).

The problem with this portrayal of female as well as male stoic self-control is that, like Rowe's Arpasia, these women must transcend the in-herent *weakness* of their gender and become, like Pope's idealized portrait of Martha Blount in *To a Lady,* little men. Behind such a trope of mas-culinized women lies latent misogyny. Even more striking is how this pas-sive acceptance of gender inferiority parallels Juba the Numidian Prince's active embrace of racial inferiority and deference to Rome's (read *Europe's*) racial and cultural superiority. Even when Juba believes he is positively describing the potential African contribution to Cato's cause, he employs metaphors of barbarism and demonic blackness that are the traditional European tropes for African inferiority:

> Did they know Cato, our remotest kings
> Would pour embattled multitudes about him;
> Their swarthy hosts would darken all our plains,
> Doubling the native horror of the war,
> And making death more grim.
>
> (II.iv.36–40)

But when he admonishes his old counselor Syphax for his views of Nu-midian martial assets, Juba articulates the rationale for European colonial and cultural imperialism:

> These all are virtues of a meaner rank,
> Perfections that are placed in bones and nerves.
> A Roman soul is bent on higher views:
> To civilize the rude, unpolished world,
> And lay it under the restraint of laws;
> To make man mild and sociable to man;
> To cultivate the wild, licentious savage
> With wisdom, discipline, and lib'ral arts—
> Th'embellishments of life; virtues like these
> Make human nature shine, reform the soul,
> And break our fierce barbarians into men.
>
> (I.iv.28–38)

In language Frantz Fanon would bitterly understand, Juba rejoices in his ability to emulate the European patriarch: in order to become worthy of his daughter, Juba pledges to Marcia, "I'll gaze forever on thy godlike father, / Transplanting, one by one, into my life, / His bright perfections, till I shine like him" (I.v.19–21). Unfortunately, no matter what white mask, his skin will always shine black. Addison's political tragedy is tragically unaware of the *liberty,* that Whig keyword touted throughout, it denies to supposedly inferior race and gender in its celebration of the triumph of bourgeois ideology.

Nicholas Rowe's *Lady Jane Gray* (1715) merits examination both because of its implicit bourgeois political theory and because of its rare positive portrait of a woman's agency—a portrait cast finally, I will argue, in disturbing shadows. The play is written during The Fifteen to support the cementing of England's Revolution (see Loftis, *Politics* 79–80). Lady Jane, grandniece to Henry VIII, is as far-fetched an heir to the throne as was George I, but the end—preserving a Protestant succession—justifies the means.

Jane's questions of Northumberland when he offers her the throne contain crucial assumptions of emergent social contract theory:

> Can *Edward*'s Will,
> Or Twenty met in Council, make a Queen?
> . . . where are those . . . who make the Law?
> Where are the Ancient Honours of the Realm,
> The Nobles, with the Mitre'd Fathers join'd?
> The Wealthy Commons solemnly Assembled?
> Where is that Voice of a Consenting People,
> To pledge the Universal Faith with mine,
> And call me justly Queen?
>
> (III, 55)

When Northumberland promises Jane that just such parliamentary approval is forthcoming, she accepts the crown. That no such approval is ever obtained implicitly explains the failure of that particular revolution. But the further implication is that when such approval is obtained (as in 1688 and again in 1715), succession can be altered—and should be in order to avoid the oppressive tyranny of absolute and therefore arbitrary monarchy. The play concludes with prophecies of future heroes (read: *William III, George I,* and *his son, the Prince of Wales,* to whose wife Rowe dedicated the play) who would finally complete the Protestant Reformation—and the bourgeois revolution—in England.

Of course, one sect's *Book of Martyrs* is another sect's *Book of Heretics,* and while Rowe's play invokes Whig rhetoric of justification—complete with villainous bishops and *Bloody* Mary—obscured is the blood of martyrs on the other side from Thomas More and John Fisher to Charles I to the Irish at the Battle of the Boyne. Once again it is not really a Parliament but an axe that rules.

In addition to its political tropes, the play portrays the bourgeois ethical trope of self-reliance in its manifestations of stoic self-mastery and constancy of mind in adversity, in short, standing firm on the fixed center of one's being, what Lady Jane calls "the settled Quiet of my Soul" (V, 83). What is remarkable about Rowe's play is that the "Divine Example" in the play (V, 87) is not the typical male (Tamerlane, Cato) but a woman. As "A Prologue to *Lady Jane Gray,* sent by an Unknown Hand" (probably Pope's) puts it,

> Nobly to bear the Changes of our State,
> To stand unmov'd against the Storms of Fate,
> A brave Contempt of Life, and Grandeur lost;
> Such glorious Toils a Female Name can boast.
> (appended, p. 94, italics omitted)

And the only reference in the text to woman's proverbial weakness is Northumberland's misogynistic complaint, which turns out to be ironic:

> What trivial Influences hold Dominion
> O'er Wise Men's Counsels, and the Fate of Empire?
> The greatest Schemes that human Wit can forge,
> Or bold Ambition dares to put in Practice,
> Depend upon our husbanding a Moment,
> And the light lasting of a Woman's Will.
> (I, 18)

Stronger than Manley's Rosalinda, Lady Jane manifests the greatest strength of "Will" in the play, constantly teaching others, especially her husband Guilford, Christian-stoic endurance. Instead of overcoming the woman in her soul (like Arpasia or Lucia or Marcia), Lady Jane boasts that, if she were sure she had legal warrant to be queen, her "Soul . . . could be more than Man, in her [England's] Defence" (III, 54). Appearing at first to accept the crown passively—"Take me, Crown me"—she quickly asserts her own agency, "I take the Lot with Joy" (56). Even the treacherous bishop of Winchester marvels at the "Command" with which Lady Jane awed the court before which she was tried offstage (V, 80). And she finally puts him in his place with two beautifully imperious imperatives: at his self-righteous condemnation of her husband's persistence in his Protestant "Heresy" (V, 86), Lady Jane commands, "Cease, thou Raven; / Nor violate, with thy profaner Malice, / My bleeding *Gilford*'s Ghost" (V, 89). Finally, when he unctuously attempts to lay the blame for her own death on her stubbornness and proclaims, "Thy Blood be on thy Head," she wonderfully retorts,

> My Blood be where it falls, let the Earth hide it,
> And may it never rise, or call for Vengeance:
> Oh, that it were the last shall fall a Victim
> To Zeal's inhumane Wrath!
>
> (V, 90)

Inspired, I believe, especially by John Banks's queens—Elizabeth; Anna Bullen; Mary, Queen of Scots—but perhaps also influenced by the first feminists of the preceding century up to Mary Astell in his own time, Rowe would seem to have provided a role model for the new bourgeois woman to emulate and a series of goals for her to aspire to: first education, then the vote, finally prime minister. But Jane's early death seems to underscore the fact that the hour of this new woman had not yet come. It was acceptable for Rowe to portray a strong woman in command because she was only queen for a day. Moreover, unlike Banks's Queen Elizabeth, despite her command presence Lady Jane never gets to really run the country. She actually becomes a figure for the new constitutional monarch in England—Anne or George I—a figurehead behind whom the Northumberlands and Harleys and Walpoles, the male prime ministers, have the real power (backed, of course, by the army and the navy).

Personal Tragedy

Restoration personal tragedy usually features a great-souled protagonist torn apart by conflicting emotions—Lee's Alexander the Great or Mithridates in plays of those titles (1677 and 1678, respectively), Dryden's Antony in *All for Love; or, The World Well Lost* (1677). In that sense alone they

seem to me to remain aristocratic.[8] One need only to contrast that aristocratic magnanimity, that capacity for great passion, with Cato's neostoic
coldness or George Lillo's portrayal of an ethic that totally suppresses passion (see below). Juxtaposed to the centrifugality of their passion and to
the mutability of their worlds and of their own wills remains generally the
aristocratic virtue of constancy to one's word, oath, vow—as I have argued
at length about not only Dryden's play but all the precedent Renaissance
treatments of the story of Antony and Cleopatra.[9]

Nevertheless, lurking within Dryden's play itself are two figures who become prominent in bourgeois personal tragedy, the self-controlled man and
the domestic woman. Although satirized in Dryden's play as a Hobbesian
pragmatist in pursuit only of his "In'trest" and a bourgeois "Usurer," "fit . . .
to buy, not conquer Kingdoms" (III.i.213–15) because he coldly refuses to
meet Antony in personal combat to decide their contestation, the unheroic
Octavius might, in bourgeois dress, become the heroic Bevil Junior of Sir
Richard Steele's *The Conscious Lovers* (see below), who refuses to fight a
duel. More interesting, perhaps, is the figure of Dryden's Cleopatra, who
has fallen off from Shakespeare's outrageously unpredictable enigma to
dwindle into a constant lover whom "Nature meant . . . / A Wife, a silly,
harmless, houshold Dove" (IV.i.93–94).

It is a critical commonplace that this figure of the domestic woman leads
to the creation of *she-tragedies* by Otway, Banks, Southerne, and Rowe,
tragedies focusing on the figure of a usually passive, pathetic, suffering,
innocent woman.[10] And it was long a theatrical commonplace to juxta-
pose against this essentially submissive woman a termagant antagonist,
from Lee's rival queens in the play of that name to Cleopatra and Octavia
in Dryden's play to the contrasts between Lavinia and Calista and Jane
Shore and Alicia in Rowe's two most famous she-tragedies. Playwrights
created such contrasting pairs to take advantage of talented actresses, no
pair more famous than Barry-Bracegirdle. If we turn to a less well known
she-tragedy—and one written by a woman—we can see earlier than Rowe
the exploitation of this pairing for the shaping of the figure of the perfect
bourgeois wife, and the complicity of a woman author in such a creation.

Catherine Trotter's *The Fatal Friendship* (1698) contrasts the fiery, passionate Lamira with the patient, submissive Felicia. The former is a wealthy
widow whose jealous husband's will enjoins her from marrying again at
the risk of forfeiture of her fortune to his sister. She is in love with the penu-
rious younger brother Gramont, who marries her hastily (and secretly, to

avoid the forfeiture) for necessary cash to pay fines unjustly levied against him and his best friend Castalio and a ransom to pirates who have kidnapped his infant son from a *previous* clandestine marriage to Felicia. In a scene that must have been an excellent vehicle for Barry, Lamira, left alone on her wedding night by the conscience-stricken Gramont, gradually surmises the presence of a rival in his affections and grows furiously vengeful in splendidly written dialogue. In contrast, Felicia is astounded but hurt by the news her husband has committed bigamy, and she becomes quickly submissive in the face of her patriarchal brother's anger at her for her secret marriage with Gramont:

> *Bellgard.*   Ay, trait'ress, weep,
>   Weep for thy shame, thy sin, thy disobedience,
>   Rebellious girl, pollution of my blood!
> *Felicia.* Oh I deserve all this, that could deceive
>   And disobey the best of brothers.
>   (III.ii, 176)

In one of those confrontational scenes between such female antagonists, Trotter brings them together for a gradual unfolding to Lamira of not just Felicia's rivalry but her prior legitimate claim. Both women are strong in this scene, Felicia having determined to "tear" Gramont from Lamira (III.ii, 178). Throughout she asserts her "right" to him, even as Lamira asserts her "right" to vengeance (178–80). But Lamira has contempt for Felicia's meek continued acceptance of Gramont: "[T]hou art so poorly spirited, / T'accept and yield t'adulterated love" (180). Yet Lamira loses the contest—at least in the ideological intentionality of the play. Her failure to control her rage leads her ignominiously to attempt to prey upon Felicia's poverty and bribe her with her fortune never to see Gramont again. Meanwhile, although she upbraids him for his perjury to their vows, Felicia forgives Gramont and even blames herself for his misery in that she in her "inconsiderate passion" revealed the "fatal secret" of their marriage to her brother:

>   it was my duty, as your wife,
>   Whate'er I suffered, not to have accused you,
>   And as I loved, I should have had no thought
>   Of my own misery whilst you were happy.
>   (IV.i, 183)

Moreover, Felicia rejects Lamira's bribe, choosing "the bitterness of poverty" and insisting, "The marriage vows are not conditional" (V.i, 191–92). To Gramont she pledges to "labour for our food, or beg an alms" (V.i, 195). This is standing by your man *without* a vengeance!

When Felicia calls her refusal of Lamira's bribe, even in the face of her husband's pleading with her to redeem their son, "the strongest trial" (V.i, 197), she underscores the real meaning of the play. Throughout *Nicholas Rowe and Christian Tragedy* I argued that *trial* is a central metaphor in the religious rhetoric of Rowe's theodicean plays. I still think it is, though I am now more interested in the ideological significance of the trope. If passion in aristocratic personal tragedy causes fatal vacillation between objects of desire, with fidelity to one's word the central test or trial, in bourgeois serious drama the trial is of one's constancy of mind (Arpasia, Marcia, Cato, Lady Jane). Let us see how these various shifts play themselves out in Trotter's tragedy.

In *The Fatal Friendship* word-as-bond remains a central theme: Gramont has perjured his vows to Felicia, yet he is praised—even by Lamira, if only grudgingly (IV.ii, 189)—for his remarkable fidelity to Felicia on the night of his wedding to Lamira by abstaining from consummation despite Lamira's abundant charms. Castalio is finally won over to reconciliation with his rival by his "superior virtue": "By Heaven, I think . . . not all my honour could / Have guarded me against so strong a trial" (V.i, 203). But Felicia's "trial"—and Gramont's most serious trial in the play—are tests of constancy of mind. More particularly, they are tests of resolve against economic exigencies, and in that sense, under the still familiar guise of an aristocratic domestic tragedy, Trotter's is a specifically bourgeois morality play.

Like the protagonists of more obvious examples of this genre—from George Barnwell (see below) to Hirstwood in Dreiser's *Sister Carrie*—Gramont is besieged by a series of financial woes. His father, the count, because he wants Felicia for himself and wants to eliminate his rival by forcing Gramont into a marriage with Lamira, blackmails Gramont by refusing to pay his or Castalio's fines. Marriage with the rich widow will give Gramont himself the means to do so. When he refuses, his father casts him out penniless. Then Gramont discovers that not only has the king not intervened with the vengeful general who holds them both hostage, the king suspects Castalio of treason. Gramont must act quickly to save his life. Then the coup de grâce: Gramont learns pirates have his son.

If Trotter has modeled her plot at least in part on Otway's *Venice Preserved* (1682), one significant difference is that Jaffeir, though bribed by Pierre's money to supply his immediate financial needs, is also prompted to join the rebellion perhaps out of principle, especially as articulated by Pierre, but certainly out of revenge. Gramont describes his motivation as "nature," that is, the natural concern of a husband, father, friend:

> I must, I must prevent at any rate
> This dismal scene of misery and ruin,
> Turn villain, any thing, when she's at stake,
> My child too, and my best friend. I could, by Heav'n,
> Suffer a thousand racking deaths for each,
> And should I sacrifice 'em all, to keep
> A little peace of mind, the pride of never straying?
> Walk on by rules, and calmly let 'em perish,
> Rather than tread one step beyond to save 'em?
> Forbid it nature!
>
> (II.ii, 167–68)

When he concludes, "[N]ot I, but fate resolves it," Trotter has made him as much as possible the passive victim of economic necessity.

Nevertheless, the moral of the play plasters over that necessity with an ethic designed to neutralize potential radicals: "[T]here's not a state / So miserable, but may with greater ease / Be suffered than dishonour" (V.i, 194). When Felicia, who as a last resort to save her son has left to plead for mercy with Gramont's father, returns with him, like Otway's Priuli, ready to help, it is too late. Gramont has accidentally killed Castalio trying to break up a duel between him and Bellgard, and he stabs himself. But not only has Felicia succeeded in softening the count; the king has learned the truth and offered satisfaction and preferment to both Castalio and Gramont. Gramont reads the lesson that underwrites the moral:

> Oh, what a wretch was I, that could not wait
> Heaven's time, the providence that never fails
> Those who dare to trust it. Durst I have been honest,
> One day had changed the scene, and made me happy.
>
> (V.i, 206)

At one point Gramont compares his behavior with that of the lower classes in a similar situation:

> Better I might have borne the worst of miseries,
> That threatened me; which not the meanest wretch,
> That begs, or toils for bread, but can support,
> And does not truck his honesty for fortune[.]
>
> (IV.i, 183)

In other words, Trotter's play is a warning to lesser members of the middle and lower classes to keep strict, neostoic resolve in the face of financial ruin, for, as with Micawber, something will turn up: God's in his heaven and all's right with the system. Both Gramont and Felicia represent the "necessity" (read *social desideratum*) for those without money and power—the lower classes and the lower gender—to endure.

In George Lillo's *The London Merchant; or, The History of George Barnwell* (1731), Barnwell and his master Thorowgood present class triumph not for the petty bourgeoisie but for the upper-middle merchant class, for although Barnwell is apprentice to Thorowgood, he may well come from the same stratum of society; in fact, as the beloved of Thorowgood's daughter Maria, he probably does.[11] (Who is, then, the London Merchant of the title?) David Wallace demonstrates how the new bourgeois ethos interpenetrates public and private realms, socioeconomic theory and ethics. Not only have merchants become respectable, as attests the opening appropriation from the aristocracy of credit for the defeat of the Spanish Armada by the London merchants (who convinced the Genoese to deny Spain a necessary loan); but capitalism is portrayed as natural, "founded in Reason, and the Nature of Things" (III.i.3–4). Because it is natural, it can be universally applied in a system of mercantile expansion that is, in effect, a justification for European, specifically British, imperialism.[12] Thorowgood's *good* apprentice Trueman, merely a bourgeois Juba, articulates colonialism rhapsodically:

> I have observ'd those Countries, where Trade is promoted and encouraged, do not make Discoveries to destroy, but to improve, Mankind,—by Love and Friendship, to tame the fierce, and polish the most savage,—to teach them the Advantages of honest Traffick,—by taking from them, with their own Consent, their useless Superfluities, and giving them, in Return, what, from their Ignorance in manual Arts, their Situation, or some other Accident, they stand in need of. (III.i.9–15)

The same rationalization for the exploitation of Third World peoples and their resources can still be heard today. In words that more nakedly justify the importation of everything from gold to oil to the Elgin marbles, Thorowgood adds, "It is the industrious Merchant's Business to collect the various Blessings of each Soil and Climate, and, with the Product of the whole, to enrich his native Country" (III.i.20–22).

What is less obvious is that the strict bourgeois ethic in the play, complete with metaphysical sanctions, portrays the simple crime of lust leading to theft and ultimately to parricide, not only because of the interpenetration of public and private, as Wallace shows, but because, as the seductress Millwood's maid Lucy puts it, "one Vice as naturally begets another, as a Father a Son" (II.xiii.7). That is, this begetting of vices is portrayed as a "natural" progression because the system such vices attack is still a patrilineal system for the transmission of power and property. Barnwell's rebellion against his "Master" and uncle/father (who raised this orphan) is called "Parricide" because it is an Oedipal rebellion against patriarchal control of the access to the inextricably connected money and sex of the play. In a bourgeois political economy, where time is money and reputation is credit, in contradistinction to the celebration of youth in Restoration comedy in particular, Thorowgood and Trueman are right to proclaim, respectively, "The State of Youth is much to be deplored," its "Idleness [the] worst of Snares" (II.iv.17–18; II.ii.77). Thus the play's insistence on absolute self-control—and the disastrous consequences when it is lost, whether that loss is a woman's loss of marketability or a young merchant's loss of credibility, or credit.

Wallace is correct to point out that while ostensibly free to marry whom she chooses, Maria would never dream of violating her father's wishes (133). Moreover, while pretending that a young man's "Merit" recommends him more as a husband for Maria than "high Birth and Titles," nevertheless, "tho' they make not a bad Man good, yet they are a real Advantage to a worthy one, and place his Virtues in the fairest Light." It is no accident that Thorowgood's drawing room is filled with "noble Lords," for Thorowgood seeks a worthy partner in his only child's inheritance of "the Fruits of many Years successful Industry" (I.ii). And at the end, when she is described as "lost" and "undone" (V.ix.4, 40), the only possible explanation is that Maria has made her love for Barnwell public, thus damaging her trade value in the marriage market. Her melancholy throughout has resulted from knowing that her father would be disappointed if she chose

Barnwell instead of one of those lords, marriage with whom, on the part of merchants' daughters, helped build those crucial estates, like the one Hogarth pictures out the window of the opening panel of *Marriage à la Mode*. Finally, even when she confesses her love to Barnwell in prison, she apologizes for *invading* "the Freedom of your Sex's Choice" (V.ix.32–33).

Splitting off his good from his bad girl, in traditional fashion but with a bourgeois twist, Lillo portrays the ultimate threat to the system as an uppity promiscuous woman, a "Sorceress," naturally—a witch (IV.xvi.18). I have already shown the character of her rebellion and the way she finally does not escape patriarchal paradigms but describes herself as Heaven's "Power to punish" (V.xi.46; see "Female Rebels" 161–62). But Millwood is not the Dark Woman of aristocratic literature (e.g., Duessa; see *Word as Bond* ch. 1 and passim). The bourgeois twist is that she exposes the rapacious Social Darwinism that lies beneath the veneer of bourgeois ideology: having flayed the system for its kickbacks and coverups, Millwood concludes, "I follow'd my Inclinations, and that the best of you does every day. All Actions seem alike natural and indifferent to Man and Beast, who devour, or are devour'd, as they meet with others weaker or stronger than themselves" (IV.xviii.33–36). And she reveals the system's enforcing metaphysic to be *man's* fiction, the devil his self-image: "That imaginary Being is an Emblem of thy cursed Sex collected. A Mirrour, wherein each particular Man may see his own Likeness, and that of all Mankind" (IV.xviii.4–6).

Lillo may have thought adding the last scene would contain Millwood's critique of capitalism. Though, as several critics have noted, Thorowgood acknowledges the "Truth" of what she says, he is referring only to religious hypocrisy, not business hypocrisy (IV.xviii.45). And Lillo may have thought that he successfully countered Millwood's negative female image with the positive one of Maria, the contaminated vessel of patriarchal seed versus the pure. Making Millwood a witch may have been the easiest way to discredit her in an essentially misogynistic culture, where power is really shared *between men*—witness the male bonding between Barnwell and Trueman. But like Lyndaraxa, Millwood is invested with too much energy to be contained, and her critique actually gains power by her being a woman, an oppressed "Slave" because she owns no "Property" (I.iii.18). In an important sense she speaks for the have-nots in capitalism, all those whom poverty drives to murder oppressors. Going beyond Trotter's Gramont, Barnwell seeks to murder his uncle/father/business patriarch for his money. Like Millwood, he has found it "necessary to be rich" in order to survive in a capitalist economy of unlimited acquisition for the few (IV.xviii.15). In short, the bourgeois ideology of the play has generated its own antithesis, which it has charmed back into the lamp of its justifying rhetorical metaphysic, where it appears to remain today: witness the condemnation of the recent shooting of a scab in West Virginia.

Tragicomic Romance

If Restoration tragicomedy in the main also reaffirms aristocratic ideology (including *Marriage à la Mode*),[13] I have already cited McKeon's dialectical reading of *Marriage*, a reading that highlights emergent bourgeois tropes such as the self-made man and freedom of marital choice (156–62). Sounding like Almanzor, Leonidas at one point exclaims, "Though meanly born, I have a Kingly Soul yet" (IV.i.22), and he and Palmyra insist on their right to choose marital partners (though not to the point of her defying her father). I would add to McKeon's tropes Doralice's threatening the male double standard as another example of the uppity woman claiming equal sexual rights—in this case, to adultery.

In the paradigm shift from aristocratic to bourgeois ideology, tragicomic form gets appropriated not only by the novel (*Pamela, Evelina*) but by that dramatic form critics have always found so off-putting, sentimental comedy. In this hybrid of somber high plot cum comic low plot similar to tragicomedy, we find as early as Shadwell's comedies of the 1680s some of those emergent bourgeois tropes already triumphing over aristocratic tropes. *The Squire of Alsatia* (1688) has long held a secure place in the history of the emergence of sentimental drama. And coming as it does at the virtual moment of revolution, it seems to me to signal a dramatic shift in ideological paradigm. Nevertheless, Shadwell's *The Lancashire Witches, and Tegue o Divelly The Irish-Priest* (1681) strikes me as a more interesting play for purposes of analyzing these ideological shifts. In it Shadwell first develops the trope of the benevolent *fratriarch* (if I may coin the term), Sir Edward Hartfort. "A worthy Hospitable true English Gentleman, of good understanding, and honest Principles," Shadwell describes him in the dramatis personae. Sir Edward merits his position in society because of his essential worthiness. Marks of this worth are his "good understanding," which consistently manifests itself in his enlightened, unsuperstitious reasonableness; his impatience with insinuating clerics; his warm affection for his daughter and the memory of his departed wife; his "honest Principles" of both domestic and national order, especially his neostoic morality and his patriotism: *I am a true English-man, I love the Princes Rights and Peoples Liberties, and will defend 'em both with the last penny in my purse, and the last drop in my veins, and dare defy the witless Plots of Papists.* For such sentiments, he is called "a Noble Patriot," a Whig keyword, and instead of familial loyalty to a father-king, he articulates a loyalty to the English "Constitution" as "the Noblest in the World." Ashamed of a decadent, Frenchified aristocracy, he agrees that "the Genius of *England*" has devolved upon the "Yeomanry" (III.47–60). But his care for building his estate through marriages between his and his neighbor's children marks him as a "true English Gentleman," one of the new country gentry upon which England will build its fame and strength (in union with its merchants).

Shadwell's young male lovers are also members of this enlightened country gentry as opposed to Restoration comedy's Town Wits. Unlike his earlier rakish pairs in *Epsom Wells* (1672) and *The Virtuoso* (1676), these lovers are already converted to true love, and while they display a faith in the new science similar to Sir Edward's, they display no wit. That is left to their female counterparts, and here Shadwell's play is most revolutionary. Yet here it is also conservative, marking the emergence of a bourgeois order but marking also its political and patriarchal limits.

The major conflict in the play is the familiar one of enforced marriage, this one to unite Sir Edward's estate with that of his neighbor, Sir Jeffrey Shackelhead, through a double marriage of their sons and daughters. The problem is that witty women are to be matched with two different kinds of fool. Sir Jeffrey is married to a status-conscious wife who would not only take on airs but impose Town airs on their son, whom she has turned into the fop Sir Timothy. And Sir Edward's own son, like so many country bumpkins in later eighteenth-century drama, loves his hunting, horses, and dogs more than women. So the arranged marriages are doomed, and the women properly rebel:

Isabella [Sir Edward's daughter]. Well, we are resolved never to Marry where we are designed, that's certain. For my part I am a free English woman, and will stand up for my Liberty, and Property of Choice.
Theodosia [Sir Jeffrey's daughter]. And Faith, Girl, I'le be a mutineer on thy side; I hate the imposition of a Husband, 'tis as bad as Popery. (I.272–76)

The reference to "Popery" is not gratuitous, for the very subtitle of the play announces the presence of the delightful Tegue o Divelly, the infamous Catholic Father Kelly of the Popish Plot, but both fathers who arrange forced marriages (Sir Edward's progressiveness is herein qualified) and the pope are traditional patriarchs who inhibit liberty.

Shadwell had been developing the figure of this resourceful English woman in *A True Widow* (1678) and *The Woman Captain* (1679), and Isabella, played by the irrepressible Elizabeth Barry, boldly proclaims, "I warrant thee, a Womans wit will naturally work about these matters" (II.429–30). She is generally the witty one, outrageously teasing Sir Timothy and even throwing stones at him, then covering up in front of the parents. Most interestingly, at one point their wit induces these female rebels to put on the disguises of the Lancashire witches of the title.

Michael Alssid has done an excellent job of detailing "the implicit parallels between feminine mischief and true sorcery" in the play (90–95). But because he sees the real witches' behavior as simply chaotic, as opposed to the rational order of Sir Edward, he seems to me to miss the profound implications of the revolutionary agency of all the witches in the play, that is, all the uppity women who would challenge patriarchal control. The ultimate liberating act of wit on the part of the heroines is to disguise themselves as witches, for in the chaotic night before their forced marriages they thus escape the reappearing representatives of patriarchal order—especially Sir Jeffrey, who is looking for his own rebellious wife, herself seeking an adulterous liaison with one of the young men. And, like Manley's Rosalinda and Trotter's Felicia, they proceed to marry their lovers clandestinely without parental, patriarchal approval and at the risk of losing their dowries and rupturing the familial warmth at least between Isabella and her father.

Agency is complicated in this night scene. Often characters attribute human agency to witches, for example when Sir Jeffrey trips over a servant upon entrance to the men's chamber, where hide the two young women and his lady (IV, 158). But it is important to note that the real witches abet the women's rebellion, providing, in the words of Alssid, "a figurative smoke screen for the harassed couples" (93). Moreover, as Alssid also notes, the real witches provide the storm that brings the young men mistakenly to the very estate that houses the women who bewitched them at the spa just in the nick of time to prevent their enforced marriage and to get the women for themselves despite "the laws of Sir Edward and Sir Jeffrey" (93).

What Alssid does not see is that the witches represent both female agency—in this case, the freedom of women to choose sexual partners—

and the limitations of that agency: the partners chosen do not finally rupture the patriarchal bonds, for the young men are themselves well bred, from good estates, and can provide superior portions for their brides. Thus Sir Edward accepts them and offers to reconcile Doubty and Theodosia to the Shackleheads. Interestingly, Sir Edward considers Doubty to "have most Injur'd [him]" (V.654). The reason is that Doubty has supplanted his son with Theodosia, thus denying him the male heir he so desperately wants to carry on his "Name" (V.663). Instead, he accepts Bellfort as his son-in-law.

Especially in the repeated references to their hidden teats whereby they suckle all manner of beast and imp, on the one hand, and to their constant involvement in infant mortality, on the other (see the ends of acts 2 and 3), the real witches are associated with the powers of fertility and impotence or barrenness, of womb and tomb. They represent the ultimate uppity women, matriarchs who threaten patriarchal control of female reproduction, the archetype of the Great Mother (see Neumann):

> Men and Beasts are in thy Power,
> Thou canst Save, and canst Devour,
> Thou canst Bless, and Curse the Earth,
> And cause Plenty, or a Dearth.
>   (III.642–45, italics omitted)

Their "*power*" is so great that "*Heaven it self can have no more*" (II.518–19). They threaten the Western male deity, the superego of Western law. Thus they must finally be subjected to that law at the end of the play, when they are sent to "Goal," that is, jail (V.564). Moreover, Shadwell tempers their threat by subjecting them to a "Master" throughout, the Devil: uppity whores must be controlled by a patriarchal superpimp.

It is no accident that one of the witches, Mother Dickenson, copulates with Tegue o Divelly in the chaotic night scene. As Alssid notes, she thus "prevents Tegue's rape of Lady Shacklehead" (93); more important, she prevents her adultery with Doubty as well: women's freedom in the play does not extend to adultery either (shades of Doralice). But most important, the copulation represents the essential similarity between witchcraft and popery [14]—not just because both are superstitious but because both threaten the emergent bourgeois order. From Marlowe's *Dr. Faustus* to Marx's interpretations of the failure of the revolutions in France (see *The Civil War in France*), the emergent middle class gains power by driving a wedge between Right and Left, between the ancien régime and any real democratic revolution. Tegue is associated not just with popery but with a clergy, a court, and a class too sympathetic with Rome and France and late European feudal aristocracy. And the witches are associated with not just female but class uppitiness. Thus through the servant Susan's potion they help bring the Anglican chaplain Smerk down, as Alssid notes without seeing the sociopolitical significance, from his "social climbing" (93) and limit him to a more proper status. Thus the human witches bring Sir Timothy— and by implication his mother—down from their unmerited status aspirations. By the end of the play not only is the country bumpkin Clod back on top of his witch and in control with *her* bridle; the benevolent fratriarch is back on top, threats to his new order banished to jail (the witches and Tegue) or put in their place. Sir Edward has earlier rationalized his disbelief in the power of witches as anti-Manichaean: " '[T]is such as you [Smerk] are Atheistical, that would equal the Devils power with that of Heaven its self" (I.356–57). Yet he does not attribute the dynamic of the denouement to Heaven, as in the typical ending of Restoration and Revolutionary drama, but instead to "Fate" (V.701). But the real dynamic is the incipient shift in power relations between one dominant class and another.

Loftis has briefly analyzed Mr. Sealand in Steele's *The Conscious Lovers* (1722) as a figure for not only the equality of the emergent middle class but (implicit in Loftis's treatment) its superiority. He notes that the play satirizes aristocratic pretensions to class superiority (*Comedy* 84–85). Loftis quotes this key statement by Sealand to Sir John Bevil, one of those who assumes class privilege, in this instance by excusing his son's putative sowing of wild oats:

> Sir, as much a Cit as you take me for—I know the Town, and the World—and give me leave to say, that we Merchants are a Species of Gentry, that have grown into the World this last Century, and are as honourable, and almost as useful, as you landed Folks, that have always thought your selves so much above us; For your trading, forsooth! is extended no farther, than a Load of Hay, or a fat Ox—You are pleasant People, indeed; because you are generally bred up to be lazy, therefore, I warrant you, Industry is dishonourable. (IV.ii.49–57)

The sneeringly sarcastic dichotomy between aristocratic laziness and middle-class industry and utility connotes not just equality but superiority.

Brown astutely analyzes the play's inherent contradiction between middle-class value based on merit and the marriage that concludes the action (170–73). While Sealand and Bevil Junior may both protest that virtue only is their concern in a marriage, as in the typical tragicomic romance each of the nubile characters turns out to be in the right class anyway, so any real challenge to the traffic in women to improve estates proves moot. If she had not been preoccupied with matters of generic form, Brown might have availed herself of more of Loftis's analysis of shifts in society to make the point that, despite Sealand's protestations, he is participating in the building of that gentry-merchant middle class Hogarth depicts as *Marriage à la Mode*. As he says in a conciliatory tone to the elder Bevil, "[L]ook you, Sir *John*, Comparisons [between our classes] are odious, and more particularly so, on Occasions of this Kind, when we are projecting Races, that are to be made out of both Sides of the Comparisons" (IV.ii.61–64).

In his contribution to this collection James Thompson nicely analyzes the relationship between sign and value especially, for my purposes here, as it relates to Indiana, the *perdita* of *The Conscious Lovers*. Supposedly, she represents inherent value to which nothing need be added. Of course, as Thompson notes of the irony of the ending, the superaddition of Sealand's vast wealth makes moot the question whether she is such a value or not. In short, the play wants to have it both ways: the bourgeois doctrine of inherent worth cum aristocratic inherited wealth, still signified by both money *and* land. And isn't it interesting that Cimberton's ostensibly satirized point turns out to be well taken: "Sir, since it is a Girl that they have, I am, for the Honour of my Family, willing to take it in again; and to sink her into our Name, and no harm done" (V.i.16–18). That is, since Lucinda Sealand's mother is herself a Cimberton cousin and since, after all, she is a "Girl" and not a male, Cimberton's marriage to her he can justify to the family patriarch Sir Geoffry, for she will not represent any real threat to patrilinearity. As in most of the plays that deal with miscegenation between gentry and merchant class, the male comes from the former and the female from the latter. Less contamination, you know. It is no accident that Indiana is the scion of a merchant, Bevil Junior that of a landed squire.

What my old friends and colleagues have omitted from their analyses, however, is, to me at least, potentially more interesting in terms of the tropes of both class and gender. Just as in *The Lancashire Witches* Shadwell drives a wedge between discredited ancien régime and excluded radical potential, so does Steele here. Cimberton is a displaced version of the Restoration rake. Beneath the veneer of his supposedly superior breeding, he is unable to control his sexual passion for Lucinda, leers and paws at her, and fears he "shan't, for many Years, have Discretion enough to give her one fallow Season"; "I must depend upon my own Reflection, and Philosophy, not to overstock my Family" (III.i.290–92, 320–22). Instead, Bevil Junior is the one who exhibits the new, middle-class concept of "breeding" (an important metaphor from the prologue on): morals, manners, taste, decorum. He reads moral authors every morning; he treats artists with magnanimity, Indiana with incredible generosity; and he exercises neostoic self-control in the face of insufferable provocation from his friend Myrtle. The point of this last display is the triumph of bourgeois ethics, sanctioned by law rather than force, over what the new dominant class portrays as the aristocratic "vice" of dueling—as if its ethics represented not just the *virtú* of the winning side, as Nietzsche would express it (*Genealogy of Morals*), but natural law.

On the other side of the wedge are the very entertaining scenes between Tom and Phillis, servants to Bevil Junior and Lucinda respectively. The two of them hilariously ape aristocratic manners of courtship and decorum. But we are never allowed to view them as the threat of any real democracy. The older, more decorous servant Humphrey makes fun of Tom's pretensions: "I hope the Fashion of being lewd and extravagant, despising of Decency and Order, is almost at an End, since it is arrived at Persons of your Quality"; when at another of Tom's extravagances he exclaims, "What will this World come to!" or when Tom himself laments aside, "The Devil's in my Master! he has always more Wit than I have," we are invited to disapprove of further social mobility than the play allows the upper-middle merchant class (I.i.166–68, 228–29; I.ii.21–22). Upstairs and Downstairs must remain firmly situated. Indeed, Tom has really only modest aspirations for himself and Phillis: "[O]ne Acre, with *Phillis*, wou'd be worth a whole County without her" (III.78–79). Note that, despite all of their pretensions, it is this lower-class couple that is satisfied with (and ends up with, we must assume) the modest little love nest—not either of the middle-class couples, who end up with money *and* status.

The play also keeps women in their place. However much she indignantly responds to Cimberton, Lucinda is really a passive object of exchange. Phillis shows more wit and agency in forestalling Mrs. Sealand and Cimberton by suggesting to Myrtle that he disguise himself as Sir Geoffry.

Indiana is as helpless as Clarissa, just luckier, lucky that her aunt's suspicions of Bevil Junior as if he were just a Lovelace prove to be, in this
instance, not true. Indiana may love Bevil but is completely dependent on
events, rationalized at the end as "Providence," for fulfillment of her desires. As Lucinda pouts to Phillis, nubile women in the system of exchange
designed to build estates "must have no Desires" (III.171–72).

Yet the play somewhat surprisingly reveals the animal desires, the real
breeding that underlies male-female relationships and that must be contained by social code. Not only can Cimberton not control his lust; Tom
can't keep his lips off Phillis. When she complains, "Lard, we have been
Fooling and Toying, and not consider'd the main Business of our Masters and Mistresses," Tom archly responds, "Why, their Business is to be
Fooling and Toying, as soon as the Parchments are ready" (III.96–99). In
other words, the business of planning marriages is an elaborate system of
control of the real biological business of coupling. People with money can
afford such elaboration, as Phillis archly reminds Lucinda, who wonders
why Phillis suffers Tom to kiss her thus: "Why, Madam, we Vulgar take it
to be a Sign of Love; we Servants, we poor People, that have nothing but
our Persons to bestow, or treat for, are forc'd to deal, and bargain by way
of Sample; and therefore, as we have no Parchments, or Wax necessary in
our Agreements, we squeeze with our Hands, and seal with our Lips, to
ratifie Vows and Promises" (III.126–31).

But even the lower classes are controlled by the patriarchal sexual system, enforced by religious sanction. And though the play shows middle-
class impatience with a double standard in this system that is an undesirable
aristocratic residual component in the new bourgeois compromise—Sealand preaches against it to Sir John, who foolishly defends it—it is not a
male who suffers the play's disapprobation for sexual transgression. After
all, Bevil Junior is not really guilty of keeping a mistress. It is Mrs. Sealand who comes in for the harshest treatment as transgressor. We learn
in act 5 that her precipitancy in getting her daughter married results from
typical mother's jealousy of a daughter who now puts her star under a
bushel. Mrs. Sealand is another Lady Wishfort, the type of the superannu-
ated woman who would continue sexual activity beyond her patriarchally
allotted time. Yet Mrs. Sealand is Sealand's second wife and is probably not
that old. Ah, but the generational law, at least in Western comedy, is cruel.

Mrs. Sealand is even more transgressive, however. In the funny scene
between her and Cimberton when he indecorously begins talking about
married couples in bed and she hides her blushes with her fan, under the

guise of advocacy for decent silence about such matters Cimberton absurdly recounts the sexual practices of the Spartans: "*Lycurgus,* Madam, instituted otherwise; among the *Lacedemonians,* the whole Female World was pregnant, but none, but the Mothers themselves, knew by whom; their Meetings were secret, and the Amorous Congress always by Stealth; and no such professed Doings between the Sexes, as are tolerated among us, under the audacious Word, Marriage." Mrs. Sealand breaks out in a rapture of wish fulfillment: "Oh! had I liv'd, in those Days, and been a Matron of *Sparta,* one might, with less Indecency, have had ten Children, according to that modest Institution, than one, under the Confusion of our modern, barefac'd manner" (III.237–46). Whatever they think they are saying, they are revealing the threat to patriarchy of uncontrolled female sexuality and therefore the need for the Western system of absolute control. If none but the mothers know, then not only is the male ego but the patriarchal control of property destroyed. At the end of the play there is no sentimental absorption of Mrs. Sealand into the concluding euphoria. She continues to be satirized as rejoicing only at no longer having her daughter around the soirees. This sentimental comedy par excellence marks the shift to a new trope of class, but it leaves much to be desired for a truly "democratic romance"—in terms of not only class but gender.

I hope to have shown by representative sampling shifting tropes of ideology from late Stuart to early Georgian serious drama. What I find most interesting is the way bourgeois ideology freezes out radical potentialities: real equality and power for women or for classes lower than the upper middle class. Bourgeois meritocracy, though dominant rhetorically, really translates in these plays into a plutocratic oligarchy, whose rapacious exploitation both at home and abroad is justified as the natural, civilizing order of things. Some of the women in these plays may be hopeful signs for the future—Manley's Rosalinda, Rowe's Lady Jane Gray, Trotter's Lamira, Lillo's Millwood. And some of the lower-class characters shine out a resilient, irrepressible spirit—Shadwell's Clod, Steele's Tom and Phillis. But for the historical nonce they are all contained in their lamps as the curtains fall.

Notes

1. Dates are first performance insofar as we know it and taken from *The London Stage.* I have analyzed *The Conquest of Granada* briefly in "Significance" 54–57 and in greater detail in *Word as Bond* 32–43.

2. Brown sees the complexity of Almanzor's character as effecting a "juxtaposi-
tion of radical challenge and royalist resolution"; but because she sees the ending
as completely arbitrary and insists on "the inherent weakness of our concern for
the ending of a heroic action" (14–19), she does not see the same legitimating sense
of an ending as do I.

3. Staves notes the similarity between Almanzor and Lyndaraxa and concludes,
"[B]ecause she exists and because her view is fully expressed, the play is an agon
where the view ultimately rejected is sufficiently interesting and persuasive to be
considered" (69–70).

4. See McKeon, *Politics* esp. 164–77. See also Thompson.

5. See my *Nicholas Rowe and Christian Tragedy* 74 n. 2.

6. Where no line numbers are available, I have given page numbers, preceded
by a comma instead of a period. In the 1720 Rowe edition, the plays have separate
pagination. *Tamerlane* is in volume 1. My readings of Rowe in this article have
been adumbrated in my contribution to Alfred W. Hesse's and my *DLB* entry on
him. My reading of *Cato* has been distantly adumbrated in *Word as Bond* (318).

7. Vortimer is a usurper, who pursues in Gallia "loyal Chiefs, / Who ill cou'd
bear the Murther of their King" (V.i, 53) and who is killed by the son of the man
whose throne he usurped. Moreover, Lucius's ascendancy is enabled by the timely
intervention of the Gallic king, Honorius. Could not a contemporary audience,
especially one familiar with Manley's Tory sentiments, read Vortimer as George I,
displaced avatar of William III and perhaps even Cromwell; Lucius as James Stuart,
son of James II, known as the Old Pretender, the King across the Water; and Honorius as the French king (Louis XIV had died in 1715 and was succeeded by the
five-year-old Louis XV)? Would not such an interpretation be especially accessible
during the later stages of the Jacobite revolution known as The Fifteen?

8. But see my argument with Staves and Brown concerning these tragedies as
well in "Royalism" 235–36.

9. See "Jewel." For an extended reading of *All for Love*, see *Word as Bond* 235–
47. My original subtitle for "Jewel" was "Mutability and Constancy in Dryden's
All for Love and Its Renaissance Predecessors."

10. I especially part company with Staves and Brown over these personal tragedies. Staves's generalization, "Christian explanations of the heroine's fate are not
only not accepted, for the most part they are not even considered" (175), seems
to me to apply only to Otway's *The Orphan* (1680), certainly not to Banks and
Southerne and Rowe. I have the same response to Brown's generalization (which
does not reach forward to Rowe but does reach backward to include Lee's *Rival
Queens* and Dryden's *All for Love*), "At its evolutionary midpoint, affective tragedy
explicitly detaches itself from any hierarchy of values, either recollected or radical, and presents simply suffering, unqualified by cause or blame" (99). All these
writers—except Otway, who is essentially a satirist whose vision is so dark as to

be virtually absurdist—assert the value of constancy in a mutable world and teach the rather traditional lesson of *contemptus mundi*.

In her recent *Ends of Empire* Brown repeats her characterization of she-tragedies as essentially vehicles for emoting over the victimization of women. She extends her argument to Rowe, whom she sees as adding to the emptiness of Otway, Banks, and Southerne bourgeois moralizing and especially the motif of commodification. Brown thereby sets up a provocative homology between the figures of women in these plays and the social history of middle- to upper-class women, emptied of significance in both material (domestic industry) and symbolic terms and made figures for the acquisitiveness of mercantile capitalist imperialism (ch. 3). While again I admire her project, I am convinced, as I have argued in the Otway and Rowe *DLB* entries and in "Female Rebels," that a great deal can be learned, including much about the ideology of patriarchy and its misogyny, by interpreting the cognitive and not just the affective aspects of these plays.

11. See Wallace 132 n. 22. Wallace's sociopolitical reading of Lillo's play is the most sophisticated to date, improving vastly on Loftis, *Politics* 125–27, and Brown 157–63, if only because Loftis concentrates solely on the portrayal of the merchant and Brown on the development of form. Wallace avails himself of recent work in social history as well as Marxist and Frankfurt School methodology.

12. Wallace slights the imperialism here, since, like Brown's, his concerns are ultimately generic as well. But Flores adeptly analyzes the play's ability to displace onto various scapegoats the contradictions within bourgeois ideology, including the rapacity of "England's own colonial exploitation" (94). In her recent *Ends of Empire* (86–88) Brown places *The London Merchant* in the context of her argument that generic transition from heroic play through she-tragedy to bourgeois morality plays is homologous to the transition from a land-based feudal economy to a trade-based bourgeois imperialist economy.

13. See my "Ideology of Restoration Tragicomedy"; I have analyzed *Marriage* briefly there (457–60) and in detail in *Word as Bond* (66–81).

14. Brown says of the witches, "They and the characters who believe in them are explicitly associated with Toryism, Popery, and the Popish Plot in particular" (107). Staves dismisses them as "merely part of an entertaining operatic and comic spectacle" (309). Neither performs an ideological analysis.

Works Cited

Addison, Joseph. *Cato. British Dramatists from Dryden to Sheridan*. Ed. George H. Nettleton and Arthur E. Case. Rev. George Winchester Stone, Jr. Boston: Houghton, 1969. 473–99.

Alssid, Michael W. *Thomas Shadwell*. Twayne's English Authors Series 50. New York: Twayne, 1967.

226 J. DOUGLAS CANFIELD

Brown, Laura. *Ends of Empire: Women and Ideology in Early Eighteenth-Century English Literature.* Ithaca, N.Y.: Cornell UP, 1993.

——. *English Dramatic Form, 1660–1760: An Essay in Generic History.* New Haven: Yale UP, 1981.

Canfield, J. Douglas. "Dramatic Shifts: Writing an Ideological History of Late Stuart Drama." *Restoration and Eighteenth-Century Theatre Research* 2nd ser. 6.1 (Summer 1991): 1–9.

——. "Female Rebels and Patriarchal Paradigms in Some Neoclassical Works." *Studies in Eighteenth-Century Culture* 18 (1988): 153–66.

——. "The Ideology of Restoration Tragicomedy." *ELH* 51 (1984): 447–64.

——. "The Jewel of Great Price: Mutability and Constancy in Dryden's *All for Love.*" *ELH* 42 (1975): 38–61.

——. "Nicholas Rowe." (With Alfred W. Hesse.) *Dictionary of Literary Biography.* Vol. 84: *Restoration and Eighteenth-Century Dramatists, Second Series.* Ed. Paula Backscheider. Detroit: Bruccoli Clark Layman–Gale, 1989. 262–89.

——. *Nicholas Rowe and Christian Tragedy.* Gainesville: UP of Florida, 1977.

——. "*Regulus* and *Cleomenes* and 1688: From Royalism to Self-Reliance." *English Culture at the End of the Seventeenth Century.* Ed. Robert P. Maccubbin and David F. Morrill. Special issue of *Eighteenth-Century Life* ns 12.3 (November 1988): 67–75.

——. "Royalism's Last Dramatic Stand: English Political Tragedy, 1679–1689." *Studies in Philology* 82 (1985): 234–63.

——. "The Significance of the Restoration Rhymed Heroic Play." *Eighteenth-Century Studies* 13 (1979): 49–62.

——. "Thomas Otway." *Dictionary of Literary Biography.* Vol. 80: *Restoration and Eighteenth-Century Dramatists, First Series.* Ed. Paula Backscheider. Detroit: Bruccoli Clark Layman–Gale, 1989. 146–71.

——. *Word as Bond in English Literature from the Middle Ages to the Restoration.* Philadelphia: U of Pennsylvania P, 1989.

Dryden, John. *The Works of John Dryden.* Ed. H. T. Swedenberg, Jr., et al. 20 vols. Berkeley and Los Angeles: U of California P, 1956– .

Fanon, Frantz. *Black Skin, White Masks.* Trans. Charles Lam Markmann. New York: Grove Weidenfeld, 1967.

Flores, Stephan P. "Mastering the Self: The Ideological Incorporation of Desire in Lillo's 'The London Merchant.'" *Essays in Theatre* 5(1987): 91–102.

Foucault, Michel. *The Order of Things: An Archaeology of the Human Sciences.* 1970. New York: Vintage, 1973.

Girard, René. *Deceit, Desire, and the Novel: Self and Other in Literary Structure.* Trans. Yvonne Freccero. Baltimore: Johns Hopkins UP, 1965.

Jameson, Fredric. *The Political Unconscious.* Ithaca, N.Y.: Cornell UP, 1981.

Kuhn, Thomas. *The Structure of Scientific Revolutions.* 2nd ed. enlarged. *International Encyclopedia of Unified Sciences.* 2.2 (1970).
</cite>

Lillo, George. *The London Merchant; or, The History of George Barnwell. The Dramatic Works of George Lillo*. Ed. James L. Steffensen. Oxford: Clarendon, 1993. 113–209.

Loftis, John. *Comedy and Society from Congreve to Fielding*. Stanford Studies in Language and Literature, 19. Stanford: Stanford UP, 1959.

———. *The Politics of Drama in Augustan England*. Oxford: Clarendon, 1963.

Loftis, John, et al., eds. *The Revels History of Drama in English*. Vol. 5: *1660–1750*. London: Methuen, 1976.

Manley, Delarivier. *Lucius, the First Christian King of Britain*. 1717. Intro. Jack M. Armistead and Debbie K. Davis. Augustan Reprint Society, 253–54. Los Angeles: Clark Library, 1989.

[Marx, Karl, and Friedrich Engels]. *The Civil War in France. The Marx-Engels Reader*. Ed. Robert C. Tucker. 2nd ed. New York: Norton, 1978. 618–52.

McKeon, Michael. "Marxist Criticism and *Marriage A La Mode*." *Eighteenth Century: Theory and Interpretation* 24 (1983): 141–62.

———. *Politics and Poetry in Restoration England: The Case of Dryden's* Annus Mirabilis. Cambridge: Harvard UP, 1975.

Neumann, Erich. *The Great Mother: An Analysis of the Archetype*. Trans. Ralph Manheim. 2nd ed. Princeton: Princeton UP, 1963.

Nietzsche, Friedrich. *The Birth of Tragedy and the Genealogy of Morals*. Trans. Francis Golffing. Garden City, N.Y.: Anchor-Doubleday, 1956.

Rowe, Nicholas. *The Dramatick Works of Nicholas Rowe, Esq.* 2 vols. 1720. Westmead, Farnborough, Hants., Eng.: Gregg, 1971. Separate pagination for each play.

Sedgwick, Eve Kosofsky. *Between Men: English Literature and Male Homosocial Desire*. New York: Columbia UP, 1985.

Shadwell, Thomas. *Thomas Shadwell's The Lancashire Witches, and Tegue o Divelly The Irish-Priest: A Critical Old-Spelling Edition*. Ed. Judith Bailey Slagle. New York: Garland, 1991.

Staves, Susan. *Players' Scepters: Fictions of Authority in the Restoration*. Lincoln: U of Nebraska P, 1979.

Steele, Richard. *The Conscious Lovers. The Plays of Richard Steele*. Ed. Shirley Strum Kenny. Oxford: Clarendon, 1971. 275–382.

Thompson, James. "Dryden's *Conquest of Granada* and the Dutch Wars." *Eighteenth Century: Theory and Interpretation* 31 (1990): 211–26.

Trotter, Catherine. *The Fatal Friendship. The Female Wits: Women Playwrights on the London Stage, 1660–1720*. Intro. and ed. Fidelis Morgan. London: Virago, 1981. 145–207.

Wallace, David. "Bourgeois Tragedy or Sentimental Melodrama? The Significance of George Lillo's *The London Merchant*." *Eighteenth-Century Studies* 25 (Winter 1991–92): 123–43.

Williams, Raymond. *Marxism and Literature*. Oxford: Oxford UP, 1977.

A Cultural Reading
of Charlotte Lennox's
Shakespear Illustrated

SUSAN GREEN

Shakespear . . . has followed pretty exactly the Thread of the Story . . . and
added some . . . which possibly may not be thought any proofs either of his
Invention or Judgment, since . . . they grow like Excrescences, and are equally
useless and disagreeable.
—CHARLOTTE LENNOX, *Shakespear Illustrated*

Resistance is a primary quality of bodies.
—CHARLES STANISLAS DUNAN, *Essais de philosophie générale*

Charlotte Lennox's *Shakespear Illustrated* (1753–54), a three-volume comparative study of Shakespeare's plays with the romance novels and historical chronicles on which they were based, resists the masculinist bias of
those plays and the consolidation of cultural authority that devolved upon
her male colleagues when their theatrical, critical, and editing projects
made of Shakespeare's dramatic works a heterogeneous, contradictory, yet
productive cultural site. Unlike her male colleagues, Lennox's engagement
with Shakespeare's text enacts a response to cultural authority that demonstrates her society's inability to recognize, identify, or discuss the cultural
significance of female abjection. In a sense, we can see in Lennox's text a
possible direction that could have been taken in the reception of Shakespeare's drama but that Lennox's culture was unable to recognize—and
that, in fact, Lennox herself could not discuss directly. As well as showing
us a response to Shakespeare unlike anything in her period, Lennox's text
opens the possibility for analyzing a textual inscription in women's writing
that gives to women's abject voice a historical trajectory that can deflect it
from a simple enunciation of itself as the repressed.

The Shakespeare Lennox constructed and responded to in her study is not the Shakespeare that emerged from Augustan culture at the end of the century. Margreta de Grazia argues in her recent study that, by the end of the eighteenth century, an individuated Shakespeare had emerged, the very pattern of an autonomous self enclosed "within his own experience, consciousness and creativity" (10). De Grazia shows in the textual apparatus of Edmond Malone's ten-volume 1790 edition of Shakespeare's works "[Shakespeare's] emergence in his modern aspect . . . a striking example of how the Enlightenment represented its constructs as Truth, inscribing factual objects and autonomous subjects (each grounded in the other) in the process of reproducing Shakespeare" (226).[1]

Lennox wrote nearly fifty years before Malone published his authoritative edition. I do not want to give the impression that she tried to block an inevitable, progressive consolidation of textual practices culminating in Malone's achievement in any self-consciously feminist way, or that there was any self-evident, inevitable progression to block. Rather, I offer a cultural reading of Lennox's neglected and maligned text so that we can imagine Shakespeare study without the institutions of scholarship, developed in his name, that now may seem so unavoidable that to remove them would be to remove the possibility for thought itself. The cultural reading that follows develops from an analysis of three approaches to Shakespeare's work taken in the eighteenth century considered in relation to what Julia Kristeva calls abjection.[2]

I am calling this essay a "cultural reading" rather than a "Kristevan reading" or a "psychoanalytic reading" because I want to situate Lennox's text in its immediate cultural context as well as to define its place in larger historical developments. Considering Kristeva's theories in relation to Lennox's text emphasizes, as Kristeva herself does, the convergence of the production of the social subject with the processes of signification. Broadly speaking, Kristeva locates in culture an "archaic mother"—the ever present figure about whom we cannot speak, the unnameable presence that is totally resistant to meaning (*Desire* 237–70). Abjection describes the approaches made to this locus of nonmeaning that begin with pre-Oedipal attempts to separate from the mother prior to acquiring the autonomy of language.

In naming and identifying abjection as principally a semiotic activity, Kristeva points out that the symbolic dimension of language by itself is not strong enough to assure an adequate separation of subject and object. Subject and object, as intimately and mutually constituted as they are, can merge or exchange places, returning the signifying process over and over again to anxieties about origins, which can only be resolved through Oedipal processes that provide entry into symbolic representation. Semiotic interventions in culture and language ensure that subject/object distinctions can be maintained because, as Kristeva describes the semiotic process, it derives from a bodily, visceral repulsion. Abjection, by means of the semiotic, offers a primary repression during which bodily, gestural responses delimit the experiential world before the emergence of the ego. The primary repressions of abjection establish corporeal boundaries in space and time that take hold so that the ego (with its secondary repressions creating attendant objects, logics, representations, and desires) can emerge. Abjection, then, is culturally productive in that it allows the drives a kind of free reign in language to keep the symbolic order from rigidifying into a too-tight hermeneutic constructed only by ego/object relations and the desire that orchestrates and connects them.

Lennox's study of Shakespeare is valuable because of the particular way that she approaches abjection in Shakespeare's text. Lennox configures Shakespeare's text as a maternal body, then speaks of her response to his text by identifying and occupying this nucleus of nonmeaning held within it. She configures Shakespeare's text in this way so that she can enact a culturally productive and transformative relationship with the narrative material of his plays, particularly in regard to his representation of women. In contrast, Alexander Pope and David Garrick configure the maternal nonmeaning of Shakespeare's text as grounds for producing their own cultural identities that can then compete with Shakespeare's. Edmond Malone and Samuel Johnson efface the possibility of nonmeaning in Shakespeare's text by developing a critical apparatus external to the plays and sufficient to their aestheticization of his work.

De Grazia emphasizes the historical contingency of Shakespearean scholarship when she writes:

Authenticity, periodization, individuation, chronology, and even interpretation are the interlocked imperatives of the study of Shakespeare, the exemplary author of the English canon. Yet if they emerged in history, they cannot be the timeless necessities of Shakespeare study; rather they are the determinate needs of a specific historical situation. (1)

While Malone's scholarship required the values of verification, histo-
ricity, and individuation, earlier treatments of Shakespeare's work, like
Lennox's, Pope's, and Garrick's, emphasized the cultural processes of discourse, power, representation, and reception. Yet Lennox's engagement
with Shakespearean drama is unique. For Lennox, Shakespeare's text does
not embody a symbolic order capable of drawing her into its processes.
Neither does she think of Shakespeare as a poetic genius with whom she
wants to compete. Rather, from within the abject, Lennox becomes Shakespeare's willing victim, fascinated yet terrified, utterly responsive but as
if to a distant and compelling voice—a voice that may or may not be
embodied by a father, a voice that may be a mother's voice. Abjection
is evident in her text when she speaks, as she does in the epigraph that
heads this essay, of something filthy, some defilement or offensive abnor-
mality in the plays that captures her imagination. As if distancing herself
from that which she deems improper to her person, Lennox responds to
the plays with repeated debasements of Shakespeare's creative efforts in
a tenaciously abusive language that declares the narrative revisions of his
source material to be "absurd" (applied to *Measure for Measure* among
several other plays, 1: 25), "injudicious" (*Cymbeline*, 1: 155), "irregular,"
and in general "greatly below" the romance novels he revised (*Measure for
Measure*, 1: 25).

Lennox's approach to Shakespeare, like the processes of abjection, exists
on a borderline where subject and object are not yet separated. At that
boundary, the abject manifests itself in the kind of visceral, bodily response we have to corpses, decayed food, fingernail parings, the skim
on milk, in Kristeva's famous examples (*Powers* 3). When I argue that
Lennox's text is a text that *resists,* I emphasize the bodily experience of resistance—the way resistance lies along the border between what is inward
and what is outward, dividing consciousness from its other that necessarily
escapes definition. That which we resist is apparently outside us. In resisting what is outside, we assume an unfettered knowledge of our mind's
material existence. For example, unlike Lennox's more inchoate resistance,
Malone, with his 1790 edition, enacts a resistance to what he assumes to
be thoroughly outside his own or Shakespeare's mind. De Grazia points
out that when Malone acknowledged the assistance of others in preparing
his edition, they were all functionaries—archivists and others with whom
Malone had professional relationships and who provided him with information. She contrasts his acknowledgments with those of earlier editors

who thanked their friends for their insights, or who, in the case of Rowe, could acknowledge persons who knew parts of Shakespeare's biography from an oral tradition (100). By means of the scholarly apparatus of his edition, Malone derived a knowledge about Shakespeare wherein subject and object are grounded within a single ontology. In producing his edition, he resisted anything that would bespeak a subjectivity different from the one being constructed in Shakespeare's name and necessarily impinging upon the authority of the criteria he established, criteria that could give Shakespeare's subjectivity primacy over all others. Malone's resistance to that which is apparently outside constitutes knowledge of Shakespeare's text as something self-evident once the proper apparatus is applied.

But, as Lennox's text attests, resistance can also be "underground," an evasive subterfuge. Our supposed immediate, conscious awareness of our mind's functioning depends upon what can only be an ambivalent interposition of a body—a body that is touched at the same time that it is touching, a body that cannot be totally incorporated or totally cast off by consciousness. When Lennox's text resists, it resists at this more unconscious, bodily level. To be able to read her resistance requires a theory like Kristeva's, whose ideas about abjection chronicle a drama at the border of what is neither thoroughly inside nor thoroughly outside. Without such a theory, Lennox's approach to Shakespeare, when compared with those of her contemporaries, simply looks faulty, naive, and inadequate as commentators on her work have persistently said.[3]

It is true enough that Lennox has not produced a perfectly discursive, accessible, readerly presentation of her insights into Shakespearean drama. Rather, I am arguing that her discourse is marked by symptoms of abjection. She speaks a language that periodically gives up and then simply starts over again. She strays, then halts only to speak of Shakespeare—and in her text, it seems to be an individual consciousness, a man "Shakespeare" (figured as maternal body) about whom she speaks—but it is as though she is speaking of, in Kristeva's words, an "unassimilable alien" (Powers 50), one whose narratives she most often calls "absurd." It is admittedly difficult to appreciate Lennox's insights about Shakespeare's plays, in part, because of the way she places her comments within her text.[4] In the first two volumes of her study, for example, Lennox provides an English translation of the Italian source story for one of Shakespeare's plays followed immediately by her summary of the play's action. Without any special heading or break in the text, she offers commentary comparing the two plots. In the third volume, Lennox, for the most part, eliminates the source story, preferring to offer her commentary without presenting the source itself. Her study, in its bulk, appears to function more as an anthology of Shakespeare's sources accompanied by her rather informal critical comparisons than it does as a self-contained analysis. Lennox's perceptions are dispersed throughout her text and somewhat buried, appearing as they do scattered throughout the three volumes without any particular headings to distinguish them. A reader must apply considerable attention to bring the elements of her critique together. Kristeva's theories help us recognize in Lennox's work the significance of her analysis that lies beyond mere compilation of sources with accompanying comments. Lennox's text gives evidence of her complex intertextual sensibility.

In *Revolution in Poetic Language,* Kristeva explains that she prefers to call intertextuality *transposition* so as to remove the connotations that would reduce intertextual processes to a simple study of sources (see Waller and Morgan). Kristeva argues that transposition, the passage from one sign system to another, is a fundamental process in the work of the unconscious along with *displacement* and *condensation,* the two identified by Freud. One could suggest that the Pope/Garrick approach I discuss in this essay emphasizes the displacement of Shakespeare's imagination in favor of one's own, while the Malone/Johnson approach emphasizes condensing Shakespeare's imagination into a discrete object suitable for aesthetic contemplation. Lennox, on the other hand, like Kristeva, treats every signifying practice as a field of transpositions—an intertext wherein displacement and condensation work together, providing passage from one sign system to another to create what Kristeva calls new *thetic* positions. Kristeva's theories about abjection, then, help us value Lennox's text precisely for the ways it cannot come to terms with its own apprehensions. The abjection of Lennox's text moves meaning back and forth across this thetic moment in signification so that Lennox never quite achieves a critical language sufficient to her insights.

Kristeva's theories and Lennox's Shakespeare study attest to the power of textuality to challenge the very grounds of its intelligibility. Kristeva makes plain the connection between textual meaning and the grounds of knowledge when she says, "All enunciation, whether of a word or of a sentence, is thetic. It requires an identification; in other words, the subject must separate from and through his image, from and through his objects" (*Revolution* 43). For Kristeva, there is no language without the

thetic; it is the precondition of the difference between signifier and signified, the necessary boundary founded in the mirror stage that is the basis
for all structural relations. As a stage attained under certain precise conditions during the signifying process, the thetic constitutes the subject on the
threshold of language but is not reducible to the subject's processes (*Revolution* 43–45). When Kristeva emphasizes the aspects of language drawn
from abjection—what she calls the "semiotic"—she is not pointing to a
stage or phase surpassed in later integrations; rather, she emphasizes that
the subject is always both semiotic and symbolic (*Revolution* 19–90).

Kristeva identifies the constitution of a thetic positionality at the moment when the subject emerges into language, but the thetic is a feature
of signification without also being a feature of subjectification. Kristeva
elaborates a theory of the thetic in order to understand the constitution
of the subject without reducing her analysis to the error of equating the
subject with the transcendental ego, or, to say it another way, without producing an analysis that denies to signification its own structuration that is
established as a thetic positionality at the same time that the subject is constituted. When the eruptions of the semiotic—the processes of abjection—
challenge the symbolic, the thetic is also challenged because abjection tries
to induce a pre-Oedipal sublimation—a *jouissance*—prior to the mirror
stage that would eliminate language. In Lennox's text we can observe the
drama of these cultural processes brought to the surface, readable in her
intertextual practice that crosses language with her prelinguistic longings,
thought with what lies both prior to and beyond her thought.

The problem in Lennox's text is that she tries to identify with and through
Shakespeare's women characters, but she cannot locate a Shakespearean
psychology of women that would underlie his narratives. In play after play,
she looks for a woman's ego structure that would require a full elaboration of denials, desires, transgressions, and narrative interests. Where she
would expect to find a consistent motivation for his women characters'
actions, she finds a void. What she notices is that, in comparison with his
sources, Shakespeare over and over again abjects women, isolates them
from their ordinary social context and makes them suffer in this isolation
for no apparent narrative purpose. That is, Lennox notices and attempts
to articulate the procedures in Shakespeare's plays that Kristeva describes
as abject, and she does so by occupying the very space of abjection that
makes of Shakespeare's women characters the fulcrum for the intertextual
procedures he uses to transpose prose narrative sources into his dramatic

plots. Lennox's comments on *Measure for Measure,* the first play she treats in volume 1, illustrate her insight and her method. She considers at length the characterization of Mariana, a figure not appearing in Shakespeare's source, which she gives as the Fifth Novel of the Eighth Decad of the *Hectomythi* of Giraldi Cinthio. Mariana becomes, in Lennox's analysis, the very image of the Shakespearean female abject. Mariana's anguished, nearly timeless presence is placed in stark relief by Lennox's approach. Repeatedly, Lennox opens a play to discussion by considering the plot from the point of view of a female character. Then Lennox questions Shakespeare's ability or willingness to represent women as fully motivated persons. In the case of *Measure for Measure,* the analysis proceeds as follows:

> How comes it to pass, that the Duke is so well acquainted with the Story of Mariana, to whom Angelo was betrothed, but abandoned by him on Account of the Loss of her Fortune? She speaks of the Duke as of a Person she had been long acquainted with. (1: 29–30)

Such is Lennox's interest in understanding Mariana's story as a coherent one that she concludes:

> [S]ome extraordinary accident . . . must have brought her [Mariana's] Story to his [the duke's] Knowledge, which we find was known to no one else; for Angelo's Reputation for Sanctity was very high, and that could not have been, if his Wrongs to Mariana were publickly known. (1: 30)

Again, Lennox probes the nature of Shakespeare's representation of women with a question:

> But why does not the Poet acquaint us with this extraordinary Accident, which happens so conveniently for his Purpose? If he is accountable to our Eyes for what he makes us see, is he not also accountable to our Judgment for what he would have us believe? (1: 30–31)

Throughout *Shakespear Illustrated,* Lennox produces these pointed, serious questions. In fact, Lennox's attention to this phenomenon of Shakespeare's isolation of heroines is exhaustive. Her analysis is consistent throughout a discussion of twenty-three of Shakespeare's women characters. In addition to Mariana, she considers Isabella, Juliet, Desdemona, Emilia, Imogen, Helena, Viola, Olivia, Lady Macbeth, Hermione, Perdita, Ophelia, Gertrude, Silvia, Cressida, Princess Katherine (in *Henry V*), Queen Margaret (in *Henry VI, Part I*), Anne Bollen and Queen Catherine (in *Henry VIII*), Hero and Margaret (in *Much Ado about Nothing*), and, finally, Cordelia.

Lennox notes that, in comparison with his source, the Ninth Novel of Bandello, Shakespeare isolates Juliet in the tomb scene, having her wake after Romeo dies rather than before his poison has taken effect as in the source. Of Perdita, she shows how much we have imaginatively to isolate her on her voyage back from Bohemia in order to believe that she is discovered for the first time in Sicily. Shakespeare invents the accidental death of Ophelia's father as well as her subsequent madness. Lennox points out that Ophelia is only temporarily the focus of Hamlet's thoughts. Lennox questions, as many subsequent critics have, Viola's motives for disguise. She thinks Olivia's passion is made ridiculous in *Twelfth Night*. Princess Katherine's being, in *Henry V*, the only one in the French court not to know English also seems absurd to Lennox. She points out that Shakespeare would have us believe Henry VIII never met Anne Bollen before Wolsey's banquet. Of Cordelia, Lennox notes how isolated from her lover she is. The prince of France falls in love with her after Lear's "absurd trial" of his daughter and does not see, as the audience does, something of Cordelia's virtue when "she gave so glorious a Testimony of it." Instead, the Prince is "touch'd by a cold Justification of her Fame, and that from herself, when he might have been charm'd with a shining Instance of her Greatness of Soul, and inviolable Regard to Truth" (3: 288). Lennox sees the hanging of Cordelia by a common soldier to be improper and debasing in comparison with the sources.

Lennox's analysis of how Shakespeare's women become isolated, and then become the focus of suffering, debasement, or just ridiculousness in comparison with how they function in his source plots, includes a perception, held within her questions, that if she produced answers she would have to shift the focus of her inquiry. In producing this study, she is not identifying with Shakespeare as an ego ideal with whom she can compete. She does not place Shakespeare's texts as an object of study within a circuit of desire wherein his representations of women could continually veil and unveil the sign of "Woman" as Truth and Beauty. She resists valorizing Shakespeare's imagination on the basis of his ability to depict "character" or on the beauty of his language. When she compares Shakespeare's plots with those in his sources, what she sees is that he consistently and radically shifts their terms to produce his representations of women. In other words, Lennox sees that when material is transposed from one signifying practice to another, the very conditions for what is representable come into question. Following this line of thought, there really are not any answers to the questions she asks. Rather, her questions, if answered seriously, would reveal a profound locus of nonmeaning within Shakespeare's text. Her discussion of *Measure for Measure* shows us the trajectory of her thinking:

> But, in short, without all this Jumble of Inconsistencies, the Comedy would have been a downright Tragedy; for Claudio's Head must have been cut off, if Isabella had not consented to redeem him; and the Duke would have wanted a Wife, if such a convenient Person as Mariana had not been introduced to supply her Place, and save her Honour. (1: 31)

And further:

> That Shakespeare made a wrong Choice of his Subject, since he was resolved to torture it into a Comedy, appears by the low Contrivance, absurd Intrigue, and improbable Incidents, he was obliged to introduce, in order to bring about three or four Weddings, instead of one good Beheading, which was the Consequence naturally expected. (1: 28)

When Lennox upbraids Shakespeare for withholding the image of a headless corpse from his narrative, we also perceive that she desires this image, feels it has been denied to her. In this wish she at once exposes the inability of Shakespeare's play to fulfill its narrative potential and places herself on the side of the "good" and "naturally expected" beheading. By speaking with and for the headless corpse that Shakespeare's play will not produce for her, Lennox's discourse hovers over a potentially new position from which to speak about her own perceptions. We can identify the emergent critical space Lennox creates as a version of Kristeva's "archaic mother"—a critic/mother who demands of interpretation that it be a grizzly, bloody, and disfiguring birth that is also a death. Such a critic wants interpretation to produce the lost object of the narrative—the site of its nonmeaning—what I might call the narrative unconscious of the text. Lennox characterizes Shakespeare's imagination as perverse, contorted, and obtuse only to demand of his narrative, with her even more abject language, a bloody image of perversity. But more than this, Lennox senses that Shakespeare's tortured representation—his women characters without "character"—depends upon sacrificing the women's stories. This is her original insight about Shakespeare's art that has gone unrecognized until our own day—an insight that has been produced by contemporary feminist criticism and that can find historical resonance in Lennox's study.[5]

Lennox's intertextual sensibility seeks those transpositional moments in Shakespeare's narrative that seem to precede or exceed textuality itself. The source of her pleasure in speaking about Shakespeare's plays comes from locating these intertextual openings through which she can approach her ephemeral and horrifying "thetic" position in regard to his representation, then abjectly condemn his representational practice. Lennox's comments on Shakespeare's treatment of Isabella further illustrate the complexity and intensity of the transpositional engagement of her critical sensibility. Unlike Mariana, Isabella's character does appear in the source, Cinthio's novel from the *Hectomythi*, so Lennox's sensitivity to the way Shakespeare shifts ground for the representation for this character further illuminates the nature of her engagement with his texts. She writes:

> The Character of Isabella in the Play seems to be an Improvement upon that of Epitia in the Novel; for Isabella absolutely refuses, and persists in her Refusal, to give up her Honour to save her Brother's Life; whereas Epitia, overcome by her own Tenderness of Nature, and the affecting Prayers of the unhappy Youth, yields to what her Soul abhors, to redeem him from a shameful Death. It is certain however, that Isabella is a mere Vixen in her Virtue; how she rates her wretched Brother, who gently urges her to save him! . . . [H]er exulting Cruelty to the dying Youth, are the Manners of an affected Prude, outrageous in her seeming Virtue; not of a pious, innocent and tender Maid.
>
> I cannot see the Use of all that Juggling and Ambiguity at the winding up of the Catastrophe; Isabella comes and demands Justice of the Duke for the Wrongs she had received from his Deputy, declaring she had sacrificed her Innocence to save her Brother's Life, whom Angelo had, notwithstanding his Promise to the contrary, caused to be executed. Upon the Duke's telling her, that he believed her Accusation to be false, she goes away in Discontent, without saying a Word more: Is this natural? Is it probable, that Isabella would thus publicly bring a false Imputation on her Honour, and, though innocent and unstained,

suffer the World to believe her violated?—She knows not that the honest Friar who advised her to this extraordinary Action, is the Duke to whom she is speaking; she knows not how the Matter will be cleared up. (1: 33–34)

If Mariana represents the image of the female abject in Shakespeare's play, Isabella, like Lennox, more actively resists. She is Lennox's other—a figure upon whom Lennox can displace her anxieties about the nature of Shakespearean representation. Like Lennox, Isabella seems a "Vixen in her Virtue." Isabella's resistance enacts an ambiguous subterfuge of the play's representation—the site of the play's unconscious embodiment of female abjection acceding to male cultural authority. Isabella faces authority throughout the play, particularly in the final scene when the duke announces she will marry him—an announcement for which Shakespeare provides no textual representation of her response. In Lennox's mind, Isabella is an "Improvement" over Epitia, upon whom she is based, and serves as evidence that Shakespeare's treatment of his source material offers, in Isabella's case, a better representation of a woman's life than in his source. Whereas Epitia succumbs to her brother's pleas, Lennox maintains that Isabella's absolute refusal makes more sense. Lennox faults Shakespeare nonetheless for spoiling the play by ignoring the reality of Isabella's perceptions—by disallowing what would more naturally follow from her resistance. Isabella listens to the discourse of her own abjection—a register tuned inward but whose clamor threatens wholesale wreckage on anything it might contact. But in Shakespeare's play, as in the reception of Lennox's Shakespeare study, we witness a seemingly inevitable silence on the part of a cultural environment that cannot identify or discuss the cultural power of female abjection.[6]

In Isabella's story, Lennox attempts to perceive a full psychology that would play itself out in Shakespeare's representation, but her inquiry only produces questions. Why is Isabella silent in the final scene? Is her suffering necessary to the outcome of the play? Lennox's questions invite us to think about how much Shakespeare's representation depends upon a particular narrative disposition of women. What would Shakespeare have us believe about women? Taking Mariana as an example, we find that women in Shakespeare's world exist in almost complete isolation from their social milieu as represented by the story's plotting. Isabella is the portrayal of a woman whose abjection produces only dissonance when she seeks some social register for her concerns and whose discourse produces her own silencing. In other words, Lennox suspects that for Shakespeare, women exist only as image—an image that must either bear all the "base Aspersions," "infamy," and "Misery" that the representation requires or be silent.

Seen in this way, Lennox's questions are not really rhetorical in the dismissive sense but heuristic. Questions are, in a sense, the only possible response to a locus of nonmeaning. But I think Lennox wants her questions answered. Answers would have to take into account the transpositional processes in Shakespeare's text that, if fully understood, would attest to a center of nonmeaning that Lennox's culture would have to acknowledge. In pointing out the inconsistencies of the plot from the point of view of the representation of a woman's story, Lennox exposes the extent to which Shakespeare was willing to go in order to create Mariana's and Isabella's suffering images. Except for her apparent desire to endure pain in Angelo's name, Mariana's every psychological connection she may have had to her social context is eliminated; there is no logic in her connection to the story. Rather than constituting a cohesive, discursive argument about the way Shakespeare treated women in his plots, Lennox's questions circle around her deep suspicion that her culture cannot adequately answer her questions—cannot produce a thetic position from which to discuss female abjection.

Kristeva suggests that with all abject positions (we can think here of Mariana's, Isabella's, and Lennox's), the apprehension is that one is responding to a voice far away yet all the while remaining enthralled. Kristeva makes it clear that from within the "horror" of abjection one offers oneself to the *jouissance* that is abjection's supplement. The sublime, in the sense of *sublimation,* exists in Lennox's Shakespeare criticism even though she does not produce an analysis that speaks directly to or about the *jouissance* of her own critical enterprise. Instead, as with Mariana, we are left to imagine Lennox's payoff. With Mariana, we puzzle over what pleasure she has in finally marrying Angelo. (Some find it difficult to imagine any joy in that marriage.) But more important to the representation of the play, Mariana's figure, as Jacqueline Rose points out, becomes the focus for that which "escapes or overwhelms the spectator" (117). In a similar way, Lennox's obsessive response to the excess that circulates around the inadequately represented women of Shakespeare's plays produces the kind of ecstatic discourse we see in her text and is the location for what we can imagine to be the sublimity of her pleasure in undertaking Shakespearean criticism.

I do not want to locate the value of Lennox's text in suppositions about any articulated or unarticulated personalized interest or pleasure she may have had in producing it. Rather, I would like to situate her text culturally so that the distinctive approach she made to Shakespeare study may be seen in both her immediate cultural context as well as in the larger trajectory of cultural history. Of overarching significance is the fact that Lennox wrote her commentary analyzing Shakespeare's use of his source material in a climate obsessed with the meaning of Shakespeare to English cultural life. His texts were fast becoming a permanent cultural summons, offering to those who approached his work any number of contradictory identities that could be constituted in his name. In order to understand the distinctiveness of Lennox's approach, which she developed in the face of the overwhelming cultural authority that devolved upon men when they produced their various Shakespeare projects in the period, I will briefly outline some of the Shakespearean projects of three of her contemporaries: David Garrick, Alexander Pope, and Samuel Johnson.

Garrick's Shakespearean projects contributed to the construction of Shakespeare as an idol of popular culture. At the beginning of the eighteenth century, Shakespeare was not a "popular" cultural figure in any sense of the word, but after one hundred years his name had achieved an iconic yet ambiguous status. Such was the impact of the multiple "Shakespeares" constituted in the eighteenth century that cultural life itself became "Shakespearean." Jonathan Bate has described this process in the context of the use of Shakespearean reference in political caricature of the period:

> Each time [Shakespeare] is cited as a figure of authority, he takes on more of a force in the culture at large. And with each appropriation it becomes more difficult to occlude the 'after life' and recover the 'original.' The 'truth' of Shakespeare thus comes to reside in the very multiplicity of his manifestations. (36–37)

That a cultural idol was being created was no secret. Most scholars agree that English Bardolatry was affirmed when Garrick held his grandiose but hilariously tawdry deification of the Bard at his jubilee in Stratford-upon-Avon in 1769. Scholars also agree that much earlier we can see intimations of the Bardomania to come. Of particular interest to Lennox's situation is the formation of the Shakespeare Ladies Club in 1736, which aimed to get theater managers to perform more Shakespeare plays. What is particularly curious is that scholars have been unable to identify the name of even a single woman involved in this club (see Bate 25–27 and Avery). We do know that the "Ladies" were aided by the earl of Burlington, Alexander Pope, Benjamin Martin, Dr. Mead, James Quinn, Lewis Theobald, the two theaters, and the dean and chapter of Westminster Abbey. The absence of women in the historical record may be just another instance of the persistent elimination of women's names from history, or it may be that no women were involved in the enterprise at all. In any case, "Ladies," perhaps as a purely textual construction, played an important role in bringing Shakespeare into public consciousness in the first half of the century. "They" were so successful, in fact, that in 1741 they financed and dedicated the statue to Shakespeare in Westminster Abbey.

Shakespeare's image and objects that could be associated with his life become commodified and fetishized in this period. Garrick's response to this appropriation of Shakespeare is particularly striking. In 1756, the Reverend Frances Gastrell, who owned New Place, Shakespeare's home in Stratford, cut down the mulberry tree that had been growing in the garden since Shakespeare's day. He sold some of the wood to a Stratford carpenter, Thomas Sharp, who carved it into "Shakespearean" objects to sell—the very beginnings of the Shakespeare souvenir industry. The next year David Garrick commissioned Roubillac to carve a marble statue of Shakespeare for which Garrick posed. A purple stain appeared on the lips—"Mulberries," they agreed.[7] When Garrick celebrated Shakespeare's cult status at the jubilee in 1769, the language of idolatry was explicit, as his "Ode upon erecting a statue to Shakespeare" written for the celebration attests: " 'Tis he! 'Tis he! / The God of our idolatry!" (quoted in England, *Jubilee* 252). The excesses of Garrick's self-promotion in the name of his admiration for Shakespeare's art was ridiculed in the magazines, notably by a reference inserted into Samuel Foote's popular play at the Haymarket, *The Devil upon Two Sticks,* which was subsequently published in *Town and Country Magazine:*

> A jubilee, as it has lately appeared, is a public invitation, urged by puffing, to go post without horses, to an obscure borough without representatives, governed by a mayor and aldermen who are not magis-

trates, to celebrate a great poet whose own works have made him immortal, by an ode without poetry, music without harmony, dinners without victuals, and lodgings without beds; a masquerade where half the people appeared bare-faced, a horse-race up to the knees in water, fireworks extinguished as soon as they were lighted, and a gingerbread amphitheatre, which like a house of cards, tumbled to pieces as soon as it was finished. (*Town and Country Magazine*, 1769, 1: 477, quoted in Bate 32)

As Bate points out, the public debate following the jubilee accomplished what the celebration itself could not. Critics of the jubilee only affirmed Shakespeare's cultural preeminence when they found fault with Garrick's excesses (see G. W. Stone).

If Lennox's approach to Shakespeare in the 1750s finds in his work a profoundly disturbing locus of nonmeaning, then Garrick's Shakespearean enterprises created an overdetermined sign whose iconic value could be employed for a number of causes, particularly for the advancement of his own privileged relationship to his predecessor. To see that Lennox did not participate in the growing idolatry of Shakespeare is an important factor in interpreting her study of his texts. At least one of her circle, John Boyle, the duke of Orrery, with whom she had an important friendship and who collaborated with her on at least one of her literary projects, *The Ladies' Museum*, a periodical for women that she published, was willing to provide materials about *Macbeth* for her Shakespeare volumes while withholding them from others precisely because of her different intentions. In a letter to Johnson, Orrery writes:

The papers which I sent to Mrs. L have long lain by me: were thrown aside because I would not walk into Mr. P[ope] and Mr. W[arburton]'s province, who seem to think that Shakespeare was the Sanctum Sanctorum where they only were sufficiently holy to enter. . . . [T]hey are hers, and she has a right to do with them as she pleases. (Isles, "Collection" 37).

Orrery is referring to Pope and Warburton's eight-volume 1747 redaction of Pope's 1725 edition of *The Works of Shakespeare*—one of a series of editions of Shakespeare produced by various editors during the eighteenth century. Lennox's study appeared, then, at a time when not only idolatry of Shakespeare provided her male colleagues a place to consolidate their cultural authority in the popular imagination, but projects in editing Shakespeare's text offered another venue for intense masculinist rivalry, with "Shakespeare" figuring as motive, prize, and authorizing genius. Orrery's letter implies as much when he characterizes Pope and Warburton's sanctification of their editing procedures. Space permits only a sketch of the complex editorial processes through which Shakespeare's text became authorized in Malone's end-of-the-century edition, but I want to suggest a linkage between the effort to use Shakespeare's texts to fix language by establishing his "best" texts and the bitter rivalry of the male editors.

That linkage can be seen, I think, in the way the editors of Shakespeare used the editing process to work out their own relationship to textual authority. Rather than acknowledging, as Lennox's study does through its disturbing enactments of abjection, that there is a profound locus of nonmeaning that lies at the center of Shakespeare's enterprise, the male editors finally authorized their relationship to the contradictory textual remains of Shakespeare's dramatic art inherited from the seventeenth century by adopting concepts exterior to it in order to objectify and "fix" the text. Eventually Shakespeare's text became an object set in the past, his authorship became the product of an original genius, and his editors became owners of his restoration.

Lennox wrote at a time when a material knowledge of Shakespeare's text—what it could or should be in a modern edition, or what principles need be applied to any editorial procedure regulating the material reproduction of that text—was uncertain in the extreme. She wrote after the Pope-Theobald fracas of the 1720s and 1730s but before Johnson's 1765 edition, which contained some unacknowledged borrowings from her own work.[8] In 1726 Theobald criticized the lack of scholarship in Pope's 1725 edition (which was based on Rowe's 1709 edition, itself little more than a modernization of the Fourth Folio). Theobald argued, in effect, for seeing the text as a material, historically contingent object. He criticized Pope for many omissions, emendations, and errors made without any regard to understanding the textual history of the various contradictory folios and quartos. Pope responded by making Theobald the original hero of his 1728 *Dunciad*. Nevertheless, Theobald's 1734 edition defined the modern role of the editor as primarily a scholar's role. He argued that modern editions should be based on the First Folio and offered a theory and practice of emendation based on collation of quarto and folio editions. Theobald's desire to re-produce what Shakespeare had written—not what he wished Shakespeare had written—distinguished his editing practice from Pope's, whose approach to editing partook of some of the elements of abjection I have been pointing to in Lennox's study.

Peter Seary, for example, intimates some of these elements of abjection in Pope's edition when he refers to what he calls Pope's "horrid fascination" for scholarship (48–64). Pope addresses the issue of the status of scholarship when he writes in his preface:

> I have discharg'd the dull duty of an Editor to my best judgment, with more labour than I expect thanks, with a religious abhorrence of all Innovation, and without any indulgence to my private sense or conjecture. (Smith 61)

In practice, Pope saw in Shakespeare's text the raw material for exercising his own art. By approaching Shakespeare's plays on the basis of a shared or comparable sensibility, he developed an editorial role chiefly to define and identify beauties and faults. As for the beauties, Pope notes, "Some of the more shining passages are distinguish'd by comma's in the margin; and where the beauty lay not in particulars but in the whole, a star is prefix'd to the scene" (Smith 61). For the faults, he indicates, "Some . . . passages which are excessively bad . . . are degraded to the bottom of the page" (Smith 61). The porter's scene in *Macbeth* was one such passage. By highlighting the great passages and stigmatizing the flaws, Pope used Shakespeare's text much as Lennox did—to sort out what seems proper and improper to his own sensibilities—in fact, the very cultural processes of abjection I have been describing in Lennox's study. Faulty as Pope's editorial procedures seem to us now, we should concede at least that his approach brought Shakespeare's text into close contact with his own discursive concerns— a process that emphasizes Shakespeare as an immediate cultural presence whose reception is precisely what is being consciously enacted. When Pope changes Shakespeare's metrical line, as he does throughout the plays, so that it conforms to his own poetic tastes, he blurs the boundaries between himself and Shakespeare, taking as his own what seems to belong to himself and suppressing or discarding the rest.[9] Pope's process does not make an object of Shakespeare's text by applying some kind of exterior apparatus that would create more apparent subject/object distinctions. Still, Pope enacts abject gestures in his Shakespeare study as part of his process of establishing his own poetic ability. Yet Pope does not speak from within the abject as Lennox does but draws from the maternal matrix of Shakespeare's plays that which he then uses to affirm his own creative sensibilities.

Pope's approach bespeaks a maternal cultural matrix in the ways I have been describing certainly to a greater extent than do Johnson's editorial procedures. Pope's preface may characterize Shakespeare as a "natural genius," but Pope insists on the concept only to the extent that the plays are capable of revealing the mind of the author:

> The Poetry of *Shakespear* was Inspiration indeed: he is not so much an Imitator, as an Instrument, of Nature; and 'tis not so just to say that he speaks from her, as that she speaks thro' him.
>
> His *Characters* are so much Nature her self, that 'tis a sort of injury to call them by so distant a name as Copies of her. (Smith 48)

Pope genders the source of Shakespeare's genius as *feminine* and claims his own interest is in the truth to be found in that female matrix that is the basis for Shakespeare's art. Johnson, on the other hand, exalts Shakespeare's authority to such an extent that Shakespeare is no longer even a subject but a phenomenon appearing fully formed at the start—an inviolable, original genius. Johnson writes in his preface:

> Shakespeare, whether life or nature be his subject, shews plainly that he has seen with his own eyes; he gives the image which he receives, not weakened or distorted by the intervention of any other mind. (Smith 140)

Or, consider the more effusive lines from the *Prologue* Johnson recited at the opening of the Drury Lane Theater in 1747:

> When Learning's Triumph o'er her barb'rous Foes
> First rear'd the Stage, immortal Shakespeare rose.
>
> (quoted in Desai 80)

Finally, the assertion of Shakespeare's originality becomes the very grounds for editorial authority over his plays. Without the categories of *originality* and *genius,* Lennox's male colleagues would have to acknowledge their constitutive role in transmitting Shakespearean drama. Their most basic fear in approaching Shakespeare is to imagine that they are the sole producers of a Shakespearean text—that they have effaced his creativity and ability altogether. Rather than thinking of culture and history as an ongoing, complex renegotiation with the past, they propped the idea of Shakespearean genius up against their anxieties about their authorship of their own culture. When Lennox attacked Shakespeare's plays because they were not original, she was displacing one of the most important criteria developed by male editors to assuage those anxieties.

Lennox paid for her criticism of the Bard. Boswell records an anecdote of Goldsmith saying to Johnson at the Club that "a person had advised him to go to hiss Mrs. Lennox's play because she had attacked Shakespeare in *Shakespear Illustrated*." The play was Lennox's *The Sister*, which was produced in 1769, fifteen years after the publication of her study. Her play was shut down by audience hooting throughout the first performance.[10]

There are a number of aspects of Lennox's textual practice that indicate that her solution to the problem of the overwhelming male cultural authority of her day was to abject herself to it. In the curious way that Lennox offered the manuscript of her novel *The Female Quixote* to her friend Samuel Johnson, allowing him to write its penultimate chapter in which a learned doctor argues Arabella, the quixotic heroine, out of her confusions about the "reality" of romance novels, so, too, when Lennox completed her Shakespeare study, which Johnson may have urged her to undertake, she asked him to write its dedication, once again allowing this important literary man of her to day to complete her task.[11]

Nowhere in Lennox's text do abjection and intertextuality meet more forcefully than in its complex and contradictory dedication. The dedication is both a pretext and a context for the volumes to follow. More famous than Lennox's study (since it is generally acknowledged to be Johnson's work), the dedication performs its own strange alienation of the material that follows it. Ventriloquized as Lennox's own voice ("My Sex, my Age, have not given me many Opportunities of mingling in the World"), the masquerading voice of the dedication seems at odds with the voice of the commentary that follows in the study itself. Seeming to take away the force of what will follow, the dedication asserts:

> It is not perhaps very necessary to enquire whether the Vehicle of so much Delight and Instruction be a Story probable, or unlikely, native, or foreign. *Shakespeare*'s Excellence is not the Fiction of a Tale, but the Representation of Life; and his Reputation is therefore safe, till Human Nature shall be changed. (1: xi)

Where Johnson in the dedication says plotting does not matter in the estimation of Shakespeare's work, Lennox, throughout an analysis of twenty-two of his plays, insists that it does.

In fact, the dedication is contradictory in its own terms. Early on, Johnson claims that the present study has been predicated upon a notion of invention—an idea seemingly at odds with the distinction between "Fiction" and "Representation" with which he concludes his remarks.[12] About invention Johnson says, "Among the Powers that must conduce to constitute a Poet, the first and most valuable is Invention" (1: iv). And further, "In the Examination of a Poet's Character it is therefore first to be enquired what Degree of Invention has been exerted by him. With this View I have very diligently read the Works of *Shakespear,* and now presume to lay the result of my Searches before your Lordship" (1: vi). Much of the fame of this piece of writing focuses on the distinction made here between "Fiction" and "Representation" (see Willems).

Faced with a study that demonstrates that claims about Shakespeare's excellence cannot be based on a notion of his wholesale "invention" of the plays that he wrote, Johnson is forced to divide our apprehension of Shakespearean genius into the separate categories of "Fiction"—here roughly equated, by inference, to "details in the plotting"—and "Representation," a larger, more encompassing term through which we locate Shakespeare's unequaled and unrivaled genius. The question that Johnson raises in the dedication is: Does *invention* include both "Fiction" and "Representation" in Shakespeare's case? Johnson implies that we can accept that Shakespeare did not invent the fictions of his plays as long as we can say that he *did* invent the *representation.* According to Johnson, therein rests Shakespeare's achievement—even the integrity of his character. But for Lennox the question is not so simple because, as her commentaries indicate, *representation* includes narration—the fiction of the plays. In fact, during the course of her comments on the place of women in Shakespearean drama, we have seen how Lennox questions precisely the integrity of Shakespeare's *representations.*

In addition to the intertextual peculiarities of the dedication to Lennox's study, there are other texts to consider when assessing Lennox's insistent and single-minded questioning of Shakespeare's art and her negotiation with the emerging masculinist bias of the Shakespeare industry. Her study of Shakespeare's plays is, in part, a response to her own encounter with the slippery, eighteenth-century notion of invention, having felt the full weight of its deployment in regard to her own writing. In 1752, the year prior to the publication of the first two volumes of *Shakespear Illustrated,* Henry Fielding, writing under the name Sir Alexander Drawcansir, reviewed Lennox's novel *The Female Quixote* in his *Covent-Garden Journal.*

In evaluating Shakespeare's plays, Lennox used the same procedure Fielding deployed the year before when evaluating her novel. After acknowledging that Lennox's book is an obvious imitation of Cervantes, Fielding writes: "I will here very frankly declare my Opinion in what Particulars the Imitation falls short; in what it equals, and in what it excels its illustrious Original" (279). Fielding makes plain the principles from which he argues: "In the first place, Cervantes has the Advantage of being the Original; and consequently is entitled to that Honour of Invention, which can never be attributed to any copy however excellent" (279). Fielding finds Lennox's work inadequate; but, more than that, he puts her work forever outside the running, permanently excluded from the possibility of being a great work of fiction. Her novel can never be "original." In flatly rejecting her achievement, Fielding's response provides a telling contrast to Lennox's more abject, more deeply connected response to Shakespearean texts.

Lennox carefully monitored the reception of her writing and worked hard to promote it. Besides the evidence of her friendship and collaboration with Johnson, Richardson, Orrery, and other important literary men of her day, we have her own words in at least one letter. She writes to Orrery asking him to promote her novels, admitting she is "not without some little ambition" (see Lennox, "To Duke of Orrery"). It is perhaps not too outrageous to suggest that Lennox would create, in her study of Shakespeare, something of a tour de force. Commentators have interpreted her objections to Shakespeare to be a result of her adherence to "rigid" neoclassical criteria (see note 3). But, the so-called criteria to which she seems to hold Shakespeare's plays can best be thought of as a screen. To take Lennox seriously on this point would be to align oneself with Johann Christoph Gottsched, Germany's most rigorous neoclassical literary critic, who found her "sharpwitted" for pointing out Shakespeare's errors to her fellow countrymen.[13] But she was not pointing out errors in a text that she could objectify by applying critical criteria that she would construct in some realm existing strictly outside herself. In comparing Shakespeare with his sources, she observed the diminished possibilities for representing women's lives. She looks closely at Shakespeare's processes of transposition in her intertextual analysis. She sees that women are the fulcrum in Shakespeare's imagination when he moves from one signifying system to another—from his source to the play he wants to produce. Identifying Shakespeare's processes of transposition, she exposes contradictions in the idolizing of Shakespeare's original genius—ironically at the very moment her own transposition of romance material was denigrated (Doody, Langbauer). Lennox shows not only that Shakespeare did not invent his fictions, which would, according to Fielding's criteria, leave him well outside the rank of "original" writers—somewhere, perhaps, in the company of Lennox herself—but, also, and Lennox is at pains to show this, that Shakespeare's representation, the very area in which Johnson's dedication indicates he can be declared "original," is inadequate to the representation of women.

Aside from the astounding suggestion that Shakespeare was "inferior" to his sources, Lennox reveals what her contemporaries refused to consider. At a time when romance novels were under attack, and, in fact, had nearly faded from the literary scene, she demonstrates that Shakespeare read them. By placing his sources beside a summary of the action of his plays, she also demonstrates that Shakespeare was far from "original" in story development. She also shows his plays to be inadequate to the representation of women. But Lennox's questions about the cultural significance of female abjection are not answered. They hang in her text both as a provocation to discussion and a resistance to Augustan critical criteria that would shut down such questioning. For us, the unanswered questions of her study offer material for a history of the female textual subject, in this case, engaged with a Shakespeare we, like Lennox's male colleagues and even Lennox herself, have yet to fully discuss.

Notes

An earlier version of this essay was presented in a Shakespeare Association of America seminar at the annual meeting in Austin, Texas, in April 1989. Special thanks to Deborah Payne and Marianne Novy for their comments on an earlier draft. Thanks go as well to Ronald Schleifer, who made suggestions on this version of the essay, and to J. Douglas Canfield for his helpful editorial guidance. Peter Donahue's encouragement was also significant and welcome.

1. See also Grady for another discussion of the construction of Shakespeare scholarship in the eighteenth century.

2. Helpful commentary on Kristeva's work may be found in Adriaens, Barzilai, Brandt, Fletcher and Benjamin, Grosz, Klein, Lechte, Moi, Nye, J. Stone, Waller, and Zepp.

3. Doody's article is the one analysis that offers a sympathetic reading of Lennox's Shakespeare study. Doody compares Lennox's Shakespeare study to her novel writing but offers no language that would locate Lennox's critical approach

within larger, more encompassing cultural processes, and in the end Doody's sympathetic reading amounts to special pleading on Lennox's behalf.

That Lennox's work does not exist in any modern edition is testimony enough that her approach to Shakespeare found few followers. Her twentieth-century biographer, Small, belittles her achievement and deprecates her judgment. Small reasons that Lennox's "equipment for Shakespearean scholarship was admittedly slight," although "according to the light granted her, she has done her work faithfully and conscientiously" (208, 196). Young says Lennox never "encounters squarely the fundamental problem of the relation of character to action with which some of our contemporary critics are largely concerned" (49). Isles contends that Lennox's critical standards are "rigid" and result in "distortion." He says a "misplaced facetiousness" is a striking feature of her study and that it is "full of illogical and imperceptive argument" ("Collection" 41). Ralli paraphrases Lennox's comments on ten of the plays and incorrectly assumes she wrote the dedication (1: 26–32). In the nineteenth century, Lennox was attacked by Douce (97). Drake says she performed her task "imperfectly" and "her notes were rather censures on the liberties which the bard had taken with the incidents to which she had traced him, than elucidatory of the exquisite manner in which he had occasionally moulded them to his purpose" (63). Goodwin says Lennox's study is "somewhat silly" (33: 50). Lounsbury contends that with her rigid canons she ought to have lived in Rymer's day: "Had she in addition become Mrs. Rymer the conjunction of these two stars, shooting madly from their spheres in the Shakespearean firmament, would have attracted the attention of observers for all time" (qtd. in Young 40). See also Anderson.

4. The contents of Lennox's volumes are given below. This is not a copy of the table of contents of each volume; rather, it is a listing of the contents that shows the order of the material presented and the number of pages given to each portion. Included in what I have called "Observations" are both Lennox's summaries of the plays and her comments that follow immediately from the summary without any break in the text.

Lennox gives fourteen source stories in all. She translated seven from Italian and one from a French translation of Plautus. Otherwise, she used English translations already available. (Lennox learned Italian in order to undertake this translation.)

She compares eight history plays with Holingshed's *Chronicles*. According to Isles, most of these sources had already been pointed out by Langbaine in his *New Catalogue of English Plays* (1688) and *Account of the English Dramatick Poets* (1691). Isles claims Lennox was familiar with Theobald's 1733 edition of Shakespeare. Her major discoveries are the use of Montemayor's *Diana* in *The Two Gentlemen of Verona*, Sidney's *Arcadia* and Spenser's *Faerie Queene* in *Lear*, and Holingshed's *Chronicles* in *Cymbeline*, and the Thirty-sixth Novel of Bandello's *Novelle* in *Twelfth Night*. He points out that she failed to notice a source in Bandello for *Much Ado about Nothing*. See Isles, "Collection" 422.

5. Contemporary feminist commentary about Shakespeare's representation of women characters is by now an impressive body of work. See Lenz et al., Bamber, Dash, Green and Swift, Kahn, Neely, and Novy.

6. Contemporary reviews of *Shakespear Illustrated* appeared in *Gentleman's Monthly* 23 (1753: 256, 250); 24 (1754: 31, 91, 233). They were favorable and asked for further comments, but evidently there were none. Samuel Richardson's response to *Shakespear Illustrated* may be found in *Letters* 264, 250. Garrick and Johnson's response may be found in Isles, "Collection" 40–42, 422–23. Isles also includes a letter from Mary Jones, a poet and prose writer and acquaintance of Lennox, that indicates her different reading of Lennox from those of Jones's male contemporaries. Jones calls Lennox "the ingenious Author of Shakespeare illustrated [*sic*]" and says that it and *The Female Quixote* can "set our Judgments right again" (Isles, "Collection" 41–43).

7. Material on Garrick's jubilee and earlier events leading to it may be found in Babcock, Bate, Deelman, both works cited by England, Holderness, Schueller, Stockholm, and Willems.

8. See Isles ("Collection" 40–41) for evidence that Johnson may have suggested to Lennox the project of comparing Shakespeare to his sources. Sherbo points out ten instances in Johnson's editing of Shakespeare in which he makes use of Lennox's opinions. While Johnson explicitly mentions Lennox's work three times in his edition, Sherbo points to seven other instances of her influence on his work. Sherbo concludes: "These similarities warrant the conclusion that Johnson's debt to Mrs. Lennox was greater than has been realized" (*Johnson* 91). Yet in Sherbo's more recent work, he never mentions Charlotte Lennox (*Birth*). I find this puzzling. Smith indicates that Lennox's work was used by Richard Farmer in his "Essay on the Learning of Shakespeare" as well as by Johnson in his preface (Smith 50–54).

9. For a discussion of how Pope changed Shakespeare's metrical line, see Bertram. For a discussion of the rivalry of Shakespeare's eighteenth-century editors, see Williams.

10. Discussed in Young 51–52.

11. Documentary evidence of Johnson's friendship with Lennox may be found in both works cited by Isles. See also Clifford. Small provides useful information, although subsequent scholarship has overturned many of her assertions. See also

Young, who discusses the Johnson-Lennox collaboration on *Shakespear Illustrated* in some detail (33–81). Eastham gives a chapter to Lennox's biography, as does Kynaston. See also Parker on Johnson's criticism of Shakespeare.

12. For a contemporary discussion of *invention*, see [Bowle] and Hurd.

13. Gottsched's review of Lennox's study may be found in his Leipzig periodical, *Das Neueste aus der anmuthigen Gelehrsamkeit* July 1775, 501–10. See Isles, "Collection" 423.

Works Cited

Adriaens, Mark. "Ideology and Literary Production: Kristeva's Poetics." *Semiotics and Dialectics: Ideology and the Text*. Ed. Peter V. Zima. Amsterdam: John Benjhamins B. V., 1981. 179–220.

Anderson, H. "The Study of Shakespeare's Sources from Langbaine to Malone." Diss. Oxford U, 1954.

Avery, Emmett L. "The Shakespeare Ladies Club." *Shakespeare Quarterly* 7 (1956): 153–58.

Babcock, Robert Witbeck. *The Genesis of Shakespeare Idolatry, 1766–1799: A Study in English Criticism of the Late Eighteenth Century*. Chapel Hill: U of North Carolina P, 1931.

Bamber, Linda. *Comic Women, Tragic Men: A Study of Gender and Genre in Shakespeare*. Stanford: Stanford UP, 1982.

Barzilai, Shuli. "Borders of Language: Kristeva's Critique of Lacan." *PMLA* 106 (1991): 294–305.

Bate, Jonathan. *Shakespearean Constitutions: Politics, Theatre, Criticism, 1730–1830*. Oxford: Clarendon, 1989.

Bertram, Paul. *White Spaces in Shakespeare: The Development of the Modern Text*. Cleveland, Ohio: Bellflower, 1981.

[Bowle, John]. *Reflections on Originality in Authors: Being Remarks on a Letter to Mr. Mason on the Marks of Imitation*. London, 1766.

Brandt, Joan. "The Systematics of a Non-System: Julia Kristeva's Revisionary Semiotics." *American Journal of Semiotics* 5 (1987): 133–50.

Clifford, James. "Johnson's First Club." *Evidence in Literary Scholarship: Essays in Memory of James Marshall Osborn*. Ed. Rene Wellek and Alvaro Ribiero. Oxford: Clarendon, 1979. 197–213.

Dash, Irene G. *Wooing, Wedding, and Power: Women in Shakespeare's Plays*. New York: Columbia UP, 1981.

Deelman, Christian. *The Great Shakespeare Jubilee*. New York: Viking, 1964.

de Grazia, Margreta. *Shakespeare Verbatim: The Reproduction of Authenticity and the 1790 Apparatus*. Oxford: Clarendon, 1991.

Desai, R. W. *Johnson on Shakespeare.* New Delhi: Orient Longman, 1979.

Doody, Margaret Anne. "Shakespeare's Novels: Charlotte Lennox Illustrated." *Studies in the Novel* 19 (1987): 296–310.

Douce, Francis. *Illustrations of Shakespeare and of Ancient Manners.* London, 1839.

Drake, Nathan. *Memorials of Shakespeare: Or, Sketches of his Character and Genius, by various writers, now first collected.* London, 1828.

Eastham, Leah Raye. "Charlotte Ramsay Lennox: A Critical Study of Her Novels." Diss. U of Arkansas, 1968.

England, Martha Winburn. *Garrick and Stratford.* New York: New York Public Library, 1962.

——. *Garrick's Jubilee.* Columbus: Ohio State UP, 1964.

[Fielding, Henry] Sir Alexander Drawcansir. *The Covent-Garden Journal.* Ed. Gerard Edward Jensen. New York: Russell and Russell, 1964.

Fletcher, John, and Andrew Benjamin, eds. *Abjection, Melancholia, and Love: The Work of Julia Kristeva.* London: Routledge, 1990.

Goodwin, Gordon. "Charlotte Lennox." *Dictionary of National Biography.*

Grady, Hugh. *The Modernist Shakespeare: Critical Texts in a Material World.* Oxford: Clarendon, 1991.

Green, Gayle, and Carolyn Ruth Swift, eds. "Feminist Criticism of Shakespeare." *Women's Studies: An Interdisciplinary Journal* 9 (1981): 1–217.

Grosz, Elizabeth. *Jacques Lacan: A Feminist Introduction.* London: Routledge, 1990.

Holderness, Graham, ed. *The Shakespeare Myth.* New York: St. Martin's, 1988.

Hurd, Richard. *A Letter to Mr. Mason, on the Marks of Imitation.* Cambridge, Eng., 1757.

Isles, Duncan. "Johnson and Charlotte Lennox." *New Rambler* 2nd ser. 3 (June 1967): 34–48.

——. "The Lennox Collection." *Harvard Library Bulletin* 18 (1970): 317–44 and 19 (1971): 36–60, 165–86, 416–35.

Kahn, Coppèlia. *Man's Estate: Masculine Identity in Shakespeare.* Berkeley and Los Angeles: U of California P, 1981.

Klein, Richard. "In the Body of the Mother." *Enclitic* 7 (1987): 66–75.

Kristeva, Julia. *Desire in Language: A Semiotic Approach to Literature and Art.* Trans. Thomas Gora, Alice Jardine, and Leon Roudiez. Ed. Leon S. Roudiez. New York: Columbia UP, 1980.

——. *Powers of Horror: An Essay on Abjection.* Trans. Leon S. Roudiez. New York: Columbia UP, 1982.

——. *Revolution in Poetic Language.* Trans. Margaret Waller. New York: Columbia UP, 1984.

Kynaston, Agnes Mary. "The Life and Writings of Charlotte Lennox, 1720–1804."
     M.A. thesis, U of London, 1937.
Langbauer, Laurie. *Women and Romance: The Consolations of Gender in the
     English Novel.* Ithaca, N.Y.: Cornell UP, 1990.
Lechte, John. *Julia Kristeva.* London: Routledge, 1990.
Lennox, Charlotte. *Shakespear Illustrated: or the Novels and Histories, on which
     the plays of Shakespear are founded, Collected and Translated from the Original
     Authors, with Critical Remarks. In two volumes.* London, 1753. *The third and
     last volume.* London, 1745.
———. "To Duke of Orrery." 29 October 1798. N.b. 42–43, 1: 85. Folger Shake-
     speare Library, Washington, D.C.
Lenz, Carolyn Ruth Swift, Gayle Greene, and Carol Thomas Neely, eds. *The
     Woman's Part: Feminist Criticism of Shakespeare.* Urbana: U of Illinois P, 1980.
Lounsbury, T. R. *Shakespeare as a Dramatic Artist.* New York: Scribners, 1901.
Moi, Toril. *Sexual/Textual Politics: Feminist Literary Theory.* London: Methuen,
     1985.
Morgan, Thaïs. "The Space of Intertextuality." O'Donnell and Davis 239–79.
Neely, Carol Thomas. *Broken Nuptials in Shakespeare's Plays.* New Haven: Yale
     UP, 1985.
Novy, Marianne. *Love's Argument: Gender Relations in Shakespeare.* Chapel Hill:
     U of North Carolina P, 1981.
Nye, Andrea. "Woman Clothed with the Sun: Julia Kristeva and the Escape from/
     to Language." *Signs* 12 (1987): 664–86.
O'Donnell, Patrick, and Robert Con Davis, eds. *Intertextuality and Contemporary
     American Fiction.* Baltimore: Johns Hopkins UP, 1989.
Parker, G. F. *Johnson's Shakespeare.* Oxford: Clarendon, 1989.
Ralli, Augustus. *A History of Shakespearian Criticism.* 2 vols. London: Oxford
     UP, 1932.
Richardson, Samuel. *Selected Letters of Samuel Richardson.* Ed. J. Carroll. Oxford:
     Oxford UP, 1964.
Rose, Jacqueline. "Sexuality in the Reading of Shakespeare: *Hamlet* and *Measure
     for Measure.*" *Alternative Shakespeares.* Ed. John Drakakis. London: Methuen,
     1985. 95–118.
Schueller, Herbert M., ed. *The Persistence of Shakespeare Idolatry: Essays in Honor
     of Robert W. Babcock.* Detroit: Wayne State UP, 1964.
Seary, Peter. *Lewis Theobald and the Editing of Shakespeare.* Oxford: Claren-
     don, 1990.
Sherbo, Arthur. *The Birth of Shakespeare Studies: Commentators from Rowe
     (1709) to Boswell-Malone (1821).* East Lansing, Mich.: Colleagues P, 1986.
———. *Samuel Johnson, Editor of Shakespeare with an Essay on "The Adven-
     turer."* Urbana: U of Illinois P, 1956.

Small, Miriam Rossiter. *Charlotte Lennox: An Eighteenth Century Lady of Letters.* 1953. New Haven: Archon, 1969.

Smith, David Nicol. *Shakespeare in the Eighteenth Century.* Oxford: Clarendon, 1928.

Stockholm, Johannes M. *Garrick's Folly: The Shakespeare Jubilee of 1769 at Stratford and Drury Lane.* New York: Barnes, 1964.

Stone, George Winchester, Jr. "David Garrick's Significance in the History of Shakespearean Criticism." *PMLA* 45 (1950): 183–97.

Stone, Jennifer. "The Horrors of Power: A Critique of 'Kristeva.'" *The Politics of Theory: Proceedings of the Essex Conference on the Sociology of Literature.* Ed. Francis Barker, Peter Hulme, and Margaret Iverson. Colchester, Eng.: U of Essex P, 1983. 38–48.

Waller, Margaret. "An Interview with Julia Kristeva." Trans. Richard Macksey. O'Donnell and Davis 280–93.

Willems, Michèle. *La genèse du mythe Shakespearien, 1660–1780.* Paris: Presses Universitaires de France, 1979.

Williams, George Walton. *The Craft of Printing and the Publishing of Shakespeare's Plays.* Washington: Folger Books, 1985.

Young, Karl. *Samuel Johnson on Shakespeare: One Aspect.* University of Wisconsin Studies in Language and Literature, 18, ser. no. 3, 1923.

Zepp, Evelyn H. "The Criticism of Julia Kristeva: A New Mode of Critical Thought." *Romantic Review* 73 (1982): 80–97.

ACTORS AND HOMOPHOBIA

KRISTINA STRAUB

From the late seventeenth to the late eighteenth century, the image of actors as represented in the British popular press is that of sexual suspects, men who are in some way outside the boundaries of culturally dominant definitions of masculinity. As sexual "others" who often stood for what masculinity was not (or was not supposed to be), actors therefore played an important role in marking the limits of what masculinity could be. The image of the actor was ambiguously positioned in relation to class hierarchies from the outset of the eighteenth century; he is represented, over the course of the century and often simultaneously as servant or gentleman, abject slave or prosperous businessman. His professional self-display and personal exhibitionism placed him at odds with the increasingly dominant image of masculinity defined as a spectating subject, rather than a specularized object. As Rousseau pointed out in his infamous and, to us, rather ironic remarks on actors, men who professionally put their bodies on display could not easily attain an authoritative or dignified masculinity. By class and gender definition, actors were liminal cases, outside and in opposition to dominant masculine roles.[1]

Actors also played an important part in the emergent organization of men into sexual "kinds" in the eighteenth century. Specifically, their representations in the popular press—theater pamphlets, biographies, histories of the theater, and overt print gossip—helped to shape the discursive formation of a male homosexual other whose definition depends on a dichotomy between "normal" manliness and effeminate "deviance." Tracing the development of the actor's sexually suspect nature over the course of the century helps us to delineate one of the discursive paths by which the effeminate homosexual male becomes a despised necessity in constructing early modern masculinity in Great Britain.

This essay maps the route by which the sexually "deviant," effeminate male emerges as a categorical other in the changing representations of

British actors in the eighteenth century. As Randolph Trumbach's work on the "birth of the molly" suggests, representations of actors were not isolated instances of "deviance" but parts of a widely articulated notion of the effeminate homosexual male as a distinct sexual type ("Birth" 134). The homoeroticism associated with the boy actors of the seventeenth century is increasingly subjected to the taxonomizing effects of a hetero/homosexual dichotomy. As a result, the actors' earlier homoeroticism is transposed into two distinct kinds of characterizations: a misogynistic discourse that subjects the "feminine" qualities of the actors to ridicule and abuse, and a homophobic discourse that divides actors, like the larger category "men" to which they belong, into "normal" and "deviant" types. I take, as a case study in this transposition, the early to midcentury fops of Colley Cibber and the later treatment of this theatrical figure in relation to the image of the actor as a sexually suspect public figure. The homoeroticism of the early fop is not unproblematic—indeed, it is in some ways as sexually suspect as the later fop was to become—but a comparison of Cibber's fops with those of David Garrick reveals the growing dominance of a masculinity increasingly defined in opposition to the effeminate homosexual other and the misogynistically defined female.

Eve Sedgwick has argued that "homophobia directed by men against men is misogynistic, and perhaps transhistorically so" (20). (By "misogynistic" she means "not only that it is oppressive of the so-called feminine in men, but that it is oppressive of women.") Speaking conversely from Sedgwick, I would say that the misogyny working through the feminization of actors as specularized sexual suspects sustained and finally enabled, as we shall see, the homophobia that was to surface in the explicit charges of homosexuality that were made against David Garrick and Samuel Foote in the 1770s. While the historically determined situations of women and gay men have been and are radically different from each other, their shared otherness to dominant modes of masculine sexuality in modern Anglo, European, and American cultures can and has linked homophobia and misogyny in the maintenance of masculinist sexual hegemonies. The misogynistically loaded feminization of actors in mid-eighteenth-century representations of their sexuality works in tandem with the association of actors with sexual "deviance" to construct a definition of actors as sexually other to dominant masculinity.

The actor's most obvious vulnerability to homophobia was, until well into the last half of the seventeenth century, the playing of female roles. While actors in drag are accepted by Samuel Pepys as late as 1661 (2: 8), and, indeed, are defended by some as morally less harmful than bringing women on the stage, seventeenth-century antitheatrical writers deployed the biblical prohibition against cross-dressing in their indictments of the stage. William Prynne's *Histrio-Mastix: The Player's Scourge* offers particularly vivid—and lengthy—indictments of the boy actors' gender ambiguity. Prynne's primary objection to theatrical cross-dressing is that it confuses the distinctions divinely ordained between male and female appearance and behavior, but aside from this sin against a scripturally based ordering of nongenital, gendered roles, Prynne also charges that a confusion of appearances might and probably does lead to a confusion of bodies: "Players and Play-hunters in their secret conclaves play the Sodomite: together with some modern examples of such, who have been desperately enamour'd with Players Boys thus clad in woman's apparell, so farre as to solicite them by words, by Letters, even actually to abuse them" (1: 211–12). The idea that the custom of boy actors playing girls encouraged sodomy was almost as common in the seventeenth-century antitheatrical literature as the idea that the representation of heterosexuality on stage encouraged adultery. The charge of sodomy was current enough to move Thomas Heywood to reject it in his defense of actors and the theater as early as 1612.

Significantly, actors who played only male roles did not escape the charge of a suspicious effeminacy even in seventeenth-century discourse. Prynne's language suggests that the very act of putting the male body on display made it somehow not-male:

A man enfeebled in all his joynts, resolved into a more than womanish effeminacy, whose art it is to speak with his hands and gestures, comes forth upon the Stage: and for this one, I know not whom, neither man nor woman, the whole citie flocke together, that so the fabulous lusts of antiquity may be acted. Yea, men . . . are unmanned on the Stage: all the honour and vigour of their sex is effeminated with the shame, the dishonesty of an unsinued body. He who is most womanish and best resembles the female sex, gives best content. (1: 168, italics omitted)

Prynne seems to hint at an actual physical condition of the body—"unsinued"—as the result of theatrical display. This physical otherness to masculinity was reinforced by assumptions about the social status of the actor that also positioned his sexuality as not fully male.

Two options for male identity defined by class position in the late seventeenth century—aristocratic or bourgeois—exclude the actor, placing him in an ambiguous, neither-nor position that works as a kind of socially enacted castration. The actor often wears the trappings of a cavalier, including a sword, but he is brutally discouraged from using that sword in the defense of "his" women. John Harold Wilson documents several of many instances in the late seventeenth century in which actors came into conflict with their betters and found themselves legally and socially without the right to protect their honor or "their" women against aristocratic insult: "[T]he fact is that actors were declassé, too, and just as fair game as the actresses for any titled rascal or his hired bullies" (28). The actor is not a full-fledged member of the aristocratic, homosocial culture based on the exchange and ownership of women. His sexuality is effectively castrated, without threat to other males.

A significant change is visible in late-seventeenth- and early-eighteenth-century representations of actors' sexuality. First, while defenses of actors' morals are certainly not new, they begin to focus more on individual actors than on actors as an undifferentiated class. Alan Bray has suggested that the figure of the sodomite changed, in the seventeenth century, from a fantastical, almost mythical creature associated with exotic crimes such as sorcery to the more everyday and, therefore, in some ways more threatening "molly."[2] The association of sodomy with individual actors is consistent with this shift from the fantastic and abstract to the concrete and nameable.

The impetus to "clean up" the theaters of the late seventeenth century, perhaps combined with the shift from mythical to mundane in homophobic formulations of the sodomite, probably helped build a growing wave of denial against the old association of sodomy with actors. Dryden links the actor Jo Haines's religious and sexual vagaries to those of the infamous "convert" and "sodomite" Titus Oates. The stage, he promises in the epilogue to *The Pilgrim*, will reform, but "neither you nor we, with all our pains, / Can make clean work; there will be some remains, / While you have still your Oates and we our Haines" (in Davies, *Dramatic* 1: 266). Sodomy and heresy are, as Bray notes, traditionally linked in English popular mythology (19); "deviance" of both kinds is invested in Haines, a "low" comedian and a type of trickster/fool figure, as a spot to be removed, albeit

by some unforeseen event attended with extreme difficulty. Tom Brown
has Haines "rehabilitate" himself by converting back from Catholicism
and apologizing for his religious and geographical wanderings to the "dear
loving Sisters of the Pit":

> [D]on't despise me now because I've liv'd
> Where . . . Boys claim your Prerogative.
> No, Sisters; no ———
> I ne'er turn'd Heretick in Love at least;
> 'Twas decent Whoring kept my Thoughts still chaste.
>
> (*Life* 213–14)

Invested in the minds and bodies of specific actors, the "homosexual
plague" previously associated with a vaguely defined class of actors could
be at worst contained and at best recuperated.

By the mid-eighteenth century, the counterattack against antitheatrical
literature was more likely to externalize the threat of male homosexuality:
this suspect form of male sexuality was "out there" in English society,
no longer a vice internal to the theater. The century's ongoing struggle to
define actors as "manly" in terms of professional status is contiguous with
an ongoing effort to define them in opposition to homosexually "tainted"
others. Theophilus Cibber argues defensively that alleged theatrical immorality is hardly a problem compared with gambling "and another most
detestable Sin, that is daily growing up amongst us." This "Sin" "calls
louder for the Regulation of the Legislature, than the Playhouses. Are not
our Youth so debauch'd with Effeminacy and Italian airs, that we daily
see Male Children of the best Families, dwindle almost into Women?" (*To
David Garrick* 73). Cibber opposes the "healthy" sexuality of the actors to
"effeminate Enunchs [*sic*], and God ____ e Italians" (76). The 1747 *Pretty
Gentleman* argues that Garrick's theater is the age's best defense against the
supposed onslaught of perverse masculinity (31). John Brown proclaims
the theater as the last bastion, in 1757, for the "Remains of manly Taste" in
an age grown effeminate and corrupt (1: 48). Homophobia is more likely
to crop up in negative definitions of what the actor is not in the mid- to
late eighteenth century than in charges leveled against the players. At the
same time, when such charges *were* made against Garrick and Foote in
the 1770s, they were posed and responded to with a legally and personally
threatening specificity unheard of in the seventeenth century. In fact, then,
homophobia against actors does not disappear in the eighteenth century;

rather, it becomes a more complex discourse by which actors' sexuality is culturally organized into an increasingly rigid gay-straight dichotomy.

Actors remain sexually suspect as a class throughout the eighteenth century, however. The primary mode of cultural suspicions about the actor's sexuality shifts its emphasis from homophobia directed against the class of actors to a misogynistic discourse that stereotypes actors as sexually other to dominant masculinities. While homophobia still arises against individual actors, misogyny takes over the cultural work of justifying the actor's social subjection as a male who makes a spectacle of himself in an age that increasingly valued men as spectating subjects rather than objects of spectatorship. Although no longer closely associated with the homophobically constructed sexuality of the cross-dressed player-boy, actors still are represented in popular theatrical discourse as sexual suspects, precisely because of the public, specularized nature of their sexuality. A pervasive stereotype of the actor as excessive in "amours" derives directly from the specularization of the actor's sexuality on stage. Theophilus Cibber's biography of Barton Booth connects his theatrical lovemaking with his behavior off the stage: "Without doubt this *actor,* who could so well express the various Passions, must have his natural Feelings; and as none could see him unmoved in a *Myron,* a *Varanes,* an *Othello,* or an *Anthony,* no wonder if he sometimes excited, off the Stage, as well as on, the tender Passions of the softer Sex" (*Lives* 26). Sergeant Eyre, speaking for the defendant William Sloper in Theophilus Cibber's suit against the latter for alienating the affections (and earnings) of Susannah Maria Cibber, is reported as saying,

> The players are a people who act and enter into all manner of characters; that their men and women are made to fall in love with each other, this day with one, tomorrow with another; that this practice in variety must give them an uncommon propensity to love without any confinement of the passion to a particular subject; 'tis very likely that this enters into their common course of life. (*Trial of Two Causes* 40)

The *Theatrical Biography* implicitly reinforces the profession's association with sexual transgression by defining "gallantry" as "a projectile feature of the histrionic character; and a player without his amour, is more seldom known than a general without his victory" (2: 80–81). Curll's *History* states that "as Mr. *Goodman* and Mr. *Hart* equally captivated the Ladies on the Stage, it is not matter of any admiration, that they should equally charm in more delightful Recesses" (Betterton 81). The memoirs of James Quinn (see *Life of Mr. James Quinn*) and Jo Haines (see Tom Brown, *Life*) both characterize their subjects' lives as a series of seductions and rapes more or less successfully staged against casually encountered women. Even relatively chaste actors, such as Robert Wilks (see *Life of the Eminent Comedian* and *Memoirs of the Life of Robert Wilks*) and David Garrick, come in for their share of "amours."

This propensity toward casual lust sometimes takes the most morally suspect forms. Hence, it is not surprising to read that Robert Baddeley was not only promiscuous but a panderer (*Theatrical Biography* 2: 151), that Colley Cibber was a "professed libertine" *and* a pimp (Davies, *Dramatic* 3: 432, 475), and that his son Theophilus not only reveled in the company of whores the night after his first wife was buried but sold the honour of his second to William Sloper.[3] The actor's sexuality is not only transgressive of chastity; more important for our purposes, it transgresses against the role of patriarchal protector so central to dominant sexual ideology. The *Theatrical Biography* gossips about the actor Vernon becoming the "beau garçon" of a woman who is, herself, a kept mistress, and one Thompson, an actor with a wife and children, is reported as going into a lady's keeping, "generously remitting," in a sort of parody of his familial responsibility, "*one sixth part* of her income for the weekly support of his family, who, from his *paternal tenderness*, he lodges in some garret in the next street" (1: 145; 2: 30). The actor's construction as oversexed functioned as much to inscribe a failed, even feminized masculinity as it did to characterize actors as virile "studs."

Working in tandem with the stereotype of the actor as excessively and rather sleazily sexual is a pervasive characterization of actors as not quite "manly," even "feminine" by profession. Given that the excessive sexuality of actors is perceived in terms of disease or the lack of dignity and control, or both, this feminization of the oversexed actor is not such a contradiction as might appear at first blush. As men who make spectacles of themselves— and their sexuality—for a living, actors are placed by popular discourse in a "feminine" relation to self-display. The actor's meticulousness about wardrobe and his love of sometimes extravagant finery were common subjects for humor throughout the century, but the turn toward less gorgeous and elaborate men's fashions in the latter half of the century rendered actors' alleged love of spangled satin and the flowing, full-bottomed periwig of the Restoration increasingly the object of ridicule. Davies writes in 1784,

The heads of the English actors were, for a long time, covered with large full-bottomed perriwigs, a fashion introduced in the reign of Charles II which was not entirely disused in public till about the year 1720. . . . Till within these twenty-five years, our Tamerlanes and Catos had as much hair on their heads as our judges on the bench. . . . We have, at length, emancipated ourselves from the usual mode of ornamenting our heroes, and are coming nearer to truth and nature. (*Dramatic* 3: 81–82)

"Truth and nature," for Davies, seem to entail toning down not just dress but theatrical style in general. Actors who showed their self-consciousness in either mode were suspect as professionals and as men. The new, "natural" style in acting and theatrical costuming demanded that the actor behave as if unaware that he was being watched—as if he were not, in short, a spectacle. Too much awareness of self-specularization on the actor's part rendered him ridiculous and "unmanly" by placing him as a "feminine" narcissist. The *Theatrical Biography* sneeringly reports in 1772 that Michael Reddish had his portrait done in character and exhibited "at spring gardens, where he regularly attended above four hours every day, for the space of six weeks, like a second Narcissus falling in love with his own reflection" (1: 107).

But even when the actor successfully avoided charges of "feminine" narcissism, his specularization entailed being seen in terms more feminine than masculine. Age, for instance, impinges on actors as it does not on men in less specularized professions. Like the actresses, old or fat actors are frequently made fun of for playing youthful parts. A 1772 *Letter to David Garrick*, who persisted in playing parts like Ranger well into middle age, asks, "Do you think you are not growing old? . . . You paint yourself well; and you move with quickness: but rouge and powder cannot give the bloom of youth; and meer quickness of motion cannot give the appearance of agility" (32). The actor's face and body are subjected to a sadistic scrutiny parallel to the culture's specularization of old women who show themselves off: "Your mouth has no sweetness; your voice is growing hoarse and hollow; your dimples are furrows; a coarse and disgustful dewlap hangs from your chin; your lips have lost their softness and pliability; the upper especially is raised all at once, like one turgid piece of leather" (34). Like actresses, actors were figured as visual commodities for the consumption of their audiences. Unlike actresses, their commodification lent a

certain air of embarrassment to their self-display. The 1786 *Green-Room
Mirror* chuckles over the actor Johnstone as "*a fine showy man to be let or
sold*" (21). In the 1743 *Dramatic Congress*, a manager tells an actor why
he was hired: "Because I found you took with the Town, and therefore I
did not care to be out of the Fashion; you were a new Face, and I was
willing to shew myself one of your Admirers." The actor replies, "Ay, and,
like a beautiful Wench, our reign won't last long" (24–25). The specularization of actors is discursively parallel to the prostitution of actresses.
The actor's exhibitionism is expressed as feminine because of its growing
inappropriateness to dominant masculine roles.

The misogyny of seventeenth-century antitheatrical discourse was closely
linked to homophobia. The feminine appearance of the player-boy was
said to instigate sodomy. Later in the eighteenth century, male theatrical
cross-dressing had become more a travesty of femininity than an imitation. Drag roles such as that of Sir John Brute were as popular in Garrick's
repertoire as in Cibber's, but responses to them suggest that performances
tended to emphasize the contrast between the actor's masculinity and the
femininity he put on. Davies, for instance, favorably compares Garrick's
cross-dressed Sir John with Cibber's because the former's "manly" voice
and appearance made the spectacle less ambiguous than the high voice and
slight frame of the latter (*Dramatic* 1: 429). Misogyny can be read in this
desire to keep gender roles "straight"; as Mary Russo points out, male
masquerade in the semblance of femininity works to reinforce misogynistic stereotypes of women and disassociate them from "real" men (216).
But one can also see an implicit homophobia in Davies's preference for the
ease with which he can separate Garrick's voice and body from the sex
roles implicit in his dress. Homophobia, as Orgel suggests, is probably responsible for the abatement of actors' impersonating females on stage after
Edward Kynaston in the late seventeenth century.

Nonetheless, I would question whether the homophobic exclusions of
ambiguous masculinity in eighteenth-century theatrical transvestism were
quite as totalizing as they would seem at first glance. In the first place,
there is some reason to believe that men and boys continued to play female
parts on the professional stage well into the eighteenth century. Kirkman,
for instance, lists several female parts in the list of Charles Macklin's roles
(2: 447–49). Kirkman also reports the bizarre accidental death of Thomas
Hallam at the hands of Macklin, who testified at his murder trial that Hallam, struck through the eye by Macklin's stick, ordered "Mr. *Arne's* son,

(who was dressed in woman's cloaths) 'whip up your clothes, you little b——h, and urine in my eye' " (1: 202). There may be reason to suspect the notion that eighteenth-century English actors had both completely given up female impersonation and had shaken off the homophobia associated with it. Feminization of actors takes the place of earlier, homophobic accusations, but misogyny directed at the "woman" in actors marks the place of a homoeroticism grown too threatening in the context of an increasingly dangerous homophobia. The exclusion of actors from full membership in male homosocial culture could be more safely expressed in terms of the misogyny that supports homosociality than it could in terms of a homoerotic language that threatens the homosocial.[4]

In the first half of the century, however, the discursive lines between the homoerotic and the homosocial are not so clearly drawn as they were to be by the 1770s. Colley Cibber takes full advantage of this fluidity in male sexual identity in his self-representations as a homoerotic spectacle. The homoerotic rhetoric of his 1740 *Apology for the Life of Mr. Colley Cibber* is too large a topic for the scope of this essay;[5] instead, I focus here on a figure that is central to Cibber's self-representation, his trademark character, Lord Foppington, of Vanbrugh's *The Relapse*, written as a sequel and in response to Cibber's *Love's Last Shift* (1696). As Helene Koon confirms in her biography of Cibber, the character of Lord Foppington served Cibber well as a mask in his public self-representations.[6] I would argue that Cibber's use of this persona is all the more explicable in the light of his particular historical position in relation to homophobic discourse about actors. The fop is a contested site in the politics of eighteenth-century spectatorship, positioned somewhere between a "feminine" spectacle and "masculine" observer. The fop roles for which Cibber was famous—Sir Novelty Fashion, Sir George Brilliant, Clodio, and Witling, as well as Lord Foppington—are important not only to the gender ideology of drama and the autobiographical rhetoric of the *Apology*. The fop, as a social construct, occupies, as Susan Staves has noted, a liminal position in the cultural imaginary of sexual possibility—and not just as confined to the stage. Staves argues that the fop was a "real," not just a theatrical, construct, and the development of Cibber's fops indicates a cultural shift in attitudes toward masculinity. Fops, according to Staves, become objects of ever gentler satire in Cibber's plays as the century goes on, suggesting that society's growing tolerance for fops indicates more "feminine" forms of dominant masculinity. I would suggest, however, that what appears from Staves's point of view to be a loosening of gender boundaries between masculine and feminine polarities can also be seen as symptomatic of a growing rigidification of the polarity between "deviate" homosexual and "normal" heterosexual masculinity. If, as Staves argues, the fop in Cibber's plays was increasingly "normalized" as heterosexual masculine within the ideologies of romantic love and companionate marriage, it was, I would argue, to subsume the fop's potential for sexual liminality within those ideologies and differentiate him from an increasingly visible gay male identity. In addition, while the fop was "real" enough in terms of having a significant ideological function, he was, at least by the time of Cibber's Apology, already a nostalgic construct, more indicative of a discursive desire for sexual liminality than of a "real" fluidity of gender roles.

Cibber writes with an air of regret in the Apology that Lord Foppington reflects a species of foppery grander and finer than his later, real-life counterparts; he has more of the "Stateliness of the Peacock," while the fashionable young men of the present have more the "pert Air of a Lapwing" (202). Later writers unanimously agree with Cibber on the progressive dwindling of the fop's dignity. Davies approves of Lord Foppington as a "man of good parts stepping beyond the bounds of sense by peculiarity of excess in dress and behavior" (Dramatic 3: 425), but he sees Garrick's caution in dropping the roles of Clodio and Lord Foppington as appropriate to his dignity as the principal actor at Drury Lane—the fop no longer coexisted with the respectable image Garrick cultivated (Memoirs 1: 59). By 1825, James Boaden writes that "the modern fop is a creature of a different kind [than Lord Foppington]—he is pert and volatile, incessantly in action, and becoming risible by awkward gestures and mere grimace. He has no dignity to keep up; you may laugh not only at him but in his face" (1: 55–56). It is probable that the modern fop's degradation is related, at least in part, to the growing tendency to connect effeminacy with homosexuality. Satires on effeminate men are more likely, after midcentury, to associate foppishness with sexual perversion. The anonymous Pretty Gentleman (1747), Humphrey Nettle's Sodom and Onan (1776), William Kenrick's Love in the Suds (1772), Garrick's The Fribbleriad (1761), and John Rubrick's The Spleen (1776), among other satires on "macaronis" and "effeminate" actors, tend to resolve the fop's sexual ambiguity all too conclusively as homosexual. The fop's "normalization" as heterosexual may, then, be read as defense against the growing danger of being defined the other way. In fact, it may well be that that contradictory being, the stately fop, was, at least from the time of Cibber's *Apology*, a nostalgic construct: whether or not he ever "really" existed, his function was, from Cibber's time on, more to mark a desire for an ambiguous or contradictory masculinity quite separate from the homophobically perceived "real-life" macaroni.

Cibber's Sir Novelty proved hard to shake from the actor's stage image. Cibber's small body and high, squeaky voice discouraged him from venturing into romantic hero parts, but it also seems likely that audiences typed him after Sir Novelty and simply would not take him seriously in heroic or romantic roles. Lois Potter suggests that Cibber tried—and failed— to pick up the romantic hero half of William Mountfort's repertoire after he was murdered in 1693. Cibber staked "a claim to the foppish half of Mountfort's repertoire" by writing and playing Sir Novelty in 1696—a claim he held for the rest of his career. But when Cibber tried to take over the romantic half by playing Longville in *Woman's Wit; or, The Lady in Fashion* in 1696, the audience laughed and hissed him off the stage. Physically better adapted to the fop than the hero, Cibber continued to lust after tragic parts, as a eunuch lusts after women, *The Laureat* cattily remarks (110), but his forays into romantic roles were few. Although the nostalgic construct of the fop marked Cibber's exclusion from roles more associated with dominant masculinity, it also, however, afforded a liminal space for representation in relation to the ideologies of romantic love and companionate marriage.

Fops, as Cibber created them, occupy a variety of more or less uneasy positions in a heterosexual economy in which women are objectified sexual commodities and men are consuming and, hence, economically and sexually empowered subjects. They are not, as Staves correctly points out, to be confused with homosexuals; rather, they muddy the distinction between sexual object and sexual subject, spectacle and spectator, commodity and consumer. While romantic love in Cibber's comedies would tend to cast women as objects, spectacles, and commodities, and men as subjects, spectators, and consumers, the fop complicates this gendering of the binaries. The fop's ambivalence—is he the object of other's desire or a desiring subject?—grants a certain ability to negotiate heterosexual romantic love without assuming a fixed position within its economy of desire.

In *Love's Last Shift*, Sir Novelty Fashion makes a spectacle of himself in spite of the play's insistent objectification of women as the "proper"

objects of romantic love. Sir Novelty is simply too busy exhibiting himself to objectify the women he rather halfheartedly pursues. Sir Novelty's
lovemaking fails because his exhibitionism works against what the sexual
economy demands—making the woman into the man's object of desire.
Instead of cataloging Narcissa's charms, Sir Novelty gives her a list of the
fashions he has created: "the Cravat-string, the Garter, the Sword-knot,
the Centurine, the Bardash, the Steinkirk, the large Button, the long Sleeve,
the Plume, and full Peruque, were all created, cry'd down, or revived by
me." Narcissa is unimpressed by Sir Novelty's exhibitionism and tries to
redirect his attention to herself: "But what have you to say to me, Sir?" The
fop, however, refuses to leave off making a spectacle of himself. Instead
he verbally exhibits his corporeal exhibitionism at the theater. He likes to
leave early, he says, in order to give "the whole Audience an Opportunity
of turning upon me at once." Sir Novelty reverses the "proper" order of
looking in the playhouse just as he reverses the proper order of desire in
his relationship with Narcissa. When Narcissa rather desperately reminds
him, "[B]ut still you ha'n't told me, why you love me," Sir Novelty replies,
"I think 'tis sufficient, if I tell a Lady, why she should love me" (II.i). Not
surprisingly, Sir William Wisewoud ultimately rejects Sir Novelty's suit for
his daughter's hand because, as he says, "you have too great a Passion for
your own Person, to have any for your Wife's" (II.i). But while Sir Novelty's
failure to assume the desire proper to a suitor excludes him from the play's
concluding marriages, it interpolates into the play's dominant sexual economy a masculine desire that is liminal to a gendered dichotomy of desire
and spectatorship—without explicitly typing Sir Novelty as homosexual.

The Relapse, Vanbrugh's follow-up to Love's Last Shift, makes even
clearer the fop's liminal position—this time both in relation to the dominant heterosexual economy and in relation to male homosexual desire.
In Vanbrugh's play, Sir Novelty has bought for himself a peerage and is
now the new-made Lord Foppington. The motif of the purchased peerage
underscores the economic side of the fop's narcissistic exhibitionism: self-
specularization, in Lord Foppington's case, is also self-commodification.
By making himself into a spectacle, Lord Foppington also makes himself
into a commodity—like a woman, an object to be desired and consumed.
Man and commodity become one, indistinguishable from each other, when
Foppington dons his full-bottomed periwig: "For a periwig to a man should
be like a mask to a woman, nothing should be seen but his eyes" (I.iii).

As the allusion to the masked prostitutes suggests, Foppington, by his desire to be seen, travesties woman as sexual commodity. At the same time, however, he is distinguished in the play from male homosexuality in the character of Coupler, an overtly gay male who pursues Foppington's desirable younger brother, Fashion. Foppington stands in an ambiguous relation to both sexual economies in the play. While certainly not a Coupler, his position within the heterosexual economy of romantic love is not clear. Cibber's version of Lord Foppington in *The Careless Husband* (1704) sustains a confusion between gendered subjects and objects while being more clearly identified as a champion of, if not always a successful participant in, heterosexual romance. Foppington, now married, is a philanderer and a rake, but his relation to women still reverses the "correct" direction of sexual desire. He "gets" women, he says, "as they get other People; I dress, and let 'em get me"; or, if "that won't do," Foppington assumes the role of the overconsumer: "[A]s I got my Title, I buy 'em" (II.ii). Yet despite this reversal and parody of masculine roles in dominant sexual ideology, Foppington serves to bring the other lovers together, literally joining Lady Betty Modish's hand to that of Lord Morelove at the play's denouement.

Cibber's fops stand in an ambivalent relationship to heterosexuality. Even though they usually have the rules of courtship all wrong, his fops often marry reasonably happily, especially, as Staves points out, in the later plays. The later fops, Clodio and Sir George Brilliant, most obviously exhibit sexually suspect behavior with other men, while also being the most energetically recuperated by the marriages that reclaim them as heterosexual. Both characters engage in homoerotic displays that are hard to see neutrally, yet both are decisively married off to attractive young women. In one particularly contradictory scene, Sir George is met by Lord Wronglove with "Ah, my Georgy! Kiss." Sir George responds with "And kiss, and kiss again, my Dear—By Ganymede there's Nectar on thy Lips," and the story of his latest heterosexual conquest (*The Lady's Last Stake* I.i). Clodio and Sir George are, unlike Sir Novelty, unequivocally reclaimed as heterosexual. Possibly the more contradictory and confusing the sexuality of the fop, the more fully he had to be subsumed into the heterosexual economy of final marriages. But however formally recuperated, especially in the later plays, the liminal sexuality of Cibber's fops results from a negotiation of a series of dichotomous positions associated with sexual desire in romantic love. The gendered positions of subject and object, spectator and spectacle, consumer and consumed all undergo reversals and returns that allow the fop a fluidity in his behavior not allowable to romantic heroes.

Cibber was able to incorporate this fluidity into his public persona as Lord Foppington; later actors are figured much less equivocally in the sexual economy. The 1770s saw two "media" events in the representation of actors' sexuality that graphically illustrate a growing danger in the actor's traditional association with the homoerotic. In 1772, Kenrick published *Love in the Suds,* an attack on Garrick, who was then well established as the most popular and personally respectable of English actors of his time. Kenrick's poem capitalized on a recent scandal involving the playwright Isaac Bickerstaff, who regularly produced work for Garrick's theater. Bickerstaff was apparently caught propositioning another man and, rather than face charges in England, fled to the Continent. Kenrick used this occasion to accuse Garrick of having an illicit relationship with Bickerstaff. This accusation, made against a highly popular and exceptionally respectable actor, did the accuser more harm than Garrick, although the latter may have taken the charge seriously enough to begin legal proceedings against Kenrick for libel.[7] Just a few years later, Samuel Foote became embroiled in a public quarrel with Elizabeth Chudleigh, the duchess of Kingston, over a satire he intended to write against her. In the course of this battle, the duchess and her henchman, a clergyman named William Jackson who controlled the *Public Ledger,* apparently set Foote up to be charged with the attempted seduction of his footman, John Sangster. The case went to trial, and Foote was acquitted, but not without, at least reportedly, some damage to his health and emotional well-being.[8] I would argue that these two events are symptomatic of a climate growing markedly less healthy for public displays of ambiguous masculine sexuality or homoeroticism such as Cibber's. These events are not causes of a growing tendency in actors to distance themselves from the fop's ambiguous eroticism; the charges against Garrick and Foote are themselves more symptomatic than causal of pervasive shifts in sexual ideology. The events of the 1770s gave dramatic public form to a process that was, in fact, already under way. Garrick, particularly, sought to distance himself from effeminate masculinities as early as the 1740s.

Garrick's self-authored fop roles in the farces *Miss in Her Teens* (1747) and *The Male Coquette* (1757) serve a very different function from Cibber's fops in the ways in which the two actors are popularly represented.

Whereas Cibber is personally identified, partly through his own efforts, with Lord Foppington, Garrick is more generally seen as the satirist who mocks a perverted masculinity that is other to his "real" identity. Instead of associating the fop's effeminacy with the actor's actual character, theatrical biography and history tend to place Garrick (and the theater) in "manly" opposition to the "real-life" effeminacy parodied by the actor. By 1801 Arthur Murphy writes of *Miss in Her Teens* that Garrick meant to satirize "the pretty gentlemen, who chose to unsex themselves, and make a display of delicacy that exceeded female softness" (1: 118). He similarly opposes the character of Daffodil in *The Male Coquette* to an even worse real-life correlative: "A single instance of the effeminate character appeared some years since at a village in Surry, and having no appearance of either the masculine or feminine gender, all who saw this motley being, agreed to give to such a phenomenon the name of *The It*" (1: 308–9). This opposition of the "manly" actor against his effeminate, offstage satiric object was made all the easier by the increasingly noticeable tendency, as we have seen, to construct the theater as a bastion of manliness in an effeminate society.

Garrick's *The Fribbleriad* (1761) is a particularly good example of how the actor's satire works to construct Garrick in opposition to ambiguous or suspect forms of masculinity. It falls in with the tendency, noted earlier, to define the actor against a "deviant" masculinity external to the acting profession. *The Fribbleriad* portrays Garrick's enemies in terms slightly less explicit than Kenrick's attack against him in *Love in the Suds* but close enough to evoke recognizable stereotypes of the effeminate, homosexual male in mannerism, dress, and an interest in the posterior anatomy. The poem was probably written in response to attacks on Garrick in *The Craftsman* in letters signed by "XYZ." The poem characterizes XYZ and his supporters as ambiguous, effeminate—and worse. The homophobic caricature of XYZ—"with a *round smirking face,* and a *jut with your bum*"— suggests that spite itself is a homosexual stereotype. The speaker decides that XYZ is neither male nor female but some of both—"Poor X,Y,Z will prove no *man.* / Nor male? nor female?—then on oath? We safely may pronounce it *Both*"—and goes on to imply its impotence and its crimes against "nature":

> What! of that wriggling, fribbling race,
> The curse of nature, and disgrace?

That mixture base, which fiends sent forth
To taint and vilify all worth—
Whose rancour knows nor bounds, nor measure,
Feels every passion, tastes no pleasure;
The want of power, all peace destroying,
For ever wishing, ne'er enjoying—[.]

(6)

Finally, the "Fribbles" speak against Garrick, who has cruelly satirized them on stage. Their officers file by in a series of recognizable stereotypes. "Fitzgig" assumes the presidency "With visage sleek and swelling chest, / With stretch'd out fingers, and a thumb / Stuck to his hips, and jutting bum . . . / Paddled away with mincing feet" (11). He wonders how the Fribbles are to revenge themselves on Garrick, "In front, my friends, or in the rear?"—a question taken up by others such as Captain Pattypan, "With kimbow'd arm, and tossing head, / He bridled up—'Wear I this red?'" (15). Garrick, in this poem, is constructed as the enemy of Fribbles: "Now, GARRICK, for the future know / Where most you have *deserv'd* a foe" (20). *The Fribbleriad* served to position him in opposition to a homophobically defined "deviate" masculine sexuality.

Kenrick's *Love in the Suds* seems, therefore, to have been aimed at a particularly well guarded, if also visible, weak spot in Garrick's public character. Theatrical histories and biographies are nearly unanimous in their defense of Garrick and condemnation of Kenrick. The fact that Kenrick tried the particular charge of homosexuality at all must be attributed to the circumstances of Bickerstaff's distress combined with the traditionally suspect nature of the actor's sexuality. Kenrick's 1772 *Letter to David Garrick, Esq. Occasioned by his moving the Court of King's Bench, for Leave to File an Information against the Author of Love in the Suds* confirms this connection. Kenrick, probably alarmed by the possibility of a lawsuit, backpedals while still maintaining the implications of his charge in *Love in the Suds*. The laws are too lenient on this "most odious of all crimes," and satire, therefore, has a public responsibility to detect and punish

those effeminate wretches, who are become so horrid a nuisance to society. If suspicion indeed be totally groundless, such delicacy is commendable; but this is seldom, if ever, the case. . . . [H]ad I conceived Roscius [Garrick] to stand in the odious predicament of Nyky, the pen of the satirist should have lain still. . . . [C]rimes of such enormous guilt [are not] proper subjects for satire. . . . [T]he plain purport of the performance in question, is most evidently and solely that of turning Roscius into ridicule, for having encouraged, as a writer, out of principles of avarice and vanity, a wretch, whom he had reason to detect, or at least, cautiously to shun as a man. (5)

Kenrick supports his insinuations by quoting Rousseau on the profession of acting: "a profession in which a man exhibits himself a publick spectacle for money: a profession in the practice of which he submits to the insults and affronts from those, who think they purchase, with pence, a right to treat him ignomeniously" (9). Besides public humiliation, Kenrick says, the actor also plays the buffoon to aristocratic patrons: "[T]heir familiarity with a player should no more excite the envy of a rational being, than his lordship's familiarity with his monkey, or my lady's fondness for her lap-dog" (10). It is not far, Kenrick implies, from this degraded object of public and private contempt and desire to the capacity to countenance—if not participate in—the homosexual activities of Bickerstaff. Kenrick's attempt to smear Garrick went too far, however, against too important and powerful a public figure. The duchess of Kingston's campaign to pin the charge of "sodomy" on Samuel Foote, while not successful in making any legal charges stick, seems to have been far more effective.

Nettle's *Sodom and Onan* (1776), like *Love in the Suds,* charged the actor with homosexuality. Unlike *Love in the Suds, Sodom and Onan* was accompanied by other print attacks as well as actual criminal charges brought by one of Foote's servants. Foote's enemies, galvanized by the duchess of Kingston, were more powerful than the solitary, unsuccessful playwright Kenrick. More effective than Kenrick *because* of their class, they were, ironically, ultimately defeated by class considerations. Cooke reports that Foote gained popular support because "no man who kept male servants in his house would be safe from such calumny" if Foote had been convicted (1: 228), an explanation confirmed by a letter in the *St. James Chronicle* of 9–10 December 1776. Although Foote was acquitted, Cooke suggests that the trial broke him mentally and physically and led to the end of his career. "The stigma of the charge still lingered in his mind," and allusions to it "preyed deeply in his heart": "The mental anxieties he had suffered during the course of the last year, had evidently preyed upon every part of him: his cheeks were lank and withered, his eyes had lost all their wonted intelligence, and his whole person appeared sunk and emaciated"

(1: 234). The *St. James Chronicle* of 18–21 May 1776 reports that Foote's performance, after his acquittal, showed the signs of strain: "Mr. Foote played languidly, except where he forced himself into a kind of exertion," despite—or because of?—the fact that "Every passage which bore the most distant Reference to his Case, was taken Notice of in such a Manner as must please him." Foote's case illustrates the full potential of the actor's vulnerability to homophobia.

In contrast to Garrick, Foote obviously had made enough enemies, both within and without the theater, to render himself vulnerable to attack. Homophobia was, in Foote's case as in many others' throughout history, a means of attacking someone for being troublesome in other respects. The particular form of the attack and its efficacy in Foote's case suggest the specific vulnerability of the actor to charges of homosexuality in an age of increasingly visible and widespread homophobia. The cases of Foote and Garrick, taken together, suggest that the growing visibility of homosexual identity as a charge to be brought against the actor meant that some actors could be more decisively recuperated into models of dominant masculinity than others. The idea of Garrick as a "sodomite" was not as tolerable as fuzzier associations of the actor with effeminacy and suspect sexuality. Brought to bear, such charges actually "masculinized" some actors—like Garrick—while leaving others—like Foote—more at risk.

The exorcism of suspect masculine sexuality in Garrick's rhetoric is "de-naturalized" and revealed as the workings of a defensive homophobia when we set it in the context of the long history of English actors as sexual suspects. Similarly, Cibber's fops take on a significant ambiguity when read in relation to the growing threat of eighteenth-century homophobia and the emergent articulation of a gay male identity. Cibber's homoerotic self-representation does not quite fit with the dichotomization of male sexual identity into gay versus straight, nor does it exactly resist it, either. It suggests, rather, an incompleteness to the dichotomy, as if some spaces are left between the poles of male sexual object choice. Read in the cultural context of a growing dichotomization of masculine sexuality into gay versus "normal," Cibber's sexually ambiguous fops point obliquely to the ongoing historical process of formulating the not-so-obvious obvious "choices" offered by dominant sexual ideologies.

Notes

This essay incorporates parts of two chapters from my book *Sexual Suspects*, published by Princeton University Press.

1. For a full treatment of the subjects of how class and gender function in the construction of the actor as spectacle, see my *Sexual Suspects*.

2. Bray's evidence is fragmentary but compelling. He asks why the charge of sodomy was, in fact, so rarely raised in the public and legal sphere when there is a good deal of evidence that male-male sodomy was fairly common before the eighteenth century. His answer is that people could not associate the mythically fearsome image of the sodomite with what their neighbors did or even with their own behavior. Bray's thesis squares with the work that establishes male homosexual identity—as opposed to behavior—as an early-eighteenth-century development. Katz is working primarily on the history of gay sexuality in America, but his observations in the *Gay/Lesbian Almanac* are useful to our purposes. Trumbach's (see all three articles cited) and Rousseau's work is primarily historical in nature, while Sedgwick and Weeks are working in gay theory. Orgel's essay on the boy-players is highly historical in its methods and is focused primarily on the theatrical context. The most closely related work to the question of gay male sexuality and the theater is Senelick's.

3. See *The Trial of Two Causes* and *An Apology for the Life of Mr. T___ C___* for information on the younger Cibber's unsavory personal life.

4. For a careful theoretical consideration of the interdependence of misogyny, homophobia, and the homosocial, see Sedgwick, especially the first two chapters, 1–66.

5. For a fuller treatment of Cibber's autobiographical representation, see my *Sexual Suspects*.

6. Koon argues that wearing the mask of Lord Foppington gave Cibber a self-protective distance on the public controversy in which he was often the subject of ridicule and attack. She does not, however, take up the implications of this role in public representations of Cibber's sexuality.

7. See Stone and Kahrl's account of this incident (601–3). Senelick gives a fuller account (58–64).

8. Fitzgerald hints at this story (231–65); Senelick fills in more details (64–67). For contemporary accounts, see the *St. James's Chronicle*, 10–12 August and 17–19 August 1775, and the *Publick Ledger*, 9 July 1776.

Works Cited

An Apology for the Life of Mr. T___ C___, Comedian. Being a Proper Sequel to the Apology for the Life of Mr. Colley Cibber, Comedian. London, 1740.

Betterton, Thomas [William Oldys?]. *The History of the English Stage, from the Restauration to the Present Time*. London, 1741.

Boaden, James. *Memoirs of the Life of John Philip Kemble, Esq.* 2 vols. London, 1825.

Bray, Alan. *Homosexuality in Renaissance England*. London: Gay Men's P, 1982.

Brown, John. *An Estimate of the Manners and Principles of the Times*. 2 vols. London, 1757.

Brown, Tom. *Amusements, Serious and Comical and Other Works*. Ed. Arthur L. Haywood. London: Routledge, 1927.

———. *The Life of the Late Famous Comedian, Jo. Hayns*. London, 1701.

Cibber, Colley. *An Apology for the life of Mr. Colley Cibber*. Ed. B. R. S. Fone. Ann Arbor: U of Michigan P, 1968.

———. *The Plays of Colley Cibber*. Ed. Rodney L. Hayley. 2 vols. New York: Garland, 1980.

Cibber, Theophilus. *The Lives and Characters of the most Eminent Actors and Actresses of Great Britain and Ireland*. London, 1753.

———. *Theophilus Cibber to David Garrick, Esq; with Dissertations on Theatrical Subjects*. London, 1759.

Cooke, William. *Memoirs of Samuel Foote, Esq.* 3 vols. London, 1805.

Davies, Thomas. *Dramatic Miscellanies*. 3 vols. London, 1784.

———. *Memoirs of the Late David Garrick, Esq.* 2 vols. London, 1784.

The Dramatic Congress: A Short State of the Stage under the Present Management. London, 1743.

Fitzgerald, Percy Hetherington. *Samuel Foote: A Biography*. London: Chatto and Windus, 1910.

Garrick, David. *The Fribbleriad*. London, 1761.

———. *The Male Coquette; or, Seventeen Hundred Fifty-Seven*. London, 1757.

———. *Miss in Her Teens*. London, 1747.

Green-Room Mirror. Clearly Delineating our Present Theatrical Performers. London, 1786.

Heywood, Thomas. *An Apology for Actors*. 1612. New York: Johnson Reprint Corporation, 1972.

Katz, Jonathan. *Gay/Lesbian Almanac: A New Documentary in Which Is Contained, in Chronological Order, Evidence of the True and Fantastical History of Those Persons Now Called Lesbians and Gay Men*. New York: Harper and Row, 1983.

Kenrick, William. *Letter to David Garrick, Esq. Occasioned by his moving the Court of King's Bench, for Leave to File an Information against the Author of Love in the Suds*. London, 1772.

———. *Love in the Suds; a Town Eclogue. Being the Lamentation of Roscius for the Loss of his Nyky*. London, 1772.

Kirkman, James Thomas. *Memoirs of the Life of Charles Macklin, Esq.* 2 vols. London, 1799.

Koon, Helene. *Colley Cibber: A Biography.* Lexington: UP of Kentucky, 1986.

The Laureat; or, The Right Side of Colley Cibber, Esq; containing Explanations, Amendments and Observations, on a Book intitled, An Apology for the Life, and Writings of Mr. Colley Cibber. London, 1740.

Letter to David Garrick, Esq. on His Conduct as Principal Manager and Actor at Drury-Lane. London, 1772.

The Life of Mr. James Quinn, Comedian. London, 1766.

The Life of the Eminent Comedian, Robert Wilks, Esq. London, 1733.

Memoirs of the Life of Robert Wilks, Esq. London, n.d.

Murphy, Arthur. *The Life of David Garrick, Esq.* 2 vols. London, 1801.

Nettle, Humphrey [William Jackson]. *Sodom and Onan.* London, 1776.

Orgel, Stephen. "Nobody's Perfect: Or Why Did the English Stage Take Boys for Women?" *South Atlantic Quarterly* 88.1 (1989): 7–30.

Pepys, Samuel. *The Diary of Samuel Pepys.* Ed. Henry B. Wheatley. 10 vols. New York: Limited Editions Club, 1942.

Potter, Lois. "Colley Cibber: The Fop as Hero." *Augustan Worlds.* Ed. J. C. Hilson, M. M. B. Jones, and J. R. Watson. Leicester, Eng.: Leicester UP, 1978. 153–64.

The Pretty Gentleman; or, Softness of Manners Vindicated. London, 1747.

Prynne, William. *Histrio-Mastix: The Player's Scourge or, Actor's Tragedy.* 2 vols. 1633. New York: Johnson Reprint Corporation, 1972.

Rousseau, G. S. "The Pursuit of Homosexuality in the Eighteenth Century: 'Utterly Confused Category' and/or Rich Repository?" *Eighteenth-Century Life* 9 (1985): 133–68.

Rubrick, John. *The Spleen; or, The Offspring of Folly.* London, 1776.

Russo, Mary. "Female Grotesques: Carnival and Theory." *Feminist Studies/Critical Studies.* Ed. Theresa de Lauretis. Bloomington: Indiana UP, 1986. 213–29.

Sedgwick, Eve Kosofsky. *Between Men: English Literature and Male Homosocial Desire.* New York: Columbia UP, 1985.

Senelick, Laurence. "Mollies or Men of Mode? Sodomy and the Eighteenth-Century London Stage." *Journal of the History of Sexuality* 1 (1990): 33–67.

Staves, Susan. "A Few Kind Words for the Fop." *Studies in English Literature* 22 (1982): 413–28.

Stone, George Winchester, Jr., and George M. Kahrl. *David Garrick: A Critical Biography.* Carbondale: Southern Illinois UP, 1979.

Straub, Kristina. *Sexual Suspects: Eighteenth-Century Players and Sexual Ideology.* Princeton: Princeton UP, 1992.

Theatrical Biography: or, Memoirs of the Principal Performers of the Three Theatres Royal. 2 vols. London, 1772.

The Trial of Two Causes: Between Theophilus Cibber, Gent., Plaintiff, and William Sloper, Esq. Defendent. 1740. London, 1887.

Trumbach, Randolph. "The Birth of the Queen: Sodomy and the Emergence of Gender Equality in Modern Culture, 1660–1750." *Hidden from History: Reclaiming the Gay and Lesbian Past.* Ed. Martin Bauml Duberman, Martha Vicinus, and George Chauncey, Jr. Markham, Ontario: New American Library, 1989. 129–40.

———. "Gender and the Homosexual Role in Modern Western Culture: The Eighteenth and Nineteenth Centuries Compared." *Homosexuality, Which Homosexuality?* International Conference on Gay and Lesbian Studies. London: GMP, 1989. 149–70.

———. "London's Sodomites: Homosexual Behavior and Western Culture in the Eighteenth Century." *Journal of Social History* 11 (1977–78): 1–33.

Vanbrugh, Sir John. *The Relapse.* Ed. Curt A. Zimansky. Lincoln: Bison–U of Nebraska P, 1970.

Weeks, Jeffrey. "Against Nature." *Homosexuality, Which Homosexuality?* International Conference on Gay and Lesbian Studies. London: GMP, 1989. 199–214.

Wilson, John Harold. *All the King's Ladies: Actresses of the Restoration.* Chicago: U of Chicago P, 1958.

"Sure I have seen that face before": Representation and Value in Eighteenth-Century Drama

JAMES THOMPSON

In the debates over the Recoinage Act of 1695–96, John Locke published *Short Observations on a Printed Paper Intituled, For encouraging the Coining Silver Money in England, and after for keeping it here* (1695), in which he argued against devaluing the coinage, for he insisted again and again that "silver is silver" whatever form it takes.[1] In the same year, William Congreve adapted the ballad catchphrase as the title of his new comedy, *Love for Love,* arguing that love does not respond to profit or loss, gain or threat, but that love is only matched by love in equal trade or barter. Locke does not reflect on romance (love for love) nor to my knowledge does Congreve allude to the Recoinage Act (silver for silver) but both texts are conservative responses to capital relations, that is, both texts are representations of and resistances to a historical moment in the development of capital. This essay is about that connection between economic and social theory in the eighteenth century, specifically in relation to the concept of value. To draw that connection, I first look at economic theorizing over the signifying process in silver coin, and, second, I explore the same issues in a series of plays that turn on the recognition or reading of value: Dryden's *Marriage à la Mode* (1671), Congreve's romance *Incognita* (1692), Steele's *The Conscious Lovers* (1722), Sheridan's *The Rivals* (1775), and Goldsmith's *She Stoops to Conquer* (1773). I am not interested in showing the coincidence of face on coin and face of the heroine in comedy, but rather I am interested in exploring the ways in which these two different discourses, political economy and comedy, work through a method of reading, a model for determining "face value." In the terminology of the period, coin can be evaluated "by weight or by tale," an opposition of evaluation and method that is also found in these plays, plays that turn on the connection between face and name: in Congreve's *Incognita* the masked heroine poses the dilemma to her would-be suitor: "[S]he gave him his choice whether he would know whom she was, or see her face" (263).

At issue is dramatic response to and representation of a specific stage in the development of money. In *English Dramatic Form, 1660–1760*, Laura Brown has analyzed the shift from a drama of social status to a drama of inner worth; so too, in *The Origins of the English Novel, 1600–1740*, Michael McKeon has explored similar shifts in the gradual recognition of the novel as a simple abstraction. Of particular relevance here are what McKeon calls "Questions of Virtue," or shifts in social evaluation from aristocratic assumptions of genealogical status to bourgeois assumptions of internal worth. How, in short, are anonymous individual subjects differentiated or, to use Louis Althusser's term, interpellated as individual, named subjects? As in economic theory, these are crucial questions of what or who authorizes an individual subject's social value and in what does this value consist. In an essay on Dryden's *Marriage à la Mode*, McKeon applies the sociological concept of "status inconsistency" to this situation of contradictions in methods of social evaluation: "[A]n easy correlation between the several external registers of place was seen no longer to be the rule. To put it most succinctly, people could no longer be dependably 'read' simply by noting one or another indicator of their outward status" ("Criticism" 171–75). In tracing a variant of plots of anonymity and recognition, I hope to show how this plot is adapted from its aristocratic origins in romance to serve bourgeois interests of the companionate marriage.

In connecting economic theory and drama, I am not trying to argue that the former causes the latter but rather that the discourse of political economy and the discourse of dramatic literature are determined by the stage of capital, and, more specifically, the stage of money. That is to say, following classic Marxist theory, I am not arguing that political economy is real and drama is fiction but rather that both political economy and drama are relatively autonomous discursive formations determined by specific historical conditions that we condense in the phrase "mode of production." Furthermore, following Althusser's structural Marxist model, I am assuming the effectivity of ideology: that is, ideology is not a reflection of the economic base or mode of production, but rather the relation between base and superstructure of a given historical formation is dialectical. Literature then performs cultural work: plays are determined by social and economic change, and in turn, plays represent and effect, solidify, or modify social change—in other words, literature can serve as a space to imagine and to represent social conditions not yet in being. In Nancy Armstrong's study of domesticity, the novel functions something like the Lacanian mirror stage, enabling a nascent, heterogeneous, and fragmentary middle class to envision itself as coherent, unitary, and stable before such coherence and stability came into being: "[T]he domestic novel antedated—was indeed necessarily antecedent to—the way of life it represented" (9); so too, these incognita plots are a kind of cultural laboratory in which various forms of social evaluation can be experimented upon. If, in Althusser's famous formulation, "ideology represents the imaginary relationship of individuals to their real conditions of existence," then, along with other institutions, literature enables the individual subject's self-representation ("Ideology" 162). I am also assuming along with Althusser that, as a "system of representation," ideology is material, that it is not a climate of opinion or an abstract body of ideas but rather that it is inscribed in material institutions, in this particular case, the theater and the "State Ideological Apparatus" of the family ("Marxism" 231–33). In short, the relation between drama and domesticity is reciprocal, effective, and dialectical. Attendance to the correspondence between the larger public economy and the private economy of the family should enable us to examine a specific historical stage in the "Traffic in Women," to use Gayle Rubin's resonant phrase, for this plot is gendered: it is invariably the female protagonist whose value is floating and that must be fixed by the process of recognition. It is not only that the specular logic of patriarchy subjects the female to a male system of representation. But rather, what is at issue are the historical particulars of the insertion of the female subject in a whole system of valuation and exchange: as Susan Staves puts it, "In the property regimes of patriarchy, descent and inheritance are reckoned in the male line; women function as procreators and as transmitters of inheritance from male to male" (4).

In the *Grundrisse*, Marx argues that money passes through three stages of development, in which it functions first as a measure of value, and second as price or a universal equivalent, a medium of exchange. In the second stage, money comes to represent accumulation or treasure, that is to say, wealth itself. Finally, in the most complex system of development, money comes to be posited in exchange per se, not merely as the measure of accumulated wealth, but rather as a means of wealth, as capital. The following passage encapsulates the dialectical relation among these three successive but interrelated stages and functions of money:

> Only with the Romans, Greeks etc. does money appear unhampered in both its first two functions, as measure and as medium of circulation, and not very far developed in either. But as soon as either their trade etc. develops, or, as in the case of the Romans, conquest brings them money in vast quantities—in short, suddenly, and at a certain stage of their economic development, money necessarily appears in its third role, and the further it develops in that role, the more the decay of their community advances. In order to function productively, money in its third role, as we have seen, must be not only the precondition but equally the result of circulation, and, as its precondition, also a moment of it, something posited by it. Among the Romans, who amassed money by stealing it from the whole world, this was not the case. It is inherent in the simple character of money itself that it can exist as a developed moment of production only where and when *wage labour* exists; that in this case, far from subverting the social formation, it is rather a condition of its development and a driving wheel for the development of all forces of production, material and mental. (223)

The historical conditions of money, its transformation into capital (what Marx calls "money in process" [*Capital* 1: 154]), in conjunction with the advent of various and disturbing new forms of paper money, provoked a semiological crisis over the concept of value: what is it and where is it located—in the signifier, in its referent, or in some signifying process? The discourse of political economy, as it is elaborated across the eighteenth century, constitutes a gradual working through of this crisis in the concept of value. As political economy comes to describe the process of capitalism (for "capital is a not a thing, but a social relation between persons, established by the instrumentality of things" [Marx, *Capital* 1: 766]) and so comes to describe the nature of capitalist exchange and its necessity of constant movement or change, by the process of the negation of the negation, the private sphere, domesticity comes to be written or represented in antithetical terms of stability, a process best described by Armstrong: conduct books and the novel "severed the language of kinship from that of political power, producing a culture divided into the respective domains of domestic woman and economic man" (60). In his theoritization of social and cultural forms of capital, Pierre Bourdieu argues that

> economic theory has allowed to be foisted upon it a definition of the economy of practices which is the historical invention of capitalism; and by reducing the universe of exchanges to mercantile exchange, which is objectively and subjectively oriented toward the maximization of profit, i.e., (economically) *self-interested,* it has implicitly defined the other forms of exchange as noneconomic, and therefore *disinterested.* (242)

It has been the principal task of Marxist and feminist analysis to show how economic exchange permeates all social relations, and here, by examining representations of value and valuation, in both civil society and the family, I want to show how the incognita plot comes to serve a peculiarly bourgeois form of the traffic in women.[2]

By the late seventeenth century, currency was in theory based on the realist premise of inherent, or as the political economists put it, "intrinsick," value in precious metal, but this theory bore little or no relation to practice because the silver coinage was both severely debased and entirely inadequate to the volume of circulation. Lord Lowndes claimed in his *Report containing an Essay for the Amendment of the Silver Coins* (1695), "[T]he Moneys commonly currant are Diminished near one Half, to wit, in a Proportion something greater than that of Ten to Twenty two. . . . [Light silver] when offered in Payments, is utterly Refused, and will not Pass, and consequently doth not serve the end or Purpose for which it was made." He goes on to describe in detail the social disruption caused by an inadequate system of coinage:

> In consequence of the Vitiating, Diminishing and Counterfeiting of the Currant Moneys, it is come to pass, That great Contentions do daily arise amongst the King's Subjects, in Fairs, Markets, Shops, and other Places throughout the Kingdom, about the Passing or Refusing of the same, to the disturbance of the Publick Peace; many Bargains, Doings and Dealings are totally prevented and laid aside, which lessens Trade in general; Persons before they conclude in any Bargains, are necessitated first to settle the Price or Value of the very Money they are to Receive for their Goods; and if it be in Guineas at a High Rate, or in

Clipt or Bad Moneys, they set the Price of their Goods accordingly,
which I think has been One great cause of Raising the Price not only
of Merchandizes, but even of Edibles, and other Necessaries for the
sustenance of the Common People, to their great Grievance.[3]

The problem of inadequate and insufficient coinage for the volume of
circulation continued throughout the century, a problem that occupied
political economists through Adam Smith. Confusion over the concept of
value was provoked not just because the value of money and the value of
commodities were floating—this happens in conditions of rapid inflation
or deflation—but because, what was more serious, just what money was
and what it represented remained unclear. In part, this confusion was determined by the advent of market capitalism; with barter exchange disappear-
ing, and full commodity exchange not yet in place, the eighteenth-century
English were daily confronted with contradictions between use value and
exchange value. The very nature of the king's image stamped on the face of
a silver coin is contradictory, for if the regal sign on the coin is a mark of
its authenticity, the use or history of that coin does not reinforce but rather
effaces the coin's authenticity. Before recoinage, coins were accepted by
"weight not by tale" (as Adam Smith puts it much later), so that it is travel,
use, wear, and clipping (one might say practice rather than theory, or better
yet, history rather than theory) that invalidate the sign or representation of
authenticity and authority. In the seventeenth century, these matters were
discussed most extensively in the debate over the Recoinage Act, which,
as J. Keith Horsefield observes, "was the last occasion on which a monetary controversy centered in the state of the coins. Immediately afterwards
the interest of economists began to move from coins to bank-notes as the
major vehicle for the conduct of trade" (xvii).

These debates foreground a whole series of theoretical issues about
money. First of all, in trying to determine how currency should be fixed
or stabilized, commentators had to ask some fundamental questions about
the nature of money: before its standard or value can be settled, it is first
necessary to ask what exactly money is and what function it is supposed
to perform. Defining money involves defining value, and clarifying the relation between money and value leads ineluctably to the question of representation: Are gold and silver inherently valuable? Do they represent some
anterior value, or is their value merely conventional and arbitrary? How
does coin of precious metal differ from coin of base metal, and does the

former embody or contain value while the latter represents value? How do coins of both sort differ from a bill of exchange that also represents value? What is the difference between a bill of exchange, a written document describing a debt, and a bank note issued by the Bank of England? Does the negotiability of paper money effect its function as money? Many of these issues turn on the common distinction between intrinsic versus extrinsic value—what a coin weighs versus what it says, the signs stamped on its surface.[4] And how are coins to be evaluated: by what they say or by what they weigh? Finally, the signs stamped on coin raise a whole series of questions about the nature of authority: Has the king the right to determine arbitrarily the value of silver coin? From Rice Vaughan in the 1630s to Adam Smith in the 1770s, the notion of the intrinsic value of silver and gold indicates the persistence of ancient notions of precious metals as incorruptible, embodying immutable value, while the notion of extrinsic value indicates the emergence of notions of nominal value. The emergence of a nominalist conception of currency is entwined with questions about the function and value of paper and other forms of symbolic money. All of these questions lead to the central one: How was the coinage to be restored and preserved? How can a monetary system be mastered or controlled?

In the eighty-year period between Locke's *Further Considerations concerning Raising the Value of Money* and Adam Smith's *The Wealth of Nations* (1776), as the theory of money is fully capitalized, that is, as it is reconceived from a thing to a process, from wealth to the representation of wealth, from inert hoard to the means of making wealth, there is a similar shift from an objective conception of money to an instrumental or functional definition. And as money is dematerialized, so its function as sign or representation is reemphasized. To Locke, silver coin has the same value as silver bullion, and so trying to increase stock by cutting more shillings from a bar of silver or by lowering interest rates is as foolish as the alchemical design to transmute lead into gold, trying to create ex nihilo: it is "like the Gold and Silver, which Old Women believe, other Conjurers bestow sometimes, by whole Lapfuls, on poor credulous Girls, which, when they bring to the light, is found to be nothing but wither'd Leaves; and the Possessors of it are still as much in want of Money as ever" (*Lowering* 124). Eighty years later, in a quintessentially capitalist conception of money as instrument and process rather than inert hoard or wealth, Adam Smith envisions money as the financial blood of civil society, necessary to a *system* of exchange:

The gold and silver money which circulates in any country may very properly be compared to a highway, which, while it circulates and carries to market all the grass and corn of the country, produces itself not a single pile of either. The judicious operations of banking, by providing, if I may be allowed so violent a metaphor, a sort of wagon-way through the air; enable the country to convert, as it were, a great part of its highways into good pastures and cornfields, and thereby to increase very considerably the annual produce of its land and labour. The commerce and industry of the country, however, it must be acknowledged, though they may be somewhat augmented, cannot be altogether so secure, when they are thus, as it were, suspended upon the Daedalian wings of paper money, as when they travel about upon the solid ground of gold and silver. (341)

In all of his economic works, Locke repeats the tautology, silver is silver no matter what outward form it takes:

Silver, which makes the Intrinsick Value of Money, compar'd with it self, under any Stamp or Denomination of the same or different Countries, cannot be *raised*. For an Ounce of Silver, whether in *Pence, Groats,* or *Crown* Pieces, *Stivers* or *Ducatoons,* or in Bullion, is and always will be of equal Value to any other Ounce of Silver, under what Stamp or Denomination soever; unless it can be shewn that any Stamp can add any new and better qualities to one parcel of Silver, which another parcel of Silver wants. ("Usury" 135)

Again, Locke makes his essential point: "*Silver, i. e.* the *quantity* of pure Silver separable from the Alloy, makes the real *value* of Money. If it does not, Coin Copper with the same Stamp and denomination, and see whether it will be of the same value" ("Usury" 145). If silver is silver, then the image of authority cannot alter its value:

The *Stamp* was a *Warranty* of the publick, that under such denomination they should receive a piece of such weight, and such a fineness; that is, they should receive so much silver. And this is the reason why counterfeiting the Stamp is made the highest Crime, and has the weight of Treason upon it: Because *the Stamp is the publick voucher* of the intrinsick value. The Royal Authority gives the stamp; the Law allows and confirms the denomination: And both together give, as it were,

the publick Faith, as a security, that Sums of Money contracted for
under such denominations, shall be of such a value, that is, shall have
in them so much silver. For 'tis Silver and not Names that pay Debts
and purchase Commodities. ("Usury" 146–47)

In *Short Observations* Locke continues to discount the significance of
the stamp: "[T]he Stamp neither does nor can take away any of the intrinsick value of the Silver, and therefore an Ounce of Coined standard
Silver, must necessarily be of equal value to an Ounce of uncoined standard Silver" (2). This tautology, silver is silver, works on a law of conservation: that nothing is ever lost and that material substance remains the
same from moment to moment. Such conservation may owe something
to Locke's interest in "new" science and corpusculan philosophy, as opposed to older aims to transform base substance into precious metal. These
laws of conservation and continuity also serve an aristocratic ideology of
genealogical and possessive continuity, as opposed to a bourgeois ideology
of progression and accumulation, a "morality of improvement" in Raymond Williams's terms.[5] The claim of conservation flies in the face of Lord
Lowndes's evidence of continual debasement, on the one hand, and the evidence of experience on the other, for Locke's law of material conservation
and continuity can be asserted only by denying or negating history. The
present state of the coinage was ample testimony that coins wear out and
that silver is lost to entropy, as it were, as well as to clipping.

In a passage that is more sophisticated and less muddled than his earliest
discussions, Locke goes on to consider three variables in evaluating silver:
weight, fineness, and stamp; the fourth variable, name, he takes up only
indirectly:

The *Coining* of Silver, or making *Money* of it, is the ascertaining of
its *quantity* by a publick mark, the better to fit it for commerce.

In *Coin'd* Silver or *Money* there are these three Things, which are
wanting in other Silver. 1. Pieces of exactly the same weight and fineness. 2. A Stamp set on those pieces by the publick Authority of that
Country. 3. A known denomination given to those pieces by the same
Authority.

The *Stamp* is a mark, and as it were a publick voucher that a piece
of such a denomination is of such a weight, and such a fineness, *i.e.*
has so much Silver in it.

That precise weight and fineness, by Law appropriated to the pieces of each denomination, is called the *Standard*. (*Further Considerations* 5)

Such an argument for a simple, unproblematic relation between stamp and silver only works if the fact of clipping is repressed. Clipping, it would seem, is only acknowledged indirectly in Locke's emphasis on authority. Here, Locke puts considerably more stress on authority, as it is represented in the stamp, its voucher of authenticity:

The use of Coin'd Silver or Money is that every Man in the Country where it is current by publick Authority, may, without the trouble of refining, essaying or weighing, be assured what *quantity* of Silver he gives, receives or contracts for, under such and such denominations. If this Security goes not along with the publick Stamp, Coining is labour to no purpose, and puts no difference between coin'd Money and un-coin'd Bullion. . . . From whence we may see, that the use and end of the publick Stamp is only to be a guard and voucher of the *quantity* of Silver which Men contract for. . . . Men in their bargains contract not for denominations or sounds, but for the intrinsick value; which is the *quantity* of Silver by publick Authority warranted to be in pieces of such denominations. (*Further Considerations* 8–9)

In such passages, Locke suggests that silver coinage works by way of a dialectic between intrinsic and extrinsic value, that currency as part of a system of exchange is the function of a matrix or interrelation between the quantity of material substance, the authority of the image, and the currency of the name. At the same time, again and again, he will return to his simplistic and contradictory assertion that silver is silver and that neither sign nor image effect the value of the material substance: "*Bullion* is silver whose workmanship has no value. And thus Foreign Coin hath no value here for its stamp, and our Coin is *Bullion* in Foreign Dominions" (*Further Considerations* 16; see also 22, 59). Locke's conservationist argument is finally a moral one: devaluation or raising the value of money is but a cheat—it is authorized clipping, a practice unworthy of an honorable prince.[6] Lowndes's tables, which detail the gradual devaluation of a shilling, from 264 grains of fine silver in the reign of Edward I down to 86 grains in the reign of Elizabeth, are evidence to Locke of the greed of kings who exploit their subjects, implying that currency follows natural and collective standards with which even kings have no right to tamper. And again he makes the analogy between clipping and raising the coin: "*Clipping* of Money is raising it without publick Authority; the same denomination remaining to the piece, that hath now less Silver in it, than it had before" (*Further Considerations* 12).

The most thorough exposition of monetary theory in between Locke and Smith is *An Essay upon Money and Coins* (1757 and 1758) by Joseph Harris, then assay-master of the Mint. Even twenty years before Smith, Harris's view of currency is tied to a material base of precious metal, for he is still using Locke's contractual language: "The public stamp upon coins, is a voucher and security to every one, that the coins that wear it, are of a certain fineness, and intrinsic value, according to their size or weight: And coins also being more distributive than bullion, are, upon that account, likewise, more convenient for trade, and in the common affairs of life" (378). After discussing the history of debasement or raising the value of money, he concludes that people knew no better: "[T]hey seem to have thought, that coins had their value, some how, from the stamp they bore" (381). Nevertheless, despite these conservative ties to the materiality of silver, Harris displays a much more sophisticated understanding of the instrumentality of money and its function as a circulating system. In a passage anticipatory of Smith's wonderful airplane metaphor, Harris envisions money as a free-flowing river, emphasizing movement and circulation in the perfect metaphor of laissez-faire economics: "Whilst it glides and circulates smoothly and freely, in its natural course and channels, money is not only a harmless but a beneficial thing; it cherishes and invigorates the whole community, and this equally, whether the stream be large or slender" (402–3).

It is Adam Smith who carries this notion of circulation to its logical conclusion, in which paper money is presented as the functional equivalent or representation of value: "[T]he substitution of paper in the room of gold and silver money, replaces a very expensive instrument of commerce with one much less costly, and sometimes equally convenient. Circulation comes to be carried on by a new wheel, which costs less both to erect and to maintain than the old one" (309). Bank notes are understood to be "promissory notes" that "come to have the same currency as gold and silver money, from the confidence that such money can at any time be had for them" (310; in this passage, the meaning of the word *currency* is clearly shifting, objectified from that which is current to a thing itself). He goes on to note

that precious metal is used principally in international trade, whereas "domestic business [is] being now transacted by paper, and the gold and silver
being converted into a fund for this new [international] trade" (312). Over
and over again, Smith dissociates money from wealth and money from
purchasing power, privileging the latter: for "money is neither a material
to work upon, nor a tool to work with; and though the wages of the work-
man are commonly paid to him in money, his real revenue, like that of all
other men, consists, not in the money, but in the money's worth; not in
the metal pieces, but in what can be got for them" (313). Rethinking of
the instrumentality of currency is ineluctably related to conceptions of the
materiality of currency and the contradictions in changing attitudes toward
paper, and finally to the question of the stamp. The authorizing stamp
grows more significant as materiality grows less significant. And of course
paper money cannot be evaluated by weight but only by tale: its signs have
to be read and interpreted. In the earlier language, paper currency ceases
to be an object per se and becomes rather more of a pledge, a promise of
authorization, rather than a self-authorizing, self-authenticating thing.

How do such matters of economic theory impinge upon language and literature? The same issues concerning the authenticating sign of authority
are bound up with questions over the divine or secular origin and nature
of language: Are there characters written by God in the hearts of men? Is
language composed of real, immanent signs, or is it merely nominal and
conventional? Desire for an older, almost purely feudal view of absolute,
transcendent authority and value is nicely condensed in Kent's offer of
service in *King Lear* (1605):

> *Lear.* Dost thou know me, fellow?
> *Kent.* No, sir; but you have that in your countenance which I would
>   fain call master.
> *Lear.* What's that?
> *Kent.* Authority. (I.ii.28–32)

In this submerged coinage metaphor, the king's face presents its own authority. Mastery, authority, and royalty are supposed to be immutable and
self-revealing, as a kind of pure or self-authorizing authority, both pledge
or assurance of and validation of ultimate authority. By the late seventeenth
century, however, the immanent recognizability of the sign of authority is
considerably more dubious. Doubt as to the face's authenticating sign of

royal genealogy and authority is apparent in Dryden's *Marriage à la Mode* (1671), where first one and then another strange child is instantly "recognized" as the royal heir, by the authenticating sign of his and then her face. The two court suitors to these potential heirs hold an embarrassing quarrel over which incognito looks the most royal, implicitly comparing bastards with counterfeits:

> *Argaleon.* Believe him not; he sees you credulous
>   And would impose his own base issue on you
>   And fix it to your crown.
> *Amalthea.* Behold his goodly shape and feature, sir;
>   Methinks he much resembles you.
> *Argaleon.* I say, if you have any issue here,
>   It must be that fair creature;
>   By all my hopes I think so.
> *Amalthea.* Yes brother, I believe you by your hopes,
>   For they are all for her.
>
>   (I.i.399–408)

Aristocratic ideology of immanent worth and romance conventions are intertwined in a trope of recognition, as here when Leonidas loftily dismisses the need for signifying costume at the masquerade in order to identify his beloved:

> I know her by a thousand other signs:
> She cannot hide so much divinity.
> Disguised, and silent, yet some graceful motion
> Breaks from her and shines round like a glory.
>
>   (IV.ii.11–14)

This trope of recognition is regularly invoked in *Marriage à la Mode,* but it is always problematic: when Palmyra replaces Leonidas as the usurping king's heir, face is no longer recognized, but instead she can only be authenticated by writing, through the agency of a "genuine" autograph. In the domestic plot as well, though they continue to speak the language of eternal recognition, the disguise of lovers is never penetrated: "I would know her in any shape" (IV.iii.58) always proves to be a false boast here. This romance trope of the discovery of familial authenticity by face or physical sign undergoes a gradual but thorough debasement in the novel, through *Joseph Andrews* and *Tom Jones,* culminating in *Humphrey Clinker* (1771), where Clinker's genteel birth is recognized by the white skin of his behind, exposed by accident in the river (see New).

In the novel, the sign of authority has been domesticated to familial and paternal rather than royal or political authority, for here authority and continuity have been transmuted into the question of marriage, while the issues of succession and genealogical continuity persist, interrelated with issues of face. Congreve's proto-novel, *Incognita: or, Love and Duty Reconciled* (1692), is an interestingly contradictory example, one that, like Dryden's *Marriage à la Mode*, seeks to uphold both the child's individual claim to desire and paternal claim to familial authority. Parents are presented as expecting their children to marry on the basis of authority, parental fiat, by reason of the family name of the prospective mate, rather than by his or her face, whereas children are presented as expecting to marry by face rather than by tale. The quarrel over valuation by name versus valuation by face becomes the stock-in-trade of later drama as in Goldsmith's *She Stoops to Conquer* (1773) and Sheridan's *The Rivals* (1775). The struggle over the recognition of royal/aristocratic power and authority in *Lear* and in the upper plot of *Marriage à la Mode* has been domesticated into a familial courtship plot in Congreve, where, again, "she gave him his choice whether he would know whom she was, or see her face."

Both monetary theory and courtship plots in this period operate on a variant of the opposition between empirical evidence and authority, or to recur to the language of political economy, intrinsic and extrinsic value.[7] In the latter, such issues are related to the fundamental question of personal identity: Of what does Congreve's Incognita consist? Of her suitor we are told, "For his part, he was strangely and insensibly fallen in love with her shape, wit and air" (254). Similarly Sheridan plays on the question of whether the prospective mate is to be valued by virtue of her intrinsic merits or to be valued by virtue of parental authority:

> *Absolute.* Pray sir, who is the lady?
> *Sir Anthony.* What's that to you, sir?—Come, give me your promise to love, and to marry her directly.
> *Absolute.* Sure, sir, this is not very reasonable, to summon my affections for a lady I know nothing of!
> *Sir Anthony.* I am sure, sir, 'tis more unreasonable in you to *object* to a lady you know nothing of! (II.i.463–71)[8]

Richard Steele's *The Conscious Lovers* (1722) has long served as the exemplary text for illustrating shifting class consciousness in drama and an attendant transition from a drama of social status to a drama of inner worth. The incognita here, Indiana, lost at birth, serves as an example of the dissociation of the individual subject from location and validation within a genealogical system of exchange—status inconsistency. Hence, she must be evaluated in and of herself, though even here Steele dwells upon the contradictions between inner and outer worth, her beauty and her virtue. In the various familiar love triangles and complications that result from the exercise of conflicting paternal authorities (representing two different classes), the play works through the rationale for choice in a marriage partner on a social and individual level, juggling the various claims of wealth, social status, beauty, and virtue, inner and outer qualities, by weight or by tale. In this play Steele insists that the female protagonist's individual worth, her beauty and virtue, must be recognized prior to elevation in class status, prior to the revelation of her birth, and in so doing he clearly ranks individual worth above class status. As in all of the texts examined here, potential conflict is resolved by romance conventions: the incognita is eventually recognized as having the requisite genealogical credentials to marry into the male protagonist's class, and so the question of whether individual qualities are determined by class and breeding is, as usual, begged. But unlike a virtuous servant character such as Cherry in George Farquhar's *The Beaux' Stratagem* (1707), a character whose beauty and virtue are recognized but whose value remains debased because of her low parentage, Steele insists that Indiana should be highly valued even if her parentage remains obscure. Class transgression in marriage is eventually avoided, and all of the couples are paired off according to their class status—servant with servant, gentry with gentry—but still Steele is at considerable pains to say that class considerations are secondary.

Thus, Indiana functions as a kind of loose sign in this play, and before it can be determined just what she signifies, the process of signification and the various fields of possibility must be considered. As a female sign in an exchange system, Indiana functions very differently than similar characters in some earlier comedies. Consider those scenes in John Vanbrugh's *The Provoked Wife* (1697) or Aphra Behn's *The Rover* (1677) in which the loose woman, that is, a woman unauthenticated by attendant male authority in the figure of brother, husband, or father, is assumed to be a prostitute and therefore subject to assault. When Willmore attacks the beautiful and virtuous but unattended Florinda, he excuses himself to her beloved Belville: "By this light, I took her for an errant harlot." Belville insists upon recognition of her individual worth: "Damn your debauched opinion! Tell me, sot, hadst thou so much sense and light about thee to distinguish her woman, and couldst not see something about her face and person to strike an awful reverence into thy soul?" But to Willmore, evaluation is purely material: "Faith no, I considered her as mere a woman as I could wish" (III.vi.21–27). Steele, however, is much more insistent on individuation, claiming that Indiana is not a sign, not finally open to interpretation, but rather she is self-evidently worthy, a subject in her own right. Thus Steele can claim that Indiana is not a sign, and not subject to exchange systems, either semiotic or economic (as is assumed by the more vulgar characters like Cimberton, who talks of marriage as a market). Rather, Indiana does not represent anything, for she is supposed to be transparently what she is, pure and constant, beautiful and virtuous—silver is silver. Her value then is not variable but fixed and apparent: "Her uncommon air, her noble modesty, the dignity of her person, and the occasion itself, drew the whole assembly together" (I.i.88–90).

Congreve's, Goldsmith's, and Sheridan's plots are connected by the same intrigue: as Captain Absolute puts it, "My father wants to *force* me to marry the very girl I am plotting to run away with!" (III.i.2–3); such a plot harmonizes face and name, parental authority and individual desire, intrinsic and extrinsic value. In between Congreve and Goldsmith, these conflicts are gradually purged of their class and social implications, and they are relocated within the family itself. The resolutions of such plots assert that the other is loved for her self, for intrinsic qualities, not for extrinsic qualities such as family name and social status. In *Incognita,* the denouement enables the reconciliation of all these contested values: paternal authority and individual desire; intrinsic and extrinsic value, name and face.[9] Father reveals daughter, bringing identity or harmony to name and face:

> *Aurelian* led *Incognita* into the room veil'd, who seeing some company there which he had not told her of, would have gone back again. But [her father] *Don Fabio* came bluntly forwards, and ere she was aware, lifted up her veil and beheld the fair *Incognita,* differing nothing from *Juliana,* but in her name. (302)

We see the same plot worked through in *She Stoops to Conquer*, where, through mistaken identity and disguise, Kate can capitalize on the dissociation of face and name: "I'm sure my family is as good as Miss Hardcastle's" (IV.i.270–71):

> *Marlow.* By heavens, madam, fortune was ever my smallest consideration. Your beauty at first caught my eye; for who could see that without emotion? But every moment that I converse with you, steals in some new grace, heightens the picture, and gives it expression. What at first seemed rustic plainness, now appears refined simplicity. What seemed forward assurance, now strikes me as the result of courageous innocence and conscious virtue. (V.iii.38–47)

Though this contradiction of evaluation is thematized directly in these incognita plots, by the end of the century it is a contradiction thematized in all courtship plots. As Elizabeth Bennett muses before the portrait of Darcy at Pemberley, of what does the beloved object consist: name, body, or character? In retrospect, we can trace the emergence of this new form of courtship plot in the transition from Dryden's Royalist and patriarchal late feudalism to Goldsmith's bourgeois ideology of individual attraction. Despite its manifest difficulties and absurdities for contemporary readers, *Marriage à la Mode* closes with its upper plot, all difficulty resolved by Royalist and patriarchal authority; the would-be adulterers and rakes of the domestic plot, Palamede and Rhodophil, repress their rivalry in royal service: "[N]o subject e'er can meet, / A nobler fate, than at his sovereign's feet" (V.i.474–75). All issues are publicized (in Habermas's sense of publicity) in Dryden and, with a graceful bow to royal authority, folded into social contract or league. As McKeon notes, there are contradictions as to which form of marriage is approved, but even in the lower, domestic world, paternal authority rules ("Criticism" 154–62). Leonidas, the new king, is allowed to flirt with romance, but even here in a thinly veiled Royalist allegory of the rightful king restored to his throne, Leonidas and Palmyra's love is a device that heals the breach between usurper and rightful heir, father-in-law and son-in-law, thereby enabling a reconciliation among the ruling elites.

   In Dryden every difficulty is referred to a public and political solution, from the top down, as it were; even the problems of envy and jealousy are contained within the political language of league.[10] But one hundred years later, in Goldsmith's *She Stoops to Conquer,* resolution is entirely privatized—the whole argument is carried out on a personal, private, and familial level.[11] Contradictions remain, for Goldsmith does not simply invert Dryden's hierarchy of town and court, but rather Goldsmith's resolutions are dependent upon the creation of a new interior world, that is, a new bourgeois subject.[12] The space accorded to the zone of the private is profoundly different in this later play. The concept of "home" has peculiar resonance in Goldsmith's works, from "The Traveller" and "The Deserted Village" to *The Vicar of Wakefield,* but nowhere is it thematized more prominently than in *She Stoops to Conquer:* travelers who think they arrive at a strange inn are in fact at home, just as travelers who think they are forty miles away on Crackskull Common are in fact at home. All lost objects—travelers, jewels, letters, inheritances, and suitors—are returned home to their rightful places and owners. The value of domesticity is in part presented in terms of a familiar opposition between country and city: "We country persons can have no manners at all. I'm in love with the Town" (II.i.618–19). Goldsmith celebrates simple homely country virtues of the natural, spontaneous, immediate, and unmediated—love, affection, family, community, common sense—and anyone who pretends to anything pretentious from Mrs. Hardcastle to Hastings is undercut. These homely, country virtues are presented as stable and constant in contrast to the city, where individuals chase after novelty and change, especially in fashion and fancy clothes. Kate's change of dress from daytime city fashion to evening housewife fare emblematizes the opposition; the city fops bring their fashion down into the country but are purged of such folly. In this contrast between the decadence and luxury of the world of London versus the humble country home, the real evils are politics, power, government, wealth, and cities. City strangers enter the redemptive home and are eventually socialized to rural community.

The values of home and country are allied to the nostalgia that runs all of the way through Goldsmith: "I love every thing that's old" (I.i.24), says Hardcastle at the opening of the play. Like Parson Primrose, there is an essential conservatism to Hardcastle, from his Marlborough stories of the good old days to the ancient shared jokes that bespeak a collective conservatism: "[W]e've laughed at that [story of Ould Gorse in the gun room] these twenty years," says the servant Diggory (II.i.45). This scene between Hardcastle and his servants exhibits a conservative, benevolent despotism: the central country value is patriarchal, obedience to authority.[13] Despite the ideology of affective individualism and individual attraction, class status, class consciousness, and hierarchy remain intact throughout *She Stoops to Conquer*. Marlow treats his father's old friend as an innkeeper and his daughter like a barmaid: "We all know the honor of the bar-maid of an inn. I don't intend to *rob* her, take my word for it; there's nothing in this house I shan't honestly *pay* for" (IV.i.60–63). Marlow is never rebuked for treating his host like an innkeeper, for it is assumed that a presuming innkeeper deserves to be snubbed, nor is there finally anything wrong with treating a barmaid like a prostitute—his is nothing more than the error of mistaken identity. As in so many eighteenth-century novels from *Pamela* and *Tom Jones* to *Humphrey Clinker*, class transgression is flirted with but is eventually averted. There are two contradictory systems of evaluation at work in *She Stoops to Conquer*: outside versus inside; social status versus inner worth; economic versus emotional; social versus individual; preconceived versus spontaneous; mediated versus natural. While the second set is privileged, the first set is never explicitly repudiated, because the social is never very far from the individual in this play—it has been relocated within the family.[14] Goldsmith's accomplishment is to retain the structure of paternal authority while appearing to privilege a free-market economy, a trick that he accomplishes by depoliticizing paternal authority and domesticating it: politics remains but one of the dimensions of the decadent world of London that are exorcised in the play. Goldsmith's *She Stoops to Conquer* is at once progressive in its representation of social relations (individualized, privatized, emotionalized) and conservative in its cover myth (rural, agricultural, nostalgic desire for a green world of the past).

It is, I think, significant that of all the plays discussed here, only Goldsmith's remains appealing and remains, along with *The Beggars' Opera*, the only dramatic text in the eighteenth-century professional's canon that has entered into the popular imagination, continually produced around the world for more than two centuries. As such it is fair to see it as the fulfillment, if that is the right word, of these recognition plots, distilled into a perfect fantasy, a fairy tale of familial benevolence, in which individual desire naturally concurs with paternal authority, where, in the end, there is no opposition between rule and desire, between law and license, between id and superego. To borrow the subtitle of Congreve's *Incognita*, here is "Love and Duty Reconciled." That is to say, all blocking in all three plots, both internal and external, eventually dissipates. This is a world in which your father and your beloved want for you, indeed labor for what you want most yourself. Yet all of this occurs without obvious sentimentality—disguised under the cloak of intrigue comedy—*The Mistakes of a Night*. In an essentially anti-Freudian and anti-Lacanian vision, the "Name of the Father" and the ego are perfectly reconciled into a domestic vision of perfect happiness: well before *The Wizard of Oz*, Goldsmith was chanting, "There's no place like home," a place of bourgeois domestic tranquillity as yet unimaginable in Dryden's day.

To conclude with the terms with which we began, there is a correspondence between the literary contradiction of name and face and the monetary contradiction of weight and tale. Valuation "by tale" corresponds to knowing the name, that is, identification of family: the sign of paternal and familial authority. By process of ideological contradiction, or negation of the negation, face comes to be construed as real, internal, what the other truly is, as opposed to the family name, which is alien, external, familial, or social, an arbitrary and therefore false label or price in the marriage market.[15] In other words, there is a fundamental contradiction between object and essence, face and character, for as method insists more and more on empirical evaluation, the object is in both cases dematerialized or, more properly, internalized in the case of character. In a sense, both the economic and social evaluation are moving toward "face value," toward tale, and away from weight: in a world of paper bank notes, weight is obsolete, for there is no inherent, physical value to be verified or validated. But still the goal of recoinage is always to make telling possible again: to recoin and so renew the royal face or stamp. Though this renewal is always the ideal, it is eventually only realized by abandoning the valuable medium, by shifting from silver to paper, when Bank of England notes become legal tender in 1797, and even then value still fluctuates. In *King Lear,* there is a longing for true but already problematic congruence between authoritative face and economic value. The graphic face that is retained on bank notes today remains vestigial, for it is the number printed on the note that signifies, not the image of the queen or, in the United States, some dead president or patriot.

In these later plays, however, and even more so in the novel, the public and private spheres are kept as separate as is possible, for individual subjects are not supposed to have economic value. Individual subjects are supposed to be valuable in and of themselves, as individuals, not as wage laborers or as gendered objects in a circulating system (as Carole Pateman shows, such objectification is what makes both slavery and prostitution so scandalous). In the plays under consideration here, from Dryden through Sheridan, it is the female character whose value is subject to fluctuation and must be verified by one method or another, and so fixed. In each of these works, the method of valuation shifts from extrinsic to intrinsic, from name to face, while monetary theory moves in the opposite direction. In part, we could view this as a quarrel between use value and exchange value: in the terms presented by courtship narrative, parents are concerned with markets, for they are the ones exchanging property (the bride's portion), whereas the children are concerned with use value, for they are the ones to extract the benefit or the use of the mate. The political economy of women is obscured by the emergent split between private and public, a demarcation that makes possible the magical boundaries of home in Goldsmith, a zone of affect from which economic value is excluded. Again, it is the incognita plot that mediates between the two zones and the two methods of valuation. The incognita plot, then, plays its part in the reconceptualization of social space and the redefinition of publicity and privacy. The discourse of publicity, as articulated in political economy, and the discourse of privacy, as articulated in conduct literature, drama, and the novel, map out, respectively, a zone of finance and a zone of affect, or money and feeling. Working in tandem with political economy through the process of differentiation and partition, domesticity constitutes or creates or maps out a private sector as a safe harbor from the public sector; this zone of affect provides refuge from the competitive world of civil society, as a place exempt from the laws of capitalist exchange. This sense of opposition and refuge helps explain how the incognita plot works as an eighteenth-century version of the traffic in women. As Pateman puts it,

> Women are incorporated into a sphere that both is and is not in civil society. The private sphere is part of civil society but is separated from the 'civil' sphere. The antinomy private/public is another expression of natural/civil and women/men. The private, womanly sphere (natural) and the public, masculine sphere (civil) are opposed but gain their meaning from each other, and the meaning of the civil freedom of public life is thrown into relief when counterposed to the natural subjection that characterizes the private realm. (11)

In a discussion of *Evelina,* a late, novelistic variant of the incognita plot, Judith Newton argues that it is the female protagonist herself who comes to be valued, not what she brings, fetches, or makes, or wills, for this female is removed from circulation. It is her destiny "to be protected rather than to act upon the world, to receive the identity of treasure rather than to create it"; "by crediting and giving value to the view that women of good family are really treasure rather than merchandise, *Evelina* reflects a renewed and widespread tendency in the late eighteenth century, especially in its literature, to idealize women of the genteel classes" (50, 33–34). That is, by process of ideological contradiction, the protagonist herself becomes the inestimable treasure, the jewel of great price, rather than a vehicle for, or representation of, portion, property, or inheritance. In the high romance plot of *She Stoops to Conquer,* despite Constance Neville's desire to retrieve her jewels, her birth right and mark of her social status, Hastings responds, "Perish the baubles! Your person is all I desire" (II.i.423). This central distinction between treasure and merchandise is intertwined with the concurrent refigurations of publicity and privacy, for merchandise only has value in public, while treasures are only valuable in private. As Kristina Straub notes in her discussion of the representation of eighteenth-century actors' sexuality, almost by definition, any public positioning of a woman, that is, any stance that is not retired, not private, and not domestic, is inevitably associated with sale and prostitution. In these plays, then, women are represented as white elephants, as inestimable treasures that cannot be traded. As "treasure" women are decapitalized, for treasure is not a commodity, and it does not circulate. Another way to put this is to argue that as political economy comes to describe and theorize civil society as a system of exchange, marriage, the traffic in women, has to be reimaged, re-presented in noncapitalist terms—enchanted and removed from or partitioned off from the soulless exchange of labor and commodities that characterizes capitalism.

The representation of the treasured wife is the linchpin to the process of removing the taint of exchange from the domestic sphere, for she functions as a deliberately archaic, decapitalized figure whose sole mode of exchange is neofeudal. I am arguing, then, that the new lease on life that the novel gives to romance, and here I mean by and large in Lawrence Stone's affective individualistic form, the transformation from the vestiges of courtly love of the old romance to its new bourgeois form in companionate marriage, is explained at least in part by its function: to cordon off the home from civil society and to keep capital relations out, to negate the fetish of the commodity, in which social relations assume the "fantastic form of a relation between things" (Marx, *Capital* 1: 72). Withdrawing from the objectified realm of exchange, the novel and its domestic space carve out a nostalgic area of "primitive exchange," of direct barter or gift, love for love, as the ballad has it, the only mode of exchange possible in the zone where love must be "freely given," naturally and spontaneously, without coercion or parental intervention, supposedly untouched by the rules of capitalist exchange, interest, profit, and constant motion.[16] As exchange (of vows, trust, or loyalty), in contrast to capitalist exchange in the outer civil society, or an unmystified vision of the traffic in women, the domestic emotional economy aspires to stasis—the end of history, or at least the end of each individual subject's history—they married and lived happily ever after.

Notes

1. References to Locke's economic works, including *Some Considerations of the Consequences of the Lowering of Interest and the Raising of the Value of Money* and "Concerning Usury" (1691); *Short Observations on a Printed Paper Intituled, For encouraging the Coining Silver Money in England, and after for keeping it here* (1695); and *Further Considerations concerning Raising the Value of Money. Wherein Mr. Lowndes Arguments for it in his late Report concerning* An Essay for the Amendment of the Silver Coins, *are particularly Examined* (2nd ed., 1696), are included in Locke, *Several Papers*.

2. In Delphy's terms, this is an analysis of a domestic mode of production and its forms of mystification.

3. Reprinted in McCulloch 228 and 233. According to Josset, "Rarely was any transaction made without an argument. No trader would sell goods without stipulating the weight of the coins in which he was to be paid. Quarrels over money values were continuous; market days and fairs were regularly scenes of brawls. Wages paid by employers to their workmen were the cause of many Saturday night disputes regarding the value of their money. Such was the result of the apathy and ignorance of the Government in so neglecting the currency" (112–13).

4. For an earlier discussion, see Rice Vaughan, *A Discourse of Coin and Coinage* (1675, written ca. 1630): "Princes can give what value they list to Gold and Silver, by enhansing and letting fall their Coins, when as in truth Gold and Silver will retain the same proportion towards other things, which are valued by them, which the general consent of other Nations doth give unto them.... [T]his universal value of Gold and Silver, the mint, even in money, do call Intrinsical, and the local value they call Extrinsical, as depending upon the impression of the mark and ordinance of the State" (McCulloch 12).

5. On the simplest level, aristocratic ideology is necessarily conservative, for it maintains the present disposition of power and of property: those families that control land, wealth, and power now will be the same families controlling land, wealth, and power in the future. For a detailed description of familial strategies of social and possessive continuity, see the Stones' controversial study of possessive continuity among the landed elite.

6. Cf. Vaughan: "[W]hat can be more dishonorable than to have the Image of the Prince, or the Mark of the Publick Attestation impressed upon false and counterfeited stuff. It is a manifest breach of publick Faith" (McCulloch 34). Similarly, in the *Speech of Sir Robert Cotton Before the Privy Council in 1626 . . . Touching on the Alteration of Coin* (1651), Sir Robert Cotton writes of experiments in raising money as "the Dishonour it laid upon the Person of the King" (McCulloch 126). After noting the effigy of the sovereign on the coin, Cotton writes, "Princes must not suffer their Faces to warrant Falsehood" (127); he terms alloying "infeebling the Coin" (128). So too, Sir William Petty, *Quantulumcunque concerning Money* (London, 1682; rpt. 1695), writes: "Honour" forbids raising the value of money (McCulloch 163). On the contrary, Lowndes argued that in the history of the mint's raising the value of money, there was not "Inconvenience, Disgrace, or Mischief" as a consequence (McCulloch 200).

7. McKeon connects Congreve's *Incognita* and the dialectic of naive empiricism and skepticism in *Origins* (61–64).

8. Citations of texts by Sheridan, Goldsmith, and Steele are to Nettleton and Case.

9. In Congreve, confusion of identity is maintained through the device of the masquerade, mistaken identity, and intrigue: "With that she pulled off her mask, and discovered to *Hippolito* (now more amaz'd than ever) the most angelick face that he had ever beheld" (256). See Castle's suggestive discussion of class and gender confusion in the phenomenon of the masquerade.

10. Canfield argues that Dryden's play should be read with the language of "league," for Dryden models domestic leagues on international, political leagues (78–79).

11. McKeon's categories of aristocratic, progressive, and conservative ideologies are useful in distinguishing between these plots of recognition, and their various strategies for resolving status inconsistency. Dryden's most clearly conforms to an aristocratic ideology because the value that is recognized in the upper-plot protagonists is innate, material, biological, and genealogical superiority; Steele's version clearly employs a progressive ideology, for the value of Indiana lies in her innate virtue, a virtue that is independent of social status. Finally, in Goldsmith, we can see a conservative ideology that displays some nostalgic desire for aristocratic status, though most of its energy is directed against unworthy parvenus, the

monied interest that here is represented primarily by the topsy-turvy world of London and its fetishizing of fashion. McKeon argues that Congreve's *Incognita* also conforms to conservative ideology, with a love plot that at once rejects paternal, traditional order but in its resolution reestablishes parental wisdom and guidance (*Origins* 263).

12. The classic study of the emergence of a bourgeois public sphere across the eighteenth century, and indeed the study from which these terms derive, is that of Habermas. More recently, Armstrong has explored the function of novels in representing privacy and domesticity: "We are taught to divide the political world in two and to detach the practices that belong to a female domain from those that govern the marketplace. In this way, we compulsively replicate the symbolic behavior that constituted a private domain of the individual outside and apart from social history" (9–10). For a Lukácsian analysis of the relation between the objectification of social relations under capital and the novelistic representation of privacy and domesticity, see my *Between Self and World*.

13. Trumbach observes that as the nuclear family grows stronger, the "patriarch ceases to be father to his servants but becomes their employer and father to his children alone," something that Hardcastle obviously resists (121).

14. These contradictions are also mediated or mystified by the multiple plots of *She Stoops to Conquer,* in a generic hierarchy of high, middle, and low courtship plots, which correspond to high, middle, and low class: a low or farcical plot with Tony Lumpkin and his barmaid, Bouncing Bett; high romance in Hastings and Constance Neville. Kate and Marlow are made normative by contrast, for virtue is found as a Horatian mean. The deal Kate strikes with her father is based on this ethical mean: "For if you should find him less impudent, and I more presuming; if you find him more respectful, and I more importunate . . ." (III.i.74–77). Kate is situated between brazen and modest, while Marlow is situated between shy and impudent.

15. In a suggestive essay on the eighteenth-century representations of character, Nussbaum argues that "the truth of character for both sexes is internal, the exterior is a falsification or a disguise: as this split between inner and outer emerges, the importance of constructing an interiority as a code to the 'real' character takes on greater significance" (149). Similarly, Armstrong argues that Richardson's first novel involves "Pamela's transformation from an object of desire into female sensibility": "As it provides the occasion for her to resist Mr. B.'s attempts to possess her body, seduction becomes the means to dislocate female identity from the body and to define it as a metaphysical object" (117). In contrast, Harriet Guest suggests, viva voce, that in the transition from evaluation by social status to evaluation by inner virtue, status is preserved or rather reappears transformed into female beauty; if this is so, then we might trace the change through the ambiguous lan-

guage of female "grace" and "charm" that figures so prominently in Pope's poems about women.

16. For a suggestive analysis of gift exchange, see Hyde.

Works Cited

Althusser, Louis. "Ideology and Ideological State Apparatuses." *Lenin and Philosophy and Other Essays.* Trans. Ben Brewster. New York: Monthly Review P, 1971. 127–86.

———. "Marxism and Humanism." *For Marx.* Trans. Ben Brewster. London: New Left Books, 1977. 219–47.

Armstrong, Nancy. *Desire and Domestic Fiction: A Political History of the Novel.* New York: Oxford UP, 1987.

Behn, Aphra. *The Rover.* Ed. Frederick M. Link. Lincoln: Bison–U of Nebraska P, 1967.

Bourdieu, Pierre. "Forms of Capital." *Handbook of Theory and Research for the Sociology of Education.* Ed. John G. Richardson. New York: Greenwood, 1986. 241–58.

Brown, Laura. "The Defenseless Woman and the Development of English Tragedy." *Studies in English Literature* 22 (1982): 429–43.

———. *English Dramatic Form, 1660–1760: An Essay in Generic History.* New Haven: Yale UP, 1981.

Burney, Frances. *Evelina.* Ed. Edward A. Bloom and Lillian D. Bloom. New York: Oxford UP, 1968.

Canfield, J. Douglas. *Word as Bond in English Literature from the Middle Ages to the Restoration.* Philadelphia: U of Pennsylvania P, 1989.

Castle, Terry. *Masquerade and Civilization.* Stanford: Stanford UP, 1986.

Congreve, William. *Incognita. Shorter Novels, Jacobean and Restoration.* London: Dent, 1930. 237–303.

Delphy, Christine. "Patriarchy, Domestic Mode of Production, Gender, and Class." *Marxism and the Interpretation of Culture.* Ed. Cary Nelson and Lawrence Grossberg. Urbana: U of Illinois P, 1988. 259–69.

Dryden, John. *Marriage à la Mode.* Ed. Mark S. Auburn. Lincoln: Bison–U of Nebraska P, 1981.

Habermas, Jürgen. *The Structural Transformation of the Public Sphere: An Inquiry into a Category of Bourgeois Society.* 1962. Trans. Thomas Burger. Cambridge: MIT P, 1989.

Harris, Joseph. *An Essay on Money and Coins.* London, 1757, 1758.

Horsefield, J. Keith. *British Monetary Experiments, 1650–1710.* London: G. Bell and Sons, 1960.

Hyde, Lewis. *The Gift: Imagination and the Erotic Life of Property.* New York: Random, 1983.

Josset, C. R. *Money in Britain: A History of the Currencies of the British Isles.* London: Frederick Warne, 1962.

Locke, John. *Several Papers Relating to Money, Interest and Trade.* 1696. New York: Augustus M. Kelley, 1968.

Marx, Karl. *Capital.* Trans. Samuel Moore and Edward Aveling. Ed. Frederick Engels. 3 vols. New York: International Publishers, 1967.

———. *Grundrisse.* Trans. Martin Nicolaus. Harmondsworth, Eng.: Penguin, 1973.

McCulloch, John R., ed. *A Select Collection of Scarce and Valuable Tracts on Money.* 1856. New York: August M. Kelley, 1966.

McKeon, Michael. "Marxist Criticism and *Marriage A La Mode.*" *Eighteenth Century: Theory and Interpretation* 24 (1983): 141–62.

———. *The Origins of the English Novel, 1600–1740.* Baltimore: Johns Hopkins UP, 1987.

Nettleton, George H., and Arthur E. Case, eds. *British Dramatists from Dryden to Sheridan.* Rev. George Winchester Stone, Jr. Carbondale: Southern Illinois UP, 1969.

New, Melvyn. "'The Grease of God': The Form of Eighteenth-Century Fiction." *PMLA* 91 (1976): 235–44.

Newton, Judith Lowder. *Women, Power, and Subversion: Social Strategies in British Fiction, 1778–1860.* Athens: U of Georgia P, 1981.

Nussbaum, Felicity. "Heteroclites." *The New Eighteenth Century.* Ed. Felicity Nussbaum and Laura Brown. New York: Methuen, 1987. 144–67.

Pateman, Carole. *The Sexual Contract.* Stanford: Stanford UP, 1988.

Rubin, Gayle. "The Traffic in Women: Notes on the 'Political Economy' of Sex." *Toward an Anthropology of Women.* Ed. Rayna R. Reiter. New York: Monthly Review P, 1975. 157–210.

Shakespeare, William. *The Complete Works of Shakespeare.* Ed. Hardin Craig. Chicago: Scott, Foresman, 1961.

Smith, Adam. *The Wealth of Nations.* Ed. Edwin Cannon. Chicago: U of Chicago P, 1976.

Staves, Susan. *Married Women's Separate Property in England, 1660–1833.* Cambridge: Harvard UP, 1990.

Stone, Lawrence, and Jeanne C. Fawtier Stone. *An Open Elite? England, 1540–1880.* Oxford: Clarendon, 1984.

Straub, Kristina. *Sexual Suspects: Eighteenth-Century Players and Sexual Ideology.* Princeton: Princeton UP, 1992.

Thompson, James. *Between Self and World: The Novels of Jane Austen.* University Park: Pennsylvania State UP, 1988.

Trumbach, Randolph. *The Rise of the Egalitarian Family: Aristocratic Kinship and Domestic Relations in Eighteenth-Century England.* New York: Academic P, 1978.

Williams, Raymond. *The Country and the City.* New York: Oxford UP, 1973.

CONTRIBUTORS

RICHARD BRAVERMAN is associate professor of English and comparative literature at Columbia University. He is the author of *Plots and Counterplots: Sexual Politics and the Body Politic in English Literature, 1660–1730*.

HELEN BURKE is assistant professor of English at Florida State University. Author of articles on eighteenth-century literature in a variety of journals, she is currently working on a book on the politics of the eighteenth-century Irish stage.

J. DOUGLAS CANFIELD is Regents Professor at the University of Arizona. Author of books on Nicholas Rowe and English literature to the Restoration, he is currently writing a book on subversive comedy and comical satire in the Restoration.

SUSAN GREEN is assistant professor of English at the University of Oklahoma and associate editor of *Genre*. Author of articles on women writers of the early modern period, she is currently writing a book on Lady Mary Wroth, Margaret Cavendish, and Aphra Behn.

RICHARD KROLL is associate professor of English at the University of California, Irvine. Author of *The Material Word: Literate Culture in the Restoration and Early Eighteenth Century* and articles on Restoration drama and culture, he is currently writing a book on eighteenth-century notions of dissent.

ROBERT MARKLEY is Jackson Professor at West Virginia University and editor of *The Eighteenth Century: Theory and Interpretation*. Author of books on Restoration comedy and the history of science in the seventeenth and eighteenth centuries, he is currently writing books on literature, gender, and exchange value and on literature, science, and postdisciplinarity.

DEBORAH C. PAYNE is associate professor of literature at American University. Author of articles on Restoration drama and theater and on such authors as Behn, Wycherley, and Pope, she is currently finishing a book entitled *Patronage, Professionalism, and the Marketplace of Restoration Theatre, 1660–1685*.

J. S. PETERS is associate professor of English, comparative literature, and theater arts at Columbia University. Author of *Congreve, the Drama, and the Printed Word,* she is currently writing a book on the relations between theater and print in Europe from 1500 to 1900.

KRISTINA STRAUB is associate professor of English at Carnegie-Mellon University. Author of books on Frances Burney and eighteenth-century actors and their role in the history of sexuality, she is currently working on two projects: an edition of Burney's *Evelina* and a book on guilt, innocence, and bodily excess in eighteenth-century British criminal biography.

JAMES THOMPSON is professor of English at the University of North Carolina at Chapel Hill and editor of *Eighteenth-Century Studies.* Author of books on Wycherley and Austen, he is currently writing a book on eighteenth-century political economy and the novel.

HAROLD WEBER is associate professor of English at the University of Alabama. Author of *The Restoration Rake Hero: Transformations in Sexual Understanding in Seventeenth-Century England,* he is currently writing a book on print culture and monarchical identity during the reign of Charles II.

INDEX

Kristeva, Julia (*continued*)
231–40; and sublimation, 240; and the
symbolic, 234; and transposition, 233
Kuhn, Thomas, 195
Kynaston, Edward, 55, 266

Lacan, Jacques, 29, 94, 110 (n. 8), 118, 138
(n. 6), 300; and "closed field of desire,"
102; *Feminine Sexuality*, 104; and the
imaginary, 102, 103; and law, 98–100,
104, 105, 108, 116; and *méconnaissance*,
theory of, 29; and mirror stage, 103, 283;
the Other in, 104; and phallic order, 104,
106, 107; and the symbolic, 94, 101
Ladies' Museum, The (Lennox), 243
Lady Jane Gray (Rowe), 205–7
*Lancashire Witches, and Tegue o Divelly
The Irish-Priest, The* (Shadwell), 215–19,
220
Langdell, Cheri Davis, 138 (n. 5)
Language: as currency, 292; Hobbes on,
48–51
Larson, Magali Sarfatti, 33–34
Lee, Nathaniel: *Lucius Junius Brutus*, 72
Lennox, Charlotte: and analysis of
Shakespeare's women characters, 234–
40; *The Female Quixote*, 247, 248–49,
253 (n. 6); and Johnson, 247–50, 253
(nn. 8, 11); *The Ladies' Museum*, 243;
and Orrery, 243, 249; and Richardson,
249, 253 (n. 6); *Shakespear Illustrated*,
228–50, 251–53 (n. 4), 253 (n. 6), 253–54
(n. 11); *The Sister*, 247
Leviathan (Hobbes), 44–55, 62–63, 64
(nn. 3, 4), 190–91 (n. 15)
Levi-Strauss, Claude, 110 (n. 10)
Libertine, 115, 119, 130, 142–44, 148,
150–57, 162–63, 164 (n. 6), 184, 186
Licensing Act, 170, 189 (n. 8)
*Life of the Late Famous Comedian, Jo.
Hayns, The* (Brown), 262
Lillo, George: *The London Merchant; or,
The History of George Barnwell*, 212–15
Locke, John, 196, 303 (n. 1); on coinage and

value, 287–91; and constitutional theory,
198; *Further Considerations concerning
Raising the Value of Money*, 287; *Short
Observations on a Printed Paper*, 281
Loftis, John, 166 (n. 19), 195, 198, 203, 205,
219–20
*London Merchant; or, The History of
George Barnwell, The* (Lillo), 212–15
Louis XIV: in *Sodom*, 80–81; in *Tamerlane*
(Rowe), 197
Lounsbury, T. R., 251
Love, Harold, 158
Love for Love (Congreve), 158–59, 174,
175, 180, 181, 184, 281
Love in the Suds (Kenrick), 272–75
Love Letters to a Gentleman (Behn), 139
(n. 13)
Love's Last Shift (Cibber), 169, 175, 176,
183, 267, 269–70
Lowndes, Lord, 285–86, 290, 304 (n. 6)
Lucius Junius Brutus (Lee), 72
Lucius, the First Christian King of Britain
(Manley), 200–201
Lucky Chance, The (Behn), 172, 174
Lucretius: *De Rerum Natura*, 48
Lynch, Kathleen, 165 (n. 10)

Macbeth (Shakespeare), 245
Macherey, Pierre, 91
MacIntyre, Alasdair, 64 (n. 4)
Macklin, Charles, 266
Macpherson, C. B., 46
Maguire, Nancy Klein, 30–31
Male Coquette, The (Garrick), 272–73
Manley, Delarivier: *Lucius, the First
Christian King of Britain*, 200–201
Man of Mode, The (Etherege), 152, 169, 175,
176, 181, 182–83
Markley, Robert, 138 (n. 3), 142, 156, 164
(n. 3), 165 (nn. 10, 11)
Marriage, 92; and property settlements,
92–93
Marriage à la Mode (Dryden), 39–40, 55–